Herodotus Reader

Annotated Passages from Books I-IX of the Histories

Herodotus Reader

Annotated Passages from Books I-IX of the Histories

Blaise Nagy

College of the Holy Cross

Focus Publishing

R Pullins Company

Newburyport, MA

Herodotus Reader: Annotated Passages from the Histories, I-IX
© 2011 Blaise Nagy

Focus Publishing/R. Pullins Company
PO Box 369
Newburyport MA 01950
www.pullins.com

Cover photo courtesy of Michael McGlin.

ISBN 13: 978-1-58510-304-1

Printed in the United States of America.

11 10 9 8 7 6 5 4 3 2

1211SP

CONTENTS

PREFACE

About a month after my contract with Focus had been signed, I asked Ron Pullins, Focus Publishing, some specific follow-up questions about the contents of this *Herodotus Reader*. His response was that I should write the kind of book *I* would want to use in the classroom. Ron's advice has guided me throughout the production of the *Reader*.

My target audience are students who have acquired a reasonable familiarity with the fundamentals of ancient Greek grammar and who have also amassed a working vocabulary in the language, but who still need help with verb forms and with certain constructions, like the genitive absolute. Such students will usually have finished two years of secondary school instruction or one year of college instruction in ancient Greek. It is also my hope that this *Reader* will be a suitable textbook in a more advanced type of a course—we call them "author level courses" at the College of the Holy Cross—on Herodotus' *Histories*, where some help with the grammar is still a major *desideratum* and where there is also a significant focus on topics in literary criticism and on historiographical issues.

The decision to produce this *Herodotus Reader* was in large part prompted by the appearance on the book market in 2007 of Robert Strassler's *Landmark Herodotus*. To say that this is a superb English-language presentation of the *Histories* is hardly an overstatement. Everything about the *Landmark*, from the translation to the splendid maps, from the helpful annotations to the engaging appendix articles, is first rate, and the price (under $20 US, the last time I checked the internet book market) makes it a real bargain. After I received my copy, I almost immediately concluded—correctly, I hope—that there was no better time for a *Herodotus Reader*, one that would take advantage of a likely resurgence of interest in Herodotus among a new generation of students. Accordingly, I have designed a *Herodotus Reader* that can be used most profitably in tandem with the *Landmark*. To this end, I have included in the *Reader* numerous references to the maps, notes, and appendix articles of the *Landmark*. Since this *Reader* presents only a portion of Herodotus' *Histories* in the original, I strongly recommend that instructors require their students to supplement and round out their readings in Greek with readings from a high-quality English translation such as the one that Andrea Purvis has provided in the *Landmark*.

In this and other ways, the present *Reader* is not a stand-alone project. What I wrote in the Preface to my *Thucydides Reader* (Focus 2005) applies here as well: "I do not envision an all-in-one, self-contained textbook, but I have in mind one where the instructor is continually called upon to provide additional background information, a more thorough historical contextualization, and a more detailed analysis of the syntax." This is especially true when it comes to the matter of the so-called New Ionic dialect of Herodotus' *Histories*. Apart from a short section in the "Students' Introduction," where I offer some tips on translating the Greek of Herodotus, there is no comprehensive section in the *Reader* that purports to explain all the differences between the Ionic and the Attic dialects. It has been my experience that these (differences) are best left for the instructor to explain over the course of an *entire* semester or at least over the course of several weeks. When their mastery is presented as a necessary pre-requisite to the reading of the *Histories*, students often feel overwhelmed and discouraged.

Another area where this *Reader* requires the regular input of instructors is in the historical contextualization of the passages from the *Histories*. All of the selections are accompanied by commentaries, but these are mere prompts to a fuller, teacher-led discussion of the many topics that a close reading of the *Histories* will elicit. Most selections will have one or two references to the venerable and extensive commentaries of W. W. How and J. Wells, which instructors can consult during their own preparation time and then bring to the attention of students. Some of the passages from Books I-IV also have references to D. Asheri's *A Commentary on Herodotus Books I-IV*, which instructors will either have in their personal libraries or can access in school libraries. The grammatical notes are brief and to the point; they too invite the added input of the instructor when the translations are gone over in class. Only rarely do the notes stray into matters that are not related to grammar, as I am convinced that students look to such notes for help with the translation and not for discussions on variant readings or similar scholarly controversies. A word list is not supplied in this *Reader*, as I very much believe in the value of having students look up words in a standard Greek-English dictionary. Only by consulting a lexicon—the *LSJ* is available on-line and even as an "app" on the I-Phone—can they be made aware of the full range of the meanings of the Greek words whose definitions they are seeking. In any case, students should have an easier time looking up verbs in this *Reader*, since the first principle parts of many inflected verb forms have been supplied.

All nine Books of the *Histories* are represented in the *Reader*. In teaching Herodotus, I have always found it impossible to limit my students to readings from only one book of the *Histories*. Having to choose between the account of Salamis and the account of Marathon, or between stories involving the fascinating Egyptians and those involving the equally fascinating Scythians, or between the morality tales of Book I and those of Book IX, has never been easy, and it is primarily for this reason that I have opted for the "selections" approach. (A. Barbour's *Selections from Herodotus*, originally published in 1929, comes closest to offering this kind of coverage, but it completely omits Books IV and IX.) At the risk of speaking heresy, I submit that the one-book approach to teaching Herodotus has this additional disadvantage: not every chapter of a given Book in the *Histories* is suitable for homework assignment and classroom recitation. In Book III, for example, Herodotus lists the amounts of tribute that came into the Persian King's coffers from the vast Persian Empire (3.90-97). These eight chapters, while invaluable to a historian of Achaemenid Persia, would have little appeal to students, especially when they could be reading instead about the gold-mining ants of India in chapter 102 or the flying snakes of Arabia in chapter 109. When there is so much fascinating material spread throughout the nine books of the *Histories*, it makes more sense—at least to me, as an instructor—to expose students to the "best of the best" and not to have to worry about whether they have read *all* of Book II or *all* of Book VII (which rarely, if ever, happens).

The almost 200 chapters that constitute this *Reader* have been selected primarily on the basis of the interest quotient of the passages. I freely acknowledge this fact, as I am convinced that Herodotus himself conducted his *historiai* or "inquiries" primarily into those subjects that he felt would most interest his audience. I have almost certainly overlooked passages that some readers, if given editorial privileges, would have insisted on including in a book like this. Indeed, I could have easily selected many more chapters, but a larger *Reader* would have resulted in greater production costs. In any case, I doubt whether anyone will be able to complain that there is not enough Herodotus here, as there is something for everybody. The passages are scrupulously identified (a feature that is missing in the above-mentioned Barbour reader); with only a very few exceptions, their integrity as chapters has been maintained; and they are presented in the order in which they appear in the nine books of the *Histories*. On the other hand, except for the long narratives that extend over multiple chapters, like the story of Croesus and Solon in Book I, instructors can feel free to skip around and assign any passage from any of the nine books, since the individual chapters are largely self-contained. In other words there are only a very few cross-references between the chapters, with the result that a grammatical form or construction will be explained anew in the notes, even if it was treated in an earlier chapter. It is my hope that students may want to keep their books even after their year or semester of formal instruction and read on their own additional passages from an author they have come to appreciate.

The Greek text for this *Reader* is K. Hude's 3rd edition (1927) of the Herodotus *OCT*, as presented in the Perseus Digital Library. I am very grateful to Prof. Gregory Crane, Perseus Editor, for giving me permission to use this version of the *Histories*.

I also offer my sincere thanks to the College of the Holy Cross for granting me a semester's leave; to Prof. Ellen Perry for supporting this project as Acting Chair of Classics at the College of the Holy Cross; to Prof. Mary Ebbott for her willingness to use a preliminary version of this *Reader* in her Intermediate Greek course at the College of the Holy Cross; to James McGovern for his generous assistance in preparing the manuscript; to Mark Wright for his help with proofreading; to Prof. Henry Bender and Prof. Lee Fratantuono for offering to read early drafts; to Prof. Gregory Nagy and Prof. Joseph Nagy for sharing with me their many insights into Herodotus; to my readers at Focus Publishing for their valuable recommendations; and to Ron Pullins, Focus Publishing, for doing so much to support the study of ancient Greek.

A STUDENTS' INTRODUCTION

"Before Herodotus there was no Herodotus" (translation from Arnaldo Momigliano, Secondo contributo alla storia degli studi classici [Rome, 1960], p. 31.)

Congratulations on having come this far in your study of ancient Greek! Your reward for all the work you have put into learning vocabulary, the principle parts of the verbs, those strange 3rd declension nouns, and everything else which makes the mastery of Greek so challenging, is the opportunity to read in the original Greek the works of Herodotus, the "Father of History" (so-called by Cicero in *Laws* 1.5) and arguably the most entertaining and informative ancient author, Greek or Roman.

I. A Herodotus Biography

Herodotus' life story is poorly attested. What few biographical materials we have from antiquity are late and not very reliable, a situation we often encounter when researching the lives of most of our best known ancient writers. Even Herodotus' birth date, c. 475 B.C., is essentially an educated guess, one that is arrived at by a calculation that our author was born sometime in the middle of the decade between the two great Persian invasions of 490 B.C. and 480 B.C. His death date of c. 430 B.C. is also an estimate, based on references that he makes to events from early in the Peloponnesian War, a Greek "world war" that was fought between Athens (and her allies) and Sparta (and her allies) from 431 B.C. to 404 B.C.

As with Herodotus' death date, the best way to reconstruct a biography of him is through the many autobiographical allusions and hints that are scattered throughout the *Histories* (the standard way of referring to his work). When reading the *Histories*, therefore, one of your tasks—and it is an enjoyable one—will be to spot those passages that shed some light on Herodotus' life-story and then put together a kind of a personal profile for our author. Here are some of the possible components to this profile:

1. *Herodotus' travels.* Scholars have debated this matter forever, but there now seems to be a consensus that Herodotus conducted many of his "inquiries" (the literal meaning of *historiai*) by actually traveling to far-away places like Egypt, Scythia, Southern Italy, and many others. (Scholars nowadays refer to these site-visits as "autopsies.") You can judge for yourself whether this scholarly consensus gets it right by looking carefully at the travelogue portions of the *Histories* and assessing the accuracy of his description of the places he allegedly visited. This type of an assessment is especially pertinent when he gives topographical information about important battle sites, like Marathon and Thermopylae, as his battle narratives can be termed reliable only if his topographical descriptions are accurate. Related to the issue of Herodotus' travels is the very practical question of how it was possible for him to range all over the Mediterranean world, given the difficulties that travelers in the 5th century B.C. would have encountered. One common-sense answer to this question has been to propose that Herodotus was a merchant whose

business travels gave him the opportunity to conduct his "inquiries" alongside his commercial activities. A good way to approach this subject is to examine carefully those passages in the *Histories* where Herodotus seems to have at his disposal the kind of information a merchant would especially want to have, like the navigability of a river, or the size of wicker-basket containers.

2. *Herodotus' religious views.* This is a topic that has evoked intense scholarly disagreements, but it is also one where even a first-time reader of the *Histories* can offer useful insights. The question that needs to be posed goes something like this: Does Herodotus believe in superhuman forces that significantly and inevitably affect the lives of human beings? Possible answers to this question can be sought in the many passages from the *Histories* which deal with Apollo's shrine at Delphi, the chief oracular site throughout antiquity for Greeks and even for non-Greeks like King Croesus, who lived on the periphery of the Greek world. Delphi played a key role in the Persian Wars, and its pronouncements were certainly taken seriously by the Greeks who received them. Did Herodotus take them seriously, as well? Stories about dreams also figure prominently in the *Histories*, and your task will be to see whether Herodotus regards these as messages from the gods or as strictly human phenomena that can be explained in human terms.

3. *A biased Herodotus.* Already in antiquity, Herodotus had the reputation of someone who, because of his pro-Athenian leanings, supposedly distorted the history of the Persian Wars. Plutarch, the early 2nd century B.C. Greek writer, best known for his *Parallel Lives* (a series of paired biographies of famous Greeks and Romans), devoted an entire essay to the subject of Herodotus' bias: it goes by the Latin title of *de Malignitate Herodoti*, "Concerning the Malice of Herodotus." In this essay (part of a collection of treatises which we call *Moralia*), Plutarch attempts to show that Herodotus, because of his bias, portrayed the Thebans as cowards who "medized" (surrendered to the Persians) at the first opportunity. To bolster his case Plutarch cites the testimony of a 4th century B.C. source (Diyllus), where it is claimed that Herodotus received 10 talents of silver (the equivalent of several million US dollars) from the Athenian state as a reward for his favorable depiction of Athens. As readers of many of the key passages in the *Histories* where Herodotus apportions praise and blame to the various Greek city states for their roles in the Persian Wars, you will be in a good position to judge for yourselves whether he was indeed biased or whether he was even-handed in his narrative.

4. *Herodotus' life philosophy.* This may be the most difficult aspect of Herodotus' biographical profile to recover. Depending on the particular passage from the *Histories*, we can see a Herodotus who views life as fraught with unpredictable change, where happiness is altogether too brief, and where death can seem to be preferable to life. Alternatively, we can catch glimpses of a Herodotus who is ebullient, who is filled with a certain *joie de vivre*, who takes obvious delight in writing about the often humorous human condition, who derives great joy from making his "inquiries" into a natural world that he clearly finds wondrous, and who, in general, has a very positive outlook on life.

II. The *Histories* of Herodotus

Besides reconstructing a personal profile for Herodotus, your other challenge when reading the *Histories* will be to assess them as history. In other words, you will want to arrive at some conclusions about just how much real (i.e., verifiably accurate) history we have in our author's magnum opus. Here are some of the specific issues you may want to consider.

1. *Herodotus' self-professed goals.* Look for passages where Herodotus specifically mentions an overarching goal or where he tells his readers about the criteria he uses for including (or not including) certain accounts. His Prologue, of course, is going to be important in this regard, but there are other passages scattered throughout the *Histories* where he will indicate, often in a seemingly incidental way, his goal(s) for conducting his "inquiries."

2. *The many hats of Herodotus.* On reading the *Histories*, you will quickly become aware that our author is not always wearing his "historian's" hat and that he occasionally dons the hat of a geographer, or that of an ethnographer, or that of a mythographer, or (for long stretches of the narrative) the hat of a story-teller. Does any of this matter in terms of Herodotus' standing as a historian? As modern readers, can we countenance a "history" where, in the same chapter, what appears to be straightforward, serious, historical narrative is followed by a story that is clearly fabulous and has to be regarded as part of some popular tradition Herodotus has tapped into?

3. *This is history?* Depending on the passage in the *Histories* you are reading, you may find yourself filled with admiration at the way the author approaches his task as a writer of "history" (in the modern sense of that word). This is especially true in those passages where Herodotus conducts an "autopsy," that is, where he "sees for himself" a battlefield, a monument, or even an inscription that was set up to commemorate an important event. In reading other passages, you may react quite differently and conclude that Herodotus' methodology is unsatisfactory and would compare unfavorably to the approach of someone writing (in the 21st century) a history of, say, the American Civil War. Perhaps the most obvious contrast between the historiographical methodology of Herodotus and that of a modern writer can be seen in the way our author avoids—not always, but for the most part—citing his sources. Another aspect of his historiography that may strike you as different is the way he incorporates into his narrative various quoted speeches, very few of which have any claim to being authentic. And then there is the matter of his overlooking issues of language. For example, he ignores the fact that when a Spartan, like the exiled king Demaratos, was in the company of Persians, there had to have been a linguistic divide which somehow (by the use of translators?) had to be bridged. Of course, I am not suggesting by these observations that you should be critical of Herodotus for his failure to implement modern historiographical methods. I am merely inviting you, as readers of the *Histories*, to appreciate what a novelty the writing of history must have been in an age when the poems of Homer were the primary way for Greeks to connect with their past. (Consider again the quotation from Arnaldo Momigliano at the start of this introduction.)

4. *Herodotus the multi-culturalist?* Your foray into the *Histories* will bring you to numerous passages where the author shows a studied admiration for non-Greek cultures, so much so that Plutarch, his ancient critic, labeled him a *philobarbaros*, or a "lover of things non-Greek" (seemingly, from Plutarch's point of view, a derogatory term). Herodotus' supposed multi-culturalism is on display throughout the *Histories*, but especially in Book II, where he takes us on a guided tour of ancient Egypt and where we are startled to read that, based on his carefully considered inquiries, the Greek pantheon was originally Egyptian. Even the Persians receive occasional praise from Herodotus as a people who are incapable of telling lies and who have a praiseworthy system of education. (Doubtless, it was this kind of a benign attitude towards Persian customs that moved Plutarch to call Herodotus a *philobarbaros*.) As is only natural, he does indulge every once in a while in a mild form of ethnocentricity and assumes that the whole world does things the Greek way, but expect to find more evidence for a multi-cultural Herodotus than for an ethnocentric one.

III. The Greek of Herodotus' *Histories*

Scholars label the Greek of the Homeric *Iliad* and *Odyssey* "Ionic," because these great epics evolved as oral poetry in the coastal region of Asia Minor, which is commonly referred to as "Ionia." The Greek of the *Histories* is in many ways similar to Homeric Greek, but it is also sufficiently different so that the term "New Ionic" has been coined to describe this variant of the older Ionic Greek. New Ionic itself eventually branches off into what experts call "Attic" Greek, the dialect that developed in Attica (the region of Athens) and that we encounter in most of the outstanding works of Greek literature from the 5th and 4th centuries B.C. from authors like Aeschylus, Sophocles, Euripides, Thucydides, Plato, Aristotle, and so on.

Your introduction to Greek grammar and vocabulary may have been facilitated by a textbook that was based on Attic Greek, or by one that was based on the Ionic of the Homeric poems. Regardless of your initial exposure to Greek, the New Ionic of Herodotus' *Histories* will appear, for the most part, familiar to you and, after a period of adjustment, should not pose any great problems. Listed below in *Part 1* are a few of the more salient features of New Ionic forms. *Part 2* is a list of some of the constructions you will frequently encounter in the *Histories*. These lists are nothing more than primers, since your best resource for mastering New Ionic will be your instructor, who, with some help from this *Reader*, will acclimate you to the features of this dialect.

Part 1. Some of the orthographical (spelling) differences between New Ionic and Attic. In the paired examples, the first form is New Ionic, the second, Attic.

  (a) Eta takes the place of a long alpha: cf. καθαρή and καθαρά.

  (b) ει takes the place of epsilon: cf. ξεῖνος and ξένος.

  (c) ου takes the place of omicron: cf. μοῦνος and μόνος.

  (d) Omega takes the place of ου: cf. ὦν and οὖν.

  (e) Kappa takes the place of pi: cf. κότερος and πότερος, κοῖος and ποῖος.

  (f) Kappa takes the place of chi: cf. δέκομαι and δέχομαι.

  (g) Pi takes the place of phi: cf. ἀπικνέομαι and ἀφικνέομαι.

  (h) Nu takes the place of γν: cf. γινώσκω and γιγνώσκω.

(i) Movable nu is not used: cf. ἐστί and ἐστίν.

(j) Temporal augment is omitted in some verbs, like ἐργάζομαι.

(k) -εω verbs are usually uncontracted: cf. φιλέει.

(l) Some forms of –μι verbs are like those of omega verbs: cf. δίδοις.

Part 2. Some observations on the syntax of the Histories.

(a) "Absolute" infinitives function as finite verbs.

(b) Iterative forms, with the infix -εσκ-, are frequently used.

(c) Articles are often used as pronouns, including relative pronouns.

(d) Indirect statements can be triggered by certain nouns, like κήρυγμα ("proclamation").

(e) Dative of respect constructions are used along with the accusative of respect.

(f) Relative pronouns often contain their antecedents.

(g) Genitive absolute constructions are very common.

(h) Accusative of extent of time constructions are common.

(i) Epexegetic infinitives are often used to explain a preceding clause.

(j) The future participle, when introduced by ὡς, indicates purpose.

(k) ἔχειν often means "to be able." With an adverb, it is the equivalent of εἶναι.

(l) κεῖμαι often means the same as εἶναι.

Abbreviations

ALC David Asheri, Alan Lloyd, Aldo Corcella: *A Commentary on Herodotus Books I-IV* (Oxford University Press, 2007).

HW W. W. How, J. Wells: *A Commentary on Herodotus*, Vols. I-II (Oxford University Press, 1936).

Landmark Robert B. Strassler, editor: *The Landmark Herodotus, The Histories* (Pantheon Books, 2007).

Guide to the Notes

Verbs are parsed in this order: tense, mood, voice, person, and number. To avoid confusion, no abbreviations are used.

Participles are parsed in this order: tense, voice, gender, case, and number. Again, no abbreviations are used.

Where they are thought to be helpful, Attic equivalents of Ionic forms are indicated with an equal (=) sign. For example: ἀπικόμενον = ἀφικόμενον.

Translations of the Greek appear inside quotation marks. For example: τὸ ποιεύμενον πρὸς τῶν Λακεδαιμονίων "That which is being done by the Lacedaemonians."

ANNOTATED PASSAGES FROM HERODOTUS' *HISTORIES*

Prologue to the Histories

In this introduction to the *Histories*, Herodotus identifies himself as a native of Halicarnassus, a Greek city in the southwest corner of Asia Minor (cf. map in Landmark *ad* 1.3). Scholars have long ago concluded that a young Herodotus probably made frequent contacts with the non-Greek population of nearby Caria, and that it is partly for this reason that he seems so open-minded towards βάρβαροι (a word that meant in the 5th century B.C. "non-Greek speakers"). Herodotus' self-proclaimed purpose for his *Histories* is to offer a "display" (ἀπόδεξις) of his "inquiry" (ἱστορίης) into a *human* past (τὰ γενόμενα ἐξ ἀνθρώπων), an inquiry which focuses on "deeds both great and wondrous" (ἔργα μεγάλα τε καὶ θωμαστά). Quite remarkably, Herodotus means to include in his inquiries the deeds not only of his fellow Greeks but also of non-Greeks (τὰ μὲν Ἕλλησι τὰ δὲ βαρβάροισι). The goal that Herodotus states last is quite noteworthy: to devise an "explanation" (αἰτίην) as to why Greeks and non-Greeks "fought against one another" (ἐπολέμησαν ἀλλήλοισι). In other words, the Father of History wants to explain the cause(s) behind the great and perhaps unending conflict between East and West.

Ἡροδότου Ἁλικαρνησέος ἱστορίης ἀπόδεξις ἥδε, ὡς μήτε τὰ γενόμενα ἐξ ἀνθρώπων τῷ χρόνῳ ἐξίτηλα γένηται, μήτε ἔργα μεγάλα τε καὶ θωμαστά, ⌐θαυμαστα τὰ μὲν Ἕλλησι, τὰ δὲ βαρβάροισι ἀποδεχθέντα, ἀκλεᾶ γένηται, τά τε ἄλλα καὶ δι᾽ ἣν αἰτίην (αιϛ) ἐπολέμησαν ἀλλήλοισι.

———————————

Ἁλικαρνησέος = Ἁλικαρνασσέως.

ἱστορίης "Inquiry" or "result of inquiry." It means "history," in the modern sense, only in 7.96.1.

ἀπόδεξις = ἀπόδειξις. "Exposition," or "display," or even "performance."

ὡς Introduces a purpose clause.

ἐξ ἀνθρώπων Equivalent of ὑπ᾽ ἀνθρώπων (genitive of agent).

θωμαστά = θαυμαστά.

ἀποδεχθέντα "Exhibited." Aorist, passive, neuter, nominative, plural participle of ἀποδείκνυμι.

○3

1.5.1-4 Herodotus Waxes Philosophical

Herodotus concludes his survey of the mythological causes for the enmity between East and West. It is not unusual for him to offer up a variant—sometimes an irreverent one—to a traditional story, as he does here with the legend of Io's abduction. Despite this tendency towards mythological revisionism, Herodotus does not stray far from the traditional world of Homer. We can see an example of this in his discussion of cities great and small (1.5.3-4), where he evokes the opening lines of the *Odyssey* (πολλῶν ἀνθρώπων ἴδεν ἄστεα). Part of the value of this passage is that it lets us see an aspect of Herodotus' modus operandi: he does not mind relating myths and legends (and often relishes doing so), and he will take a historical stand only in those instances where he can have at least a degree of certainty. Finally, near the end of the passage, Herodotus stakes out a philosophical position on the cyclical nature of human history. This "rise and fall" theme will appear elsewhere in the *Histories* (cf. 7.46).

οὕτω μὲν Πέρσαι λέγουσι γενέσθαι, καὶ διὰ τὴν Ἰλίου ἅλωσιν εὑρίσκουσι σφίσι ἐοῦσαν τὴν ἀρχὴν τῆς ἔχθρης τῆς ἐς τοὺς Ἕλληνας. [2] περὶ δὲ τῆς Ἰοῦς οὐκ ὁμολογέουσι Πέρσῃσι οὕτω Φοίνικες· οὐ γὰρ ἁρπαγῇ σφέας χρησαμένους λέγουσι ἀγαγεῖν αὐτὴν ἐς Αἴγυπτον, ἀλλ᾽ ὡς ἐν τῷ Ἄργεϊ ἐμίσγετο τῷ ναυκλήρῳ τῆς νεός· ἐπεὶ δ᾽ ἔμαθε ἔγκυος ἐοῦσα, αἰδεομένη τοὺς τοκέας, οὕτω δὴ ἐθελοντὴν αὐτὴν τοῖσι Φοίνιξι συνεκπλῶσαι, ὡς ἂν μὴ κατάδηλος γένηται. [3] ταῦτα μέν νυν Πέρσαι τε καὶ Φοίνικες λέγουσι. ἐγὼ δὲ περὶ μὲν τούτων οὐκ ἔρχομαι ἐρέων ὡς οὕτω ἢ ἄλλως κως ταῦτα ἐγένετο, τὸν δὲ οἶδα αὐτὸς πρῶτον ὑπάρξαντα ἀδίκων ἔργων ἐς τοὺς Ἕλληνας, τοῦτον σημήνας προβήσομαι ἐς τὸ πρόσω τοῦ λόγου, ὁμοίως σμικρὰ καὶ μεγάλα ἄστεα ἀνθρώπων ἐπεξιών. [4] τὰ γὰρ τὸ πάλαι μεγάλα ἦν, τὰ πολλὰ σμικρὰ αὐτῶν γέγονε, τὰ δὲ ἐπ᾽ ἐμεῦ ἦν μεγάλα, πρότερον ἦν σμικρά. τὴν ἀνθρωπηίην ὦν ἐπιστάμενος εὐδαιμονίην οὐδαμὰ ἐν τὠυτῷ μένουσαν ἐπιμνήσομαι ἀμφοτέρων ὁμοίως.

═══════════════

1.5.1
Ἰλίου Troy.
ἐοῦσαν = οὖσαν.

1.5.2
ἁρπαγῇ...χρησαμένους "Using violence."
ἐμίσγετο "She had sex." Imperfect, indicative, passive, 3rd, singular of μίγνυμι.
νεός Genitive of νηῦς (= ναῦς).
ἔγκυος "Pregnant."

αὐτήν...συνεκπλῶσαι Accusative and infinitive in indirect statement.

κατάδηλος The form is feminine.

1.5.3

οὐκ ἔρχομαι Translate with the future participle ἐρέων. "I do not come to say," or "I'm not here to say."

οὕτω ἢ ἄλλως "This way or that way."

κως = πως.   *How / somehow*

τόν A relative pronoun and its antecedent combined.

σημήνας Aorist, active, masculine, nominative, singular participle of σημαίνω.

προβήσομαι Future, indicative, middle, 1st, singular of προβαίνω.

1.5.4

ἐπ' ἐμεῦ "In my time."

ὦν = οὖν.   *therefore*

τὠυτῷ Crasis (two words combined into one) for τῷ αὐτῷ.

ἐπιμνήσομαι Future, indicative, middle, 1st, singular of ἐπιμιμνήσκομαι. "I will make mention of."

☙

1.8.1-4 Gyges, the Unwilling Peeping Tom, Part I

We are told in 1.5 that Croesus, the king of a Lydia, was responsible for the original conflict between Greeks and Asia. In 1.6, Herodotus begins his story of the Lydians and their rulers, including the Heraklid ("claiming descent from Herakles") Candaules (c. late 8th century B.C.). The episode related here has everything which could possibly have appealed to an ancient audience; it may have actually been one of the so-called "performance pieces" which Herodotus would have "performed" or recited in a theatrical setting. As is often the case, Homeric touches are never distant: for example, we are told that τὰ καλά ("things beautiful") constitute the chief moral principle humans must live by (1.8.4). There is also something of a Greek tragedy in this "piece," as we are made aware of Candaules' excesses (ὑπερεπαινέων) and of the inevitability of his tragic downfall (χρῆν γὰρ Κανδαύλῃ γενέσθαι κακῶς). The folksy sayings in this passage are, of course charming, but one in particular (1.8.2) may be seen as Herodotus' guiding principle for the way he conducted his inquiries: ὦτα γὰρ τυγχάνει ἀνθρώποισι ἐόντα ἀπιστότερα ὀφθαλμῶν ("eyes happen to be more reliable than ears").

οὗτος δὴ ὦν ὁ Κανδαύλης ἠράσθη τῆς ἑωυτοῦ γυναικός, ἐρασθεὶς δὲ ἐνόμιζέ οἱ εἶναι γυναῖκα πολλὸν πασέων καλλίστην. ὥστε δὲ ταῦτα νομίζων, ἦν γάρ οἱ τῶν αἰχμοφόρων Γύγης ὁ Δασκύλου ἀρεσκόμενος μάλιστα, τούτῳ τῷ Γύγῃ καὶ τὰ σπουδαιέστερα τῶν πρηγμάτων ὑπερετίθετο ὁ Κανδαύλης καὶ δὴ καὶ τὸ εἶδος τῆς γυναικὸς ὑπερεπαινέων. [2] χρόνου δὲ οὐ πολλοῦ διελθόντος, χρῆν γὰρ Κανδαύλῃ γενέσθαι κακῶς, ἔλεγε πρὸς τὸν Γύγην τοιάδε · "Γύγη, οὐ γὰρ σε δοκέω πείθεσθαί μοι λέγοντι περὶ τοῦ εἴδεος τῆς γυναικός (ὦτα γὰρ τυγχάνει ἀνθρώποισι ἐόντα ἀπιστότερα ὀφθαλμῶν), ποίεε ὅκως ἐκείνην θεήσεαι γυμνήν." [3] ὃ δ' ἀμβώσας εἶπε· "Δέσποτα, τίνα λέγεις λόγον οὐκ ὑγιέα, κελεύων με δέσποιναν τὴν ἐμὴν θεήσασθαι γυμνήν; ἅμα δὲ κιθῶνι ἐκδυομένῳ συνεκδύεται καὶ τὴν αἰδῶ γυνή. [4] πάλαι δὲ τὰ καλὰ ἀνθρώποισι ἐξεύρηται, ἐκ τῶν μανθάνειν δεῖ · ἐν τοῖσι ἓν τόδε ἐστί, σκοπέειν τινὰ τὰ ἑωυτοῦ. ἐγὼ δὲ πείθομαι ἐκείνην εἶναι πασέων γυναικῶν καλλίστην, καί σεο δέομαι μὴ δέεσθαι ἀνόμων."

1.8.1

ἠράσθη Aorist, indicative, passive, 3rd, singular of ἔραμαι.

ἑωυτοῦ = ἑαυτοῦ.

οἱ Dative of possession.

πολλὸν "By far."

πασέων = πασῶν.

ἦν γάρ οἱ "For there was to him," or "he had."

καὶ δὴ καὶ "And especially."

ὑπερεπαινέων "Praising excessively."

1.8.2

ὦτα Neuter, nominative, plural of οὖς.

ὀφθαλμῶν Genitive of comparison.

ὅκως = ὅπως.

θεήσεαι Aorist, subjunctive, middle, 2nd, singular of θεάομαι.

1.8.3

ἅμα δὲ κιθῶνι ἐκδυομένῳ "As soon as her clothes are removed."

κιθῶνι = κιτῶνι.

ἐξεύρηται Perfect, indicative, passive, 3rd, singular of ἐξευρίσκω.

τῶν Translate as a relative pronoun.

σκοπέειν τινὰ τὰ ἑωυτοῦ "To mind one's own business."

☙

1.9.1-3 Gyges, the Unwilling Peeping Tom, Part II

One mark of a good storyteller is the ability to pile on the details and still keep the narrative brisk. Herodotus excels in this skill, and, through the accumulation of detail, even manages to impart credibility to a story that is otherwise ahistorical. Perhaps it is in this passage that Herodotus perhaps comes closest to indulging the prurient taste of his audience, particularly in the way he describes the disrobing of Candaules' wife.

ὃ μὲν δὴ λέγων τοιαῦτα ἀπεμάχετο, ἀρρωδέων μή τί οἱ ἐξ αὐτῶν γένηται κακόν. ὁ δ᾽ ἀμείβετο τοισίδε· "Θάρσει, Γύγη, καὶ μὴ φοβεῦ μήτε ἐμέ, ὥς σεο πειρώμενος λέγω λόγον τόνδε, μήτε γυναῖκα τὴν ἐμήν, μή τί τοι ἐξ αὐτῆς γένηται βλάβος. ἀρχὴν γὰρ ἐγὼ μηχανήσομαι οὕτω ὥστε μηδὲ μαθεῖν μιν ὀφθεῖσαν ὑπὸ σεῦ. [2] ἐγὼ γάρ σε ἐς τὸ οἴκημα ἐν τῷ κοιμώμεθα ὄπισθε τῆς ἀνοιγομένης θύρης στήσω. μετὰ δ᾽ ἐμὲ ἐσελθόντα παρέσται καὶ ἡ γυνὴ ἡ ἐμὴ ἐς κοῖτον. κεῖται δὲ ἀγχοῦ τῆς ἐσόδου θρόνος· ἐπὶ τοῦτον τῶν ἱματίων κατὰ ἓν ἕκαστον ἐκδύνουσα θήσει, καὶ κατ᾽ ἡσυχίην πολλὴν παρέξει τοι θεήσασθαι. [3] ἐπεὰν δὲ ἀπὸ τοῦ θρόνου στείχῃ ἐπὶ τὴν εὐνὴν κατὰ νώτου τε αὐτῆς γένῃ, σοὶ μελέτω τὸ ἐνθεῦτεν ὅκως μή σε ὄψεται ἰόντα διὰ θυρέων."

1.9.1

ἀρρωδέων = ὀρρωδῶν.

οἱ Dative case.

φοβεῦ Present, imperative, middle, 2nd, singular of φοβέομαι.

ἀρχήν "To start with."

ὀφθεῖσαν Aorist, passive, feminine, accusative, singular participle of ὁράω.

1.9.2

ἐν τῷ κοιμώμεθα "Where we sleep."

ἀνοιγομένης Present, passive, feminine, genitive, singular participle of ἀνοίγνυμι.

κατ᾽ ἡσυχίην πολλὴν "At your complete leisure."

παρέξει Translate as an impersonal: "It will be possible."

1.9.3

ἐπεάν = ἐπειδάν.

κατὰ νώτου τε αὐτῆς γένῃ "And she has her back turned to you."

γένῃ = Aorist, subjunctive, middle, 2nd, singular of γίγνομαι.

ἐνθεῦτεν = ἐντεῦθεν.

ὅκως = ὅπως.

∞

1.10.1-3 Gyges, the Unwilling Peeping Tom, Part III

As we approach the denouement to the story of Candaules, we see our author donning yet another hat, that of the ethnographer. Indeed, research into the "customs of individual peoples and cultures" is a regular (and welcome) feature of the *Histories*. It has often been remarked that Herodotus, because of his multi-cultural background in Halicarnassus, was open-minded and non-judgmental, even when describing customs that may have seemed to him strange and thoroughly un-Greek. In the so-called "Archaeology" section of his *Histories* (1.6.5), the historian Thucydides also takes up the subject of nakedness and notes that in earlier times even Greeks wore loincloths during athletic competitions, such as the Olympic Games. By the fifth century, however, only non-Greeks wore such clothing during wrestling and boxing matches.

ὁ μὲν δὴ ὡς οὐκ ἐδύνατο διαφυγεῖν, ἦν ἕτοιμος· ὁ δὲ Κανδαύλης, ἐπεὶ ἐδόκεε ὥρη τῆς κοίτης εἶναι, ἤγαγε τὸν Γύγεα ἐς τὸ οἴκημα, καὶ μετὰ ταῦτα αὐτίκα παρῆν καὶ ἡ γυνή. ἐσελθοῦσαν δὲ καὶ τιθεῖσαν τὰ εἵματα ἐθηεῖτο ὁ Γύγης. [2] ὡς δὲ κατὰ νώτου ἐγένετο ἰούσης τῆς γυναικὸς ἐς τὴν κοίτην, ὑπεκδὺς ἐχώρεε ἔξω, καὶ ἡ γυνὴ ἐπορᾷ μιν ἐξιόντα. μαθοῦσα δὲ τὸ ποιηθέν ἐκ τοῦ ἀνδρὸς οὔτε ἀνέβωσε αἰσχυνθεῖσα οὔτε ἔδοξε μαθεῖν, ἐν νόῳ ἔχουσα τίσεσθαι τὸν Κανδαύλεα. [3] παρὰ γὰρ τοῖσι Λυδοῖσι, σχεδὸν δὲ καὶ παρὰ τοῖσι ἄλλοισι βαρβάροισι, καὶ ἄνδρα ὀφθῆναι γυμνὸν ἐς αἰσχύνην μεγάλην φέρει.

1.10.1

δή This particle indicates that the story is about to resume.

μετὰ ταῦτα αὐτίκα "Soon after these things," or "soon thereafter."

ἐθηεῖτο Imperfect, indicative, middle, 3rd, singular of θηέομαι (= θεάομαι).

1.10.2

ἐγένετο Subject is Gyges.

ἰούσης τῆς γυναικός Genitive absolute construction.

ὑπεκδὺς Aorist, active, masculine, nominative, singular participle of ὑπεκδύομαι.

ἐπορᾷ = ἐφορᾷ.

τὸ ποιηθέν "That which had been done."

ἐν νόῳ ἔχουσα "Having it in mind," or "intending." Takes complementary infinitive.

τίσεσθαι τὸν Κανδαύλεα "To make Candaules pay."

τίσεσθαι Future, middle infinitive of τίνω.

1.10.3

σχεδὸν "Almost."

ὀφθῆναι Aorist, passive infinitive of ὁράω. It is the subject of φέρει.

CB

1.11.1-5 Gyges, the Unwilling Peeping Tom, Part IV

Yet another spirited and lively installment to the story of Gyges. The continued use of the dialogue format contributes greatly to the sense that the reader is actually watching a theatrical production. Herodotus' skills as a writer can also be seen in the way he comes up with some pithy and effective lines for his characters (e.g., the queen's ἴδης τὰ μὴ σε δεῖ). Commentators have attempted to see in this story some indication of the rules of succession for Lydian monarchs (e.g., whoever marries a widowed queen automatically becomes king), but the most recent scholarship (ALC ad 1.11.2) cautions against this interpretation.

τότε μὲν δὴ οὕτως οὐδὲν δηλώσασα ἡσυχίην εἶχε· ὡς δὲ ἡμέρη τάχιστα ἐγεγόνεε, τῶν οἰκετέων τοὺς μάλιστα ὥρα πιστοὺς ἐόντας ἑωυτῇ, ἑτοίμους ποιησαμένη ἐκάλεε τὸν Γύγεα. ὁ δὲ οὐδὲν δοκέων αὐτὴν τῶν πρηχθέντων ἐπίστασθαι ἦλθε καλεόμενος· ἐώθεε γὰρ καὶ πρόσθε, ὅκως ἡ βασίλεια καλέοι, φοιτᾶν. [2] ὡς δὲ ὁ Γύγης ἀπίκετο, ἔλεγε ἡ γυνὴ τάδε. "Νῦν τοι δυῶν ὁδῶν παρεουσέων, Γύγη, δίδωμι αἵρεσιν, ὁκοτέρην βούλεαι τραπέσθαι. ἢ γὰρ Κανδαύλεα ἀποκτείνας ἐμέ τε καὶ τὴν βασιληίην ἔχε τὴν Λυδῶν, ἢ αὐτόν σε αὐτίκα οὕτω ἀποθνήσκειν δεῖ, ὡς ἂν μὴ πάντα πειθόμενος Κανδαύλῃ τοῦ λοιποῦ ἴδης τὰ μή σε δεῖ. [3] ἀλλ' ἤτοι κεῖνόν γε τὸν ταῦτα βουλεύσαντα δεῖ ἀπόλλυσθαι ἢ σὲ τὸν ἐμὲ γυμνὴν θεησάμενον καὶ ποιήσαντα οὐ νομιζόμενα." ὁ δὲ Γύγης τέως μὲν ἀπεθώμαζε τὰ λεγόμενα, μετὰ δὲ ἱκέτευε μή μιν ἀναγκαίῃ ἐνδέειν διακρῖναι τοιαύτην αἵρεσιν. [4] οὔκων δὴ ἔπειθε, ἀλλ' ὥρα ἀναγκαίην ἀληθέως προκειμένην ἢ τὸν δεσπότεα ἀπολλύναι ἢ αὐτὸν ὑπ' ἄλλων ἀπόλλυσθαι: αἱρέεται αὐτὸς περιεῖναι. ἐπείρωτα δὴ λέγων τάδε· "Ἐπεί με ἀναγκάζεις δεσπότεα τὸν ἐμὸν κτείνειν οὐκ ἐθέλοντα, φέρε ἀκούσω, τέῳ καὶ τρόπῳ ἐπιχειρήσομεν αὐτῷ." [5] ἡ δὲ ὑπολαβοῦσα ἔφη "Ἐκ τοῦ αὐτοῦ μὲν χωρίου ἡ ὁρμὴ ἔσται ὅθεν περ καὶ ἐκεῖνος ἐμὲ ἐπεδέξατο γυμνήν, ὑπνωμένῳ δὲ ἡ ἐπιχείρησις ἔσται."

1.11.1

ὡς δὲ ἡμέρη τάχιστα ἐγεγόνεε "As soon as it had become day."

τῶν οἰκετέων τοὺς "Those of her attendants whom…"

ὥρα Imperfect, indicative, active, 3rd, singular of ὁράω.

ἑωυτῇ = ἑαυτῇ.

πρηχθέντων Aorist, passive, neuter, genitive, plural participle of πρήσσω (= πράσσω).

ἐώθεε Pluperfect, indicative, active, 3rd, singular of ἔθω. Translate as an imperfect.

καὶ πρόσθε "Even on earlier occasions."

1.11.2

ἀπίκετο = ἀφίκετο.

παρεουσέων = παρουσῶν.

ὁκοτέρην = ὁποτέραν.

ὡς Introduces a purpose clause.

τοῦ λοιποῦ Genitive of time within which. "In the future."

1.11.3

κεῖνον = ἐκεῖνον.

θηησάμενον Aorist, middle, masculine, accusative, singular participle of θεάομαι.

οὐ νομιζόμενα "Things that defy [our] customs."

τέως μέν Correlative with μετὰ δὲ.

μιν ἀναγκαίη ἐνδέειν διακρῖναι τοιαύτην αἵρεσιν "To tie him to the necessity of making such a choice."

1.11.4

οὔκων = οὔκουν.

ἐπειρώτα Imperfect, indicative, active, 3rd, singular of ἐπερωτάω.

φέρε The imperative is used like an adverb: "Well."

ἀκούσω "May I hear."

τέῳ = τῷ (τίνι).

ἐπεδέξατο Aorist, indicative, middle, 3rd, singular of ἐπιδείκνυμι.

℺

1.12.1-2 Gyges, the Unwilling Peeping Tom, Part V

There are no real surprises in this concluding segment to the story of Gyges, except for the "footnote" towards the end, which cites Archilochos of Paros, the outstanding Greek lyric poet of the 8th and 7th centuries B.C. At first blush, this citation seems to have the purpose of imparting some credibility to Herodotus' story. However, as scholars have long ago pointed out (cf. HW ad 1.12.2), the reference to Archilochos is probably an interpolation, since the technical expression ἐν ἰάμβῳ τριμέτρῳ comes from a later period than Herodotus. (That the Archilochos poem actually refers to Gyges is not, of course, what is contested.)

ὡς δὲ ἤρτυσαν τὴν ἐπιβουλήν, νυκτὸς γενομένης (οὐ γὰρ ἐμετίετο ὁ Γύγης, οὐδέ οἱ ἦν ἀπαλλαγὴ οὐδεμία, ἀλλ᾽ ἔδεε ἢ αὐτὸν ἀπολωλέναι ἢ Κανδαύλεα) εἵπετο ἐς τὸν θάλαμον τῇ γυναικί. καὶ μιν ἐκείνη ἐγχειρίδιον δοῦσα κατακρύπτει ὑπὸ τὴν αὐτὴν θύρην. [2] καὶ μετὰ ταῦτα ἀναπαυομένου Κανδαύλεω ὑπεκδύς τε καὶ ἀποκτείνας αὐτὸν ἔσχε καὶ τὴν γυναῖκα καὶ τὴν βασιληίην Γύγης, τοῦ καὶ Ἀρχίλοχος ὁ Πάριος, κατὰ τὸν αὐτὸν χρόνον γενόμενος, ἐν ἰάμβῳ τριμέτρῳ ἐπεμνήσθη.

1.12.1

ἤρτυσαν Aorist, indicative, active, 3rd, plural of ἀρτύω.

νυκτὸς γενομένης Genitive absolute construction.

ἐμετίετο Imperfect, indicative, passive, 3rd, singular of μετίημι (= μεθίημι).

οἱ Dative case.

ἀπολωλέναι Perfect, active infinitive of ἀπόλλυμι.

εἵπετο Imperfect, indicative, middle, 3rd, singular of ἔπομαι.

1.12.2

ἀναπαυομένου Κανδαύλεω Genitive absolute construction.

ὑπεκδύς "Having slipped out." Aorist, active, masculine, nominative, singular participle of ὑπεκδύομαι.

ἐπεμνήσθη "Makes mention of." Aorist, indicative, passive, 3rd, singular of ἐπιμιμνήσκομαι.

☙

1.14.1-3 A Grateful Gyges

We learn in 1.13 that Gyges secured the approval of the Delphic Oracle for his accession to the Lydian throne. In this current chapter, Gyges is described making spectacular offerings at Delphi to thank Apollo (the patron of the Delphic Oracle) and to guarantee the continued good will of the god. The topic of oracles is huge in the *Histories*, and readers are challenged to recover at least a semblance of Herodotus' real views on their validity and/or efficacy. His position seems to be this: since oracular utterances are seldom (if ever) straightforward, it is the responsibility of the humans who consult the oracles to figure out their actual meaning as opposed to their apparent meaning. It should be noted that Herodotus often quotes these utterances and, in so doing, provides us with historical data of some importance. Moreover, we can be fairly confident that Herodotus "knew" his Delphi. In other words, it seems all but certain that he had visited Delphi (perhaps on more than one occasion) and that he was familiar with the votive offerings that a visitor or tourist would see there. He actually shows off his knowledge of Delphi in this section by making a correction of an erroneous claim, according to which certain votive offerings at Delphi resided in the Treasury of Corinth and not in the treasury of the tyrant Cypselos (1.14.2).

τὴν μὲν δὴ τυραννίδα οὕτω ἔσχον οἱ Μερμνάδαι τοὺς Ἡρακλείδας ἀπελόμενοι, Γύγης δὲ τυραννεύσας ἀπέπεμψε ἀναθήματα ἐς Δελφοὺς οὐκ ὀλίγα, ἀλλ᾽ ὅσα μὲν ἀργύρου ἀναθήματα, ἔστι οἱ πλεῖστα ἐν Δελφοῖσι, πάρεξ δὲ τοῦ ἀργύρου χρυσὸν ἄπλετον ἀνέθηκε ἄλλον τε καὶ τοῦ μάλιστα μνήμην ἄξιον ἔχειν ἐστί, κρητῆρές οἱ ἀριθμὸν ἓξ χρύσεοι ἀνακέαται. [2] ἑστᾶσι δὲ οὗτοι ἐν τῷ Κορινθίων θησαυρῷ σταθμὸν ἔχοντες τριήκοντα τάλαντα·

ἀληθέϊ δὲ λόγῳ χρεωμένῳ οὐ Κορινθίων τοῦ δημοσίου ἐστὶ ὁ θησαυρός, ἀλλὰ Κυψέλου τοῦ Ἠετίωνος. οὗτος δὲ ὁ Γύγης πρῶτος βαρβάρων τῶν ἡμεῖς ἴδμεν ἐς Δελφοὺς ἀνέθηκε ἀναθήματα μετὰ Μίδην τὸν Γορδίεω, Φρυγίης βασιλέα. [3] ἀνέθηκε γὰρ δὴ καὶ Μίδης τὸν βασιλήιον θρόνον ἐς τὸν προκατίζων ἐδίκαζε, ἐόντα ἀξιοθέητον· κεῖται δὲ ὁ θρόνος οὗτος ἔνθα περ οἱ τοῦ Γύγεω κρητῆρες. ὁ δὲ χρυσὸς οὗτος καὶ ὁ ἄργυρος, τὸν ὁ Γύγης ἀνέθηκε, ὑπὸ Δελφῶν καλέεται Γυγάδας ἐπὶ τοῦ ἀναθέντος ἐπωνυμίην.

1.14.1

οἱ Μερμνάδαι The family of Gyges.

τοὺς Ἡρακλείδας The family of Candaules; they claimed descent from Herakles.

ἀπελόμενοι Aorist, middle, masculine, nominative, plural participle of ἀπαιρέω (= ἀφαιρέω). Note how this participle takes the double accusative.

ἀλλ᾽ ὅσα μὲν ἀργύρου ἀναθήματα, ἔστι οἱ πλεῖστα ἐν Δελφοῖσι "But as many offerings as there were of silver, most of these in Delphi were from him [Gyges]."

ἀριθμὸν Accusative of respect.

ἀνακέαται = ἀνάκεινται.

1.14.2

τάλαντα As a unit of weight in Athens, a talent was the equivalent of about 57 pounds.

ἀληθέϊ δὲ λόγῳ χρεωμένῳ "To one speaking truthfully," or "If one were to speak the truth."

Κυψέλου Cypselos was a tyrant of Corinth (657-627 B.C.) at a time when the city enjoyed great wealth. His son Periander (627-587 B.C.) succeeded him as tyrant and also enjoyed a long, prosperous reign.

τόν Once again, a relative pronoun.

προκατίζων = προκαθίζων.

ἐπὶ τοῦ ἀναθέντος ἐπωνυμίην "As an eponym [a term or nickname derived from the personal name of someone] of the one who dedicated them."

☙

1.24.1-8 The Best Singer in the World and the Dolphin

Herodotus is clearly wearing the hat of a story-teller in this chapter. The delightful account of Arion's incredible escape from predatory sailors and his subsequent confrontation with his captors is beyond perfect in its timing (the narrative is well-paced), amount of detail (note how Herodotus doesn't waste any time telling us what Arion did in Sicily and Italy), humor (Arion shows up in Corinth wearing the same performer's suit he had on when he jumped overboard), and implied message (Corinthians cannot be trusted). Although the story (certainly older than Herodotus) has all the earmarks of a fairy tale, Herodotus clothes it with some historicity by adding the detail (1.24.8) of the small bronze statue at Tainaron (cf. map in Landmark *ad* 1.24). Twice he indicates that this is a story that others tell (λέγουσι), but this kind of a disclaimer does not quite let him off the hook. Indeed, it reminds us that Herodotus was irresistibly drawn to great stories, no matter the consequences to his reputation as an "inquirer" into great events. This being said, the passage is a gold mine for information on one of the earliest types of lyric poetry (dithyramb), on Arion (no longer considered ahistorical), and on communication between mainland Greece and Magna Graecia (the portions of southern Italy and Sicily that had been colonized by the Greeks beginning in the 8th century B.C.).

τοῦτον τὸν Ἀρίονα λέγουσι, τὸν πολλὸν τοῦ χρόνου διατρίβοντα παρὰ Περιάνδρῳ, ἐπιθυμῆσαι πλῶσαι ἐς Ἰταλίην τε καὶ Σικελίην, ἐργασάμενον δὲ χρήματα μεγάλα θελῆσαι ὀπίσω ἐς Κόρινθον ἀπικέσθαι. [2] ὁρμᾶσθαι μέν νυν ἐκ Τάραντος, πιστεύοντα δὲ οὐδαμοῖσι μᾶλλον ἢ Κορινθίοισι μισθώσασθαι πλοῖον ἀνδρῶν Κορινθίων· τοὺς δὲ ἐν τῷ πελάγεϊ ἐπιβουλεύειν τὸν Ἀρίονα ἐκβαλόντας ἔχειν τὰ χρήματα· τὸν δὲ συνέντα τοῦτο λίσσεσθαι, χρήματα μέν σφι προϊέντα, ψυχὴν δὲ παραιτεόμενον. [3] οὔκων δὴ πείθειν αὐτὸν τούτοισι, ἀλλὰ κελεύειν τοὺς πορθμέας ἢ αὐτὸν διαχρᾶσθαί μιν, ὡς ἂν ταφῆς ἐν γῇ τύχῃ, ἢ ἐκπηδᾶν ἐς τὴν θάλασσαν τὴν ταχίστην· [4] ἀπειληθέντα δὲ τὸν Ἀρίονα ἐς ἀπορίην παραιτήσασθαι, ἐπειδή σφι οὕτω δοκέοι, περιιδεῖν αὐτὸν ἐν τῇ σκευῇ πάσῃ στάντα ἐν τοῖσι ἐδωλίοισι ἀεῖσαι· ἀείσας δὲ ὑπεδέκετο ἑωυτὸν κατεργάσασθαι. [5] καὶ τοῖσι ἐσελθεῖν γὰρ ἡδονὴν εἰ μέλλοιεν ἀκούσεσθαι τοῦ ἀρίστου ἀνθρώπων ἀοιδοῦ, ἀναχωρῆσαι ἐκ τῆς πρύμνης ἐς μέσην νέα. τὸν δὲ ἐνδύντα τε πᾶσαν τὴν σκευὴν καὶ λαβόντα τὴν κιθάρην, στάντα ἐν τοῖσι ἐδωλίοισι διεξελθεῖν νόμον τὸν ὄρθιον, τελευτῶντος δὲ τοῦ νόμου ῥῖψαί μιν ἐς τὴν θάλασσαν ἑωυτὸν ὡς εἶχε σὺν τῇ σκευῇ πάσῃ. [6] καὶ τοὺς μὲν ἀποπλέειν ἐς Κόρινθον, τὸν δὲ δελφῖνα λέγουσι ὑπολαβόντα ἐξενεῖκαι ἐπὶ Ταίναρον. ἀποβάντα δὲ αὐτὸν χωρέειν ἐς Κόρινθον σὺν τῇ σκευῇ καὶ ἀπικόμενον ἀπηγέεσθαι πᾶν τὸ γεγονός. [7] Περίανδρον δὲ ὑπὸ ἀπιστίης Ἀρίονα μὲν ἐν φυλακῇ ἔχειν οὐδαμῇ μετιέντα, ἀνακῶς δὲ ἔχειν τῶν πορθμέων· ὡς δὲ ἄρα παρεῖναι αὐτούς, κληθέντας ἱστορέεσθαι εἴ τι λέγοιεν περὶ Ἀρίονος. φαμένων δὲ ἐκείνων ὡς εἴη τε σῶς περὶ Ἰταλίην καί μιν εὖ πρήσσοντα λίποιεν ἐν Τάραντι, ἐπιφανῆναί σφι τὸν Ἀρίονα ὥσπερ ἔχων ἐξεπήδησε· καὶ τοὺς ἐκπλαγέντας οὐκ ἔχειν ἔτι ἐλεγχομένους ἀρνέεσθαι. [8] ταῦτα μέν νυν Κορίνθιοί τε καὶ Λέσβιοι λέγουσι, καὶ Ἀρίονός ἐστι ἀνάθημα χάλκεον οὐ μέγα ἐπὶ Ταινάρῳ, ἐπὶ δελφῖνος ἐπέων ἄνθρωπος.

1.24.1

λέγουσι The verb's subject, "Corinthians," carries over from the previous chapter. Much of the present chapter is in indirect discourse (oratio obliqua).

παρὰ Περιάνδρῳ "At the court of Periander." He was tyrant at Corinth from 627 to 587 B.C.

ἀπικέσθαι = ἀφίκεσθαι. Aorist, middle infinitive of ἀφικνέομαι.

1.24.2

Τάραντος Taras (the Roman Tarentum and the modern Taranto) was a Spartan colony in the "arch" of the Italian "boot."

συνέντα "Realizing." Aorist, active, masculine, accusative, singular participle of συνίημι.

1.24.3

οὔκων = οὔκουν.

διαχρᾶσθαί "Kill."

τύχῃ Aorist, subjunctive, active, 3rd, singular of τυγχάνω. It takes the genitive.

τὴν ταχίστην "By the quickest [way]."

1.24.4

ἀπειληθέντα Aorist, passive, masculine, accusative, singular participle of ἀπειλέω. "Having been driven."

ἐδωλίοισι The "raised deck in the stern" of a ship.

ἀεῖσαι Aorist, active infinitive of ἀείδω.

ἀείσας δὲ ὑπεδέκετο There is a pause in the indirect statement construction.

ἑωυτὸν = ἑαυτὸν.

1.24.5

νόμον τὸν ὄρθιον "A high-pitched melody."

ὡς εἶχε σὺν τῇ σκευῇ πάσῃ "Just as he was, with his entire performer's garb [still] on."

1.24.6

ἐξενεῖκαι (= ἐξενέγκαι) Aorist, active infinitive of ἐκφέρω.

Ταίναρον The tip of the most southern promontory of the Peloponnese and a purported entrance to the underworld.

ἀπηγέεσθαι Aorist, middle infinitive of ἀπηγέομαι (= ἀφηγέομαι). "He led off," or "he related."

1.24.7

ἀνακῶς δὲ ἔχειν "He was wary of." When ἔχω is used with an adverb, it is the equivalent of the verb "to be."

κληθέντας Aorist, passive, masculine, accusative, plural participle of καλέω.

φαμένων δὲ ἐκείνων Genitive absolute construction.

ἐπιφανῆναί Aorist, passive infinitive of ἐπιφαίνω.

ὥσπερ ἔχων ἐξεπήδησε "Looking as he did when he leapt overboard."

οὐκ ἔχειν "Were unable."

☙

1.29.1-2 Croesus and Solon, Part I

Herein begins one of the most spectacular "performance pieces" of the *Histories*. Four generations after Gyges, Croesus became king of Lydia (560-546 B.C.) and enjoyed tremendous prosperity. To hear Herodotus tell the story, Croesus, like Candaules, was destined for a tragic downfall, one that was eventually brought about by his excessive self-confidence. It is a story that pre-dates Herodotus, but it is also one he tells more brilliantly than probably anyone before him. Perhaps more than any other section of the *Histories*, the story of Croesus and Solon shows us something of Herodotus' philosophy of life, one which regards human happiness as fragile and transitory. The historicity of the meeting between Croesus and the Athenian "wise man" (σοφιστής) has been rightly questioned, as Croesus' reign in Lydia began in 560 B.C., while Solon's archonship (during which he reformed the laws of Athens) was in 594 B.C. In other words, Solon would have been too old to travel to Sardis and visit with Croesus during the king's glory days.

ἀπικνέονται ἐς Σάρδις ἀκμαζούσας πλούτῳ ἄλλοι τε οἱ πάντες ἐκ τῆς Ἑλλάδος σοφισταί, οἳ τοῦτον τὸν χρόνον ἐτύγχανον ἐόντες, ὡς ἕκαστος αὐτῶν ἀπικνέοιτο, καὶ δὴ καὶ Σόλων ἀνὴρ Ἀθηναῖος, ὃς Ἀθηναίοισι νόμους κελεύσασι ποιήσας ἀπεδήμησε ἔτεα δέκα, κατὰ θεωρίης πρόφασιν ἐκπλώσας, ἵνα δὴ μή τινα τῶν νόμων ἀναγκασθῇ λῦσαι τῶν ἔθετο. [2] αὐτοὶ γὰρ οὐκ οἷοί τε ἦσαν αὐτὸ ποιῆσαι Ἀθηναῖοι· ὁρκίοισι γὰρ μεγάλοισι κατείχοντο δέκα ἔτεα χρήσεσθαι νόμοισι τοὺς ἄν σφι Σόλων θῆται.

1.29.1

ἀπικνέονται = ἀφικνοῦνται.

σοφισταί Not "Sophists" in the historical and technical sense, but "wise men" or "sages."

ὡς ἕκαστος αὐτῶν ἀπικνέοιτο "For whatever reasons each of them might come."

Ἀθηναίοισι νόμους κελεύσασι "For the Athenians who requested the laws."

ἔτεα δέκα Accusative of extent of time.

ἀναγκασθῇ Aorist, subjunctive, passive, 3rd, singular of ἀναγκάζω.

τῶν Here, a relative pronoun.

1.29.2

οὐκ οἷοί τε ἦσαν "Were not able."

χρήσεσθαι Future, middle infinitive of χράω.

θῆται Aorist, subjunctive, middle, 3rd, singular of τίθημι.

☙

1.30.1-5 Croesus and Solon, Part II

The story of Solon's encounter with Croesus continues at a brisk pace. Herodotus skips over the sage's visit to Amasis in Egypt, even though it is a backdrop to the legend of Atlantis (cf. Plato, *Timaeus* 20d-27b), and focuses instead on the famous dialogue at the court of Croesus. It is hard to say how much of this visit is historical, given the chronological problems it entails (as Solon may have been dead by the time Croesus came to power in 560 B.C.). Even so, Herodotus' story of why Tellus was the happiest man on earth is replete with valuable insights into the Greek value system, certain aspects of which may actually strike a modern reader as quite familiar (e.g., the blessing of being outlived by your children and their children: cf. 1.30.4).

αὐτῶν δὴ ὦν τούτων καὶ τῆς θεωρίης ἐκδημήσας ὁ Σόλων εἵνεκεν ἐς Αἴγυπτον ἀπίκετο παρὰ Ἄμασιν καὶ δὴ καὶ ἐς Σάρδις παρὰ Κροῖσον. ἀπικόμενος δὲ ἐξεινίζετο ἐν τοῖσι βασιληίοισι ὑπὸ τοῦ Κροίσου· μετὰ δέ, ἡμέρῃ τρίτῃ ἢ τετάρτῃ, κελεύσαντος Κροίσου τὸν Σόλωνα θεράποντες περιῆγον κατὰ τοὺς θησαυροὺς καὶ ἐπεδείκνυσαν πάντα ἐόντα μεγάλα τε καὶ ὄλβια. [2] θηησάμενον δέ μιν τὰ πάντα καὶ σκεψάμενον, ὥς οἱ κατὰ καιρὸν ἦν, εἴρετο ὁ Κροῖσος τάδε· "Ξεῖνε Ἀθηναῖε, παρ' ἡμέας γὰρ περὶ σέο λόγος ἀπίκται πολλὸς καὶ σοφίης εἵνεκεν τῆς σῆς καὶ πλάνης, ὡς φιλοσοφέων γῆν πολλὴν θεωρίης εἵνεκεν ἐπελήλυθας· νῦν ὦν ἐπειρέσθαι με ἵμερος ἐπῆλθέ σε εἴ τινα ἤδη πάντων εἶδες ὀλβιώτατον." [3] ὁ μὲν ἐλπίζων εἶναι ἀνθρώπων ὀλβιώτατος ταῦτα ἐπείρώτα, Σόλων δὲ οὐδὲν ὑποθωπεύσας, ἀλλὰ τῷ ἐόντι χρησάμενος λέγει· "ὦ βασιλεῦ, Τέλλον Ἀθηναῖον." [4] ἀποθωμάσας δὲ Κροῖσος τὸ λεχθὲν εἴρετο ἐπιστρεφέως· "κοίῃ δὴ κρίνεις Τέλλον εἶναι ὀλβιώτατον;" ὁ δὲ εἶπε· "Τέλλῳ τοῦτο μὲν τῆς πόλιος εὖ ἡκούσης παῖδες ἦσαν καλοί τε κἀγαθοί, καὶ σφι εἶδε ἅπασι τέκνα ἐκγενόμενά καὶ πάντα παραμείναντα· τοῦτο δὲ τοῦ βίου εὖ ἥκοντι, ὡς τὰ παρ' ἡμῖν, τελευτὴ τοῦ βίου λαμπροτάτη ἐπεγένετο· [5] γενομένης γὰρ Ἀθηναίοισι μάχης πρὸς τοὺς ἀστυγείτονας ἐν Ἐλευσῖνι βοηθήσας καὶ τροπὴν ποιήσας τῶν πολεμίων ἀπέθανε κάλλιστα, καὶ μίν Ἀθηναῖοι δημοσίῃ τε ἔθαψαν αὐτοῦ τῇ περ ἔπεσε καὶ ἐτίμησαν μεγάλως."

1.30.1

ὦν = οὖν.

εἵνεκεν = ἕνεκα. When this preposition follows its object (anastrophe), several words can intervene.

ἀπίκετο = ἀφίκετο.

παρὰ Ἄμασιν "At the court of Amasis." Amasis was a pharaoh of the Saite Dynasty and ruled c. 569-525 B.C. For the story of his friendship with another famous Greek, Polycrates of Samos, see below the commentary for 3.40.

καὶ δὴ καὶ With these three words, Herodotus puts emphasis on the second item in a series of two, the first of which (the visit to Egypt) is not as important as the second (the visit to Sardis). Translate: "But especially."

Σάρδις See map in Landmark *ad* 1.28.

παρὰ Κροῖσον Croesus' dates as king are c. 560-546 B.C.

ἡμέρῃ τρίτῃ ἢ τετάρτῃ A standard unit of time in Herodotus.

κελεύσαντος Κροίσου Genitive absolute construction.

1.30.2

ὥς οἱ κατὰ καιρὸν ἦν "When the right moment had arrived."

ἐπελήλυθας Perfect, indicative, active, 2nd, singular of ἐπέρχομαι.

ἐπειρέσθαι Aorist, middle infinitive of ἐπείρομαι (= ἐπέρομαι).

εἴ τινα ἤδη πάντων εἶδες ὀλβιώτατον A compressed clause where a verb phrase needs to be supplied. Translate: "If anyone of all the people you have seen [can be judged to be] happiest."

1.30.3

ἐπειρώτα = ἐπέρωτα.

τῷ ἐόντι Literally, "that which is." Idiomatically, "reality."

1.30.4

τὸ λεχθὲν "What had [just] been said."

κοίη = ποίη. "In what [way]?"

τοῦτο μὲν Translate with τοῦτο δὲ: "For one thing...for another."

τῆς πόλιος εὖ ἡκούσης Genitive absolute construction.

κἀγαθοί Crasis (two words combined into one) for καὶ ἀγαθοί.

παραμείναντα "Outliving [him]."

τοῦ βίου εὖ ἥκοντι "Prospering in his occupation."

γενομένης γὰρ Ἀθηναίοισι μάχης Genitive absolute construction.

☙

1.31.1-4 Croesus and Solon, Part III

To place second in Homer's heroic world was unacceptable (cf. *Odyssey* 9.159-64). We see in this passage, however, that Croesus would have gladly settled for the title of second happiest man on earth, one which Solon confers instead on Cleobis and Biton. Although the story of these two Argive youths is peppered with mythological details, it manages to pass as quasi-historical as a result of Herodotus' reference to the two statues which were set up at Delphi in their honor. Two *kouroi* which now reside in the museum at Delphi have been identified by scholars as representing Cleobis and Biton and give "striking confirmation" (cf. HW *ad* 1.31.5) of Herodotus' account (but see also ALC *ad* 1.31.1). The philosophy which underpins the story of Cleobis and Biton and which is summarized with this one sentence, ὡς ἄμεινον εἴη ἀνθρώπῳ τεθνάναι μᾶλλον ἢ ζώειν, may certainly be characterized as pessimistic, and it may even incline a reader to label Herodotus' own life-view as pessimistic. It is not, however, a simple advocacy of death over life but is part of a calculation, that it may be better to die at the peak of one's success and glory than to continue living and run the risk of a reversal of fortune. (There is a similar sentiment in the famous choral ode which comes at the end of Sophocles' *Oedipus Tyrannus*.)

ὡς δὲ τὰ κατὰ τὸν Τέλλον προετρέψατο ὁ Σόλων τὸν Κροῖσον εἴπας πολλά τε καὶ ὄλβια, ἐπειρώτα τίνα δεύτερον μετ᾽ ἐκεῖνον ἴδοι, δοκέων πάγχυ δευτερεῖα γῶν οἴσεσθαι. ὁ δ᾽ εἶπε· "Κλέοβίν τε καὶ Βίτωνα. [2] τούτοισι γὰρ ἐοῦσι γένος Ἀργείοισι βίος τε ἀρκέων ὑπῆν καὶ πρὸς τούτῳ ῥώμη σώματος τοιήδε· ἀεθλοφόροι τε ἀμφότεροι ὁμοίως ἦσαν, καὶ δὴ καὶ λέγεται ὅδε ὁ λόγος· ἐούσης ὁρτῆς τῇ Ἥρῃ τοῖσι Ἀργείοισι ἔδεε πάντως τὴν μητέρα αὐτῶν ζεύγεϊ κομισθῆναι ἐς τὸ ἱρόν, οἱ δέ σφι βόες ἐκ τοῦ ἀγροῦ οὐ παρεγίνοντο ἐν ὥρῃ· ἐκκληιόμενοι δὲ τῇ ὥρῃ οἱ νεηνίαι ὑποδύντες αὐτοὶ ὑπὸ τὴν ζεύγλην εἷλκον τὴν ἅμαξαν, ἐπὶ τῆς ἁμάξης δέ σφι ὠχέετο ἡ μήτηρ· σταδίους δὲ πέντε καὶ τεσσεράκοντα διακομίσαντες ἀπίκοντο ἐς τὸ ἱρόν. [3] ταῦτα δέ σφι ποιήσασι καὶ ὀφθεῖσι ὑπὸ τῆς πανηγύριος τελευτὴ τοῦ βίου ἀρίστη ἐπεγένετο, διέδεξέ τε ἐν τούτοισι ὁ θεὸς ὡς ἄμεινον εἴη ἀνθρώπῳ τεθνάναι μᾶλλον ἢ ζώειν. Ἀργεῖοι μὲν γὰρ περιστάντες ἐμακάριζον τῶν νεηνιέων τὴν ῥώμην, αἱ δὲ Ἀργεῖαι τὴν μητέρα αὐτῶν, οἵων τέκνων ἐκύρησε· [4] ἡ δὲ μήτηρ περιχαρὴς ἐοῦσα τῷ τε ἔργῳ καὶ τῇ φήμῃ, στᾶσα ἀντίον τοῦ ἀγάλματος εὔχετο Κλεόβι τε καὶ Βίτωνι τοῖσι ἑωυτῆς τέκνοισι, οἵ μιν ἐτίμησαν μεγάλως, τὴν θεὸν δοῦναι τὸ ἀνθρώπῳ τυχεῖν ἄριστόν ἐστι. [5] μετὰ ταύτην δὲ τὴν εὐχὴν ὡς ἔθυσάν τε καὶ εὐωχήθησαν, κατακοιμηθέντες ἐν αὐτῷ τῷ ἱρῷ οἱ νεηνίαι οὐκέτι ἀνέστησαν, ἀλλ᾽ ἐν τέλεϊ τούτῳ ἔσχοντο. Ἀργεῖοι δὲ σφεων εἰκόνας ποιησάμενοι ἀνέθεσαν ἐς Δελφοὺς ὡς ἀνδρῶν ἀρίστων γενομένων."

1.31.1

τὰ κατὰ τὸν Τέλλον "In the matters concerning Tellus."

προετρέψατο "Incited."

τίνα δεύτερον μετ᾽ ἐκεῖνον ἴδοι "Whom he [Solon] might see, after him [Croesus], as second."

γῶν = γοῦν.

οἴσεσθαι Future, middle infinitive of φέρω.

1.31.2

γένος Accusative of respect.

βίος τε ἀρκέων ὑπῆν "Life was sufficiently prosperous."

ἐούσης ὁρτῆς Genitive absolute construction.

ὁρτῆς = ἑορτῆς.

ἱρόν = ἱερόν.

ἐν ὥρῃ "On time."

ἐκκληιόμενοι δὲ τῇ ὥρῃ Literally, "Being excluded by time." More idiomatically, "Being thwarted by the [lack of] time."

ἐκκληιόμενοι = ἐκκλειόμενοι.

σταδίους δὲ πέντε καὶ τεσσεράκοντα Approximately 5 miles.

ἀπίκοντο = ἀφίκοντο.

1.31.3

ὀφθεῖσι Aorist, passive, masculine, dative, plural participle of ὁράω.

διέδεξέ Aorist, indicative, active, 3rd, singular of διαδείκνυμι.

τεθνάναι Perfect, active, infinitive of θνήσκω.

οἵων τέκνων ἐκύρησε "[For] the kind of sons she had raised."

1.31.4

τὴν θεὸν δοῦναι Translate with εὔχετο.

τὸ ἀνθρώπῳ τυχεῖν ἄριστόν ἐστι "The thing which for a human being is best to obtain."

1.31.5

εὐωχήθησαν Aorist, indicative, passive, 3rd, plural of εὐωχέω.

ἐν τέλεϊ τούτῳ ἔσχοντο The middle (ἔσχοντο) functions here as a passive. "They were held in this finality." In other words, "They died."

ὡς ἀνδρῶν ἀρίστων γενομένων A causal expression: "Because they were the best men." When ὡς introduces a phrase like this, it means that the reason given is not necessarily that of the author.

☙

1.32.1-9 Croesus and Solon, Part IV

The paradox from the previous chapter is here resolved. What Solon (Herodotus?) meant when he said ὡς ἄμεινον εἴη ἀνθρώπῳ τεθνάναι μᾶλλον ἢ ζώειν is summed up with this second maxim: σκοπέειν δὲ χρὴ παντὸς χρήματος τὴν τελευτήν. We also learn that the reason one has to "look to the end" is because of the mercurial and determinative nature of fortune, which often gives men a glimpse of happiness only to destroy them utterly. There is much to recommend this passage, including the sobering calculations that Solon makes about the number of days a human can expect to live. That he should make such a calculation (albeit, possibly an erroneous one: cf. HW *ad* 1.32.3) is in keeping with the tradition that Solon reformed the Athenian calendar during his year as archon eponymous (594 B.C.). The popularity of Herodotus' account can be seen in the way

Aristotle (*Nicomachean Ethics* 1178 b33) quotes the passage. As for the larger philosophical themes here, they are echoed in Sophocles' *Philoctetes* (lines 305-6). Finally, it should be mentioned that Herodotus' use of the singular ὁ θεός, here (1.32.9) and elsewhere (1.31.3), need not be taken as an indication of some incipient monotheism, but is most likely an alternative to τὸ θεῖον (seen in 1.32.1) or "divinity" (cf. ALC *ad* 31.3).

Σόλων μὲν δὴ εὐδαιμονίης δευτερεῖα ἔνεμε τούτοισι, Κροῖσος δὲ σπερχθεὶς εἶπε· "ὦ ξεῖνε Ἀθηναῖε, ἡ δ᾽ ἡμετέρη εὐδαιμονίη οὕτω τοι ἀπέρριπται ἐς τὸ μηδὲν ὥστε οὐδὲ ἰδιωτέων ἀνδρῶν ἀξίους ἡμέας ἐποίησας;" ὁ δὲ εἶπε· "ὦ Κροῖσε, ἐπιστάμενόν με τὸ θεῖον πᾶν ἐὸν φθονερόν τε καὶ ταραχῶδες ἐπειρωτᾷς ἀνθρωπηίων πρηγμάτων πέρι. [2] ἐν γὰρ τῷ μακρῷ χρόνῳ πολλὰ μὲν ἔστι ἰδεῖν τὰ μή τις ἐθέλει, πολλὰ δὲ καὶ παθεῖν. ἐς γὰρ ἑβδομήκοντα ἔτεα οὖρον τῆς ζόης ἀνθρώπῳ προτίθημι. [3] οὗτοι ἐόντες ἐνιαυτοὶ ἑβδομήκοντα παρέχονται ἡμέρας διηκοσίας καὶ πεντακισχιλίας καὶ δισμυρίας, ἐμβολίμου μηνὸς μὴ γινομένου· εἰ δὲ δὴ ἐθελήσει τοὔτερον τῶν ἐτέων μηνὶ μακρότερον γίνεσθαι, ἵνα δὴ αἱ ὧραι συμβαίνωσι παραγινόμεναι ἐς τὸ δέον, μῆνες μὲν παρὰ τὰ ἑβδομήκοντα ἔτεα οἱ ἐμβόλιμοι γίνονται τριήκοντα πέντε, ἡμέραι δὲ ἐκ τῶν μηνῶν τούτων χίλιαι πεντήκοντα. [4] τουτέων τῶν ἁπασέων ἡμερέων τῶν ἐς τὰ ἑβδομήκοντα ἔτεα, ἐουσέων πεντήκοντα καὶ διηκοσιέων καὶ ἑξακισχιλιέων καὶ δισμυριέων, ἡ ἑτέρη αὐτέων τῇ ἑτέρῃ ἡμέρῃ τὸ παράπαν οὐδὲν ὅμοιον προσάγει πρῆγμα. οὕτω ὦν, Κροῖσε, πᾶν ἐστι ἄνθρωπος συμφορή. [5] ἐμοὶ δὲ σὺ καὶ πλουτέειν μέγα φαίνεαι καὶ βασιλεὺς πολλῶν εἶναι ἀνθρώπων· ἐκεῖνο δὲ τὸ εἴρεό με οὔ κώ σε ἐγὼ λέγω, πρὶν τελευτήσαντα καλῶς τὸν αἰῶνα πύθωμαι. οὐ γάρ τι ὁ μέγα πλούσιος μᾶλλον τοῦ ἐπ᾽ ἡμέρην ἔχοντος ὀλβιώτερός ἐστι, εἰ μή οἱ τύχη ἐπίσποιτο πάντα καλὰ ἔχοντα εὖ τελευτῆσαι τὸν βίον. πολλοὶ μὲν γὰρ ζάπλουτοι ἀνθρώπων ἀνόλβοί εἰσι, πολλοὶ δὲ μετρίως ἔχοντες βίου εὐτυχέες. [6] ὁ μὲν δὴ μέγα πλούσιος ἀνόλβιος δὲ δυοῖσι προέχει τοῦ εὐτυχέος μοῦνον, οὗτος δὲ τοῦ πλουσίου καὶ ἀνόλβου πολλοῖσι· ὁ μὲν ἐπιθυμίην ἐκτελέσαι καὶ ἄτην μεγάλην προσπεσοῦσαν ἐνεῖκαι δυνατώτερος, ὁ δὲ τοισίδε προέχει ἐκείνου· ἄτην μὲν καὶ ἐπιθυμίην οὐκ ὁμοίως δυνατὸς ἐκείνῳ ἐνεῖκαι, ταῦτα δὲ ἡ εὐτυχίη οἱ ἀπερύκει, ἄπηρος δέ ἐστι, ἄνουσος, ἀπαθὴς κακῶν, εὔπαις, εὐειδής· [7] εἰ δὲ πρὸς τούτοισι ἔτι τελευτήσει τὸν βίον εὖ, οὗτος ἐκεῖνος τὸν σὺ ζητέεις, ὁ ὄλβιος κεκλῆσθαι ἄξιός ἐστι· πρὶν δ᾽ ἂν τελευτήσῃ, ἐπισχεῖν μηδὲ καλέειν κω ὄλβιον, ἀλλ᾽ εὐτυχέα. [8] τὰ πάντα μέν νυν ταῦτα συλλαβεῖν ἄνθρωπον ἐόντα ἀδύνατον ἐστι, ὥσπερ χώρη οὐδεμία καταρκέει πάντα ἑωυτῇ παρέχουσα, ἀλλὰ ἄλλο μὲν ἔχει, ἑτέρου δὲ ἐπιδέεται· ἣ δὲ ἂν τὰ πλεῖστα ἔχῃ, αὕτη ἀρίστη. ὣς δὲ καὶ ἀνθρώπου σῶμα ἓν οὐδὲν αὔταρκες ἐστι· τὸ μὲν γὰρ ἔχει, ἄλλου δὲ ἐνδεές ἐστι· [9] ὃς δ' ἂν αὐτῶν πλεῖστα ἔχων διατελέῃ καὶ ἔπειτα τελευτήσῃ εὐχαρίστως τὸν βίον, οὗτος παρ' ἐμοὶ τὸ οὔνομα τοῦτο, ὦ βασιλεῦ, δίκαιος ἐστι φέρεσθαι. σκοπέειν δὲ χρὴ παντὸς χρήματος τὴν τελευτὴν κῇ ἀποβήσεται· πολλοῖσι γὰρ δὴ ὑποδέξας ὄλβον ὁ θεὸς προρρίζους ἀνέτρεψε."

1.32.1

σπερχθείς Aorist, passive, masculine, nominative, singular participle of σπέρχω. "Irritated."

ἀπέρριπται ἐς τὸ μηδέν "Has been rejected as worthless."

ἀπέρριπται Perfect, indicative, passive, 3rd, singular of ἀπορρίπτω.

ταραχῶδες "Given to making trouble."

ἐπειρωτᾷς = ἐπερωτᾷς.

πέρι An instance of anastrophe, where the postpositive preposition governs the preceding word (note the position of the accent).

1.32.2

τά Here, a relative pronoun.

οὖρον = ὅρον.

1.32.3

ἐμβολίμου μηνὸς This "intercalary month" was regularly added to the lunar year to synchronize it with the solar year.

ἐθελήσει Future, indicative, middle, 2nd, singular of ἐθέλω.

τοὔτερον Crasis (two words combined into one) for τὸ ἕτερον.

ἐς τὸ δέον "To what is necessary." In other words, so that the calendar and the agricultural seasons could be synchronized.

1.32.4

πᾶν ἐστὶ ἄνθρωπος συμφορή "Human existence is all about chance."

1.32.5

οὐ γάρ τι A strong negative expression: "Not in the least."

τοῦ ἐπ' ἡμέρην ἔχοντος A genitive of comparison construction. Idiomatically, "than one who just gets by from one day to the next."

τύχη Synonymous with the earlier συμφορή.

ἐπίσποιτο Aorist, optative, middle, 3rd, singular of ἐφέπω.

1.32.6

δυοῖσι προέχει τοῦ εὐτυχέος μοῦνον "Has an advantage over the fortunate one only in two things."

ὁ That is, the wealthy person.

ἐκτελέσαι Translate both this infinitive and the following ἐνεῖκαι (aorist, active infinitive of
    φέρω) as complements to δυνατώτερος.

ταῦτα δὲ ἡ εὐτυχίη οἱ ἀπερύκει "But good luck wards off these things for him."

1.32.7

ἐπισχεῖν…καλέειν The infinitives are used here as commands.

κω = πω.

1.32.8

ἑωυτῇ = ἑαυτῇ.

σῶμα Here, "person" (and not "body").

1.32.9

κῇ = πῇ.

ἀποβήσεται Subject is τελευτή.

ὑποδέξας "Having given a glimpse."

☙

1.33.1 Croesus and Solon, Epilogue

Croesus will have to learn the hard way that he should have taken to heart Solon's
advice, "Look to the end." The following story of his son Atys will amply confirm the
wisdom of Solon's prescription as to what constitutes human happiness.

ταῦτα λέγων τῷ Κροίσῳ οὔ κως οὔτε ἐχαρίζετο, οὔτε λόγου μιν ποιησάμενος
οὐδενὸς ἀποπέμπεται, κάρτα δόξας ἀμαθέα εἶναι, ὃς τὰ παρεόντα ἀγαθὰ
μετεὶς τὴν τελευτὴν παντὸς χρήματος ὁρᾶν ἐκέλευε.

1.33.1

κως = πως.

λόγου Genitive of value. "Worth."

ἀποπέμπεται The subject has switched from Solon to Croesus.

μετεὶς Aorist, active, masculine, nominative, singular participle of μετίημι (= μεθίημι).

☙

1.34.1-3 Atys and the Boar Hunt, Part I

This chapter begins another of Herodotus' so-called "performance pieces," extended
sections of the *Histories* which may have been delivered orally to appreciative audiences
even before they appeared in written form. It has often been pointed out that the story
of Croesus is like a mini-tragedy in which the Lydian king could pass for a "tragic hero"

(cf. ALC *ad* 34-45). Indeed, certain features of Herodotus' tale remind us of Sophocles' *Oedipus Tyrannus*. For example, the dilemma of Oedipus is the same for Croesus, insofar as both bring about the very calamity they want so desperately to avoid. Although it is the prediction of a dream which Croesus wishes to thwart, and not that of an oracle, both tragic heroes have in common the inability to interpret correctly a dream or an oracle.

μετὰ δὲ Σόλωνα οἰχόμενον ἔλαβε ἐκ θεοῦ νέμεσις μεγάλη Κροῖσον, ὡς εἰκάσαι, ὅτι ἐνόμισε ἑωυτὸν εἶναι ἀνθρώπων ἁπάντων ὀλβιώτατον. αὐτίκα δέ οἱ εὕδοντι ἐπέστη ὄνειρος, ὅς οἱ τὴν ἀληθείην ἔφαινε τῶν μελλόντων γενέσθαι κακῶν κατὰ τὸν παῖδα. [2] ἦσαν δὲ τῷ Κροίσῳ δύο παῖδες, τῶν οὕτερος μὲν διέφθαρτο, ἦν γὰρ δὴ κωφός, ὁ δὲ ἕτερος τῶν ἡλίκων μακρῷ τὰ πάντα πρῶτος· οὔνομα δέ οἱ ἦν Ἄτυς. τοῦτον δὴ ὦν τὸν Ἄτυν σημαίνει τῷ Κροίσῳ ὁ ὄνειρος, ὡς ἀπολέει μιν αἰχμῇ σιδηρέῃ βληθέντα. [3] ὁ δ' ἐπείτε ἐξηγέρθη καὶ ἑωυτῷ λόγον ἔδωκε, καταρρωδήσας τὸν ὄνειρον ἄγεται μὲν τῷ παιδὶ γυναῖκα, ἐωθότα δὲ στρατηγέειν μιν τῶν Λυδῶν οὐδαμῇ ἔτι ἐπὶ τοιοῦτο πρῆγμα ἐξέπεμπε· ἀκόντια δὲ καὶ δοράτια καὶ τὰ τοιαῦτα πάντα τοῖσι χρέωνται ἐς πόλεμον ἄνθρωποι, ἐκ τῶν ἀνδρεώνων ἐκκομίσας ἐς τοὺς θαλάμους συνένησε, μή τί οἱ κρεμάμενον τῷ παιδὶ ἐμπέσῃ.

1.34.1
Σόλωνα οἰχόμενον "Solon's departure."
ὡς εἰκάσαι "As I suppose." The infinitive here is used absolutely.
ἑωυτὸν = ἑαυτὸν.

1.34.2
οὕτερος Crasis (two words combined into one) for ὁ ἕτερος.
διέφθαρτο Pluperfect, indicative, passive, 3rd, singular of διαφθείρω.
μακρῷ Dative of degree of difference.
τὰ πάντα Accusative of respect.
ὦν = οὖν.
ἀπολέει Future, indicative, active, 3rd, singular of ἀπόλλυμι. "Will lose."
βληθέντα Aorist, passive, masculine, accusative, singular participle of βάλλω.

1.34.3
ἐξηγέρθη Aorist, indicative, passive, 3rd, singular of ἐξεγείρω.
ἑωυτῷ λόγον ἔδωκε "He consulted with himself."
ἐωθότα "Although he was accustomed."
Λυδῶν Genitive after στρατηγέειν.
τοῖσι Translate as a relative pronoun.
συνένησε Aorist, indicative, active, 3rd, singular of συννέω.

☙

1.35.1-4 Atys and the Boar Hunt, Part II

Adrastos, an exile from Phrygia, shows up at Croesus' court and asks that he be given purification rites. Herodotus the ethnographer takes this opportunity to point out that Lydian and Greek rites of purification were essentially the same (1.35.2), but he does not go into any detail, probably because he did not want to slow down his story. The Croesus we see in this passage is quite different from the arrogant king who angrily sent Solon on his way in the earlier chapter. His words of welcome and assurance to Adrastos are quite moving and help illustrate what a wonderfully humane code of conduct the Greek concept of *xenia* represented. (That Herodotus should put these welcoming words into the mouth of a Lydian and not a Greek is perhaps to be expected.) Equally striking is the wisdom that has come over Croesus, who is shown giving some very Solonian advice to Adrastos in the last sentence of this chapter.

ἔχοντος δέ οἱ ἐν χερσὶ τοῦ παιδὸς τὸν γάμον ἀπικνέεται ἐς τὰς Σάρδις ἀνὴρ συμφορῇ ἐχόμενος καὶ οὐ καθαρὸς χεῖρας, ἐὼν Φρὺξ μὲν γενεῇ, γένεος δὲ τοῦ βασιληίου. παρελθὼν δὲ οὗτος ἐς τὰ Κροίσου οἰκία κατὰ νόμους τοὺς ἐπιχωρίους καθαρσίου ἐδέετο ἐπικυρῆσαι, Κροῖσος δέ μιν ἐκάθηρε. [2] ἔστι δὲ παραπλησίη ἡ κάθαρσις τοῖσι Λυδοῖσι καὶ τοῖσι Ἕλλησι. ἐπείτε δὲ τὰ νομιζόμενα ἐποίησε ὁ Κροῖσος, ἐπυνθάνετο ὁκόθεν τε καὶ τίς εἴη, λέγων τάδε· [3] "ὤνθρωπε, τίς τε ἐὼν καὶ κόθεν τῆς Φρυγίης ἥκων ἐπίστιός μοι ἐγένεο; τίνα τε ἀνδρῶν ἢ γυναικῶν ἐφόνευσας;" ὁ δὲ ἀμείβετο· "ὦ βασιλεῦ, Γορδίεω μὲν τοῦ Μίδεω εἰμὶ παῖς, ὀνομάζομαι δὲ Ἄδρηστος, φονεύσας δὲ ἀδελφεὸν ἐμεωυτοῦ ἀέκων πάρειμι ἐξεληλαμένος τε ὑπὸ τοῦ πατρὸς καὶ ἐστερημένος πάντων." [4] Κροῖσος δέ μιν ἀμείβετο τοισίδε· "ἀνδρῶν τε φίλων τυγχάνεις ἔκγονος ἐὼν καὶ ἐλήλυθας ἐς φίλους, ἔνθα ἀμηχανήσεις χρήματος οὐδενὸς μένων ἐν ἡμετέρου. συμφορήν δὲ ταύτην ὡς κουφότατα φέρων κερδανέεις πλεῖστον."

1.35.1
χεῖρας Accusative of respect.
γενεῇ Dative of respect. Both the accusative and the dative can have this function.
καθαρσίου Genitive after κυρῆσαι.

1.35.2
τὰ νομιζόμενα "The required rituals."
ὀκόθεν = ὁπόθεν.

1.35.3
ὤνθρωπε Crasis (two words combined into one) for ὦ ἄνθρωπε.

κόθεν τῆς Φρυγίης "From where in Phrygia."

κόθεν = πόθεν.

ἐμεωυτοῦ = ἐμαυτοῦ.

ἐξεληλαμένος Perfect, passive, masculine, nominative, singular participle of ἐξελαύνω.

1.35.4

τυγχάνεις ἔκγονος ἐών "You happen to be a relative."

ἐν ἡμετέρου Supply οἴκῳ.

☙

1.36.1-3 Atys and the Boar Hunt, Part III

The boar hunt was a popular theme in Greek literature as far back as Homer. In the Calydonian Boar hunt, the most celebrated instance of such a venture, every important legendary hero (Bacchylides referred to them as "the best of the Greeks"), with the exception of Herakles, took part in the event. The boar hunt which Herodotus presents here was arranged to track down a "great thing of a boar" (1.36.1), which terrorized the people of Mysia (a region in the northwest of Asia Minor). Doubtless, a story like this added a level of excitement to Herodotus' "performance piece." Note also the extensive dialogue in this chapter: it resembles speaking parts of a play and would have allowed the "audience" to comprehend fully the irony of what was being said.

ὁ μὲν δὴ δίαιταν εἶχε ἐν Κροίσου, ἐν δὲ τῷ αὐτῷ χρόνῳ τούτῳ ἐν τῷ Μυσίῳ Ὀλύμπῳ ὑὸς χρῆμα γίνεται μέγα· ὁρμώμενος δὲ οὗτος ἐκ τοῦ ὄρεος τούτου τὰ τῶν Μυσῶν ἔργα διαφθείρεσκε, πολλάκις δὲ οἱ Μυσοὶ ἐπ' αὐτὸν ἐξελθόντες ποιέεσκον μὲν κακὸν οὐδέν, ἔπασχον δὲ πρὸς αὐτοῦ. [2] τέλος δὲ ἀπικόμενοι παρὰ τὸν Κροῖσον τῶν Μυσῶν ἄγγελοι ἔλεγον τάδε· "ὦ βασιλεῦ, ὑὸς χρῆμα μέγιστον ἀνεφάνη ἡμῖν ἐν τῇ χώρῃ, ὃς τὰ ἔργα διαφθείρει. τοῦτον προθυμεόμενοι ἑλεῖν οὐ δυνάμεθα. νῦν ὦν προσδεόμεθά σευ τὸν παῖδα καὶ λογάδας νεηνίας καὶ κύνας συμπέμψαι ἡμῖν, ὡς ἄν μιν ἐξέλωμεν ἐκ τῆς χώρης." [3] οἱ μὲν δὴ τούτων ἐδέοντο, Κροῖσος δὲ μνημονεύων τοῦ ὀνείρου τὰ ἔπεα ἔλεγέ σφι τάδε· "παιδὸς μὲν περὶ τοῦ ἐμοῦ μὴ μνησθῆτε ἔτι· οὐ γὰρ ἂν ὑμῖν συμπέμψαιμι· νεόγαμός τε γάρ ἐστι καὶ ταῦτά οἱ νῦν μέλει. Λυδῶν μέντοι λογάδας καὶ τὸ κυνηγέσιον πᾶν συμπέμψω, καὶ διακελεύσομαι τοῖσι ἰοῦσι εἶναι ὡς προθυμοτάτοισι συνεξελεῖν ὑμῖν τὸ θηρίον ἐκ τῆς χώρης."

1.36.1

ὁ Adrastos.

ἐν Κροίσου Supply οἴκῳ.

Μυσίῳ Ὀλύμπῳ Mysia is in the northwest section of Asia Minor. For the location of Mt. Olympus in Mysia, see map in Landmark *ad* 1.46.

ὑὸς χρῆμα γίνεται μέγα "A giant monster of a boar appeared."

γίνεται = γίγνεται.

ἔργα "Fields and crops."

διαφθείρεσκε The infix -εσκ, inserted before the personal ending, marks this verb as an iterative imperfect. Note that there is no augment.

ποιέεσκον Another iterative imperfect.

πρὸς αὐτοῦ Here, the preposition πρὸς expresses agency.

1.36.2

τέλος Adverbial accusative.

ἀπικόμενοι = ἀφικόμενοι.

ἀνεφάνη Aorist, indicative, passive, 3rd, singular of ἀναφαίνω.

ἑλεῖν Aorist, active infinitive of αἱρέω.

ὦν = οὖν.

1.36.3

μὴ μνησθῆτε "Don't mention."

συμπέμψαιμι Potential optative. "I would [not] send."

ࢤ

1.37.1-3 Atys and the Boar Hunt, Part IV

This chapter drives home the point that the hunt was an important arena for the ancient aristocratic code of conduct, insofar as it confirmed the reputation of the hunter in the eyes of the community (and even in the eyes of his wife). The speech put into the mouth of Atys is persuasive, as are most of the speeches in Herodotus, and even reasonable, especially in the part where the son asks the father to show him why it was that staying at home was the better option (1.37.3).

ταῦτα ἀμείψατο· ἀποχρεωμένων δὲ τούτοισι τῶν Μυσῶν ἐπεσέρχεται ὁ τοῦ Κροίσου παῖς ἀκηκοὼς τῶν ἐδέοντο οἱ Μυσοί. οὐ φαμένου δὲ τοῦ Κροίσου τόν γε παῖδά σφι συμπέμψειν λέγει πρὸς αὐτὸν ὁ νεηνίης τάδε· [2] "ὦ πάτερ, τὰ κάλλιστα πρότερόν κοτε καὶ γενναιότατα ἡμῖν ἦν ἔς τε πολέμους καὶ ἐς ἄγρας φοιτέοντας εὐδοκιμέειν· νῦν δὲ ἀμφοτέρων με τούτων ἀποκληίσας ἔχεις, οὔτε τινὰ δειλίην μοι παριδὼν οὔτε ἀθυμίην. νῦν τε τέοισί με χρὴ ὄμμασι ἔς τε ἀγορὴν καὶ ἐξ ἀγορῆς φοιτέοντα φαίνεσθαι; [3] κοῖος μέν τις τοῖσι πολιήτῃσι δόξω εἶναι, κοῖος δέ τις τῇ νεογάμῳ γυναικί; κοίῳ δὲ ἐκείνη δόξει ἀνδρὶ συνοικέειν; ἐμὲ ὦν σὺ ἢ μέθες ἰέναι ἐπὶ τὴν θήρην, ἢ λόγῳ ἀνάπεισον ὅκως μοι ἀμείνω ἐστὶ ταῦτα οὕτω ποιεόμενα."

1.37.1

ἀμείψατο Subject is Croesus.

ἀποχρεωμένων δὲ τούτοισι τῶν Μυσῶν Genitive absolute construction. "With the Mysians being content regarding these things."

οὐ φαμένου δὲ τοῦ Κροίσου This genitive absolute is followed by an indirect statement (τόν γε παῖδά σφι συμπέμψειν).

1.37.2

τὰ κάλλιστα...καὶ γενναιότατα The infinitive εὐδοκιμέειν explains (as an epexegetic infinitive) what constitutes "the most beautiful and most noble things."

κοτέ = ποτέ.

ἀποκληΐσας ἔχεις A periphrastic or roundabout way of forming the perfect tense: "You have prevented."

παριδὼν Modifies the subject ("you") of ἔχεις.

τέοισί = τίσι.

ὄμμασι "Face."

1.37.3

κοῖος = ποῖος.

ὦν = οὖν.

μέθες Aorist, imperative, active, 2nd, singular of μεθίημι.

ἀνάπεισον Aorist, imperative, active, 2nd, singular of ἀναπείθω.

ὅκως = ὅπως.

ἀμείνω = ἀμείνονα. Translate with ταῦτα.

☙

1.38.1-2 Atys and the Boar Hunt, Part V

The back and forth between Croesus and his son Atys continues. The modern reader may well be jolted by the gross insensitivity of Croesus, who is made to say in the last sentence that, as far as he is concerned, he has but one son.

ἀμείβεται Κροῖσος τοισίδε· "ὦ παῖ, οὔτε δειλίην οὔτε ἄλλο οὐδὲν ἄχαρι παριδὼν, τοι ποιέω ταῦτα, ἀλλά μοι ὄψις ὀνείρου ἐν τῷ ὕπνῳ ἐπιστᾶσα ἔφη σε ὀλιγοχρόνιον ἔσεσθαι· ὑπὸ γὰρ αἰχμῆς σιδηρέης ἀπολέεσθαι. [2] πρὸς ὦν τὴν ὄψιν ταύτην τόν τε γάμον τοι τοῦτον ἔσπευσα καὶ ἐπὶ τὰ παραλαμβανόμενα οὐκ ἀποπέμπω, φυλακὴν ἔχων, εἴ κως δυναίμην ἐπὶ τῆς ἐμῆς σε ζόης διακλέψαι. εἷς γὰρ μοι μοῦνος τυγχάνεις ἐὼν παῖς· τὸν γὰρ δὴ ἕτερον διεφθαρμένον τὴν ἀκοὴν οὐκ εἶναί μοι λογίζομαι."

1.38.1

ἄχαρι Neuter, accusative, singular.

ἀπολέεσθαι Future, middle infinitive of ἀπόλλυμι.

1.38.2

κως = πως.

διακλέψαι Aorist, active infinitive of διακλέπτω. "Steal your life back," or "save you by means of stealth."

τὴν ἀκοὴν Accusative of respect.

03

1.39.1-2 Atys and the Boar Hunt, Part VI

In the *Histories*, dreams and oracles are shown to be difficult to interpret. Herodotus' audience, which probably knew the outcome of this story, would have appreciated the almost Sophoclean irony implicit in the arguments Atys makes as a result of his ignorance of the true meaning of his father's dream.

ἀμείβεται ὁ νεηνίης τοισίδε. "συγγνώμη μὲν ὦ πάτερ τοι, ἰδόντι γε ὄψιν τοιαύτην, περὶ ἐμὲ φυλακὴν ἔχειν· τὸ δὲ οὐ μανθάνεις, ἀλλὰ λέληθέ σε τὸ ὄνειρον, ἐμέ τοι δίκαιόν ἐστι φράζειν. [2] φής τοι τὸ ὄνειρον ὑπὸ αἰχμῆς σιδηρέης φάναι ἐμὲ τελευτήσειν· ὑὸς δὲ κοῖαι μέν εἰσι χεῖρες, κοίη δὲ αἰχμὴ σιδηρέη τὴν σὺ φοβέαι; εἰ μὲν γὰρ ὑπὸ ὀδόντος τοι εἶπε τελευτήσειν με ἢ ἄλλου τευ ὅ τι τούτῳ οἶκε, χρῆν δή σε ποιέειν τὰ ποιέεις· νῦν δὲ ὑπὸ αἰχμῆς. ἐπείτε ὦν οὐ πρὸς ἄνδρας ἡμῖν γίνεται ἡ μάχη, μέθες με."

1.39.1

τὸ δὲ οὐ μανθάνεις ἀλλὰ λέληθέ σε τὸ ὄνειρον "That which you do not understand but in regard to which your dream has eluded you."

λέληθέ Perfect, indicative, active, 3rd, singular of λανθάνω.

1.39.2

κοῖαι = ποῖαι.

τευ = τινος.

ὦν = οὖν.

γίνεται = γίγνεται.

μέθες Aorist, imperative, active, 2nd, singular of μεθίημι.

03

1.40.1 Atys and the Boar Hunt, Part VII

The same Croesus who could not be convinced by the wise Solon is readily won over by his son.

ἀμείβεται Κροῖσος· "ὦ παῖ, ἔστι τῇ με νικᾷς γνώμην ἀποφαίνων περὶ τοῦ ἐνυπνίου· ὡς ὢν νενικημένος ὑπὸ σέο μεταγινώσκω, μετίημί τέ σε ἰέναι ἐπὶ τὴν ἄγρην."

1.40.1

ἔστι τῇ "There is [a way] in which," or "Somehow."
ὢν = οὖν.

☙

1.41.1-3 Atys and the Boar Hunt, Part VIII

Hospitality works both ways. Croesus summons Adrastos (whose name literally means, rather significantly, "he who cannot run away") and demands that he pay back χρηστά with χρηστοῖσι. Note the way Croesus tries to appeal to what he assumes is Adrastos' desire to enhance his own fame and that of his father.

εἴπας δὲ ταῦτα ὁ Κροῖσος μεταπέμπεται τὸν Φρύγα Ἄδρηστον, ἀπικομένῳ δέ οἱ λέγει τάδε· "Ἄδρηστε, ἐγώ σε συμφορῇ πεπληγμένον ἀχάριτι, τήν τοι οὐκ ὀνειδίζω, ἐκάθηρα καὶ οἰκίοισι ὑποδεξάμενος ἔχω παρέχων πᾶσαν δαπάνην· [2] νῦν ὦν, ὀφείλεις γὰρ ἐμεῦ προποιήσαντος χρηστὰ ἐς σὲ χρηστοῖσί με ἀμείβεσθαι φύλακα παιδός σε τοῦ ἐμοῦ χρηίζω γενέσθαι ἐς ἄγρην ὁρμωμένου, μή τινες κατ' ὁδὸν κλῶπες κακοῦργοι ἐπὶ δηλήσι φανέωσι ὑμῖν. [3] πρὸς δὲ τούτῳ καὶ σέ τοι χρεόν ἐστι ἰέναι ἔνθα ἀπολαμπρυνέαι τοῖσι ἔργοισι· πατρώιόν τε γάρ τοι ἐστι καὶ προσέτι ῥώμη ὑπάρχει."

1.41.1

ἀπικομένῳ = ἀφικομένῳ.
πεπληγμένον Perfect, passive, masculine, accusative singular participle of πλήσσω.
τήν τοι οὐκ ὀνειδίζω "For which I don't blame you."
ὑποδεξάμενος ἔχω A periphrasis for the perfect: "I have received."

1.41.2

ὢν = οὖν.
ἐπὶ δηλήσι Idiomatically, "to do harm."

φανέωσι Aorist, subjunctive, passive, 3rd, plural of φαίνω.

1.41.3

τοι "Surely."

ἐστι Supply as subject "to win fame."

☙

1.42.1-2 Atys and the Boar Hunt, Part IX

A reluctant Adrastos agrees to Croesus' request, solely on the grounds that he owes Croesus repayment. His words, ὀφείλω γάρ σε ἀμείβεσθαι χρηστοῖσι, drip with tragic irony, something that Herodotus' audience would have surely picked up on.

ἀμείβεται ὁ Ἄδρηστος· "ὦ βασιλεῦ, ἄλλως μὲν ἔγωγε ἂν οὐκ ἤια ἐς ἄεθλον τοιόνδε· οὔτε γὰρ συμφορῇ τοιῇδε κεχρημένον οἰκός ἐστι ἐς ὁμήλικας εὖ πρήσσοντας ἰέναι, οὔτε τὸ βούλεσθαι πάρα, πολλαχῇ τε ἂν ἶσχον ἐμεωυτόν. [2] νῦν δέ, ἐπείτε σὺ σπεύδεις καὶ δεῖ τοί χαρίζεσθαι (ὀφείλω γάρ σε ἀμείβεσθαι χρηστοῖσι), ποιέειν εἰμὶ ἕτοιμος ταῦτα, παῖδά τε σόν, τὸν διακελεύεαι φυλάσσειν, ἀπήμονα τοῦ φυλάσσοντος εἵνεκεν προσδόκα τοι ἀπονοστήσειν."

1.42.1

ἤια Imperfect, indicative, active, 1st, singular of εἶμι.

κεχρημένον Perfect, middle, masculine, accusative, singular participle of χράομαι.

οἰκός = ἐοικός. "Fitting."

τὸ βούλεσθαι Articular infinitive used as subject of πάρα (shortened form of πάρεστι). "The desire."

ἐμεωυτόν = ἐμαυτόν.

1.42.2

τόν Here, a relative pronoun.

τοῦ φυλάσσοντος εἵνεκεν "On account of my guardianship."

εἵνεκεν = ἕνεκα.

☙

1.43.1-3 Atys and the Boar Hunt, Part X

Events take a turn for the worse at the wild boar hunt on Mysian Mount Olympus. Herodotus re-introduces Adrastos (καλεόμενος δὲ Ἄδρηστος) and in so doing drives home the point that his very name (which literally means "he who cannot run away") should have warned Croesus that it was a bad idea to appoint someone with such a foreboding name as the guardian to his son.

τοιούτοισι ἐπείτε οὗτος ἀμείψατο Κροῖσον, ἤισαν μετὰ ταῦτα ἐξηρτυμένοι λογάσι τε νεηνίῃσι καὶ κυσί. ἀπικόμενοι δὲ ἐς τὸν Ὄλυμπον τὸ ὄρος ἐζήτεον τὸ θηρίον, εὑρόντες δὲ καὶ περιστάντες αὐτὸ κύκλῳ ἐσηκόντιζον. [2] ἔνθα δὴ ὁ ξεῖνος, οὗτος δὴ ὁ καθαρθεὶς τὸν φόνον, καλεόμενος δὲ Ἄδρηστος, ἀκοντίζων τὸν ὗν τοῦ μὲν ἁμαρτάνει, τυγχάνει δὲ τοῦ Κροίσου παιδός. [3] ὁ μὲν δὴ βληθεὶς τῇ αἰχμῇ ἐξέπλησε τοῦ ὀνείρου τὴν φήμην, ἔθεε δέ τις ἀγγελέων τῷ Κροίσῳ τὸ γεγονός, ἀπικόμενος δὲ ἐς τὰς Σάρδις τήν τε μάχην καὶ τὸν τοῦ παιδὸς μόρον ἐσήμηνέ οἱ.

1.43.1

ἀμείψατο Subject is Adrastos.
ἤισαν Imperfect, indicative, active, 3rd, plural of εἶμι.
ἀπικόμενοι = ἀφικόμενοι.

1.43.2

τὸν φόνον Accusative of respect.

1.43.3

βληθεὶς Aorist, passive, masculine, nominative, singular participle of βάλλω.
ἐξέπλησε Aorist, indicative, active, 3rd, singular of ἐκπίμπλημι.
ἀγγελέων A future participle indicating purpose.
τὸ γεγονός "That which happened."

 CB

1.44.1-2 Atys and the Boar Hunt, Part XI

This chapter and the next constitute the "discovery scene," if we view this lengthy "performance piece" as a mini-tragedy. Croesus' reaction to the death of his son consists of a triple appeal to Zeus, who is represented here in three of his guises: as the patron of purification, as the patron of the guest-host relationship, and as the patron of friendship. That a Lydian king should be making appeals to a very Greek Zeus with very Greek functions seems of little concern to Herodotus.

ὁ δὲ Κροῖσος τῷ θανάτῳ τοῦ παιδὸς συντεταραγμένος μᾶλλόν τι ἐδεινολογέετο ὅτι μιν ἀπέκτεινε τὸν αὐτὸς φόνου ἐκάθηρε· [2] περιημεκτέων δὲ τῇ συμφορῇ δεινῶς ἐκάλεε μὲν Δία καθάρσιον, μαρτυρόμενος τὰ ὑπὸ τοῦ ξείνου πεπονθὼς εἴη, ἐκάλεε δὲ ἐπίστιόν τε καὶ ἑταιρήιον, τὸν αὐτὸν τοῦτον ὀνομάζων θεόν, τὸν μὲν ἐπίστιον καλέων, διότι δὴ οἰκίοισι ὑποδεξάμενος τὸν ξεῖνον φονέα τοῦ παιδὸς ἐλάνθανε βόσκων, τὸν δὲ ἑταιρήιον, ὡς φύλακα συμπέμψας αὐτὸν εὑρήκοι πολεμιώτατον.

1.44.1

συντεταραγμένος Perfect, passive, masculine, nominative, singular participle of συνταράσσω.

μᾶλλόν τι "Even more."

1.44.2

περιημεκτέων "Being aggrieved over."

Δία καθάρσιον "Zeus who presides over purification."

πεπονθὼς εἴη A periphrastic, it is used as the perfect, optative, active, 3rd, singular of πάσχω. This optative, and the other optative in this sentence (εὑρήκοι), are triggered by the indirect discourse implied by μαρτυρόμενος.

ἐπίστιόν "[Zeus] who presides over hospitality."

ἑταιρήιον "[Zeus] who presides over friendships."

ἐλάνθανε βόσκων "He accidentally entertained." When λανθάνω is used with a supplementary participle, the participle contains the main idea and λανθάνω is reduced to having the function of an adverb.

εὑρήκοι Perfect, optative, active, 3rd, singular of εὑρίσκω.

1.45.1-3 Atys and the Boar Hunt, Conclusion

The concluding chapter to our "performance piece" shows us a Croesus who is quite remarkable for his sense of compassion (he forgives Adrastos), for his sense of justice (he tells Adrastos that he has already paid his penalty), and for his wisdom (he allows that he should have known better than to go against the dream). This is certainly not the same Croesus who angrily sent Solon away from his court (1.33). Though Croesus has yet to recall in his tragic situation the words of Solon ("Look to the end")—and he will not until much later in Book I—he is well on his way to recognizing the truth of the sage's advice. As befits a mini-tragedy, this concluding chapter comes with a couple of resolutions (the burial of Atys and the desperate act of Adrastos) and even a touch of the *deus ex machina*, as Croesus ponders the role of a god in all that has happened.

παρῆσαν δὲ μετὰ τοῦτο οἱ Λυδοὶ φέροντες τὸν νεκρόν, ὄπισθε δὲ εἵπετό οἱ ὁ φονεύς. στὰς δὲ οὗτος πρὸ τοῦ νεκροῦ παρεδίδου ἑωυτὸν Κροίσῳ προτείνων τὰς χεῖρας, ἐπικατασφάξαι μιν κελεύων τῷ νεκρῷ, λέγων τήν τε προτέρην ἑωυτοῦ συμφορήν, καὶ ὡς ἐπ᾽ ἐκείνῃ τὸν καθήραντα ἀπολωλεκὼς εἴη, οὐδέ οἱ εἴη βιώσιμον. [2] Κροῖσος δὲ τούτων ἀκούσας τόν τε Ἄδρηστον κατοικτίρει,

καίπερ ἐὼν ἐν κακῷ οἰκηίῳ τοσούτῳ, καὶ λέγει πρὸς αὐτόν· "ἔχω, ὦ ξεῖνε,
παρὰ σεῦ πᾶσαν τὴν δίκην, ἐπειδὴ σεωυτοῦ καταδικάζεις θάνατον. εἰς δὲ
οὐ σύ μοι τοῦδε τοῦ κακοῦ αἴτιος, εἰ μὴ ὅσον ἀέκων ἐξεργάσαο, ἀλλὰ θεῶν
κού τις, ὅς μοι καὶ πάλαι προεσήμαινε τὰ μέλλοντα ἔσεσθαι." [3] Κροῖσος
μέν νυν ἔθαψε, ὡς οἰκὸς ἦν, τὸν ἑωυτοῦ παῖδα· Ἄδρηστος δὲ ὁ Γορδίεω τοῦ
Μίδεω, οὗτος δὴ ὁ φονεὺς μὲν τοῦ ἑωυτοῦ ἀδελφεοῦ γενόμενος, φονεὺς
δὲ τοῦ καθήραντος, ἐπείτε ἡσυχίη τῶν ἀνθρώπων ἐγένετο περὶ τὸ σῆμα,
συγγινωσκόμενος ἀνθρώπων εἶναι τῶν αὐτὸς ᾔδεε βαρυσυμφορώτατος,
ἐπικατασφάζει τῷ τύμβῳ ἑωυτόν.

1.45.1

ἑωυτὸν = ἑαυτὸν.
τῷ νεκρῷ Dative object of the ἐπι- in ἐπικατασφάξαι.
ἐπ᾽ ἐκείνῃ "In addition to that [first misfortune]."
ἀπολωλεκὼς εἴη The perfect, active participle of ἀπόλλυμι and the present optative of the verb
   "to be" constitute the perfect optative (used here in indirect discourse).
οὐδέ οἱ εἴη βιώσιμον "Nor would it be right for him to live."

1.45.2

εἷς = εἶ.
εἰ μὴ ὅσον "Except insofar as."

1.45.3

ὡς οἰκός = ὡς ἐοικός. "As was fitting."
ἐπείτε ἡσυχίη τῶν ἀνθρώπων ἐγένετο "When calm had returned."
συγγινωσκόμενος = συγγιγνωσκόμενος.

☙

1.47.1-3 Croesus Puts Oracles to the Test, Part I

Herodotus reports (1.46) that Croesus mourned his son's death for two years before
he decided to deal with the growing power of the Persian empire. Before undertaking a
war with Persia, Croesus was determined to test the accuracy of several oracles, including
the one at Delphi. He did this because he wanted to make sure his subsequent inquiry
(about whether or not he should go to war) was from the most reliable of the oracles.
Delphi is a huge topic in the *Histories* and is mentioned prominently in all nine books.
Herodotus' position regarding Delphi is varied, and readers should exercise caution before
they draw any conclusions concerning his stance (see the important article by D. Lateiner
in Landmark, Appendix P). The very historicity of this passage may well be called into
question, as it is either unlikely or impossible for Croesus' scheme to have worked, given

the limited availability ("office hours") of the oracles (Delphi was open only one day a year during the archaic period: cf. ALC *ad* 47.1). The oracular response which is cited in this chapter is the first of many in the *Histories*.

ἐντειλάμενος δὲ τοῖσι Λυδοῖσι τάδε ἀπέπεμπε ἐς τὴν διάπειραν τῶν χρηστηρίων,
ἀπ' ἧς ἂν ἡμέρης ὁρμηθέωσι ἐκ Σαρδίων, ἀπὸ ταύτης ἡμερολογέοντας τὸν
λοιπὸν χρόνον ἑκατοστῇ ἡμέρῃ χρᾶσθαι τοῖσι χρηστηρίοισι, ἐπειρωτῶντας
ὅ τι ποιέων τυγχάνοι ὁ Λυδῶν βασιλεὺς Κροῖσος ὁ Ἀλυάττεω· ἄσσα δ'
ἂν ἕκαστα τῶν χρηστηρίων θεσπίσῃ, συγγραψαμένους ἀναφέρειν παρ'
ἑωυτόν. [2] ὅ τι μέν νυν τὰ λοιπὰ τῶν χρηστηρίων ἐθέσπισε, οὐ λέγεται
πρὸς οὐδαμῶν· ἐν δὲ Δελφοῖσι ὡς ἐσῆλθον τάχιστα ἐς τὸ μέγαρον οἱ Λυδοὶ
χρησόμενοι τῷ θεῷ καὶ ἐπείρωτων τὸ ἐντεταλμένον, ἡ Πυθίη ἐν ἑξαμέτρῳ
τόνῳ λέγει τάδε.

[3] "οἶδα δ' ἐγὼ ψάμμου τ' ἀριθμὸν καὶ μέτρα θαλάσσης,
καὶ κωφοῦ συνίημι καὶ οὐ φωνεῦντος ἀκούω.
ὀδμή μ' ἐς φρένας ἦλθε κραταιρίνοιο χελώνης
ἑψομένης ἐν χαλκῷ ἅμ' ἀρνείοισι κρέεσσιν,
ᾗ χαλκὸς μὲν ὑπέστρωται, χαλκὸν δ' ἐπιέσται."

1.47.1

τοῖσι Λυδοῖσι These Lydians were the emissaries Croesus had sent to the various oracles.

ὁρμηθέωσι Aorist, subjunctive, passive, 3rd, plural of ὁρμάω. Literally, "they were put into motion." Idiomatically, "they started out."

ἀπὸ ταύτης "From this [day forward]."

χρᾶσθαι Infinitive in an indirect command following ἐντειλάμενος ("having instructed").

ἄσσα = ἄττα (variant of ἅτινα). Direct object of θεσπίσῃ.

1.47.2

ὡς…τάχιστα "As soon as possible."

ἐπείρωτων Imperfect, indicative, active, 3rd, plural of ἐπειρωτάω (= ἐπερωτάω).

ἡ Πυθίη The priestess or μάντις, who was the direct recipient of the oracle at Delphi.

1.47.3

What follows is A. H. Sayce's excellent translation in *The Ancient Empires of the East: Herodotus I-III* (New York: 1886) of the oracular response which Herodotus reports here:

> I number the sand and I measure the sea,
> And the dumb and the voiceless speak to me;
> The flesh of a tortoise, hard of shell,

Boiled with a lamb is the smell I smell,
In a caldron of brass with brass cover as well.

CB

1.48.1-2 Croesus Puts Oracles to the Test, Part II

The enigmatic oracle from Delphi, cited in the previous chapter, is here declared the winner by an overjoyed Croesus. Only the Delphic Pythia was able to divine what Croesus had done on the appointed day, namely, make a noxious stew in a bronze caldron. Although this story, as told by Herodotus, may seem like a confirmation of the validity of the Delphic oracle, it could also be seen as just the opposite, given the fact that Croesus, whose track record with dreams and oracles was notoriously poor, is the one who is endorsing Delphi. A side note: Croesus, a Lydian, is made to seem well-versed in Greek, as he is depicted reading aloud the hexameters of the Pythia.

ταῦτα οἱ Λυδοὶ θεσπισάσης τῆς Πυθίης συγγραψάμενοι οἴχοντο ἀπιόντες ἐς τὰς Σάρδις. ὡς δὲ καὶ ὧλλοι οἱ περιπεμφθέντες παρῆσαν φέροντες τοὺς χρησμούς, ἐνθαῦτα ὁ Κροῖσος ἕκαστα ἀναπτύσσων ἐπώρα τῶν συγγραμμάτων. τῶν μὲν δὴ οὐδὲν προσίετό μιν· ὁ δὲ ὡς τὸ ἐκ Δελφῶν ἤκουσε, αὐτίκα προσεύχετό τε καὶ προσεδέξατο, νομίσας μοῦνον εἶναι μαντήιον τὸ ἐν Δελφοῖσι, ὅτι οἱ ἐξευρήκεε τὰ αὐτὸς ἐποίησε. [2] ἐπείτε γὰρ δὴ διέπεμψε παρὰ τὰ χρηστήρια τοὺς θεοπρόπους, φυλάξας τὴν κυρίην τῶν ἡμερέων ἐμηχανᾶτο τοιάδε· ἐπινοήσας τὰ ἦν ἀμήχανον ἐξευρεῖν τε καὶ ἐπιφράσασθαι, χελώνην καὶ ἄρνα κατακόψας ὁμοῦ ἧψεε αὐτὸς ἐν λέβητι χαλκέῳ, χάλκεον ἐπίθημα ἐπιθείς.

1.48.1

θεσπισάσης τῆς Πυθίης Genitive absolute construction.

ὧλλοι Crasis (two words combined into one) for οἱ ἄλλοι.

ἀναπτύσσων "Unfolding [the writing tablets]."

ἐπώρα Imperfect, indicative, active, 3rd, singular of ἐποράω (= ἐφοράω).

προσίετό Imperfect, indicative, middle, 3rd, singular of προσίημι. "Satisfied."

ἐξευρήκεε Pluperfect, indicative, active, 3rd, singular of ἐξευρίσκω.

1.48.2

τὴν κυρίην τῶν ἡμερέων "The ordained day."

τὰ ἦν ἀμήχανον "Things which were impossible." Translate with the following infinitives.

ἧψεε Imperfect of ἕψω.

CB

1.53.1-3 Delphi is Ambiguous

Following his experiment with the oracles, Croesus sent massive votive offerings to Delphi and also to Amphiaraus, an oracular shrine in Boeotia (see map in Landmark *ad* 1.46) which also passed his test. Based on the very accurate descriptions (1.51) which Herodotus gives of the offerings in Delphi, including that of a gold lion which weighed the equivalent of 570 pounds, we need not doubt that he conducted an autopsy for this part of his narrative. The current chapter contains the story of the notoriously ambiguous oracular response which Delphi gave to Croesus to his question of whether he should go to war against Persia. Some modern scholars question the genuineness of this Delphic oracle: cf. ALC *ad* 1.53.3.

τοῖσι δὲ ἄγειν μέλλουσι τῶν Λυδῶν ταῦτα τὰ δῶρα ἐς τὰ ἱρὰ ἐνετέλλετο ὁ Κροῖσος ἐπειρωτᾶν τὰ χρηστήρια εἰ στρατεύηται ἐπὶ Πέρσας Κροῖσος καὶ εἴ τινα στρατὸν ἀνδρῶν προσθέοιτο φίλον. [2] ὡς δὲ ἀπικόμενοι ἐς τὰ ἀπεπέμφθησαν, οἱ Λυδοὶ ἀνέθεσαν τὰ ἀναθήματα, ἐχρέωντο τοῖσι χρηστηρίοισι λέγοντες· "Κροῖσος ὁ Λυδῶν τε καὶ ἄλλων ἐθνέων βασιλεύς, νομίσας τάδε μαντήια εἶναι μοῦνα ἐν ἀνθρώποισι, ὑμῖν τε ἄξια δῶρα ἔδωκε τῶν ἐξευρημάτων, καὶ νῦν ὑμέας ἐπειρωτᾷ εἰ στρατεύηται ἐπὶ Πέρσας καὶ εἴ τινα στρατὸν ἀνδρῶν προσθέοιτο σύμμαχον." [3] οἱ μὲν ταῦτα ἐπειρώτων, τῶν δὲ μαντηίων ἀμφοτέρων ἐς τώυτὸ αἱ γνῶμαι συνέδραμον, προλέγουσαι Κροίσῳ, ἢν στρατεύηται ἐπὶ Πέρσας, μεγάλην ἀρχήν μιν καταλύσειν· τοὺς δὲ Ἑλλήνων δυνατωτάτους συνεβούλευόν οἱ ἐξευρόντα φίλους προσθέσθαι.

1.53.1

ταῦτα τὰ δῶρα The incredibly rich gifts are described in 1.51.

ἱρά = ἱερά.

ἐπειρωτᾶν Present, active infinitive of ἐπειρωτάω (= ἐπερωτάω).

προσθέοιτο "Should ally to himself." Aorist, optative, middle, 3rd, singular of προστίθημι.

1.53.2

ἀπικόμενοι = ἀφικόμενοι.

ἐς τὰ "To the places [oracles] where…."

ἄξια…τῶν ἐξευρημάτων "Worthy of the discoveries" that the oracles had made when Croesus put them to the test.

1.53.3

συνέδραμον Aorist, indicative, active, 3rd, plural of συντρέχω. Literally, "ran together." Idiomatically, "concurred."

ἐξευρόντα Aorist, active, masculine, accusative, singular participle of ἐξευρίσκω.

☙

1.60.1-5 Peisistratos and "Athena" Ride into Athens

We recall (from 1.53.3) that Delphi instructed Croesus to seek allies from the most powerful Greek states, if he was to wage a war against Persia. This gives Herodotus the opportunity to do what Croesus is described as doing, namely, making inquiries into the histories of Sparta and Athens. The passage here is a long excursus into the history of 6th century Athens, specifically into the period when the city was ruled by Peisistratos and, after him, by his sons Hippias and Hipparchos. These "Peisistratids" ruled as *tyrannoi*, a word that had yet to have any strongly negative connotations in the 6th century. Along with a passage in Thucydides (6.54-9) and the Aristotelian *Athenaion Politeia*, this section of Herodotus' *Histories* helps fill some of the void in our information for 6th century B.C. Athenian history. Since oral tradition must have been a major source of information for Herodotus, some less than credible stories, such as the one in this chapter on the ruse of Peisistratos, have found their way into his narrative. Even so, much can be learned from his description of a political scene which was dominated by the great Athenian families, such as the Alcmaeonids (represented by Megacles in this account). We also catch a glimpse of the political divisions that plagued the city in the 6th century B.C., divisions which were the result of strong regionalism in Attica. This type of incidental history forms a backdrop to the main story of the pseudo-Athena's ride into Athens.

μετὰ δὲ οὐ πολλὸν χρόνον τὠυτὸ φρονήσαντες οἵ τε τοῦ Μεγακλέος στασιῶται καὶ οἱ τοῦ Λυκούργου ἐξελαύνουσί μιν. οὕτω μὲν Πεισίστρατος ἔσχε τὸ πρῶτον Ἀθήνας καὶ τὴν τυραννίδα οὔ κω κάρτα ἐρριζωμένην ἔχων ἀπέβαλε, οἱ δὲ ἐξελάσαντες Πεισίστρατον αὖτις ἐκ νέης ἐπ᾽ ἀλλήλοισι ἐστασίασαν. [2] περιελαυνόμενος δὲ τῇ στάσι ὁ Μεγακλῆς ἐπεκηρυκεύετο Πεισιστράτῳ, εἰ βούλοιτό οἱ τὴν θυγατέρα ἔχειν γυναῖκα ἐπὶ τῇ τυραννίδι. [3] ἐνδεξαμένου δὲ τὸν λόγον καὶ ὁμολογήσαντος ἐπὶ τούτοισι Πεισιστράτου μηχανῶνται δὴ ἐπὶ τῇ κατόδῳ πρῆγμα εὐηθέστατον, ὡς ἐγὼ εὑρίσκω, μακρῷ (ἐπεί γε ἀπεκρίθη ἐκ παλαιτέρου τοῦ βαρβάρου ἔθνεος τὸ Ἑλληνικὸν ἐὸν καὶ δεξιώτερον καὶ εὐηθίης ἠλιθίου ἀπηλλαγμένον μᾶλλον), εἰ καὶ τότε γε οὗτοι ἐν Ἀθηναίοισι τοῖσι πρώτοισι λεγομένοισι εἶναι Ἑλλήνων σοφίην μηχανῶνται τοιάδε. [4] ἐν τῷ δήμῳ τῷ Παιανιέι ἦν γυνή, τῇ οὔνομα ἦν Φύη, μέγαθος ἀπὸ τεσσέρων πηχέων ἀπολείπουσα τρεῖς δακτύλους καὶ ἄλλως εὐειδής· ταύτην τὴν γυναῖκα σκευάσαντες πανοπλίῃ, ἐς ἅρμα ἐσβιβάσαντες καὶ προδέξαντες σχῆμα οἷόν τι ἔμελλε εὐπρεπέστατον φανέεσθαι ἔχουσα ἤλαυνον ἐς τὸ ἄστυ, προδρόμους κήρυκας προπέμψαντες· οἳ τὰ ἐντεταλμένα ἠγόρευον ἀπικόμενοι ἐς τὸ ἄστυ, λέγοντες τοιάδε· [5] "ὦ Ἀθηναῖοι, δέκεσθε ἀγαθῷ νόῳ Πεισίστρατον, τὸν αὐτὴ ἡ Ἀθηναίη τιμήσασα ἀνθρώπων μάλιστα κατάγει ἐς τὴν ἑωυτῆς ἀκρόπολιν." οἳ μὲν δὴ ταῦτα διαφοιτέοντες ἔλεγον· αὐτίκα δὲ ἔς τε τοὺς δήμους φάτις ἀπίκετο ὡς Ἀθηναίη Πεισίστρατον κατάγει, καὶ οἱ ἐν τῷ ἄστεϊ πειθόμενοι τὴν γυναῖκα εἶναι αὐτὴν τὴν θεὸν προσεύχοντό τε τὴν ἄνθρωπον, καὶ ἐδέκοντο Πεισίστρατον.

1.60.1

τὠυτό Crasis (two words combined into one) for τὸ αὐτό.

τὠυτὸ φρονήσαντες "Having made an alliance."

μιν Peisistratos.

κάρτα ἐρριζωμένην "Strongly rooted."

ἀπέβαλε Object is τὴν τυραννίδα.

αὖτις ἐκ νέης "Once more."

1.60.2

περιελαυνόμενος δὲ τῇ στάσι "Troubled by the civil strife."

ἐπὶ τῇ τυραννίδι "In addition to the tyranny."

1.60.3

ἐνδεξαμένου δὲ τὸν λόγον καὶ ὁμολογήσαντος ἐπὶ τούτοισι Πεισιστράτου Genitive absolute construction.

ἐπεί "Insofar as." It introduces a clause which explains why Herodotus regarded the scheme concocted by Megacles and Peisistratos as beyond ridiculous (εὐηθέστατον).

εὐηθείης ἠλιθίου ἀπηλλαγμένον μᾶλλον "Further removed from mindless foolishness." The participle is the perfect, passive, neuter, nominative, singular of ἀπαλλάσσω. It takes the genitive.

εἰ καί "If in fact."

πρώτοισι λεγομένοισι εἶναι Ἑλλήνων σοφίην "Said to be the first of the Greeks in wisdom."

1.60.4

Παιανιέϊ For the location of this village in Attica (home of Demosthenes), see map in Landmark ad 1.59.

μέγαθος ἀπὸ τεσσέρων πηχέων ἀπολείπουσα τρεῖς δακτύλους "In height missing three finger widths from [being] four cubits tall." In other words, Phye was about 5'10" tall (and, by ancient standards, very tall).

προδέξαντες σχῆμα οἷόν τι ἔμελλε εὐπρεπέστατον φανέεσθαι ἔχουσα "Teaching her the kind of bearing, having which, she would appear most comely."

τὰ ἐντεταλμένα "Their orders."

ἀπικόμενοι = ἀφικόμενοι.

1.60.5

ἑωυτῆς = ἑαυτῆς.

☙

1.68.1-6 The Tomb of Orestes is Discovered

Just as Delphi recommended, Croesus next investigates Sparta before asking the city for an alliance. There is also some valid history in this chapter, as Herodotus shows us a Sparta which was extending its hegemony over much of the Peloponnese in the 6th century B.C. Fortunately for readers of the *Histories*, Croesus' inquiry is really Herodotus' inquiry, and so the result is yet another magnificent tale, this time involving the discovery of a giant skeleton. It seems that during a long, drawn out war with Tegea, a polis in Arcadia (see the map in Landmark *ad* 1.67), the Spartans themselves had consulted Delphi about what they needed to do to secure victory. They received a response in the form of a riddle (nothing unusual about that), which stipulated that, for victory to be achieved, the remains of Orestes had to be brought to Sparta. The theme of finding the remains of heroes as a way of securing their protection is a familiar one (cf. the story in Pausanias 3.3.7 of the return to Athens of the bones of Theseus), and some scholars have seen the story of the return of Orestes' bones as a "fact" (HW *ad* 67.2). More recent commentators are less convinced (cf. ALC *ad* 68.3: "The entire story is, of course, an aetiological legend"). Since this is the first section of the *Histories* where Herodotus deals extensively with Sparta, one may begin to form some ideas about his attitude towards Sparta and the Spartans. If the story of the recovery of Orestes' bones is any indication, we can at least tentatively conclude that some Spartans could be quite clever and resourceful.

τούτων ὦν τῶν ἀνδρῶν Λίχης ἀνεῦρε ἐν Τεγέῃ καὶ συντυχίῃ χρησάμενος καὶ σοφίῃ. ἐούσης γὰρ τοῦτον τὸν χρόνον ἐπιμειξίης πρὸς τοὺς Τεγεήτας ἐλθὼν ἐς χαλκήιον ἐθηεῖτο σίδηρον ἐξελαυνόμενον, καὶ ἐν θώματι ἦν ὁρῶν τὸ ποιεόμενον. [2] μαθὼν δέ μιν ὁ χαλκεὺς ἀποθωμάζοντα εἶπε παυσάμενος τοῦ ἔργου· "ἦ κου ἄν, ὦ ξεῖνε Λάκων, εἴ περ εἶδες τό περ ἐγώ, κάρτα ἂν ἐθώμαζες, ὅκου νῦν οὕτω τυγχάνεις θῶμα ποιεύμενος τὴν ἐργασίην τοῦ σιδήρου. [3] ἐγὼ γὰρ ἐν τῇδε θέλων τῇ αὐλῇ φρέαρ ποιήσασθαι, ὀρύσσων ἐπέτυχον σορῷ ἑπταπήχεϊ· ὑπὸ δὲ ἀπιστίης μὴ μὲν γενέσθαι μηδαμὰ μέζονας ἀνθρώπους τῶν νῦν ἄνοιξα αὐτὴν καὶ εἶδον τὸν νεκρὸν μήκεϊ ἴσον ἐόντα τῇ σορῷ· μετρήσας δὲ συνέχωσα ὀπίσω." ὁ μὲν δή οἱ ἔλεγε τά περ ὀπώπεε, ὁ δὲ ἐννώσας τὰ λεγόμενα συνεβάλλετο τὸν Ὀρέστεα κατὰ τὸ θεοπρόπιον τοῦτον εἶναι, τῇδε συμβαλλόμενος· [4] τοῦ χαλκέος δύο ὁρέων φύσας τοὺς ἀνέμους εὕρισκε ἐόντας, τὸν δὲ ἄκμονα καὶ τὴν σφῦραν τόν τε τύπον καὶ τὸν ἀντίτυπον, τὸν δὲ ἐξελαυνόμενον σίδηρον τὸ πῆμα ἐπὶ πήματι κείμενον, κατὰ τοιόνδε τι εἰκάζων, ὡς ἐπὶ κακῷ ἀνθρώπου σίδηρος ἀνεύρηται. [5] συμβαλόμενος δὲ ταῦτα καὶ ἀπελθὼν ἐς Σπάρτην ἔφραζε Λακεδαιμονίοσσι πᾶν τὸ πρῆγμα. οἱ δὲ ἐκ λόγου πλαστοῦ ἐπενείκαντές οἱ αἰτίην ἐδίωξαν. ὁ δὲ ἀπικόμενος ἐς Τεγέην καὶ φράζων τὴν ἑωυτοῦ συμφορὴν πρὸς τὸν χαλκέα

ἐμισθοῦτο παρ' οὐκ ἐκδιδόντος τὴν αὐλήν· [6] χρόνῳ δὲ ὡς ἀνέγνωσε,
ἐνοικίσθη, ἀνορύξας δὲ τὸν τάφον καὶ τὰ ὀστέα συλλέξας οἴχετο φέρων
ἐς Σπάρτην. καὶ ἀπὸ τούτου τοῦ χρόνου, ὅκως πειρῴατο ἀλλήλων, πολλῷ
κατυπέρτεροι τῷ πολέμῳ ἐγίνοντο οἱ Λακεδαιμόνιοι· ἤδη δέ σφι καὶ ἡ πολλὴ
τῆς Πελοποννήσου ἦν κατεστραμμένη.

1.68.1

τούτων...τῶν ἀνδρῶν A special unit of Spartans called "Agathoergoi," whose task it was to
carry out special operations for the state.

ὦν = οὖν.

ἐούσης γὰρ τοῦτον τὸν χρόνον ἐπιμιξίης A genitive absolute construction and an accusative
of extent of time. Presumably there was a truce between Tegea and Sparta, so that
communication (ἐπιμιξίης) between the two was possible.

ἐθηεῖτο Imperfect, indicative, middle, 3rd, singular of θηέομαι (= θεάομαι).

ἐξελαυνόμενον "Forged."

1.68.2

ὁ χαλκεὺς Curiously, though the man was forging iron, he is still referred to as a
"bronzesmith."

κου = που.

ἄν It signals and belongs to the "if clause."

τό περ ἐγώ "That which truly I [have seen]."

ὅκου νῦν "Since now."

ὅκου = ὅπου.

τυγχάνεις θῶμα ποιεύμενος "You happen to be amazed."

θῶμα = θαῦμα.

1.68.3

ἐπέτυχον Aorist, indicative, active, 1st, singular of ἐπιτυγχάνω.

ἑπταπήχεϊ Seven cubits are the equivalent of about twelve feet.

ἀπιστίης "Disbelief that...." The word triggers an indirect statement.

τῶν νῦν Genitive of comparison. "Than men [alive] today."

συνέχωσα ὀπίσω "I piled the earth back."

ὀπώπεε Pluperfect, indicative, active, 3rd, singular of ὁράω.

συνεβάλλετο "Concluded."

κατὰ τὸ θεοπρόπιον A reference to the second oracle which the Spartans received from
Delphi in the matter of their war with Tegea and which Herodotus quotes in 1.67:

ἔστι τις Ἀρκαδίης Τεγέη λευρῷ ἐνὶ χώρῳ,
ἔνθ' ἄνεμοι πνείουσι δύω κρατερῆς ὑπ' ἀνάγκης,
καὶ τύπος ἀντίτυπος, καὶ πῆμ' ἐπὶ πήματι κεῖται.
ἔνθ' Ἀγαμεμνονίδην κατέχει φυσίζοος αἶα·
τὸν σὺ κομισσάμενος Τεγέης ἐπιτάρροθος ἔσση.

A translation from A. H. Sayce (*The Ancient Empires of the East: Herodotus I-III* [New York, 1896]) follows:

> Arcadian Tegea lies upon a plain;
> There blow two winds driven by might and main,
> Blow upon blow and stroke on stroke again.
> The fruitful soil holds Agamemnon's son;
> Fetch him to thee and Tegea is won.

τῇδε "In the following way."

1.68.4

φύσας "Bellows."

κείμενον "Being."

κατὰ τοιόνδε τι εἰκάζων "Reckoning in this way."

ἀνεύρηται Perfect, indicative, passive, 3rd, singular of ἀνευρίσκω.

1.68.5

ἐδίωξαν "They exiled [him]." Apparently, the Spartans brought Lichas up on false charges and banished him so that he could return to Tegea, whose treaty with Sparta had expired.

ἀπικόμενος = ἀφικόμενος.

ἑωυτοῦ = ἑαυτοῦ.

1.68.6

ἐνοικίσθη "He took up residence." Aorist, indicative, passive, 3rd, singular of ἐνοικίζω.

ἐγίνοντο = ἐγίγνοντο.

κατεστραμμένη Perfect, passive, feminine, nominative, singular participle of καταστρέφω.

☙

1.86.1-6 Croesus at the Pyre, Part I

In the preceding chapters, Herodotus narrates the story of the war which Croesus, confident that he would destroy a great empire, launched against Persia. We see in the opening sentence of this chapter that things did not go well for Croesus: in the 14th year of his tyranny and the 14th day of the Persian siege, Sardis, the main population center of Lydia, was taken by the army of Cyrus, the Persian king. Herodotus presents us with yet another of the "many faces" of Croesus, whose personality seems to change from one episode to the next. Indeed, it would be hard not to admire the long-suffering and sage-like Croesus who appears in this part of the long Croesus saga of Book I. As often happens when Herodotus weaves a miracle into his narrative, he tones down the "miraculous" to make his story seem more credible. (In contrast, Croesus is magically transported to the land of the Hyperboreans in Bacchylides, *Ode* 3.58 ff.) It is difficult to determine what actually happened to Croesus once he lost his empire. Xenophon (*Cyropaedia* 7.2.9), for one, skips the story of the pyre and the rescue altogether and writes that Croesus became a consultant to Cyrus.

οἱ δὲ Πέρσαι τάς τε δὴ Σάρδις ἔσχον καὶ αὐτὸν Κροῖσον ἐζώγρησαν, ἄρξαντα ἔτεα τεσσερεσκαίδεκα καὶ τεσσερεσκαίδεκα ἡμέρας πολιορκηθέντα, κατὰ τὸ χρηστήριόν τε καταπαύσαντα τὴν ἑωυτοῦ μεγάλην ἀρχήν. λαβόντες δὲ αὐτὸν οἱ Πέρσαι ἤγαγον παρὰ Κῦρον. [2] ὁ δὲ συννήσας πυρὴν μεγάλην ἀνεβίβασε ἐπ' αὐτὴν τὸν Κροῖσόν τε ἐν πέδῃσι δεδεμένον καὶ δὶς ἑπτὰ Λυδῶν παρ' αὐτὸν παῖδας, ἐν νόῳ ἔχων εἴτε δὴ ἀκροθίνια ταῦτα καταγιεῖν θεῶν ὅτεῳ δή, εἴτε καὶ εὐχὴν ἐπιτελέσαι θέλων, εἴτε καὶ πυθόμενος τὸν Κροῖσον εἶναι θεοσεβέα τοῦδε εἵνεκεν ἀνεβίβασε ἐπὶ τὴν πυρήν, βουλόμενος εἰδέναι εἴ τίς μιν δαιμόνων ῥύσεται τοῦ μὴ ζῶντα κατακαυθῆναι. [3] τὸν μὲν δὴ ποιεῖν ταῦτα· τῷ δὲ Κροίσῳ ἑστεῶτι ἐπὶ τῆς πυρῆς ἐσελθεῖν, καίπερ ἐν κακῷ ἐόντι τοσούτῳ, τὸ τοῦ Σόλωνος, ὥς οἱ εἴη σὺν θεῷ εἰρημένον, τὸ μηδένα εἶναι τῶν ζωόντων ὄλβιον. ὡς δὲ ἄρα μιν προσστῆναι τοῦτο, ἀνενεικάμενόν τε καὶ ἀναστενάξαντα ἐκ πολλῆς ἡσυχίης ἐς τρὶς ὀνομάσαι "Σόλων." [4] καὶ τὸν Κῦρον ἀκούσαντα κελεῦσαι τοὺς ἑρμηνέας ἐπειρέσθαι τὸν Κροῖσον τίνα τοῦτον ἐπικαλέοιτο, καὶ τοὺς προσελθόντας ἐπειρωτᾶν· Κροῖσον δὲ ἕως μὲν σιγὴν ἔχειν εἰρωτώμενον, μετὰ δέ, ὡς ἠναγκάζετο, εἰπεῖν· "τὸν ἂν ἐγὼ πᾶσι τυράννοισι προετίμησα μεγάλων χρημάτων ἐς λόγους ἐλθεῖν." ὡς δέ σφι ἄσημα ἔφραζε, πάλιν ἐπειρώτων τὰ λεγόμενα. [5] λιπαρεόντων δὲ αὐτῶν καὶ ὄχλον παρεχόντων, ἔλεγε δὴ ὡς ἦλθε ἀρχὴν ὁ Σόλων ἐὼν Ἀθηναῖος, καὶ θεησάμενος πάντα τὸν ἑωυτοῦ ὄλβον ἀποφλαυρίσειε (οἷα δὴ εἴπας), ὥς τε αὐτῷ πάντα ἀποβεβήκοι τῇ περ ἐκεῖνος εἶπε, οὐδέν τι μᾶλλον ἐς ἑωυτὸν λέγων ἢ οὐκ ἐς ἅπαν τὸ ἀνθρώπινον καὶ μάλιστα τοὺς παρὰ σφίσι αὐτοῖσι ὀλβίους δοκέοντας εἶναι. τὸν μὲν Κροῖσον ταῦτα ἀπηγέεσθαι, τῆς δὲ πυρῆς ἤδη ἁμμένης καίεσθαι τὰ περιέσχατα. [6] καὶ τὸν Κῦρον ἀκούσαντα τῶν ἑρμηνέων τὰ Κροῖσος εἶπε, μεταγνόντα τε καὶ ἐννώσαντα ὅτι καὶ αὐτὸς ἄνθρωπος ἐὼν ἄλλον ἄνθρωπον, γενόμενον ἑωυτοῦ εὐδαιμονίῃ οὐκ ἐλάσσω, ζῶντα πυρὶ διδοίη, πρός τε τούτοισι δείσαντα τὴν τίσιν καὶ ἐπιλεξάμενον ὡς οὐδὲν εἴη τῶν ἐν ἀνθρώποισι ἀσφαλέως ἔχον, κελεύειν σβεννύναι τὴν ταχίστην τὸ καιόμενον πῦρ καὶ καταβιβάζειν Κροῖσόν τε καὶ τοὺς μετὰ Κροίσου. καὶ τοὺς πειρωμένους οὐ δύνασθαι ἔτι τοῦ πυρὸς ἐπικρατῆσαι.

1.86.1

ἑωυτοῦ = ἑαυτοῦ.

1.86.2

παῖδας Accusative, because it is also the object of ἀνεβίβασε.

εἴτε Herodotus offers three possible explanations for what Cyrus had in mind (ἐν νόῳ ἔχων) when he decided to place Croesus and the Lydian youths on the pyre; each explanation is introduced by εἴτε.

ὅτεῳ = ὅτῳ.

ῥύσεται τοῦ μὴ ζῶντα κατακαυθῆναι "Would rescue him from being burned alive." The verb ῥύσεται is followed by a genitive of separation, τοῦ μὴ ζῶντα κατακαυθῆναι, which is in the form of an articular infinitive construction.

1.86.3

τὸν μὲν δὴ ποιέειν The narrative switches to an indirect statement; something like λέγεται needs to be supplied.

ἐόντι Modifies Κροίσῳ.

τὸ τοῦ Σόλωνος ὥς οἱ εἴη σὺν θεῷ εἰρημένον "How the thing which Solon had spoken to him was as though from a god."

τὸ μηδένα εἶναι τῶν ζωόντων ὄλβιον In apposition to τὸ τοῦ Σόλωνος…εἰρημένον.

ἀνενεικάμενόν Aorist, middle, masculine, accusative, singular participle of ἀναφέρω. "Having brought up [a sigh]."

1.86.4

ἐπειρέσθαι = ἐπερέσθαι.

τίνα τοῦτον ἐπικαλέοιτο "Who it was whom he was calling."

τὸν ἂν ἐγὼ πᾶσι τυράννοισι… "The one whom I would have valued over much treasure to enter into conversation with every tyrant." In other words, "I'd give all the money in the world if every tyrant could talk with this man."

1.86.5

λιπαρεόντων δὲ αὐτῶν καὶ ὄχλον παρεχόντων Genitive absolute constructions.

ὄχλον παρεχόντων "Being annoyingly persistent."

ἀρχὴν Used adverbially.

οἷα δὴ εἴπας "Having said the sorts of things [that one might have expected him to say]." The participle εἴπας modifies "Croesus."

ὥς τε αὐτῷ πάντα ἀποβεβήκοι τῇ περ ἐκεῖνος εἶπε This clause expands on οἷα.

τῇ περ "In exactly the way in which."

οὐδέν τι μᾶλλον ἐς ἑωυτὸν λέγων… In other words, Croesus claims that Solon said nothing more to him than he might have said to all of mankind.

παρὰ σφίσι αὐτοῖσι "As far as they are concerned."

ἁμμένης Perfect, passive, feminine, genitive, singular participle of ἅπτω. Translate with τῆς δὲ πυρῆς as a genitive absolute construction.

1.86.6

ἐπιλεξάμενον "Reflecting."

τὴν ταχίστην "The quickest [way] possible."

☙

1.87.1-4 Croesus at the Pyre, Part II

The miraculous deliverance of Croesus is the subject of this passage. The storyteller Herodotus seems incapable of resisting a story as good as this one, but the historian Herodotus also tries to distance himself from the story by adding one of his usual disclaimers: λέγεται ὑπὸ Λυδῶν (1.87.1). Though he was saved by Apollo (in Bacchylides' version, it is Zeus who sends the rain), Croesus is later (1.90) described as sending an offering of shackles to Delphi (Apollo's shrine) as a symbol of his outrage over the faulty information that the Pythia had given him. Delphi's response, which Herodotus merely paraphrases in 1.91, points out that it was Croesus' own fault that he did not go back and ask for a clarification of the original oracle ("If you go to war, a mighty empire will fall"). The current passage ends with a stunningly effective condemnation of war (1.87.4) which, though placed in the mouth of Croesus, may represent Herodotus' own views.

ἐνθαῦτα λέγεται ὑπὸ Λυδῶν Κροῖσον μαθόντα τὴν Κύρου μετάγνωσιν, ὡς ὥρα πάντα μὲν ἄνδρα σβεννύντα τὸ πῦρ, δυναμένους δὲ οὐκέτι καταλαβεῖν, ἐπιβώσασθαι τὸν Ἀπόλλωνα ἐπικαλεόμενον, εἴ τί οἱ κεχαρισμένον ἐξ αὐτοῦ ἐδωρήθη, παραστῆναι καὶ ῥύσασθαι ἐκ τοῦ παρεόντος κακοῦ. [2] τὸν μὲν δακρύοντα ἐπικαλέεσθαι τὸν θεόν, ἐκ δὲ αἰθρίης τε καὶ νηνεμίης συνδραμεῖν ἐξαπίνης νέφεα καὶ χειμῶνά τε καταρραγῆναι καὶ ὗσαι ὕδατι λαβροτάτῳ, κατασβεσθῆναί τε τὴν πυρήν. οὕτω δὴ μαθόντα τὸν Κῦρον ὡς εἴη ὁ Κροῖσος καὶ θεοφιλὴς καὶ ἀνὴρ ἀγαθός, καταβιβάσαντα αὐτὸν ἀπὸ τῆς πυρῆς εἰρέσθαι τάδε· [3] "Κροῖσε, τίς σε ἀνθρώπων ἀνέγνωσε ἐπὶ γῆν τὴν ἐμὴν στρατευσάμενον πολέμιον ἀντὶ φίλου ἐμοὶ καταστῆναι; ὁ δὲ εἶπε· "ὦ βασιλεῦ, ἐγὼ ταῦτα ἔπρηξα τῇ σῇ μὲν εὐδαιμονίῃ, τῇ ἐμεωυτοῦ δὲ κακοδαιμονίῃ· αἴτιος δὲ τούτων ἐγένετο ὁ Ἑλλήνων θεὸς ἐπάρας ἐμὲ στρατεύεσθαι. [4] οὐδεὶς γὰρ οὕτω ἀνόητός ἐστι ὅστις πόλεμον πρὸ εἰρήνης αἱρέεται· ἐν μὲν γὰρ τῇ οἱ παῖδες τοὺς πατέρας θάπτουσι, ἐν δὲ τῷ οἱ πατέρες τοὺς παῖδας. ἀλλὰ ταῦτα δαίμονί κου φίλον ἦν οὕτω γενέσθαι."

1.87.1

ὥρα Imperfect, indicative, active, 3rd, singular of ὁράω.

καταλαβεῖν "To extinguish."

τί οἱ κεχαρισμένον "Anything pleasing to him [Apollo]."

ἐδωρήθη Aorist, indicative, passive, 3rd, singular of δωρέω.

1.87.2

καταρραγῆναι "Broke out." Aorist, passive infinitive of καταρρήγνυμι.

κατασβεσθῆναί Aorist, passive infinitive of κατασβέννυμι.

1.87.3

τῇ σῇ μὲν εὐδαιμονίη "Unto a blessing for you."

ἐμεωυτοῦ = ἐμαυτοῦ.

ἐπάρας "Having persuaded." Aorist, active, masculine, nominative, singular participle of
ἐπαείρω (= ἐπαίρω).

1.87.4

κου = που.

φίλον ἦν "Was pleasing."

ଔ

1.94.1-7 Lydians Devise Ways to Deal with a Famine

This passage, part of a series of chapters in Book I where Herodotus writes about the customs of the Lydians, contains the very famous account of how the Lydians, faced with a serious famine of long duration, invented games as a way of dealing with their hunger. Although this story has many of the features of a folk tale, it may be that Herodotus, a native of Halicarnassus, a city on the periphery of Caria, which was next door to Lydia, had access to some valid information about these regions of Asia Minor. Throughout the *Histories*, we occasionally see a Herodotus who is quite willing to give credit to non-Greeks for any number of discoveries they may have made: here, it is the discovery of the kind of games which were popular among ancient Greeks. Also of significance is Herodotus' claim that the Lydians were the first to mint coins in gold and silver, a claim which represents the opinion of most current scholars. Finally, this is the chapter where Herodotus formulates his famous theory, that the Etruscans of ancient Italy originally came from Lydia. While this notion has never been universally accepted, it remains today one of the more widely held and legitimate theories concerning the mysterious Etruscans.

Λυδοὶ δὲ νόμοισι μὲν παραπλησίοισι χρέωνται καὶ Ἕλληνες, χωρὶς ἢ ὅτι τὰ θήλεα τέκνα καταπορνεύουσι, πρῶτοι δὲ ἀνθρώπων τῶν ἡμεῖς ἴδμεν νόμισμα χρυσοῦ καὶ ἀργύρου κοψάμενοι ἐχρήσαντο, πρῶτοι δὲ καὶ κάπηλοι ἐγένοντο. [2] φασὶ δὲ αὐτοὶ Λυδοὶ καὶ τὰς παιγνίας τὰς νῦν σφίσι τε καὶ Ἕλλησι κατεστεῶσας ἑωυτῶν ἐξεύρημα γενέσθαι· ἅμα δὲ ταύτας τε ἐξευρεθῆναι παρὰ σφίσι λέγουσι καὶ ἑωυτῶν Τυρσηνίην ἀποικίσαι, ὧδε περὶ αὐτῶν λέγοντες· [3] ἐπὶ Ἄτυος τοῦ Μάνεω βασιλέος σιτοδείην ἰσχυρὴν ἀνὰ τὴν Λυδίην πᾶσαν γενέσθαι· καὶ τοὺς Λυδοὺς ἕως μὲν διάγειν λιπαρέοντας, μετὰ δέ, ὡς οὐ παύεσθαι, ἄκεα δίζησθαι, ἄλλον δὲ ἄλλο ἐπιμηχανᾶσθαι αὐτῶν. ἐξευρεθῆναι δὴ ὦν τότε καὶ τῶν κύβων καὶ τῶν ἀστραγάλων καὶ τῆς σφαίρης καὶ τῶν ἀλλέων πασέων παιγνιέων τὰ εἴδεα, πλὴν πεσσῶν· τούτων γὰρ ὦν τὴν ἐξεύρεσιν οὐκ οἰκηιοῦνται Λυδοί. [4] ποιέειν δὲ ὧδε πρὸς τὸν λιμὸν ἐξευρόντας· τὴν μὲν ἑτέρην τῶν ἡμερέων παίζειν πᾶσαν, ἵνα δὴ μὴ ζητέοιεν σιτία, τὴν δὲ ἑτέρην σιτέεσθαι παυομένους τῶν παιγνιέων. τοιούτῳ τρόπῳ διάγειν ἐπ᾽ ἔτεα δυῶν δέοντα εἴκοσι. [5] ἐπείτε δὲ οὐκ ἀνιέναι τὸ κακόν, ἀλλ᾽ ἔτι ἐπὶ μᾶλλον βιάζεσθαι, οὕτω δὴ τὸν βασιλέα αὐτῶν δύο μοίρας διελόντα Λυδῶν πάντων κληρῶσαι τὴν μὲν ἐπὶ μόνῃ, τὴν δὲ ἐπὶ ἐξόδῳ ἐκ τῆς χώρης, καὶ ἐπὶ μὲν τῇ μένειν αὐτοῦ λαγχανούσῃ τῶν μοιρέων ἑωυτὸν τὸν βασιλέα προστάσσειν, ἐπὶ δὲ τῇ ἀπαλλασσομένῃ τὸν ἑωυτοῦ παῖδα, τῷ οὔνομα εἶναι Τυρσηνόν. [6] λαχόντας δὲ αὐτῶν τοὺς ἑτέρους ἐξιέναι ἐκ τῆς χώρης [καὶ] καταβῆναι ἐς Σμύρνην καὶ μηχανήσασθαι πλοῖα, ἐς τὰ ἐσθεμένους τὰ πάντα, ὅσα σφι ἦν χρηστὰ ἐπίπλοα, ἀποπλέειν κατὰ βίου τε καὶ γῆς ζήτησιν, ἐς ὃ ἔθνεα πολλὰ παραμειψαμένους ἀπικέσθαι ἐς Ὀμβρικούς, ἔνθα σφέας ἐνιδρύσασθαι πόλιας καὶ οἰκέειν τὸ μέχρι τοῦδε. [7] ἀντὶ δὲ Λυδῶν μετονομασθῆναι αὐτοὺς ἐπὶ τοῦ βασιλέος τοῦ παιδός, ὅς σφεας ἀνήγαγε· ἐπὶ τούτου τὴν ἐπωνυμίην ποιευμένους ὀνομασθῆναι Τυρσηνούς.

1.94.1

χωρὶς ἢ ὅτι "Apart from the fact that."
νόμισμα "Coins."

1.94.2

ἑωυτῶν = ἑαυτῶν.
ἅμα...καὶ "At the same time that...they also."

1.94.3

Ἄτυος Obviously, this is not Atys, the son of Croesus.
ἄλλον δὲ ἄλλο ἐπιμηχανᾶσθαι αὐτῶν "One [Lydian] would devise one of these [cures], while another [Lydian] would devise another of these [cures]." In other words, the Lydians devised various remedies for the famine.
ἐξευρεθῆναι Aorist, passive infinitive of ἐξευρίσκω.
ὦν = οὖν.

1.94.4

πᾶσαν Supply ἡμέρην. Accusative of extent of time.

1.94.5

διελόντα Aorist, active, masculine, accusative, singular participle of διαιρέω.
τὴν μὲν ἐπὶ μόνῃ "One portion [of the population] to remain."
ἐπὶ μὲν τῇ μένειν αὐτοῦ λαγχανούσῃ "For the portion [of the population] that drew the lot to stay."

1.94.6

Σμύρνην For the location of Smyrna, see map in Landmark *ad* 1.92.

ἀπικέσθαι = ἀφικέσθαι.

Ὀμβρικούς Perhaps a reference to the Umbrian region of Italy.

πόλιας = πόλεις.

CB

1.131.1-3 The Religion of the Persians, Part I

Comparative Religion is clearly a favorite topic for Herodotus. In this chapter, he begins his long discourse (1.131-40) on the manners and institutions of the Persians by presenting a short description of their religion. Note the way Herodotus manages to stay impartial in his description of a belief system which, unlike that of the Greeks, did not see its gods as human-like (anthropomorphic). As a firm believer in the syncretic nature of religions, Herodotus mentions here the Assyrian and Arab influences on the Persian pantheon; in the process, he finds an opportunity to display his knowledge of languages other than Greek.

Πέρσας δὲ οἶδα νόμοισι τοιοισίδε χρεωμένους, ἀγάλματα μὲν καὶ νηοὺς καὶ βωμοὺς οὐκ ἐν νόμῳ ποιευμένους ἰδρύεσθαι, ἀλλὰ καὶ τοῖσι ποιεῦσι μωρίην ἐπιφέρουσι, ὡς μὲν ἐμοὶ δοκέειν, ὅτι οὐκ ἀνθρωποφυέας ἐνόμισαν τοὺς θεοὺς κατά περ οἱ Ἕλληνες εἶναι· [2] οἱ δὲ νομίζουσι Διὶ μὲν ἐπὶ τὰ ὑψηλότατα τῶν ὀρέων ἀναβαίνοντες θυσίας ἔρδειν, τὸν κύκλον πάντα τοῦ οὐρανοῦ Δία καλέοντες· θύουσι δὲ ἡλίῳ τε καὶ σελήνῃ καὶ γῇ καὶ πυρὶ καὶ ὕδατι καὶ ἀνέμοισι. [3] τούτοισι μὲν δὴ θύουσι μούνοισι ἀρχῆθεν, ἐπιμεμαθήκασι δὲ καὶ τῇ Οὐρανίῃ θύειν, παρά τε Ἀσσυρίων μαθόντες καὶ Ἀραβίων. καλέουσι δὲ Ἀσσύριοι τὴν Ἀφροδίτην Μύλιττα, Ἀράβιοι δὲ Ἀλιλάτ, Πέρσαι δὲ Μίτραν.

1.131.1

οὐκ ἐν νόμῳ ποιευμένους "Not considering [these things] to be lawful."

μωρίην ἐπιφέρουσι "They chalk it up as folly on the part of...."

δοκέειν The infinitive is used absolutely; translate as a finite verb.

1.131.2

Διὶ Herodotus is referring here to Ahura Mazda, the supreme god of the Persians.

1.131.3

ἐπιμεμαθήκασι Perfect, indicative, active, 3rd, plural of ἐπιμανθάνω.

CB

1.132.1-3 The Religion of the Persians, Part II

By the estimate of modern scholars, Herodotus provides very valuable information in this passage. Given the specificity of his narrative, it is safe to assume that he actually witnessed the performance of a Persian sacrifice: in other words, he conducted an autopsy. G. Rawlinson, the great 19th century commentator on Herodotus, concluded that open-air sacrifices, the boiling and sharing of sacrificial meat, and the special sacrificial hymn were all genuine features of Persian ritual from Herodotus' day (cf. HW *ad* 1.132.1). As usual, Herodotus does not pass judgment on customs different from his own and actually seems to express his approval of the way Persians are allowed to do whatever they choose with the sacrificial meat.

θυσίη δὲ τοῖσι Πέρσῃσι περὶ τοὺς εἰρημένους θεοὺς ἥδε κατέστηκε· οὔτε βωμοὺς ποιεῦνται οὔτε πῦρ ἀνακαίουσι μέλλοντες θύειν· οὐ σπονδῇ χρέωνται, οὐκὶ αὐλῷ, οὐ στέμμασι, οὐκὶ οὐλῇσι· τῶν δὲ ὡς ἑκάστῳ θύειν θέλῃ, ἐς χῶρον καθαρὸν ἀγαγὼν τὸ κτῆνος καλέει τὸν θεόν, ἐστεφανωμένος τὸν τιάραν μυρσίνῃ μάλιστα. [2] ἑωυτῷ μὲν δὴ τῷ θύοντι ἰδίῃ μούνῳ οὔ οἱ ἐγγίνεται ἀρᾶσθαι ἀγαθά, ὁ δὲ τοῖσι πᾶσι Πέρσῃσι κατεύχεται εὖ γίνεσθαι καὶ τῷ βασιλέϊ· ἐν γὰρ δὴ τοῖσι ἅπασι Πέρσῃσι καὶ αὐτὸς γίνεται. ἐπεὰν δὲ διαμιστύλας κατὰ μέλεα τὸ ἱρήιον ἑψήσῃ τὰ κρέα ὑποπάσας ποίην ὡς ἁπαλωτάτην, μάλιστα δὲ τὸ τρίφυλλον, ἐπὶ ταύτης ἔθηκε ὦν πάντα τὰ κρέα. [3] διαθέντος δὲ αὐτοῦ μάγος ἀνὴρ παρεστεὼς ἐπαείδει θεογονίην, οἵην δὴ ἐκεῖνοι λέγουσι εἶναι τὴν ἐπαοιδήν· ἄνευ γὰρ δὴ μάγου οὔ σφι νόμος ἐστὶ θυσίας ποιέεσθαι. ἐπισχὼν δὲ ὀλίγον χρόνον ἀποφέρεται ὁ θύσας τὰ κρέα καὶ χρᾶται ὅ τι μιν λόγος αἱρέει.

1.132.1
κατέστηκε Perfect, indicative, active, 3rd, singular of κατίστημι (= καθίστημι).
τῶν...ἑκάστῳ "To each of the gods."
θέλῃ Supply τις as subject.

1.132.2
ἑωυτῷ = ἑαυτῷ.
ἐγγίνεται = ἐγγίγνεται. "Is [not] allowed." Subject is ἀρᾶσθαι ἀγαθά.
γίνεσθαι = γίγνεσθαι.
ἐπεάν = ἐπειδάν.
ἱρήιον = ἱερεῖον.
κατὰ μέλεα "Limb by limb."
ὡς ἁπαλωτάτην "As soft as possible."

1.132.3

διαθέντος δὲ αὐτοῦ Genitive absolute construction. "Once he has arranged the sacrificial meat."

Μάγος The Magi were members of the Persian priestly caste.

θεογονίην A hymn recounting the genealogy of the Persian gods.

ὀλίγον χρόνον Accusative of extent of time.

ὅ τι μιν λόγος αἱρέει "However reason moves him." In other words, "However he chooses."

☙

1.133.1-4 The Persian Diet

Herodotus the ethnographer is at his best in this chapter. In describing the eating habits of the Persians, he seems to endorse the way the Persian meal was supplemented with side-dishes and desserts. He even seems to imply that the Greek way of dining was inferior: while noting the Persian taboo on public vomiting and urinating during a banquet, he may be suggesting that such actions were acceptable by Greek standards. The passage concludes with an observation on Persian drunkenness, one which may have served as the model for Tacitus' description (*Germania* 22.2-4) of ancient Germanic customs: *Deliberant dum fingere nesciunt, constituunt dum errare non possunt* ("They deliberate while they are incapable of lying; they make decisions when they are incapable of erring").

ἡμέρην δὲ ἁπασέων μάλιστα ἐκείνην τιμᾶν νομίζουσι τῇ ἕκαστος ἐγένετο. ἐν ταύτῃ δὲ πλέω δαῖτα τῶν ἀλλέων δικαιεῦσι προτίθεσθαι· ἐν τῇ οἱ εὐδαίμονες αὐτῶν βοῦν καὶ ἵππον καὶ κάμηλον καὶ ὄνον προτίθεαται ὅλους ὀπτοὺς ἐν καμίνοισι, οἱ δὲ πένητες αὐτῶν τὰ λεπτὰ τῶν προβάτων προτιθέαται. [2] σίτοισι δὲ ὀλίγοισι χρέωνται, ἐπιφορήμασι δὲ πολλοῖσι καὶ οὐκ ἁλέσι· καὶ διὰ τοῦτό φασι Πέρσαι τοὺς Ἕλληνας σιτεομένους πεινῶντας παύεσθαι, ὅτι σφι ἀπὸ δείπνου παραφορέεται οὐδὲν λόγου ἄξιον· εἰ δέ τι παραφέροιτο, ἐσθίοντας ἂν οὐ παύεσθαι. [3] οἴνῳ δὲ κάρτα προσκέαται, καί σφι οὐκ ἐμέσαι ἔξεστι, οὐκὶ οὐρῆσαι ἀντίον ἄλλου. ταῦτα μέν νυν οὕτω φυλάσσεται, μεθυσκόμενοι δὲ ἐώθασι βουλεύεσθαι τὰ σπουδαιέστατα τῶν πρηγμάτων· [4] τὸ δ' ἂν ἄδῃ σφι βουλευομένοισι, τοῦτο τῇ ὑστεραίῃ νήφουσι προτιθεῖ ὁ στέγαρχος, ἐν τοῦ ἂν ἐόντες βουλεύωνται. καὶ ἢν μὲν ἄδῃ καὶ νήφουσι, χρέωνται αὐτῷ, ἢν δὲ μὴ ἄδῃ, μετιεῖσι. τὰ δ' ἂν νήφοντες προβουλεύσωνται, μεθυσκόμενοι ἐπιδιαγινώσκουσι.

1.133.1

τῇ ἕκαστος ἐγένετο That is, on his birthday.

πλέω δαῖτα Accusative forms.

τῶν ἀλλέων Genitive of comparison.

οἱ εὐδαίμονες αὐτῶν "The rich among them."

τὰ λεπτὰ τῶν προβάτων That is, sheep and goats.

1.133.2

ἐπιφορήμασι "Side dishes" and/or "desserts."

οὐκ ἁλέσι "Not all at the same time [but spread out over the course of an extended meal]."

ἐσθίοντας ἂν οὐ παύεσθαι "They wouldn't stop eating."

1.133.3

προσκέαται "They are attached to…."

ἔξεστι "It is [not] permitted."

1.133.4

ἐν τοῦ ἂν ἐόντες βουλεύωνται "In whose house they were while they deliberated."

ἅδη Aorist, subjunctive, active, 3rd, singular of ἀνδάνω.

☙

1.134.1-2 Persian Neighborliness

We have here a fascinating glimpse into the social distinctions that existed among Persians in the 5th century B.C. Most likely, Herodotus learned about these through personal observation (autopsy) during his travels in the Persian Empire. A revealing bit of information emerges in 1.134.1, where we read that debasement by prostration (προσπίπτων προσκυνέει τὸν ἕτερον), even when it was done in the presence of the Great King, was all about social rank and not worship. Although Herodotus is usually noncommittal when describing the customs of non-Greeks, here he seems to show some slight admiration for the way Persians make social distinctions.

ἐντυγχάνοντες δ᾽ ἀλλήλοισι ἐν τῆσι ὁδοῖσι, τῷδε ἄν τις διαγνοίη εἰ ὅμοιοί εἰσι οἱ συντυγχάνοντες· ἀντὶ γὰρ τοῦ προσαγορεύειν ἀλλήλους φιλέουσι τοῖσι στόμασι· ἢν δὲ ᾖ οὕτερος ὑποδεέστερος ὀλίγῳ, τὰς παρειὰς φιλέονται· ἢν δὲ πολλῷ ᾖ οὕτερος ἀγεννέστερος, προσπίπτων προσκυνέει τὸν ἕτερον. [2] τιμῶσι δὲ ἐκ πάντων τοὺς ἄγχιστα ἑωυτῶν οἰκέοντας μετά γε ἑωυτούς, δεύτερα δὲ τοὺς δευτέρους· μετὰ δὲ κατὰ λόγον προβαίνοντες τιμῶσι· ἥκιστα δὲ τοὺς ἑωυτῶν ἑκαστάτω οἰκημένους ἐν τιμῇ ἄγονται, νομίζοντες ἑωυτοὺς εἶναι ἀνθρώπων μακρῷ τὰ πάντα ἀρίστους, τοὺς δὲ ἄλλους κατὰ λόγον τῆς ἀρετῆς ἀντέχεσθαι, τοὺς δὲ ἑκαστάτω οἰκέοντας ἀπὸ ἑωυτῶν κακίστους εἶναι.

1.134.1

εἰσι οἱ συντυγχάνοντες "Happen to be."

ἀντὶ γὰρ τοῦ προσαγορεύειν ἀλλήλους Articular infinitive construction.

φιλέουσι "They kiss."

1.134.2

ἑωυτῶν = ἑαυτῶν.

δεύτερα "Second of all." In contrast to ἄγχιστα ("most of all").

τοὺς δευτέρους "[Those living] next closest."

κατὰ λόγον "According to [this] principle."

τὰ πάντα Accusative of respect.

ଔ

1.136.1-2 Persian Educational System

This passage contains the famous remark concerning the value that Persians place on the virtue of honesty. Although Herodotus is adamant on the subject (cf. 1.138), recent scholarship has questioned the validity of this assertion (cf. ALC *ad* 1.136.1)

ἀνδραγαθίη δὲ αὕτη ἀποδέδεκται, μετὰ τὸ μάχεσθαι εἶναι ἀγαθόν, ὃς ἂν πολλοὺς ἀποδέξῃ παῖδας· τῷ δὲ τοὺς πλείστους ἀποδεικνύντι δῶρα ἐκπέμπει βασιλεὺς ἀνὰ πᾶν ἔτος. τὸ πολλὸν δ' ἡγέαται ἰσχυρὸν εἶναι. [2] παιδεύουσι δὲ τοὺς παῖδας ἀπὸ πενταέτεος ἀρξάμενοι μέχρι εἰκοσαέτεος τρία μοῦνα, ἱππεύειν καὶ τοξεύειν καὶ ἀληθίζεσθαι. πρὶν δὲ ἢ πενταέτης γένηται, οὐκ ἀπικνέεται ἐς ὄψιν τῷ πατρί, ἀλλὰ παρὰ τῇσι γυναιξὶ δίαιταν ἔχει. τοῦδε δὲ εἵνεκα τοῦτο οὕτω ποιέεται, ἵνα ἢν ἀποθάνῃ τρεφόμενος, μηδεμίαν ἄσην τῷ πατρὶ προσβάλῃ.

1.136.1

μετὰ τὸ μάχεσθαι εἶναι ἀγαθόν "Next to being brave in battle."

ἀποδέξῃ Aorist, subjunctive, active, 3rd, singular of ἀποδείκνυμι. "Produce."

τὸ πολλὸν "Numbers."

1.136.2

ἀπικνέεται = ἀφικνεῖται.

τρεφόμενος "While still being cared for by a nurse."

ଔ

1.137.1-2 Persian Laws on Justifiable Homicide and Parricide

Herodotus begins this passage by explicitly endorsing the Persian custom (mentioned in 1.136) whereby children are kept away from their fathers until they reach a certain age. He also indicates his approval of the custom he describes here, whereby a Persian king cannot put to death one of his subjects on the basis of just a single offence. He follows this observation with an extraordinary statement: no legitimate child of Persian parents has ever murdered a parent. Note that when Herodotus is hesitant about an outlandish claim such as this, he often makes sure to insert "they say," or a variation thereof. There are three such disclaimers in just this one chapter!

αἰνέω μέν νυν τόνδε τὸν νόμον, αἰνέω δὲ καὶ τόνδε, τὸ μὴ μιῆς αἰτίης εἵνεκα μήτε αὐτὸν τὸν βασιλέα μηδένα φονεύειν, μήτε μηδένα τῶν ἄλλων Περσέων μηδένα τῶν ἑωυτοῦ οἰκετέων ἐπὶ μιῇ αἰτίῃ ἀνήκεστον πάθος ἔρδειν· ἀλλὰ λογισάμενος ἢν εὑρίσκῃ πλέω τε καὶ μέζω τὰ ἀδικήματα ἐόντα τῶν ὑπουργημάτων, οὕτω τῷ θυμῷ χρᾶται. [2] ἀποκτεῖναι δὲ οὐδένα κω λέγουσι τὸν ἑωυτοῦ πατέρα οὐδὲ μητέρα, ἀλλὰ ὁκόσα ἤδη τοιαῦτα ἐγένετο, πᾶσαν ἀνάγκην φασὶ ἀναζητεόμενα ταῦτα ἂν εὑρεθῆναι ἤτοι ὑποβολιμαῖα ἐόντα ἢ μοιχίδια· οὐ γὰρ δή φασι οἰκὸς εἶναι τόν γε ἀληθέως τοκέα ὑπὸ τοῦ ἑωυτοῦ παιδὸς ἀποθνήσκειν.

1.137.1

τὸ μὴ μιῆς αἰτίης εἵνεκα μήτε αὐτὸν τὸν βασιλέα μηδένα φονεύειν Articular infinitive construction.

ἑωυτοῦ = ἑαυτοῦ.

ἔρδειν Takes a double accusative (μηδένα…πάθος).

ἢν εὑρίσκῃ The verb is subjunctive in a present general condition.

τῷ θυμῷ χρᾶται "He [the master of a slave] gives in to his anger."

1.137.2

κω = πω.

ὁκόσα = ὁπόσα.

ταῦτα Supply τέκνα.

ἀνευρεθῆναι Aorist, passive infinitive of ἀνευρίσκω.

τόν γε ἀληθέως τοκέα "A legitimate parent."

ಬ

1.138.1-2 On Lying, Debt, Leprosy, Doves, Rivers

As he is about to conclude his long excursus into the customs of the Persians, Herodotus seems to want to pack in a lot of topics into his remaining chapters. By his estimation, the (alleged) Persian aversion to lying is such a major feature of the Persian life style that he feels justified in mentioning it again (it was briefly touched upon in 1.136). Because of the rapid-fire way in which he treats the rather disparate subjects of this paragraph, we never get to learn why it is that white doves were considered to carry some kind of contagion.

ἄσσα δέ σφι ποιέειν οὐκ ἔξεστι, ταῦτα οὐδὲ λέγειν ἔξεστι. αἴσχιστον δὲ αὐτοῖσι τὸ ψεύδεσθαι νενόμισται, δεύτερα δὲ τὸ ὀφείλειν χρέος, πολλῶν μὲν καὶ ἄλλων εἵνεκα, μάλιστα δὲ ἀναγκαίην φασὶ εἶναι τὸν ὀφείλοντα καί τι ψεῦδος λέγειν. ὃς ἂν δὲ τῶν ἀστῶν λέπρην ἢ λεύκην ἔχῃ, ἐς πόλιν οὗτος οὐ κατέρχεται οὐδὲ συμμίσγεται τοῖσι ἄλλοισι Πέρσῃσι· φασὶ δέ μιν ἐς τὸν ἥλιον ἁμαρτόντα τι ταῦτα ἔχειν. [2] ξεῖνον δὲ πάντα τὸν λαμβανόμενον ὑπὸ τουτῶν πολλοὶ ἐξελαύνουσι ἐκ τῆς χώρης, καὶ τὰς λευκὰς περιστεράς, τὴν αὐτὴν αἰτίην ἐπιφέροντες. ἐς ποταμὸν δὲ οὔτε ἐνουρέουσι οὔτε ἐμπτύουσι, οὐ χεῖρας ἐναπονίζονται οὐδὲ ἄλλον οὐδένα περιορῶσι, ἀλλὰ σέβονται ποταμοὺς μάλιστα.

1.138.1

ἄσσα = ἅτινα.

τὸν ὀφείλοντα "The debtor."

λεύκην Some mild form of leprosy (cf. HW *ad* 1.138.1).

1.138.2

λευκὰς περιστεράς "White doves."

ଓଃ

1.187.1-5 The Strange Tomb of a Babylonian Queen

In chapter 1.178, Herodotus turns his attention to King Cyrus' conquest of the great city of Babylon (539 B.C.). Before he gets down to the business of narrating the actual military campaign, he allows himself an opportunity to describe some of the more amazing monuments of the city. The following passage is a digression from that digression, where Herodotus tells about the strange tomb of a Queen Nitocris, a woman whom he characterizes (1.185.1) as συνετωτέρη ("rather intelligent"). (On the question of her historicity, see HW *ad* 1.185.2.) According to our author, the Queen's intelligence could be seen in the way she ordered the Babylonians to build defensive structures in anticipation of a Persian attack (1.185-6) and also in the way she designed a rather strange tomb for herself. Herodotus certainly made room in his *Histories* for women characters, and this passage allows us to see that, on occasion at least, they can elicit some admiration from him (cf. Landmark, Appendix U, "On Women and Marriage in Herodotus").

ἡ δ' αὐτὴ αὕτη βασίλεια καὶ ἀπάτην τοιήνδε τινὰ ἐμηχανήσατο· ὑπὲρ τῶν μάλιστα λεωφόρων πυλέων τοῦ ἄστεος τάφον ἑωυτῇ κατεσκευάσατο μετέωρον ἐπιπολῆς αὐτέων τῶν πυλέων, ἐνεκόλαψε δὲ ἐς τὸν τάφον γράμματα λέγοντα τάδε· [2] "τῶν τις ἐμεῦ ὕστερον γινομένων Βαβυλῶνος βασιλέων ἢν σπανίσῃ χρημάτων, ἀνοίξας τὸν τάφον λαβέτω ὁκόσα βούλεται χρήματα· μὴ μέντοι γε μὴ σπανίσας γε ἄλλως ἀνοίξῃ· οὐ γὰρ ἄμεινον." [3] οὗτος ὁ τάφος ἦν ἀκίνητος μέχρι οὗ ἐς Δαρεῖον περιῆλθε ἡ βασιληίη· Δαρείῳ δὲ καὶ δεινὸν ἐδόκεε εἶναι τῇσι πύλῃσι ταύτῃσι μηδὲν χρᾶσθαι καὶ χρημάτων κειμένων καὶ αὐτῶν τῶν γραμμάτων ἐπικαλεομένων, μὴ οὐ λαβεῖν αὐτά· [4] τῇσι δὲ πύλῃσι ταύτῃσι οὐδὲν ἐχρᾶτο τοῦδε εἵνεκα, ὅτι ὑπὲρ κεφαλῆς οἱ ἐγίνετο ὁ νεκρὸς διεξελαύνοντι. [5] ἀνοίξας δὲ τὸν τάφον εὗρε χρήματα μὲν οὔ, τὸν δὲ νεκρὸν καὶ γράμματα λέγοντα τάδε· "εἰ μὴ ἄπληστός τε ἔας χρημάτων καὶ αἰσχροκερδής, οὐκ ἂν νεκρῶν θήκας ἀνέῳγες." αὕτη μέν νυν ἡ βασίλεια τοιαύτη τις λέγεται γενέσθαι.

1.187.1

τῶν μάλιστα λεωφόρων "The most busily traveled."

ἑωυτῇ = ἑαυτῇ.

μετέωρον "High up."

ἐπιπολῆς "On top of" (+ genitive).

1.187.2

γινομένων = γιγνομένων.

ἢν Note how this "if" is postponed to mid-sentence.

ὁκόσα = ὁπόσα.

ἄλλως "For any other reason"

ἀνοίξῃ Aorist, subjunctive, active, 3rd, singular of ἀνοίγνυμι.

οὐ γὰρ ἄμεινον "It will not be better [for him]." That is, things will get rather bad.

1.187.3

μέχρι οὗ "Until the time when."

χρημάτων κειμένων καὶ αὐτῶν τῶν γραμμάτων ἐπικαλεομένων Genitive absolute constructions.

μὴ οὐ λαβεῖν αὐτά "Not to take it." The double negative is for emphasis; translate only one of the two.

1.187.4

εἵνεκα = ἕνεκα.

1.187.5

ἔας = ἦσθα.

ἀνέῳγες Imperfect, indicative, active, 2nd, singular of ἀνοίγνυμι.

☙

1.196.1-5 The Babylonian Bride-Auction

Herodotus is usually content to describe the customs and practices of non-Greeks without passing judgment on them. Here, however, we see him actually endorsing a custom which, by modern standards, would seem abhorrent. This endorsement can even be characterized as "resounding," as on two occasions, at the beginning and end of the passage, Herodotus uses superlative adjectives (σοφώτατος and κάλλιστος) to describe the Babylonian practice of bride auctions. Other than its value as a passage that lets us look inside the mind of our author, this chapter probably has little historical value (cf. ALC *ad* 1.196.1: "No Babylonian evidence exists for such a custom, and the entire description gives the impression of a utopian, half-comic Greek fantasy.") For a balanced assessment of the topic of "Women" in the *Histories*, see Landmark, Appendix U, "On Women and Marriage in Herodotus."

αὕτη μὲν δή σφι ἄρτισις περὶ τὸ σῶμά ἐστι· νόμοι δὲ αὐτοῖσι οἵδε κατεστέασι, ὁ μὲν σοφώτατος ὅδε κατὰ γνώμην τὴν ἡμετέρην, τῷ καὶ Ἰλλυριῶν Ἐνετοὺς πυνθάνομαι χρᾶσθαι. κατὰ κώμας ἑκάστας ἅπαξ τοῦ ἔτεος ἑκάστου ἐποιέετο τάδε· ὡς ἂν αἱ παρθένοι γινοίατο γάμων ὡραῖαι, ταύτας ὅκως συναγάγοιεν πάσας, ἐς ἓν χωρίον ἐσάγεσκον ἁλέας, πέριξ δὲ αὐτὰς ἵστατο ὅμιλος ἀνδρῶν. [2] ἀνιστὰς δὲ κατὰ μίαν ἑκάστην κῆρυξ πωλέεσκε, πρῶτα μὲν τὴν εὐειδεστάτην ἐκ πασέων· μετὰ δέ, ὅκως αὕτη εὑροῦσα πολλὸν χρυσίον πρηθείη, ἄλλην ἀνεκήρυσσε ἣ μετ' ἐκείνην ἔσκε εὐειδεστάτη· ἐπωλέοντο δὲ ἐπὶ συνοικήσι. ὅσοι μὲν δὴ ἔσκον εὐδαίμονες τῶν Βαβυλωνίων ἐπίγαμοι, ὑπερβάλλοντες ἀλλήλους ἐξωνέοντο τὰς καλλιστευούσας· ὅσοι δὲ τοῦ δήμου ἔσκον ἐπίγαμοι, οὗτοι δὲ εἶδεος μὲν οὐδὲν ἐδέοντο χρηστοῦ, οἱ δ' ἂν χρήματά τε καὶ αἰσχίονας παρθένους ἐλάμβανον. [3] ὡς γὰρ δὴ διεξέλθοι ὁ κῆρυξ πωλέων τὰς εὐειδεστάτας τῶν παρθένων, ἀνίστη ἂν τὴν ἀμορφεστάτην ἢ εἴ τις αὐτέων ἔμπηρος ἦν, καὶ ταύτην ἀνεκήρυσσε, ὅστις θέλοι ἐλάχιστον χρυσίον λαβὼν συνοικέειν αὐτῇ, ἐς ὃ τῷ τὸ ἐλάχιστον ὑπισταμένῳ προσέκειτο. τὸ δὲ ἂν χρυσίον ἐγίνετο ἀπὸ τῶν εὐειδέων παρθένων, καὶ οὕτως αἱ εὔμορφοι τὰς ἀμόρφους καὶ ἐμπήρους ἐξεδίδοσαν. ἐκδοῦναι δὲ τὴν ἑωυτοῦ θυγατέρα ὅτεῳ βούλοιτο ἕκαστος οὐκ ἐξῆν οὐδὲ ἄνευ ἐγγυητέω ἀπαγαγέσθαι τὴν παρθένον πριάμενον, ἀλλ' ἐγγυητὰς χρῆν καταστήσαντα ἦ μὲν συνοικήσειν αὐτῇ, οὕτω ἀπάγεσθαι· [4] εἰ δὲ μὴ συμφεροίατο, ἀποφέρειν τὸ χρυσίον ἔκειτο νόμος. ἐξῆν δὲ καὶ ἐξ ἄλλης ἐλθόντα κώμης τὸν βουλόμενον ὠνέεσθαι. [5] ὁ μέν νυν κάλλιστος νόμος οὗτός σφι ἦν, οὐ μέντοι νῦν γε διετέλεε ἐών, ἄλλο δέ τι ἐξευρήκασι νεωστὶ γενέσθαι [ἵνα μὴ ἀδικοῖεν αὐτὰς μηδ' εἰς ἑτέραν πόλιν ἄγωνται]· ἐπείτε γὰρ ἁλόντες ἐκακώθησαν καὶ οἰκοφθορήθησαν, πᾶς τις τοῦ δήμου βίου σπανίζων καταπορνεύει τὰ θήλεα τέκνα.

1.196.1

αὕτη μὲν δή σφι ἄρτισις περὶ τὸ σῶμά ἐστι This sentence concludes the section on Babylonian clothing (begun in 1.195).

Ἰλλυριῶν Ἐνετοὺς The Eneti of Illyria lived on the coasts of the northern reach of the Adriatic Sea. Cf. map in Landmark *ad* 1.166.

γάμων ὡραῖαι "Of a suitable age for marriage."

ὅκως = ὅπως.

ἐσάγεσκον Imperfect, indicative, active, 3rd, plural of ἐσάγω (= εἰσάγω). The -εσκ- infix emphasizes the iterative aspect of the imperfect.

1.196.2

πωλέεσκε Another iterative imperfect.

εὑροῦσα "Having commanded."

πρηθείη Aorist, optative, passive, 3rd, singular of πιπράσκω.

ἔσκε Iterative imperfect of εἰμί.

ἐπὶ συνοικήσι "For the purpose of sharing a household [as husband and wife]."

ὑπερβάλλοντες "Outbidding."

εἴδεος μὲν οὐδὲν ἐδέοντο χρηστοῦ "Did not require good looks [on the grounds that it was not] useful."

αἰσχίονας "Rather unattractive."

1.196.3

ἐς ὃ τῷ τὸ ἐλάχιστον ὑπισταμένῳ προσέκειτο "Until she belonged to him who offered to take the least [money]."

ἐξεδίδοσαν "Paid the dowries for…."

οὐκ ἐξῆν "It was not permitted."

ἐγγυητέω The form is genitive. This person was a kind of bondsman who would guarantee that the purchaser of a bride would indeed treat her as a wife (and not as a slave).

ἦ μὲν "Truly."

1.196.4

συμφεροίατο "If they [the couple] did [not] get along." Present, optative, passive, 3rd, plural of συμφέρω.

ἔκειτο νόμος "It was the custom."

1.196.5

διατελέει ἐών "Continue existing."

☙

2.2.1-5 The Language Experiment of King Psammetichos

This story of how King Psammetichos of Egypt (7th century B.C.) conducted his linguistic experiment shows Herodotus as the consummate story teller and is one of the most cherished of all the tales in the *Histories*. Apparently, the story had such an impact on Frederick II (King of Prussia) and James I (King of Scotland) that they repeated Psammetichos' experiment (see HW *ad* 2.2.2). A few additional things to note here. One is that Herodotus allows that his fellow Greeks are NOT the most ancient of peoples (in fact, they are not even in the running). Another is that Herodotus seems, quite pointedly, to make Psammetichos carry out the kind of inquiries that Herodotus himself would conduct (cf. the repeated use of forms of πυνθάνομαι). Finally, note Herodotus' harsh dismissal of a variant to this story, which he attributes to unnamed Greeks (Ἕλληνες δὲ λέγουσι ἄλλα τε μάταια πολλά).

οἱ δὲ Αἰγύπτιοι, πρὶν μὲν ἢ Ψαμμήτιχον σφέων βασιλεῦσαι, ἐνόμιζον ἑωυτοὺς πρώτους γενέσθαι πάντων ἀνθρώπων· ἐπειδὴ δὲ Ψαμμήτιχος βασιλεύσας ἠθέλησε εἰδέναι οἵτινες γενοίατο πρῶτοι, ἀπὸ τούτου νομίζουσι Φρύγας προτέρους γενέσθαι ἑωυτῶν, τῶν δὲ ἄλλων ἑωυτούς. [2] Ψαμμήτιχος δὲ ὡς οὐκ ἐδύνατο πυνθανόμενος πόρον οὐδένα τούτου ἀνευρεῖν, οἳ γενοίατο πρῶτοι ἀνθρώπων, ἐπιτεχνᾶται τοιόνδε· παιδία δύο νεογνὰ ἀνθρώπων τῶν ἐπιτυχόντων διδοῖ ποιμένι τρέφειν ἐς τὰ ποίμνια τροφήν τινα τοιήνδε, ἐντειλάμενος μηδένα ἀντίον αὐτῶν μηδεμίαν φωνὴν ἱέναι, ἐν στέγῃ δὲ ἐρήμῃ ἐπ' ἑωυτῶν κεῖσθαι αὐτά, καὶ τὴν ὥρην ἐπαγινέειν σφι αἶγας, πλήσαντα δὲ γάλακτος τἆλλα διαπρήσσεσθαι· [3] ταῦτα δὲ ἐποίεέ τε καὶ ἐνετέλλετο Ψαμμήτιχος θέλων ἀκοῦσαι τῶν παιδίων, ἀπαλλαχθέντων τῶν ἀσήμων κνυζημάτων, ἥντινα φωνὴν ῥήξουσι πρώτην· τά περ ὦν καὶ ἐγένετο. ὡς γὰρ διέτης χρόνος ἐγεγόνεε ταῦτα τῷ ποιμένι πρήσσοντι, ἀνοίγοντι τὴν θύρην καὶ ἐσιόντι τὰ παιδία ἀμφότερα προσπίπτοντα βεκὸς ἐφώνεον ὀρέγοντα τὰς χεῖρας. [4] τὰ μὲν δὴ πρῶτα ἀκούσας ἥσυχος ἦν ὁ ποιμήν· ὡς δὲ πολλάκις φοιτῶντι καὶ ἐπιμελομένῳ πολλὸν ἦν τοῦτο τὸ ἔπος, οὕτω δὴ σημήνας τῷ δεσπότῃ ἤγαγε τὰ παιδία κελεύσαντος ἐς ὄψιν τὴν ἐκείνου. ἀκούσας δὲ καὶ αὐτὸς ὁ Ψαμμήτιχος ἐπυνθάνετο οἵτινες ἀνθρώπων βεκός τι καλέουσι, πυνθανόμενος δὲ εὕρισκε Φρύγας καλέοντας τὸν ἄρτον. [5] οὕτω συνεχώρησαν Αἰγύπτιοι καὶ τοιούτῳ σταθμησάμενοι πρήγματι τοὺς Φρύγας πρεσβυτέρους εἶναι ἑωυτῶν. ὧδε μὲν γενέσθαι τῶν ἱρέων τοῦ Ἡφαίστου τοῦ ἐν Μέμφι ἤκουον. Ἕλληνες δὲ λέγουσι ἄλλα τε μάταια πολλὰ καὶ ὡς γυναικῶν τὰς γλώσσας ὁ Ψαμμήτιχος ἐκταμὼν τὴν δίαιταν οὕτως ἐποιήσατο τῶν παίδων παρὰ ταύτῃσι τῇσι γυναιξί.

2.2.1

εἰδέναι Perfect, active infinitive of οἶδα.

γενοίατο = γένοιντο. Aorist, optative, middle, 3rd, plural of γίγνομαι.

ἀπὸ τούτου "From this time forward."

2.2.2

ἀνευρεῖν Aorist, active infinitive of ἀνευρίσκω.

ἀνθρώπων τῶν ἐπιτυχόντων "People who happened by." In other words, "randomly selected people."

μηδεμίαν φωνὴν ἱέναι "Utter any sound."

ἑωυτῶν = ἑαυτῶν.

αὐτά Refers to παιδία.

τὴν ὥρην "At the appropriate time."

τἄλλα Crasis (two words combined into one) for τὰ ἄλλα.

2.2.3

ἀπαλλαχθέντων τῶν ἀσήμων κνυζημάτων Genitive absolute construction. "Once the boys outgrew their meaningless babblings."

ὦν = οὖν.

ἐγεγόνεε = ἐγεγόνει. Pluperfect, indicative, active, 3rd, singular of γίγνομαι.

πρήσσοντι, ἀνοίγοντι …ἐσιόντι All three participles modify τῷ ποιμένι.

2.2.4

τά…πρῶτα "At first."

κελεύσαντος ἐς ὄψιν τὴν ἐκείνου Genitive absolute construction.

2.2.5

ὧδε μὲν γενέσθαι Translate with ἤκουον. "I heard …that this is the way it happened."

τῶν ἱρέων Translate with ἤκουον.

ἐκταμὼν Aorist, active, masculine, nominative, singular participle of ἐκτέμνω.

☙

2.20.1-3 On Why the Nile Floods Annually

In this part of Book II, Herodotus undertakes to explore some of the mysteries surrounding the great Nile River. (The oft-quoted expression, "Egypt, gift of the Nile," occurs earlier, in 2.5.) He notes in 2.19 that the reasons for the annual flooding of the river were beyond the grasp of his Egyptian informants. In this chapter, he emphasizes how certain unnamed and vainglorious Greeks have themselves been incapable of coming up with an explanation. The reasons why he rejects the Etesian Wind theory—the Etesian Winds, which blow from the north, keep the river from flowing into the sea and thus make it flood—are themselves problematic (cf. note in Landmark *ad* 2.20.3), but they do illustrate the kind of scientific reasoning our author often employs.

ἀλλὰ Ἑλλήνων μέν τινες ἐπίσημοι βουλόμενοι γενέσθαι σοφίην ἔλεξαν περὶ τοῦ ὕδατος τούτου τριφασίας ὁδούς· τῶν τὰς μὲν δύο τῶν ὁδῶν οὐδ᾽ ἀξιῶ μνησθῆναι εἰ μὴ ὅσον σημῆναι βουλόμενος μοῦνον·[2] τῶν ἡ ἑτέρη μὲν λέγει τοὺς ἐτησίας ἀνέμους εἶναι αἰτίους πληθύειν τὸν ποταμόν, κωλύοντας ἐς θάλασσαν ἐκρέειν τὸν Νεῖλον. πολλάκις δὲ ἐτησίαι μὲν οὐκ ὦν ἔπνευσαν, ὁ δὲ Νεῖλος τὠυτὸ ἐργάζεται. [3] πρὸς δέ, εἰ ἐτησίαι αἴτιοι ἦσαν, χρῆν καὶ τοὺς ἄλλους ποταμούς, ὅσοι τοῖσι ἐτησίῃσι ἀντίοι ῥέουσι, ὁμοίως πάσχειν καὶ κατὰ τὰ αὐτὰ τῷ Νείλῳ, καὶ μᾶλλον ἔτι τοσούτῳ ὅσῳ ἐλάσσονες ἐόντες ἀσθενέστερα τὰ ῥεύματα παρέχονται. εἰσὶ δὲ πολλοὶ μὲν ἐν τῇ Συρίῃ ποταμοί, πολλοὶ δὲ ἐν τῇ Λιβύῃ, οἳ οὐδὲν τοιοῦτο πάσχουσι οἷόν τι καὶ ὁ Νεῖλος.

2.20.1

ἐπίσημοι "Seeking distinction."

ὁδούς "Explanations."

εἰ μὴ ὅσον σημῆναι βουλόμενος μοῦνον "Except for my merely wanting to mention them."

2.20.2

οὔκων = οὔκουν.

τὠυτό Crasis (two words combined into one) for τὸ αὐτό.

2.20.3

πρὸς δέ "In addition."

ὁμοίως πάσχειν καὶ κατὰ τὰ αὐτὰ τῷ Νείλῳ "To experience likewise the same things that the Nile experiences."

τοσούτῳ ὅσῳ "For this reason, insofar as."

πολλοί It is not clear what these "many" rivers of Libya and Syria are.

☙

2.35.1-4 Marvelous Egypt

This is the much-celebrated passage where Herodotus expounds—perhaps excessively—on the great contrasts between the Egyptian way of life and the Greek way. It begins with a display of the author's unbridled enthusiasm for the marvels of Egypt, which by his estimation eclipse those of any other land. In pointing out the contrasts between Egyptian and Greek customs, he emphasizes how Egyptian woman are familiar with the ways of the marketplace. This aspect of Egyptian life may have been of special interest to Herodotus, who quite possibly made his living as a merchant and, as such, was familiar with marketplaces all over the Mediterranean. The section where Egyptian men are said to stay at home and weave is echoed in Sophocles' *Oedipus at Colonus*, where a blind Oedipus laments the weakness of his sons (337 ff.). While some commentators (cf. note in Landmark *ad* 2.35.4 and ALC *ad* 2.35.1) are eager to point out the mistakes in this section, others allow that it is perhaps the "most valuable part of Book II" (HW *ad* 2.35).

Νείλου μέν νυν πέρι τοσαῦτα εἰρήσθω· ἔρχομαι δὲ περὶ Αἰγύπτου μηκυνέων τὸν λόγον, ὅτι πλεῖστα θωμάσια ἔχει ἢ ἡ ἄλλη πᾶσα χώρη καὶ ἔργα λόγου μέζω παρέχεται πρὸς πᾶσαν χώρην· τούτων εἵνεκα πλέω περὶ αὐτῆς εἰρήσεται. [2] Αἰγύπτιοι ἅμα τῷ οὐρανῷ τῷ κατὰ σφέας ἐόντι ἑτεροίῳ καὶ τῷ ποταμῷ φύσιν ἀλλοίην παρεχομένῳ ἢ οἱ ἄλλοι ποταμοί, τὰ πολλὰ πάντα ἔμπαλιν τοῖσι ἄλλοισι ἀνθρώποισι ἐστήσαντο ἤθεά τε καὶ νόμους· ἐν τοῖσι αἱ μὲν γυναῖκες ἀγοράζουσι καὶ καπηλεύουσι, οἱ δὲ ἄνδρες κατ' οἴκους ἐόντες ὑφαίνουσι· ὑφαίνουσι δὲ οἱ μὲν ἄλλοι ἄνω τὴν κρόκην ὠθέοντες, Αἰγύπτιοι δὲ κάτω. [3] τὰ ἄχθεα οἱ μὲν ἄνδρες ἐπὶ τῶν κεφαλέων φορέουσι, αἱ δὲ γυναῖκες ἐπὶ τῶν ὤμων. οὐρέουσι αἱ μὲν γυναῖκες ὀρθαί, οἱ δὲ ἄνδρες κατήμενοι. εὐμαρείη χρέωνται ἐν τοῖσι οἴκοισι, ἐσθίουσι δὲ ἔξω ἐν τῆσι ὁδοῖσι, ἐπιλέγοντες ὡς τὰ μὲν αἰσχρὰ ἀναγκαῖα δὲ ἐν ἀποκρύφῳ ἐστὶ ποιέειν χρεόν, τὰ δὲ μὴ αἰσχρὰ ἀναφανδόν. [4] ἱρᾶται γυνὴ μὲν οὐδεμία οὔτε ἔρσενος θεοῦ οὔτε θηλέης, ἄνδρες δὲ πάντων τε καὶ πασέων. τρέφειν τοὺς τοκέας τοῖσι μὲν παισὶ οὐδεμία ἀνάγκη μὴ βουλομένοισι, τῇσι δὲ θυγατράσι πᾶσα ἀνάγκη καὶ μὴ βουλομένῃσι.

2.35.1

πέρι Note the position of the accent.

εἰρήσθω "Let what has been said be enough."

2.35.2

ἅμα Used here as a preposition.

τῷ ποταμῷ φύσιν ἀλλοίην παρεχομένῳ "The river displaying a nature that is different."

τὰ πολλὰ πάντα "In most all respects."

ἄνω τὴν κρόκην ὠθέοντες "Pushing the thread of the weft in an upward direction."

2.35.3

ὀρθαί…κατήμενοι "Standing up…sitting down."

εὐμαρείῃ χρέωνται A euphemism comparable to "they relieve themselves."

2.37.1-5 Religious Practices of the Egyptians

In the Egypt section of the *Histories* (much of Book II), Herodotus is almost incapable of being dull. A large part of the interest in this passage is generated by the exquisite detail with which Herodotus describes the religious customs of Egyptians and their priests: e.g., the priests could eat all the goose meat they wanted but could not even look at beans. The strong opening statement about the Egyptians being the most religious of all mankind finds confirmation in additional ancient sources (cf. Cicero, *Tusculan Disputations* 5.27). Some of the specific statements in this passage, however, have been discredited by modern commentators: cf. the note in Landmark *ad* 2.36.2, where Herodotus' claim that the Egyptians regarded chickpea (ὄσπριον) as unclean is rejected.

θεοσεβέες δὲ περισσῶς ἐόντες μάλιστα πάντων ἀνθρώπων νόμοισι τοιοῖσδε χρέωνται. ἐκ χαλκέων ποτηρίων πίνουσι, διασμῶντες ἀνὰ πᾶσαν ἡμέρην, οὐκ ὁ μέν, ὁ δ' οὔ, ἀλλὰ πάντες. [2] εἵματα δὲ λίνεα φορέουσι αἰεὶ νεόπλυτα, ἐπιτηδεύοντες τοῦτο μάλιστα. τά τε αἰδοῖα περιτάμνονται καθαρειότητος εἵνεκεν, προτιμῶντες καθαροὶ εἶναι ἢ εὐπρεπέστεροι. οἱ δὲ ἱρέες ξυρῶνται πᾶν τὸ σῶμα διὰ τρίτης ἡμέρης, ἵνα μήτε φθεὶρ μήτε ἄλλο μυσαρὸν μηδὲν ἐγγίνηταί σφι θεραπεύουσι τοὺς θεούς. [3] ἐσθῆτα δὲ φορέουσι οἱ ἱρέες λινέην μούνην καὶ ὑποδήματα βύβλινα· ἄλλην δέ σφι ἐσθῆτα οὐκ ἔξεστι λαβεῖν οὐδὲ ὑποδήματα ἄλλα. λοῦνται δὲ δίς τε τῆς ἡμέρης ἑκάστης ψυχρῷ καὶ δὶς ἑκάστης νυκτός. ἄλλας τε θρησκηίας ἐπιτελέουσι μυρίας ὡς εἰπεῖν λόγῳ. [4] πάσχουσι δὲ καὶ ἀγαθὰ οὐκ ὀλίγα· οὔτε τι γὰρ τῶν οἰκηίων τρίβουσι οὔτε δαπανῶνται, ἀλλὰ καὶ σιτία σφί ἐστι ἱρὰ πεσσόμενα, καὶ κρεῶν βοέων καὶ χηνέων πλῆθός τι ἑκάστῳ γίνεται πολλὸν ἡμέρης ἑκάστης, δίδοται δέ σφι καὶ οἶνος ἀμπέλινος· ἰχθύων δὲ οὔ σφι ἔξεστι πάσασθαι. [5] κυάμους δὲ οὔτε τι μάλα σπείρουσι Αἰγύπτιοι ἐν τῇ χώρῃ, τούς τε γινομένους οὔτε τρώγουσι οὔτε ἕψοντες πατέονται· οἱ δὲ δὴ ἱρέες οὐδὲ ὁρέοντες ἀνέχονται, νομίζοντες οὐ καθαρὸν εἶναί μιν ὄσπριον. ἱρᾶται δὲ οὐκ εἰς ἑκάστου τῶν θεῶν ἀλλὰ πολλοί, τῶν εἷς ἐστι ἀρχιερεύς· ἐπεὰν δέ τις ἀποθάνῃ, τούτου ὁ παῖς ἀντικατίσταται.

─────────────────

2.37.1

θεοσεβέες δὲ περισσῶς ἐόντες "Being extraordinarily religious."

οὐκ ὁ μέν, ὁ δ᾽ οὔ "Not merely this one or that one."

2.37.2

τά τε αἰδοῖα περιτάμνονται "They practice circumcision."

εἵνεκεν = ἕνεκα.

ἐγγίνηται = ἐγγίγνηται.

2.37.3

ὑποδήματα βύβλινα "Sandals made of papyrus."

ὡς εἰπεῖν λόγῳ This phrase tones down the exaggeration implicit in μυρίας.

2.37.4

ἱρά = ἱερά.

πάσασθαι Translate with ἔξεστι.

2.37.5

τούς τε γινομένους "[Beans] that grow in the wild."

ὄσπριον "chickpea."

ἐπεάν = ἐπειδάν.

ଔ

2.44.1-5 Herodotus Travels Great Distances to Conduct his Inquiries

In this chapter, Herodotus supplies his readers with some valuable autobiographical information. He explicitly states that he traveled to Tyre in Phoenicia and then to the island of Thasos in the northern Aegean—long journeys, to be sure—in order to gain "secure knowledge" (σαφές τι εἰδέναι) concerning the Phoenician counterpart to the Greek hero-god, Herakles. That Herodotus could travel such great distances in order to make his inquiries indicates that he had the financial means to do so. It is also possible that Herodotus was a merchant who traveled extensively because of his trade and who was thus able to make his inquiries alongside his business dealings. The inquiry that he conducts in this passage shows us a very open-minded Herodotus, who wants to see Greek religion as an off-shoot of Middle Eastern, especially Egyptian, religions. (For a survey of recent research concerning the "Egyptian Herakles" and the "Phoenician Herakles," see ALC ad 2.44.)

καὶ θέλων δὲ τούτων πέρι σαφές τι εἰδέναι ἐξ ὧν οἷόν τε ἦν, ἔπλευσα καὶ ἐς Τύρον τῆς Φοινίκης, πυνθανόμενος αὐτόθι εἶναι ἱρὸν Ἡρακλέος ἅγιον. [2] καὶ εἶδον πλουσίως κατεσκευασμένον ἄλλοισί τε πολλοῖσι ἀναθήμασι, καὶ ἐν αὐτῷ ἦσαν στῆλαι δύο, ἡ μὲν χρυσοῦ ἀπέφθου, ἡ δὲ σμαράγδου λίθου λάμποντος τὰς νύκτας μέγαθος· ἐς λόγους δὲ ἐλθὼν τοῖσι ἱρεῦσι τοῦ θεοῦ εἰρόμην ὁκόσος χρόνος εἴη ἐξ οὗ σφι τὸ ἱρὸν ἵδρυται. [3] εὗρον δὲ οὐδὲ τούτους τοῖσι Ἕλλησι συμφερομένους· ἔφασαν γὰρ ἅμα Τύρῳ οἰκιζομένῃ καὶ τὸ ἱρὸν τοῦ θεοῦ ἱδρυθῆναι, εἶναι δὲ ἔτεα ἀπ' οὗ Τύρον οἰκέουσι τριηκόσια καὶ δισχίλια. εἶδον δὲ ἐν τῇ Τύρῳ καὶ ἄλλο ἱρὸν Ἡρακλέος ἐπωνυμίην ἔχοντος Θασίου εἶναι· [4] ἀπικόμην δὲ καὶ ἐς Θάσον, ἐν τῇ εὗρον ἱρὸν Ἡρακλέος ὑπὸ Φοινίκων ἱδρυμένον, οἳ κατ' Εὐρώπης ζήτησιν ἐκπλώσαντες Θάσον ἔκτισαν· καὶ ταῦτα καὶ πέντε γενεῇσι ἀνδρῶν πρότερά ἐστι ἢ τὸν Ἀμφιτρύωνος Ἡρακλέα ἐν τῇ Ἑλλάδι γενέσθαι. [5] τὰ μὲν νυν ἱστορημένα δηλοῖ σαφέως παλαιὸν θεὸν Ἡρακλέα ἐόντα, καὶ δοκέουσι δέ μοι οὗτοι ὀρθότατα Ἑλλήνων ποιέειν, οἳ διξὰ Ἡράκλεια ἱδρυσάμενοι ἔκτηνται, καὶ τῷ μὲν ὡς ἀθανάτῳ, Ὀλυμπίῳ δὲ ἐπωνυμίην θύουσι, τῷ δὲ ἑτέρῳ ὡς ἥρωι ἐναγίζουσι.

2.44.1

ἐξ ὧν οἷόν τε ἦν "From whatever source it was possible."
ἱρὸν Ἡρακλέος ἅγιον "A shrine sacred to Herakles."
ἱρόν = ἱερόν.

2.44.2

χρυσοῦ ἀπέφθου "Of refined gold."
ἐς λόγους δὲ ἐλθών "Entering into conversation."
ὁκόσος = ὁπόσος.
ἵδρυται Perfect, indicative, passive, 3rd, singular of ἱδρύω.

2.44.3

συμφερομένους "In agreement."
ἅμα Τύρῳ οἰκιζομένῃ "At the same time that Tyre was founded."
ἐπωνυμίην "Epithet."
Θασίου Thasos is an island in the northern Aegean (see map in Landmark *ad* 2.48).

2.44.4

ἀπικόμην = ἀφικόμην.
πέντε γενεῇσι ἀνδρῶν πρότερα "Earlier by five generations of men."

2.44.5

τὰ ...ἱστορημένα "These inquiries."
διξὰ Ἡράκλεια "Two separate shrines to Herakles."
ἐναγίζουσι "They bring offerings to the dead."

∞

2.66.1-4 The Cats of Egypt

Herodotus' inexhaustible curiosity often has him exploring animal behavior. Egyptian cats, or cats in general, would have been of special interest to him, as there were no domestic cats in fifth century Greece (cf. note in Landmark *ad* 2.66.4). The privileged status of Egyptian cats is corroborated by an account in Diodorus Siculus (1.83), who writes that a Roman, after he had accidentally killed a cat in Egypt during the time of Ptolemy XII Auletes (the father of Cleopatra VII), was executed in spite of the efforts of Ptolemy to save him. The claim that Egyptian cats would run into burning buildings is supported in HW *ad* 2.66.3 and dismissed in Landmark *ad* 2.66.4.

πολλῶν δὲ ἐόντων ὁμοτρόφων τοῖσι ἀνθρώποισι θηρίων πολλῷ ἂν ἔτι πλέω ἐγίνετο, εἰ μὴ κατελάμβανε τοὺς αἰελούρους τοιάδε· ἐπεὰν τέκωσι αἱ θήλεαι, οὐκέτι φοιτῶσι παρὰ τοὺς ἔρσενας· οἱ δὲ διζήμενοι μίσγεσθαι αὐτῇσι οὐκ ἔχουσι. [2] πρὸς ὦν ταῦτα σοφίζονται τάδε· ἁρπάζοντες ἀπὸ τῶν θηλέων καὶ ὑπαιρεόμενοι τὰ τέκνα κτείνουσι, κτείναντες μέντοι οὐ πατέονται. αἱ δὲ στερισκόμεναι τῶν τέκνων, ἄλλων δὲ ἐπιθυμέουσαι, οὕτω δὴ ἀπικνέονται παρὰ τοὺς ἔρσενας· φιλότεκνον γὰρ τὸ θηρίον. [3] πυρκαϊῆς δὲ γινομένης θεῖα πρήγματα καταλαμβάνει τοὺς αἰελούρους· οἱ μὲν γὰρ Αἰγύπτιοι διαστάντες φυλακὰς ἔχουσι τῶν αἰελούρων, ἀμελήσαντες σβεννύναι τὸ καιόμενον, οἱ δὲ αἰέλουροι διαδύνοντες καὶ ὑπερθρῴσκοντες τοὺς ἀνθρώπους ἐσάλλονται ἐς τὸ πῦρ. [4] ταῦτα δὲ γινόμενα πένθεα μεγάλα τοὺς Αἰγυπτίους καταλαμβάνει. ἐν ὁτέοισι δ᾽ ἂν οἰκίοισι αἰέλουρος ἀποθάνῃ ἀπὸ τοῦ αὐτομάτου, οἱ ἐνοικέοντες πάντες ξυρῶνται τὰς ὀφρύας μούνας, παρ᾽ ὁτέοισι δ᾽ ἂν κύων, πᾶν τὸ σῶμα καὶ τὴν κεφαλήν.

2.66.1

πολλῶν δὲ ἐόντων ὁμοτρόφων τοῖσι ἀνθρώποισι θηρίων Genitive absolute construction.
ἐγίνετο = ἐγίγνετο
τοιάδε Subject of the conditional clause.
ἐπεάν = ἐπειδάν.
τέκωσι Aorist, subjunctive, active, 3rd, plural of τίκτω.
φοιτέουσι "Copulate."
μίσγεσθαι Present, passive infinitive of μίγνυμι. "To mate."
οὐκ ἔχουσι "Are unable."

2.66.2

ὦν = οὖν.

ὑπαιρεόμενοι = ὑφαιρούμενοι.

ἄλλων Genitive case after ἐπιθυμέουσαι.

ἀπικνέονται = ἀφικνοῦνται.

2.66.3

πυρκαϊῆς δὲ γενομένης Genitive absolute construction. "When a fire breaks out."

θεῖα πρήγματα "Supernatural forces."

διαστάντες "Standing at regular intervals from one another."

ἀμελήσαντες σβεννύναι τὸ καιόμενον "Not paying attention to putting out whatever is burning."

ἐσάλλονται = εἰσάλλονται.

2.66.4

ἀποθάνῃ Aorist, subjunctive, active, 3rd, singular of ἀποθνήσκω.

ταῦτα δὲ γινόμενα Treat as though it were a genitive absolute construction. "When these things happen [i.e., cats running into a burning building]."

☙

2.68.1-5 Egyptian Crocodiles and Plovers

This a very interesting passage, where Herodotus describes the Egyptian crocodile and its symbiotic relationship with the Egyptian plover. Never one to miss an opportunity to write in considerable detail about such fascinating topics, our author has made himself the target of modern writers who have rejected his observation that the Egyptian crocodile does not have a tongue (it does, albeit only a small one), or his finding that leeches abound in the Nile (there are other kinds of parasites, but not leeches). In antiquity, at least, Herodotus' expertise in biological matters was acknowledged by scientific writers as important as Aristotle, whose account of the Egyptian crocodile (*Historia Animalium* 2.10) largely follows that of Herodotus.

τῶν δὲ κροκοδείλων φύσις ἐστὶ τοιήδε· τοὺς χειμεριωτάτους μῆνας τέσσερας ἐσθίει οὐδέν, ἐὸν δὲ τετράπουν χερσαῖον καὶ λιμναῖόν ἐστι· τίκτει μὲν γὰρ ᾠὰ ἐν γῇ καὶ ἐκλέπει, καὶ τὸ πολλὸν τῆς ἡμέρης διατρίβει ἐν τῷ ξηρῷ, τὴν δὲ νύκτα πᾶσαν ἐν τῷ ποταμῷ· θερμότερον γὰρ δή ἐστι τὸ ὕδωρ τῆς τε αἰθρίης καὶ τῆς δρόσου. [2] πάντων δὲ τῶν ἡμεῖς ἴδμεν θνητῶν τοῦτο ἐξ ἐλαχίστου μέγιστον γίνεται· τὰ μὲν γὰρ ᾠὰ χηνέων οὐ πολλῷ μέζονα τίκτει, καὶ ὁ νεοσσὸς κατὰ λόγον τοῦ ᾠοῦ γίνεται, αὐξανόμενος δὲ γίνεται καὶ ἐς ἑπτακαίδεκα πήχεας καὶ μέζων ἔτι. [3] ἔχει δὲ ὀφθαλμοὺς μὲν ὑός, ὀδόντας δὲ μεγάλους καὶ χαυλιόδοντας κατὰ λόγον τοῦ σώματος. γλῶσσαν δὲ μοῦνον θηρίων οὐκ ἔφυσε. οὐδὲ κινέει τὴν κάτω γνάθον, ἀλλὰ καὶ τοῦτο μοῦνον θηρίων τὴν ἄνω γνάθον προσάγει τῇ κάτω. [4] ἔχει δὲ καὶ ὄνυχας καρτεροὺς καὶ δέρμα λεπιδωτὸν ἄρρηκτον ἐπὶ τοῦ νώτου. τυφλὸν δὲ ἐν ὕδατι, ἐν δὲ τῇ αἰθρίῃ ὀξυδερκέστατον. ἅτε δὴ ὦν ἐν ὕδατι δίαιταν ποιεύμενον, τὸ στόμα ἔνδοθεν φορέει πᾶν μεστὸν βδελλέων. τὰ μὲν δὴ ἄλλα ὄρνεα καὶ θηρία φεύγει μιν, ὁ δὲ τροχίλος εἰρηναῖόν οἱ ἐστι ἅτε ὠφελεομένῳ πρὸς αὐτοῦ· [5] ἐπεὰν γὰρ ἐς τὴν γῆν ἐκβῇ ἐκ τοῦ ὕδατος ὁ κροκόδειλος καὶ ἔπειτα χάνῃ (ἔωθε γὰρ τοῦτο ὡς ἐπίπαν ποιέειν πρὸς τὸν ζέφυρον), ἐνθαῦτα ὁ τροχίλος ἐσδύνων ἐς τὸ στόμα αὐτοῦ καταπίνει τὰς βδέλλας· ὁ δὲ ὠφελεύμενος ἥδεται καὶ οὐδὲν σίνεται τὸν τροχίλον.

2.68.1

τοὺς χειμεριωτάτους μῆνας τέσσερας Accusative of extent of time.

ἐὸν δὲ τετράπουν "Being a four-footed beast."

2.68.2

γίνεται = γίγνεται.

μέζονα = μείζονα.

ὁ νεοσσὸς κατὰ λόγον τοῦ ᾠοῦ γίνεται "[The size of] the hatchling is proportionate [to the size] of the egg."

ἑπτακαίδεκα πήχεας "Seventeen cubits," or over 25 feet. A cubit is the distance from the end of the middle finger to the tip of the elbow.

2.68.3

κατὰ λόγον τοῦ σώματος "In proportion [to the size] of the body."

μοῦνον = μόνον.

τὴν ἄνω γνάθον προσάγει τῇ κάτω "Brings its upper jaw down upon its lower jaw."

2.68.4

ἅτε "Inasmuch as." Translate with the participle ποιεύμενον.

ὦν = οὖν.

τροχίλος The Egyptian plover.

ἅτε ὠφελεομένῳ πρὸς αὐτοῦ "Inasmuch as it [the crocodile] benefits from it [the plover]."

2.68.5

ἐπεάν = ἐπειδάν.

ἔωθε "Is accustomed."

ἐνθαῦτα = ἐνταῦθα.

☙

2.69.1-3 More on the Egyptian Crocodile

Herodotus continues his marvelous account of the Egyptian crocodile. The accuracy of his description of the way select crocodiles were outfitted with glass and gold earrings is at least partially confirmed by finds of mummified crocodiles, whose skulls appear to have been pierced (cf. HW *ad* 2.69.2). The passage ends with a brief discussion of the Greek word κροκόδειλος and its original meaning, "lizard." It presents us with a Herodotus who has some linguistic insights which, in this case at least, are "gratifyingly accurate" (ALC *ad* 2.69.3). It also shows a Herodotus who could readily transport his readers' imaginations to the magical world of the Mediterranean with its ancient stone walls and scurrying lizards.

τοῖσι μὲν δὴ τῶν Αἰγυπτίων ἱροί εἰσι οἱ κροκόδειλοι, τοῖσι δὲ οὔ, ἀλλ᾽ ἅτε πολεμίους περιέπουσι· οἱ δὲ περί τε Θήβας καὶ τὴν Μοίριος λίμνην οἰκέοντες καὶ κάρτα ἥγηνται αὐτοὺς εἶναι ἱρούς·[2] ἐκ πάντων δὲ ἕνα ἑκάτεροι τρέφουσι κροκόδειλον, δεδιδαγμένον εἶναι χειροήθεα, ἀρτήματά τε λίθινα χυτὰ καὶ χρύσεα ἐς τὰ ὦτα ἐσθέντες καὶ ἀμφιδέας περὶ τοὺς ἐμπροσθίους πόδας καὶ σιτία ἀποτακτὰ διδόντες καὶ ἱρήια καὶ περιέποντες ὡς κάλλιστα ζῶντας· ἀποθανόντας δὲ θάπτουσι ταριχεύσαντες ἐν ἱρῇσι θήκῃσι. [3] οἱ δὲ περὶ Ἐλεφαντίνην πόλιν οἰκέοντες καὶ ἐσθίουσι αὐτούς οὐκ ἡγεόμενοι ἱροὺς εἶναι. καλέονται δὲ οὐ κροκόδειλοι ἀλλὰ χάμψαι· κροκοδείλους δὲ Ἴωνες ὠνόμασαν, εἰκάζοντες αὐτῶν τὰ εἴδεα τοῖσι παρὰ σφίσι γινομένοισι κροκοδείλοισι τοῖσι ἐν τῇσι αἱμασιῇσι.

2.69.1

ἱροί = ἱεροί.

ἅτε "As if."

Θήβας καὶ τὴν Μοίριος λίμνην For locations, see map in Landmark *ad* 2.67.

ἥγηνται Perfect, indicative, middle, 3rd, plural of ἡγέομαι. Translate as a present: "They regard."

2.69.2

δεδιδαγμένον Perfect, passive, masculine, accusative, singular participle of διδάσκω.

λίθινα χυτὰ "Glass." Literally, "melted stone."

ἀμφιδέας "Anklets."

ζῶντας "While living."

ταριχεύσαντες "Mummifying."

2.69.3

γινομένοισι = γιγνομένοισι.

☙

2.70.1-2 Egyptian Crocodiles…One More Time

This passage has attracted the special interest of scholars, since it seems likely that Herodotus drew on the Ionian geographer Hecataeus for information concerning crocodile hunting in Egypt (cf. ALC *ad* 2.70.1-2). Of course, the rules for acknowledging the works of other writers were quite different in ancient times. As mentioned in the introduction to 2.68, Aristotle freely re-used material from Herodotus when describing the Egyptian crocodile in his *Historia Animalium*.

ἄγραι δέ σφεων πολλαὶ κατεστᾶσι καὶ παντοῖαι· ἣ δ' ὦν ἔμοιγε δοκέει ἀξιωτάτη ἀπηγήσιος εἶναι, ταύτην γράφω. ἐπεὰν νῶτον ὑὸς δελεάσῃ περὶ ἄγκιστρον, μετίει ἐς μέσον τὸν ποταμόν, αὐτὸς δὲ ἐπὶ τοῦ χείλεος τοῦ ποταμοῦ ἔχων δέλφακα ζωὴν ταύτην τύπτει. [2] ἐπακούσας δὲ τῆς φωνῆς ὁ κροκόδειλος ἵεται κατὰ τὴν φωνήν, ἐντυχὼν δὲ τῷ νώτῳ καταπίνει· οἱ δὲ ἕλκουσι. ἐπεὰν δὲ ἐξελκυσθῇ ἐς γῆν, πρῶτον ἁπάντων ὁ θηρευτὴς πηλῷ κατ' ὦν ἔπλασε αὐτοῦ τοὺς ὀφθαλμούς· τοῦτο δὲ ποιήσας κάρτα εὐπετέως τὰ λοιπὰ χειροῦται, μὴ ποιήσας δὲ τοῦτο σὺν πόνῳ.

2.70.1

κατεστᾶσι Perfect, indicative, active, 3rd, plural of κατίστημι (= καθίστημι). "Are established," or simply "exist."

ὦν = οὖν.

ἀπηγήσιος = ἀφηγήσεως. The form is genitive.

ἐπεάν = ἐπειδάν.

νῶτον ὑὸς δελεάσῃ περὶ ἄγκιστρον "Placed on a hook the back of a pig." Supply "hunter" as the subject of δελεάσῃ.

μετίει = μεθίει.

2.70.2

κατὰ τὴν φωνήν "In the direction of the noise."

οἱ δὲ When an article (οἱ) is followed by δέ or μέν, it is translated as a pronoun.

ἐξελκυσθῇ Aorist, subjunctive, passive, 3rd, singular of ἐξέλκω.

☙

2.75.1-4 The Flying Snakes of Arabia

This chapter on the flying snakes of Arabia has strained the credulity of readers from antiquity to the present. It should be noted, however, that when Herodotus states he had conducted an autopsy in Arabia (a claim that is itself questioned by some modern commentators: cf. ALC *ad* 2.75.1), he vouches merely for the existence of the heaps of snake skeletons, and nothing more. In fact, he clearly says that the story of the ibises intercepting the snakes in mid-flight is something he had merely heard (λόγος δὲ ἐστὶ) and not witnessed. Leaving aside the veracity of this account, it has to be admitted that few stories in Herodotus capture the imagination quite as much as the one of ibises waylaying the flying snakes at a narrow pass leading from Arabia into Egypt.

ἔστι δὲ χῶρος τῆς Ἀραβίης κατὰ Βουτοῦν πόλιν μάλιστά κη κείμενος, καὶ ἐς τοῦτο τὸ χωρίον ἦλθον πυνθανόμενος περὶ τῶν πτερωτῶν ὀφίων· ἀπικόμενος δὲ εἶδον ὀστέα ὀφίων καὶ ἀκάνθας πλήθεϊ μὲν ἀδύνατα ἀπηγήσασθαι, σωροὶ δὲ ἦσαν τῶν ἀκανθέων καὶ μεγάλοι καὶ ὑποδεέστεροι καὶ ἐλάσσονες ἔτι τούτων, πολλοὶ δὲ ἦσαν οὗτοι. [2] ἔστι δὲ ὁ χῶρος οὗτος, ἐν τῷ αἱ ἄκανθαι κατακεχύαται, τοιόσδε τις· ἐσβολὴ ἐξ ὀρέων στεινῶν ἐς πεδίον μέγα, τὸ δὲ πεδίον τοῦτο συνάπτει τῷ Αἰγυπτίῳ πεδίῳ. [3] λόγος δέ ἐστι ἅμα τῷ ἔαρι πτερωτοὺς ὄφις ἐκ τῆς Ἀραβίης πέτεσθαι ἐπ᾽ Αἰγύπτου, τὰς δὲ ἴβις τὰς ὄρνιθας ἀπαντώσας ἐς τὴν ἐσβολὴν ταύτης τῆς χώρης οὐ παριέναι τοὺς ὄφις ἀλλὰ κατακτείνειν. [4] καὶ τὴν ἴβιν διὰ τοῦτο τὸ ἔργον τετιμῆσθαι λέγουσι Ἀράβιοι μεγάλως πρὸς Αἰγυπτίων· ὁμολογέουσι δὲ καὶ Αἰγύπτιοι διὰ ταῦτα τιμᾶν τὰς ὄρνιθας ταύτας.

2.75.1

κατὰ Βουτοῦν πόλιν μάλιστά κη κείμενος "Situated more or less near the city of Bouto." For the identity and location of this city, see map in Landmark *ad* 2.67.

ἀπικόμενος = ἀφικόμενος.

ἀκάνθας "Backbones."

πλήθεϊ "In terms of their multitude."

ἀπηγήσασθαι = ἀφηγήσασθαι. Aorist, middle, infinitive of ἀπηγέομαι (=ἀφηγέομαι). Translate with ἀδύνατα.

2.75.2

κατακεχύαται Perfect, indicative, passive, 3rd, plural of καταχέω. "Are spread over the ground."

2.75.3

πτερωτοὺς ὄφις Look to the adjective πτερωτοὺς to determine the case, number, gender of ὄφις.

παριέναι Present, active, infinitive of παρίημι. "Allow to pass" or "admit."

☙

2.77.1-5 Healthy Egyptians

The passage opens with a statement in which Herodotus expresses his appreciation for the way Egyptians, more than any other people, cultivate a memory of the past. He calls those Egyptians who specialize in preserving the past λογιώτατοι, "most learned." The rest of the passage concerns the healthy life-style of the Egyptians. Next to the Libyans (whose health is accounted for by a practice which calls for the cauterization of the veins on the head: cf. 4.187), the Egyptians are said to be the healthiest of all humans. Commentators point out that some of what Herodotus writes on the subject of health and diet parallels the medical writings of his contemporary Hippocrates (cf. HW *ad* 77.3). In describing the ingredient of the bread that Egyptians consume, Herodotus calls it by its Egyptian name (κυλλήστις) and shows that he does in fact have some knowledge of the Egyptian language.

αὐτῶν δὲ δὴ Αἰγυπτίων οἳ μὲν περὶ τὴν σπειρομένην Αἴγυπτον οἰκέουσι, μνήμην ἀνθρώπων πάντων ἐπασκέοντες μάλιστα λογιώτατοί εἰσι μακρῷ τῶν ἐγὼ ἐς διάπειραν ἀπικόμην. [2] τρόπῳ δὲ ζόης τοιῷδε διαχρέωνται· συρμαΐζουσι τρεῖς ἡμέρας ἐπεξῆς μηνὸς ἑκάστου, ἐμέτοισι θηρώμενοι τὴν ὑγιείην καὶ κλύσμασι, νομίζοντες ἀπὸ τῶν τρεφόντων σιτίων πάσας τὰς νούσους τοῖσι ἀνθρώποισι γίνεσθαι. [3] εἰσὶ μὲν γὰρ καὶ ἄλλως Αἰγύπτιοι μετὰ Λίβυας ὑγιηρέστατοι πάντων ἀνθρώπων τῶν ὡρέων δοκέειν ἐμοὶ εἵνεκα, ὅτι οὐ μεταλλάσσουσι αἱ ὧραι· ἐν γὰρ τῇσι μεταβολῇσι τοῖσι ἀνθρώποισι αἱ νοῦσοι μάλιστα γίνονται, τῶν τε ἄλλων πάντων καὶ δὴ καὶ τῶν ὡρέων μάλιστα. [4] ἀρτοφαγέουσι δὲ ἐκ τῶν ὀλυρέων ποιεῦντες ἄρτους, τοὺς ἐκεῖνοι κυλλήστις ὀνομάζουσι. οἴνῳ δὲ ἐκ κριθέων πεποιημένῳ διαχρέωνται· οὐ γάρ σφι εἰσι ἐν τῇ χώρῃ ἄμπελοι. ἰχθύων δὲ τοὺς μὲν πρὸς ἥλιον αὐήναντες ὠμοὺς σιτέονται, τοὺς δὲ ἐξ ἅλμης τεταριχευμένους. [5] ὀρνίθων δὲ τούς τε ὄρτυγας καὶ τὰς νήσσας καὶ τὰ σμικρὰ τῶν ὀρνιθίων ὠμὰ σιτέονται προταριχεύσαντες· τὰ δὲ ἄλλα ὅσα ἢ ὀρνίθων ἢ ἰχθύων σφί ἐστι ἐχόμενα, χωρὶς ἢ ὁκόσοι σφι ἱροὶ ἀποδεδέχαται, τοὺς λοιποὺς ὀπτοὺς καὶ ἑφθοὺς σιτέονται.

2.77.1

τὴν σπειρομένην Αἴγυπτον "The agricultural part of Egypt."

μνήμην ἀνθρώπων πάντων ἐπασκέοντες μάλιστα "Cultivating, more than any other humans, a memory [of the past]."

ἀπικόμην = ἀφικόμην.

2.77.2

τρεῖς ἡμέρας Accusative of extent of time.

μηνὸς ἑκάστου Genitive of time within which.

θηρώμενοι "Seeking after."

κλύσμασι "Enemas."

γίνεσθαι = γίγνεσθαι.

2.77.3

μετὰ Λίβυας "After the Libyans." The reasons for the extraordinary health of the Libyans are explained in 4.187.

τῶν ὠρέων Genitive case with εἵνεκα (= ἕνεκα).

δοκέειν ἐμοὶ "As far as I can tell."

ἄλλων πάντων Translate with ἐν…τῇσι μεταβολῇσι.

2.77.4

κυλλήστις Ostensibly, an Egyptian word transliterated into Greek.

οἴνῳ δὲ ἐκ κριθέων πεποιημένῳ "Wine made from barley." That is, beer.

τεταριχευμένους "Preserved."

2.77.5

προταριχεύσαντες "Curing [with salt]."

ὁκόσοι = ὁπόσοι.

ἱροί = ἱεροί.

ἀποδεδέχαται Perfect, indicative, passive, 3rd, plural of ἀποδέχομαι.

 CB

2.86.1-7 On Embalming…the Expensive Way

While writing on the process of mummification, Herodotus describes how Egyptian embalmers extract human brain tissue through the nostrils with an iron hook. It should be emphasized that at no point does Herodotus exhibit an untoward interest in gory matters but displays instead the reserve of a scientist who is taking field notes on an apparently important cultural aspect of ancient Egypt. Modern scholars have given Herodotus high marks for the overall accuracy of his reportage in this section (cf. ALC *ad* 2.86.2: "Herodotus' description is the most informative account of mummification in any language"). One example of Herodotus' accuracy can be seen from the evidence of Egyptian mummies, which exhibit holes drilled through the nostrils. A modern reader, accustomed to being shown "models" of appliances, cars, computers, etc., might find a touch of gallows humor (where, of course, none was intended) when Herodotus describes the embalmers showing "models" of mummification to customers.

εἰσὶ δὲ οἳ ἐπ' αὐτῷ τούτῳ κατέαται καὶ τέχνην ἔχουσι ταύτην. [2] οὗτοι, ἐπεάν σφι κομισθῇ νεκρός, δεικνύουσι τοῖσι κομίσασι παραδείγματα νεκρῶν ξύλινα, τῇ γραφῇ μεμιμημένα, καὶ τὴν μὲν σπουδαιοτάτην αὐτέων φασὶ εἶναι τοῦ οὐκ ὅσιον ποιεῦμαι τὸ οὔνομα ἐπὶ τοιούτῳ πρήγματι ὀνομάζειν,

τὴν δὲ δευτέρην δεικνύουσι ὑποδεεστέρην τε ταύτης καὶ εὐτελεστέρην,
τὴν δὲ τρίτην εὐτελεστάτην· φράσαντες δὲ πυνθάνονταί παρ’ αὐτῶν κατὰ
ἥντινα βούλονταί σφι σκευασθῆναι τὸν νεκρόν. [3] οἱ μὲν δὴ ἐκποδὼν
μισθῷ ὁμολογήσαντες ἀπαλλάσσονται, οἱ δὲ ὑπολειπόμενοι ἐν οἰκήμασι
ὧδε τὰ σπουδαιότατα ταριχεύουσι· πρῶτα μὲν σκολιῷ σιδήρῳ διὰ τῶν
μυξωτήρων ἐξάγουσι τὸν ἐγκέφαλον, τὰ μὲν αὐτοῦ οὕτω ἐξάγοντες, τὰ δὲ
ἐγχέοντες φάρμακα· [4] μετὰ δὲ λίθῳ Αἰθιοπικῷ ὀξέϊ παρασχίσαντες παρὰ
τὴν λαπάρην ἐξ ὧν εἷλον τὴν κοιλίην πᾶσαν, ἐκκαθήραντες δὲ αὐτὴν καὶ
διηθήσαντες οἴνῳ φοινικηίῳ αὖτις διηθέουσι θυμιήμασι τετριμμένοισι: [5]
ἔπειτα τὴν νηδὺν σμύρνης ἀκηράτου τετριμμένης καὶ κασίης καὶ τῶν ἄλλων
θυμιημάτων, πλὴν λιβανωτοῦ, πλήσαντες συρράπτουσι ὀπίσω. ταῦτα δὲ
ποιήσαντες, ταριχεύουσι λίτρῳ κρύψαντες ἡμέρας ἑβδομήκοντα· πλεῦνας
δὲ τουτέων οὐκ ἔξεστι ταριχεύειν. [6] ἐπεὰν δὲ παρέλθωσι αἱ ἑβδομήκοντα,
λούσαντες τὸν νεκρὸν κατειλίσσουσι πᾶν αὐτοῦ τὸ σῶμα σινδόνος
βυσσίνης τελαμῶσι κατατετμημένοισι, ὑποχρίοντες τῷ κόμμι, τῷ δὴ ἀντὶ
κόλλης τὰ πολλὰ χρέωνται Αἰγύπτιοι. [7] ἐνθεῦτεν δὲ παραδεξάμενοί μιν
οἱ προσήκοντες ποιεῦνται ξύλινον τύπον ἀνθρωποειδέα, ποιησάμενοι δὲ
ἐσεργνῦσι τὸν νεκρόν, καὶ κατακληίσαντες οὕτω θησαυρίζουσι ἐν οἰκήματι
θηκαίῳ, ἱστάντες ὀρθὸν πρὸς τοῖχον.

2.86.1

ἐπ’ αὐτῷ τούτῳ Refers to the type of funeral mentioned in the previous chapter.

κατέαται Present, indicative, middle, 3rd, plural of κάτημαι (= κάθημαι). “Are employed.”

2.86.2

ἐπεάν = ἐπειδάν.

τῇ γραφῇ “Painting.”

καὶ τὴν μὲν σπουδαιοτάτην αὐτέων φασὶ εἶναι τοῦ οὐκ ὅσιον ποιεῦμαι τὸ οὔνομα ἐπὶ τοιούτῳ
    πρήγματι ὀνομάζειν A somewhat convoluted sentence: “They say that the most excellent
    type of these is of him whose name I regard as forbidden to be mentioned in such a
    matter.” Presumably, the name is that of Osiris.

ἥντινα Modifies τέχνην.

σκευασθῆναι Aorist, passive infinitive of σκευάζω.

2.86.3

μισθῷ Dative of price.

οἱ δὲ ὑπολειπόμενοι Referring to the embalmers.

τὰ σπουδαιότατα “In the best possible way.”

2.86.4

μετά Here, an adverb. "Next."

παρὰ τὴν λαπάρην "Along the side."

ἐξ... εἷλον An instance of tmesis (prepositional prefix is separated from the verb).

ὦν = οὖν.

τὴν κοιλίην πᾶσαν "All of the intestines."

θυμιήμασι τετριμμένοισι "With crushed spices."

2.86.5

πλήσαντες Aorist, active, masculine, nominative, plural participle of πίμπλημι.

λίτρῳ = νίτρῳ. "Natron."

πλεῦνας = πλειόνας.

ἡμέρας Accusative of extent of time.

2.86.6

παρέλθωσι Aorist, subjunctive, active, 3rd, plural of παρέρχομαι.

κατειλίσσουσι = καθελίσσουσι.

κατατετμημένοισι Perfect, passive, masculine, dative, plural participle of κατατέμνω.

τὰ πολλὰ "For the most part."

2.86.7

ἐνθεῦτεν = ἐντεῦθεν.

ξύλινον τύπον ἀνθρωποειδέα "Wooden figure in the shape of a man."

ἐσεργνῦσι Present, indicative, active, 3rd, plural of εἰσέργνυμι. "Enclose inside."

κατακληίσαντες Aorist, active, masculine, nominative, plural participle of κατακλείω.

03

2.107.1-2 How Sesostris Escaped From a Burning Building

Starting with 2.99, Herodotus ends his eyewitness reports. The rest of Book II consists of stories he heard—cf. the words ἔλεγον οἱ ἱρέες in the opening sentence of this chapter—and which he felt compelled to pass on to his readers. The story of Sesostris' deliverance, though it has many of the earmarks of a folktale (like the theme of the conniving brother), is about an authentic king of Egypt (see ALC *ad* 2.102-10.), and it rings historically true in its description of a pharaoh who brings prisoners of war back to Egypt, presumably for use in public works projects (cf. *Exodus* 1.11). Herodotus' tendency to impute Greek values to non-Greeks can be seen in the way the invitation of the treacherous brother was extended out of deference to ξενία, a cardinal Greek virtue which pertains to the sacred bond between hosts and their guests.

τοῦτον δὴ τὸν Αἰγύπτιον Σέσωστριν ἀναχωρέοντα καὶ ἀνάγοντα πολλοὺς ἀνθρώπους τῶν ἐθνέων τῶν τὰς χώρας κατεστρέψατο, ἔλεγον οἱ ἱρέες, ἐπείτε ἐγίνετο ἀνακομιζόμενος ἐν Δάφνῃσι τῇσι Πηλουσίῃσι, τὸν ἀδελφεὸν αὐτοῦ, τῷ ἐπέτρεψε Σέσωστρις τὴν Αἴγυπτον, τοῦτον ἐπὶ ξείνια αὐτὸν καλέσαντα καὶ πρὸς αὐτῷ τοὺς παῖδας περινῆσαι ἔξωθεν τὴν οἰκίην ὕλῃ, περινήσαντα δὲ ὑποπρῆσαι. [2] τὸν δὲ ὡς μαθεῖν τοῦτο, αὐτίκα συμβουλεύεσθαι τῇ γυναικί· καὶ γὰρ δὴ καὶ τὴν γυναῖκα αὐτὸν ἅμα ἄγεσθαι· τὴν δέ οἱ συμβουλεῦσαι τῶν παίδων ἐόντων ἕξ τοὺς δύο ἐπὶ τὴν πυρὴν ἐκτείναντα γεφυρῶσαι τὸ καιόμενον, αὐτοὺς δ᾽ ἐπ᾽ ἐκείνων ἐπιβαίνοντας ἐκσῴζεσθαι. ταῦτα ποιῆσαι τὸν Σέσωστριν, καὶ δύο μὲν τῶν παίδων κατακαῆναι τρόπῳ τοιούτῳ, τοὺς δὲ λοιποὺς ἀποσωθῆναι ἅμα τῷ πατρί.

2.107.1

Σέσωστριν Accusative in indirect statement. The whole passage is in indirect statement, because of ἔλεγον οἱ ἱρέες.

τῶν τὰς χώρας τῶν is a used a relative pronoun.

ἱρέες = ἱερῆς.

ἐπείτε = ἐπεί.

ἐγίνετο = ἐγίγνετο.

ἐν Δάφνῃσι τῇσι Πηλουσίῃσι See map in Landmark *ad* 2.107.

ἑωυτοῦ = ἑαυτοῦ.

τῷ Here, a relative pronoun.

ξεινία = ξενία.

περινῆσαι "Surrounded."

ὑποπρῆσαι Aorist, active, infinitive of ὑποπίμπρημι.

2.107.2

γεφυρῶσαι τὸ καιόμενον "To make a bridge over the burning [wood]."

κατακαῆναι Aorist, passive infinitive of κατακαίω.

☙

2.111.1-4 An Unusual Cure for Blindness

This chapter comes from the part of Book II (beginning with chapter 99) in which Herodotus relies on others for his information. (This is emphasized by the repeated appearance of the verb ἔλεγον.) We see in the story of the pharaoh's blindness some recognizable folktale motifs: the deceptively simple oracular command, the difficulty of finding chaste women, and the spear as an instrument of hubris, all of which detract from the story's historicity (cf. ALC *ad* 2.111.2). Diodorus Siculus, a Greek historian from the time of Augustus, saw enough historical merit in this story to include it in his universal history (1.59), albeit with the additional bit of information that the one chaste woman in the entire kingdom was a simple gardener. Herodotus ends his account by specifying the sizes of the two spectacular obelisks which the pharaoh is said to have dedicated in gratitude for his recovery. These dimensions are probably exaggerations, as the world's largest extant obelisk, situated in front of the church of San Giovanni in Laterano in Rome, is a bit over 100 feet tall, while the ones in Herodotus' tale were supposedly around 150 feet tall.

Σεσώστριος δὲ τελευτήσαντος ἐκδέξασθαι ἔλεγον τὴν βασιληίην τὸν παῖδα αὐτοῦ Φερῶν, τὸν ἀποδέξασθαι μὲν οὐδεμίαν στρατηίην, συνενειχθῆναι δέ οἱ τυφλὸν γενέσθαι διὰ τοιόνδε πρῆγμα· τοῦ ποταμοῦ κατελθόντος μέγιστα δὴ τότε ἐπ᾽ ὀκτωκαίδεκα πήχεας, ὡς ὑπερέβαλε τὰς ἀρούρας, πνεύματος ἐμπεσόντος κυματίης ὁ ποταμὸς ἐγένετο· [2] τὸν δὲ βασιλέα λέγουσι τοῦτον ἀτασθαλίῃ χρησάμενον λαβόντα αἰχμὴν βαλεῖν ἐς μέσας τὰς δίνας τοῦ ποταμοῦ, μετὰ δὲ αὐτίκα καμόντα αὐτὸν τοὺς ὀφθαλμοὺς τυφλωθῆναι. δέκα μὲν δὴ ἔτεα εἶναί μιν τυφλόν, ἑνδεκάτῳ δὲ ἔτεϊ ἀπικέσθαι οἱ μαντήιον ἐκ Βουτοῦς πόλιος ὡς ἐξήκει τέ οἱ ὁ χρόνος τῆς ζημίης καὶ ἀναβλέψει γυναικὸς οὔρῳ νιψάμενος τοὺς ὀφθαλμούς, ἥτις παρὰ τὸν ἑωυτῆς ἄνδρα μοῦνον πεφοίτηκε, ἄλλων ἀνδρῶν ἐοῦσα ἄπειρος. [3] καὶ τὸν πρώτης τῆς ἑωυτοῦ γυναικὸς πειρᾶσθαι, μετὰ δέ, ὡς οὐκ ἀνέβλεπε, ἐπεξῆς πασέων πειρᾶσθαι· ἀναβλέψαντα δὲ συναγαγεῖν τὰς γυναῖκας τῶν ἐπειρήθη, πλὴν ἢ τῆς τῷ οὔρῳ νιψάμενος ἀνέβλεψε, ἐς μίαν πόλιν, ἣ νῦν καλέεται Ἐρυθρὴ βῶλος· ἐς ταύτην συναλίσαντα ὑποπρῆσαι πάσας σὺν αὐτῇ τῇ πόλι· [4] τῆς δὲ νιψάμενος τῷ οὔρῳ ἀνέβλεψε, ταύτην δὲ ἔσχε αὐτὸς γυναῖκα. ἀναθήματα δὲ ἀποφυγὼν τὴν πάθην τῶν ὀφθαλμῶν ἄλλα τε ἀνὰ τὰ ἱρὰ πάντα τὰ λόγιμα ἀνέθηκε καὶ τοῦ γε λόγου μάλιστα ἄξιόν ἐστι ἔχειν, ἐς τοῦ Ἡλίου τὸ ἱρὸν ἀξιοθέητα ἀνέθηκε ἔργα, ὀβελοὺς δύο λιθίνους, ἐξ ἑνὸς ἐόντα ἑκάτερον λίθου, μῆκος μὲν ἑκάτερον πήχεων ἑκατόν, εὖρος δὲ ὀκτὼ πήχεων.

2.111.1

ἐκδέξασθαι Aorist, middle infinitive of ἐκδέχομαι.

ἔλεγον This verb sets in motion a series of indirect statement constructions.

συνενειχθῆναι Aorist, passive infinitive of συμφέρω. "It came to pass that..."

πρῆγμα = πρᾶγμα.

ὀκτωκαίδεκα πήχεας "Eighteen cubits," or about 27 feet.

ἐμπεσόντος Aorist, active, neuter, genitive, singular participle of ἐμπίπτω.

2.111.2

ἀτασθαλίῃ χρησάμενον "Having resorted to recklessness."

τυφλωθῆναι Aorist, passive infinitive of τυφλόω.

ἔτεα Accusative of extent of time.

ἀπικέσθαι Aorist, middle infinitive of ἀπικνέομαι (=ἀφικνέομαι).

Βουτοῦς For the location of Bouto, see map in Landmark *ad* 2.112.

ἑωυτῆς = ἑαυτῆς.

πεφοίτηκε "Had intercourse." Perfect, indicative, active, 3rd, singular of φοιτάω.

2.111.3

μετά Adverb.

Ἐρυθρὴ βῶλος Location of this "Red Glebe" is unknown.

2.111.4

τῆς Here, a relative pronoun. Antecedent is ταύτην.

πήχεων ἑκατόν About 150 feet.

ὀκτὼ πήχεων About 12 feet.

ଐ

2.114.1-3 The Real Story of Helen, Part I

Herodotus challenges the traditional story of Helen in Troy and presents a version which enjoyed some popularity in 5th-century Greece. (Euripides, for example, based his play *Helen* on the premise that Helen never left Egypt.) In 2.116, Herodotus will even speculate that Homer, although he knew of the story of Helen staying behind in Egypt, chose to have her go to Troy simply because it made for a better story. In other ways, however, the version that Herodotus presents is thoroughly Homeric, even in the way he calls the Egyptian ruler who interrogates Alexander (Paris) "Proteus," a name which was likely inspired by the mythological sea god who figures in the *Odyssey* (cf. HW *ad* 2.113). Note once more the way Herodotus imputes a Greek (and Homeric) value system to non-Greeks…in this case, to the Egyptian Proteus.

ἀκούσας δὲ τούτων ὁ Θῶνις πέμπει τὴν ταχίστην ἐς Μέμφιν παρὰ Πρωτέα ἀγγελίην λέγουσαν τάδε· [2] "ἥκει ξεῖνος, γένος μὲν Τευκρός, ἔργον δὲ ἀνόσιον ἐν τῇ Ἑλλάδι ἐξεργασμένος· ξείνου γὰρ τοῦ ἑωυτοῦ ἐξαπατήσας τὴν γυναῖκα αὐτήν τε ταύτην ἄγων ἥκει καὶ πολλὰ κάρτα χρήματα, ὑπὸ ἀνέμων ἐς γῆν σὴν ἀπενειχθείς· κότερα δῆτα τοῦτον ἐῶμεν ἀσινέα ἐκπλέειν ἢ ἀπελώμεθα τὰ ἔχων ἦλθε;" [3] ἀντιπέμπει πρὸς ταῦτα ὁ Πρωτεὺς λέγων τάδε· "ἄνδρα τοῦτον, ὅστις κοτέ ἐστι ἀνόσια ἐξεργασμένος ξεῖνον τὸν ἑωυτοῦ, συλλαβόντες ἀπάγετε παρ' ἐμέ, ἵνα εἰδέω τί κοτε καὶ λέξει."

2.114.1

Θῶνις Identified in 2.113 as an Egyptian official in charge of the Canobic Mouth of the Nile.

2.114.2

ξεῖνος = ξένος.

γένος Accusative of respect.

ἑωυτοῦ = ἑαυτοῦ.

ἀπενειχθείς Aorist, passive, masculine, nominative, singular participle of ἀποφέρω.

κότερα = πότερα.

ἀπελώμεθα = ἀφελώμεθα. Aorist, subjunctive, middle, 1st, plural of ἀφαιρέω.

2.114.3

ὅστις κοτέ ἐστι Note the disdain conveyed by these words.

κοτέ = ποτέ.

附

2.115.1-6 The Real Story of Helen, Part II

Herodotus' revisionist story of what "really" happened to Helen continues here. As in Part I (2.114), he throws out a challenge of sorts to Homer and his version of Helen's tale, but he nevertheless clothes his account with Homeric touches, like the speech of Proteus in *oratio recta* (direct address). He does not try to make the speech seem authentic, but is content to have his Egyptian character proclaim the strongly held Greek (and Homeric) view that any crime is made more vile and reprehensible when it is committed in the context of the guest-host relationship (ξενία). The whole story of what really happened to Helen is, of course, a tangent to the larger theme of the Persian conquest of Egypt. But then again, so is much of Book II.

ἀκούσας δὲ ταῦτα ὁ Θῶνις συλλαμβάνει τὸν Ἀλέξανδρον καὶ τὰς νέας αὐτοῦ κατίσχει, μετὰ δὲ αὐτόν τε τοῦτον ἀνήγαγε ἐς Μέμφιν καὶ τὴν Ἑλένην τε καὶ τὰ χρήματα, πρὸς δὲ καὶ τοὺς ἱκέτας. [2] ἀνακομισθέντων δὲ πάντων εἰρώτα τὸν Ἀλέξανδρον ὁ Πρωτεὺς τίς εἴη καὶ ὁκόθεν πλέοι. ὁ δέ οἱ καὶ τὸ γένος κατέλεξε καὶ τῆς πάτρης εἶπε τὸ οὔνομα καὶ δὴ καὶ τὸν πλόον ἀπηγήσατο ὁκόθεν πλέοι. [3] μετὰ δὲ ὁ Πρωτεὺς εἰρώτα αὐτὸν ὁκόθεν τὴν Ἑλένην λάβοι· πλανωμένου δὲ τοῦ Ἀλεξάνδρου ἐν τῷ λόγῳ καὶ οὐ λέγοντος τὴν ἀληθείην ἤλεγχον οἱ γενόμενοι ἱκέται ἐξηγεύμενοι πάντα λόγον τοῦ ἀδικήματος. [4] τέλος δὲ δή σφι λόγον τόνδε ἐκφαίνει ὁ Πρωτεύς, λέγων ὅτι "ἐγὼ εἰ μὴ περὶ πολλοῦ ἡγεύμην μηδένα ξείνων κτείνειν, ὅσοι ὑπ' ἀνέμων ἤδη ἀπολαμφθέντες ἦλθον ἐς χώρην τὴν ἐμήν, ἐγὼ ἄν σε ὑπὲρ τοῦ Ἕλληνος ἐτεισάμην, ὅς, ὦ κάκιστε ἀνδρῶν, ξεινίων τυχὼν ἔργον ἀνοσιώτατον ἐργάσαο· παρὰ τοῦ σεωυτοῦ ξείνου τὴν γυναῖκα ἦλθες· καὶ μάλα ταῦτά τοι οὐκ ἤρκεσε, ἀλλ' ἀναπτερώσας αὐτὴν οἴχεαι ἔχων ἐκκλέψας. [5] καὶ οὐδὲ ταῦτά τοι μοῦνα ἤρκεσε, ἀλλὰ καὶ τὰ οἰκία τοῦ ξείνου κεραΐσας ἥκεις. [6] νῦν ὦν ἐπειδὴ περὶ πολλοῦ ἥγημαι μὴ ξεινοκτονέειν, γυναῖκα μὲν ταύτην καὶ τὰ χρήματα οὔ τοι προήσω ἀπάγεσθαι, ἀλλ᾽ αὐτὰ ἐγὼ τῷ Ἕλληνι ξείνῳ φυλάξω, ἐς ὃ ἂν αὐτὸς ἐλθὼν ἐκεῖνος ἀπαγαγέσθαι ἐθέλῃ· αὐτὸν δέ σε καὶ τοὺς σοὺς συμπλόους τριῶν ἡμερέων προαγορεύω ἐκ τῆς ἐμῆς γῆς ἐς ἄλλην τινὰ μετορμίζεσθαι, εἰ δὲ μή, ἅτε πολεμίους περιέψεσθαι."

2.115.1

τοὺς ἱκέτας After Alexander's (Paris') ships had been blown off course to Egypt, his crew sought refuge as "supplicants" at a shrine to Herakles. The Thonis in this sentence is described as a local governor.

2.115.2

ἀνακομισθέντων δὲ πάντων Genitive absolute construction.

ὁκόθεν = ὁπόθεν.

2.115.3

μετά Here, an adverb.

πλανωμένου δὲ τοῦ Ἀλεξάνδρου ἐν τῷ λόγῳ καὶ οὐ λέγοντος τὴν ἀληθείην Genitive absolute construction.

ἱκέται The crew of Alexander's (Paris') ships.

πάντα λόγον "The complete story."

2.115.4

τέλος "At last."

περὶ πολλοῦ ἡγεόμην "If I didn't think it important."

ἡγεόμην Imperfect, indicative, middle, 1st, singular of ἡγέομαι. "Regard," or "consider."

ἀπολαμφθέντες = ἀποληφθέντες. Aorist, passive, masculine, nominative, plural participle of ἀπολαμβάνω.

σε... ἐτεισάμην "I would have punished you."

ἐτεισάμην Aorist, indicative, middle, 1st, singular of τίνω.

ξεινίων = ξενίων.

τυχὼν Aorist, active, masculine, nominative, singular participle of τυγχάνω.

παρὰ τοῦ σεωυτοῦ ξείνου τὴν γυναῖκα ἦλθες "You had sex with the wife of your very own host."

σεωυτοῦ = σεαυτοῦ.

ἤρκεσε Aorist, indicative, active, 3rd, singular of ἀρκέω. "Were [not] enough."

ἀναπτερώσας Literally, "Having given [her] wings." Idiomatically, "Having emboldened [her]."

2.115.5

κεραΐσας "Having looted."

2.115.6

ὦν = οὖν.

προήσω Future, indicative, active, 1st, singular of προΐημι.

ἐς ὅ "Until the time when."

τριῶν ἡμερέων Genitive of time within which.

μετορμίζεσθαι = μεθορμίζεσθαι.

☙

2.125.1-7 The Construction of the Pyramid of Cheops

This fascinating passage on the building of the Great Pyramid at Gizeh during the Fourth Dynasty (3rd millennium B.C.) has been the frequent target of criticisms from modern commentators. In the preceding chapter (2.124), Herodotus gives the dimensions of Cheops' pyramid (c. 800 feet at the base on all four sides and 800 feet in height: cf. Landmark *ad* 2.124.5) and notes that it took 20 years to build. In this chapter, he writes about the actual construction and claims that cranes (μηχαναί) were used to position the stones, some weighing as much as 50 tons, into place. This assertion, according to experts, is yet another instance of Herodotus assuming that construction projects in Egypt were done the "Greek way," that is, with cranes, even when there is no evidence to support such an assumption. (Cf. ALC *ad* 2.125, where it is argued that cranes were not used in Egypt during the Fourth Dynasty, and that the only way builders could vertically move blocks of stone was by the inclined plane method.) Another criticism leveled at Herodotus is—ironically—the result of (1) his acknowledgement that he used an interpreter (a good thing, at first blush, as Herodotus is often oblivious to matters of language), and (2) his citation of an inscription (in theory, always a laudable feature in any ancient history). Critics have insisted that the Great Pyramid most likely did NOT have an inscription and that, even if it did have one, the translation provided to Herodotus by his interpreter could not have possibly been correct. There is no way, critics point out, that 1600 talents of silver (an enormous amount) could have been spent solely on the "radishes, onions, and garlic" which were consumed by the workers. (There is also the problem of Herodotus' implication that some form of money was used in the pre-monetary society of Egypt of the Fourth Dynasty.) It is at least possible that Herodotus' interpreter himself could not read the inscription (if in fact there was one) or that he was "pulling the leg of the father of history" (Landmark *ad* 2.125.6).

ἐποιήθη δὲ ὧδε αὕτη ἡ πυραμίς, ἀναβαθμῶν τρόπον, τὰς μετεξέτεροι κρόσσας, οἱ δὲ βωμίδας ὀνομάζουσι· [2] τοιαύτην τὸ πρῶτον ἐπείτε ἐποίησαν αὐτήν, ἤειρον τοὺς ἐπιλοίπους λίθους μηχανῇσι ξύλων βραχέων πεποιημένῃσι, χαμᾶθεν μὲν ἐπὶ τὸν πρῶτον στοῖχον τῶν ἀναβαθμῶν ἀείροντες· [3] ὅκως δὲ ἀνίοι ὁ λίθος ἐπ᾽ αὐτόν, ἐς ἑτέρην μηχανὴν ἐτίθετο ἑστεῶσαν ἐπὶ τοῦ πρώτου στοίχου, ἀπὸ τούτου δὲ ἐπὶ τὸν δεύτερον εἵλκετο στοῖχον ἐπ᾽ ἄλλης μηχανῆς· [4] ὅσοι γὰρ δὴ στοῖχοι ἦσαν τῶν ἀναβαθμῶν, τοσαῦται καὶ μηχαναὶ ἦσαν, εἴτε καὶ τὴν αὐτὴν μηχανὴν ἐοῦσαν μίαν τε καὶ εὐβάστακτον μετεφόρεον ἐπὶ στοῖχον ἕκαστον, ὅκως τὸν λίθον ἐξέλοιεν·

λελέχθω γὰρ ἡμῖν ἐπ᾽ ἀμφότερα, κατά περ λέγεται. [5] ἐξεποιήθη δ᾽ ὦν τὰ ἀνώτατα αὐτῆς πρῶτα, μετὰ δὲ τὰ ἐχόμενα τούτων ἐξεποίευν, τελευταῖα δὲ αὐτῆς τὰ ἐπίγαια καὶ τὰ κατωτάτω ἐξεποίησαν. [6] σεσήμανται δὲ διὰ γραμμάτων Αἰγυπτίων ἐν τῇ πυραμίδι ὅσα ἔς τε συρμαίην καὶ κρόμμυα καὶ σκόροδα ἀναισιμώθη τοῖσι ἐργαζομένοισι· καὶ ὡς ἐμὲ εὖ μεμνῆσθαι τὰ ὁ ἑρμηνεύς μοι ἐπιλεγόμενος τὰ γράμματα ἔφη, ἑξακόσια καὶ χίλια τάλαντα ἀργυρίου τετελέσθαι. [7] εἰ δ᾽ ἔστι οὕτω ἔχοντα ταῦτα, κόσα οἰκὸς ἄλλα δεδαπανῆσθαί ἐστι ἔς τε σίδηρον τῷ ἐργάζοντο καὶ σιτία καὶ ἐσθῆτα τοῖσι ἐργαζομένοισι, ὁκότε χρόνον μὲν οἰκοδόμεον τὰ ἔργα τὸν εἰρημένον, ἄλλον δέ, ὡς ἐγὼ δοκέω, ἐν τῷ τοὺς λίθους ἔταμνον καὶ ἦγον καὶ τὸ ὑπὸ γῆν ὄρυγμα ἐργάζοντο, οὐκ ὀλίγον χρόνον.

2.125.1

κρόσσας…βωμίδας Both appear to be technical terms to describe steps.

2.125.2

ἐπείτε = ἐπεί.

ἤειρον Imperfect, indicative, active, 3rd, plural of ἀείρω.

μηχανῇσι Crane-like "machines."

στοῖχον "Landing" or "tier."

2.125.3

ὅκως = ὅπως.

ἀνίοι Present, optative, active, 3rd, singular of ἄνειμι.

ἐτίθετο "It [the stone] was fitted."

εἵλκετο Imperfect, indicative, passive, 3rd, singular of ἕλκω.

2.125.4

κατά περ = καθάπερ

κατά περ λέγεται "Exactly as it has been said [to me]."

2.125.5

ἐξεποιήθη "Were finished off." In other words, the angles of the steps were fitted with stones so that a smooth surface could be achieved.

ὦν = οὖν.

μετά Here, an adverb.

τὰ ἐχόμενα τούτων "The ones supporting these."

2.125.6

σεσήμανται Perfect, indicative, passive, 3rd, singular of σημαίνω.

ἀναισιμώθη Aorist, indicative, passive, 3rd, singular of ἀναισιμόω.

2.125.7

κόσα = πόσα.

οἰκὸς...ἐστὶ "It is likely."

οἰκός = εἰκός.

ὁκότε = ὁπότε.

ἐν τῷ "During which."

⋘

2.133.1-5 Mykerinos Turns Nights into Days

A charming story, with several features of a folktale. It comes from that part of Book II (beginning with chapter 99) where Herodotus relies on what his informants told him and not on autopsy. (Note that most of the passage is narrated in indirect statement.) Herodotus' superb skills as a storyteller are on display here: we are called on to suspend our historiographical expectations and enjoy this tale of the pharaoh Mykerinos and his defiance of destiny. The last stanza of Matthew Arnold's "Mycerinus" perfectly captures the mood of Herodotus' folktale:

> So six long years he revell'd, night and day.
> And when the mirth wax'd loudest, with dull sound
> Sometimes from the grove's centre echoes came,
> To tell his wondering people of their king;
> In the still night, across the steaming flats,
> Mix'd with the murmur of the moving Nile.

μετὰ δὲ τῆς θυγατρὸς τὸ πάθος δεύτερα τούτῳ τῷ βασιλέι τάδε γενέσθαι· ἐλθεῖν οἱ μαντήιον ἐκ Βουτοῦς πόλιος ὡς μέλλοι ἓξ ἔτεα μοῦνον βιοὺς τῷ ἑβδόμῳ τελευτήσειν· [2] τὸν δὲ δεινὸν ποιησάμενον πέμψαι ἐς τὸ μαντήιον τῷ θεῷ ὀνείδισμά ἀντιμεμφόμενον ὅτι ὁ μὲν αὐτοῦ πατὴρ καὶ πάτρως ἀποκληίσαντες τὰ ἱρὰ καὶ θεῶν οὐ μεμνημένοι, ἀλλὰ καὶ τοὺς ἀνθρώπους φθείροντες, ἐβίωσαν χρόνον ἐπὶ πολλόν, αὐτὸς δ' εὐσεβέων μέλλοι ταχέως οὕτω τελευτήσειν. [3] ἐκ δὲ τοῦ χρηστηρίου αὐτῷ δεύτερα ἐλθεῖν λέγοντα τούτων εἵνεκα καὶ συνταχύνειν αὐτὸν τὸν βίον· οὐ γὰρ ποιῆσαί μιν τὸ χρεὸν ἦν ποιέειν· δεῖν γὰρ Αἴγυπτον κακοῦσθαι ἐπ' ἔτεα πεντήκοντά τε καὶ ἑκατόν, καὶ τοὺς μὲν δύο τοὺς πρὸ ἐκείνου γενομένους βασιλέας μαθεῖν τοῦτο, κεῖνον δὲ οὔ. [4] ταῦτα ἀκούσαντα τὸν Μυκερῖνον, ὡς κατακεκριμένων ἤδη οἱ τούτων, λύχνα ποιησάμενον πολλά, ὅκως γίνοιτο νύξ, ἀνάψαντα αὐτὰ πίνειν τε καὶ εὐπαθέειν, οὔτε ἡμέρης οὔτε νυκτὸς ἀνιέντα, ἔς τε τὰ ἕλεα καὶ τὰ ἄλσεα πλανώμενον καὶ ἵνα πυνθάνοιτο εἶναι ἐνηβητήρια ἐπιτηδεότατα.

[5] ταῦτα δὲ ἐμηχανᾶτο θέλων τὸ μαντήιον ψευδόμενον ἀποδέξαι, ἵνα οἱ δυώδεκα ἔτεα ἀντὶ ἓξ ἐτέων γένηται, αἱ νύκτες ἡμέραι ποιεύμεναι.

2.133.1

γενέσθαι The indirect statement continues from the previous passage.

ἐκ Βουτοῦς For the location, see map in Landmark *ad* 2.140.

μοῦνον Adverb.

2.133.2

τὸν δὲ δεινὸν ποιησάμενον "Being disturbed."

ἱρά = ἱερά.

2.133.3

εἵνεκα = ἕνεκα.

τὸ χρεὸν ἦν ποιέειν "That which he was supposed to do."

κεῖνον = ἐκεῖνον.

2.133.4

ὡς κατακεκριμένων ἤδη οἱ τούτων Genitive absolute construction.

κατακεκριμένων Perfect, passive, neuter, genitive, plural participle of κατακρίνω.

οὔτε ἡμέρης οὔτε νυκτὸς ἀνιέντα "Stopping during neither day nor night."

2.133.5

ἀποδέξαι Aorist, active infinitive of ἀποδείκνυμι.

જી

2.143.1-4 A Challenge to Hecataeus and his Supposed Divine Ancestry

Starting with 2.142 and continuing to 2.146, Herodotus takes a break from his survey of the history of Egyptian pharaohs. His intent in this passage is to share with his readers his appreciation of the enormous antiquity of Egypt and to deride his predecessor Hecataeus, who apparently claimed (in *Heroologia*, his work on genealogy) that a god could be identified in his family's history if he went back a mere 16 generations. This is the first instance in the *Histories* that Herodotus mentions by name Hecataeus of Miletus, a late 6th century B.C. prose writer, best known for geographical accounts (*Periegesis*), which Herodotus knew well. Greek anthropomorphism had as one of its tenets the belief that humans were descended from gods; for Herodotus to have challenged this view represents an important break from tradition. It should also be noted that Herodotus shows some linguistic awareness in this chapter, as he uses in a transliterated form the Egyptian word *tiromis*, which, he assures us, means a "good and noble man."

πρότερον δὲ Ἑκαταίῳ τῷ λογοποιῷ ἐν Θήβῃσι γενεηλογήσαντί τε ἑωυτὸν καὶ ἀναδήσαντι τὴν πατριὴν ἐς ἑκκαιδέκατον θεὸν ἐποίησαν οἱ ἱρέες τοῦ

Διὸς οἷόν τι καὶ ἐμοὶ οὐ γενεηλογήσαντι ἐμεωυτόν· [2] ἐσαγαγόντες ἐς τὸ μέγαρον ἔσω ἐὸν μέγα ἐξηρίθμεον δεικνύντες κολοσσοὺς ξυλίνους τοσούτους ὅσους περ εἶπον· ἀρχιερεὺς γὰρ ἕκαστος αὐτόθι ἱστᾷ ἐπὶ τῆς ἑωυτοῦ ζόης εἰκόνα ἑωυτοῦ· [3] ἀριθμέοντες ὦν καὶ δεικνύντες οἱ ἱρέες ἐμοὶ ἀπεδείκνυσαν παῖδα πατρὸς ἑωυτῶν ἕκαστον ἐόντα, ἐκ τοῦ ἄγχιστα ἀποθανόντος τῆς εἰκόνος διεξιόντες διὰ πασέων, ἐς οὗ ἀπέδεξαν ἁπάσας αὐτάς. [4] Ἑκαταίῳ δὲ γενεηλογήσαντι ἑωυτὸν καὶ ἀναδήσαντι ἐς ἑκκαιδέκατον θεὸν ἀντεγενεηλόγησαν ἐπὶ τῇ ἀριθμήσι, οὐ δεκόμενοι παρ' αὐτοῦ ἀπὸ θεοῦ γενέσθαι ἄνθρωπον· ἀντεγενεηλόγησαν δὲ ὧδε, φάμενοι ἕκαστον τῶν κολοσσῶν πίρωμιν ἐκ πιρώμιος γεγονέναι, ἐς ὃ τοὺς πέντε καὶ τεσσεράκοντα καὶ τριηκοσίους ἀπέδεξαν κολοσσοὺς [πίρωμιν ἐπονομαζόμενον], καὶ οὔτε ἐς θεὸν οὔτε ἐς ἥρωα ἀνέδησαν αὐτούς. πίρωμις δέ ἐστι κατ' Ἑλλάδα γλῶσσαν καλὸς κἀγαθός.

2.143.1

πρότερον Hecataeus was born around the middle of the 6th cenury. His visit to Egypt, therefore, would have been quite a bit earlier than that of Herodotus.

ἑωυτόν = ἑαυτόν.

ἀναδήσαντι τὴν πατριὴν ἐς ἑκκαιδέκατον θεὸν "Linking a god to his family from 16 generations ago."

ἱρέες = ἱερῆς.

ἐποίησαν...οἷόν τι καὶ ἐμοὶ "Gave him [a tour or explanation] like the one they gave me."

ἐμεωυτόν = ἐμαυτόν.

2.143.2

ἐξηρίθμεον "They counted out."

τοσούτους ὅσους περ εἶπον "As many as I have mentioned." In 2.142, the number given is 341.

ἱστᾷ The verb ἱστάω is a variant of ἵστημι.

2.143.3

ὦν = οὖν.

ἕως οὗ "Until they reached the point when...."

2.143.4

δεκόμενοι = δεχόμενοι.

☙

2.148.1-7 The Fabulous Labyrinth Near the "City of the Crocodiles"

While Herodotus may have made some mistakes in this description of the much celebrated Egyptian Labyrinth (cf. HW, *ad* 2.148.4: "It would be impossible to construct a building according to the description of Herodotus..."), his account, when combined with those of Strabo (17.1.37) and Pliny the Elder (*Natural Histories* 6.13), gives us at least an idea of what this fabulous building, now in ruins, may have looked like. The wide-eyed amazement which Herodotus displays as he describes the myriad hallways and columned rooms is balanced by the seemingly careful and detailed descriptions he provides. It should be observed that, more so in this passage than anywhere else in Book II, Herodotus is very careful to distinguish those portions of his narrative which are based on what he actually saw and those which are based on what others told him. Finally, we see in this passage more of the same enthusiasm for things Egyptian, which may have earned him the sobriquet of *philobarbaros* from Plutarch (*Moralia* 2.857a), his severest critic in antiquity.

καὶ δή σφι μνημόσυνα ἔδοξε λιπέσθαι κοινῇ, δόξαν δέ σφι ἐποιήσαντο λαβύρινθον, ὀλίγον ὑπὲρ τῆς λίμνης τῆς Μοίριος κατὰ Κροκοδείλων καλεομένην πόλιν μάλιστά κη κείμενον· τὸν ἐγὼ ἤδη εἶδον λόγου μέζω. [2] εἰ γάρ τις τὰ ἐξ Ἑλλήνων τείχεά τε καὶ ἔργων ἀπόδεξιν συλλογίσαιτο, ἐλάσσονος πόνου τε ἂν καὶ δαπάνης φανείη ἐόντα τοῦ λαβυρίνθου τούτου. καίτοι ἀξιόλογός γε καὶ ὁ ἐν Ἐφέσῳ ἐστὶ νηὸς καὶ ὁ ἐν Σάμῳ. [3] ἦσαν μέν νυν καὶ αἱ πυραμίδες λόγου μέζονες καὶ πολλῶν ἑκάστη αὐτέων Ἑλληνικῶν ἔργων καὶ μεγάλων ἀνταξίη, ὁ δὲ δὴ λαβύρινθος καὶ τὰς πυραμίδας ὑπερβάλλει· [4] τοῦ γὰρ δυώδεκα μέν εἰσι αὐλαὶ κατάστεγοι, ἀντίπυλοι ἀλλήλῃσι, ἓξ μὲν πρὸς βορέω, ἓξ δὲ πρὸς νότον τετραμμέναι, συνεχέες· τοῖχος δὲ ἔξωθεν ὁ αὐτός σφεας περιέργει. οἰκήματα δ' ἔνεστι διπλά, τὰ μὲν ὑπόγαια, τὰ δὲ μετέωρα ἐπ' ἐκείνοισι, τρισχίλια ἀριθμόν, πεντακοσίων καὶ χιλίων ἑκάτερα. [5] τὰ μέν νυν μετέωρα τῶν οἰκημάτων αὐτοί τε ὡρῶμεν διεξιόντες καὶ αὐτοὶ θεησάμενοι λέγομεν, τὰ δὲ αὐτῶν ὑπόγαια λόγοισι ἐπυνθανόμεθα. οἱ γὰρ ἐπεστεῶτες τῶν Αἰγυπτίων δεικνύναι αὐτὰ οὐδαμῶς ἤθελον, φάμενοι θήκας αὐτόθι εἶναι τῶν τε ἀρχὴν τὸν λαβύρινθον τοῦτον οἰκοδομησαμένων βασιλέων καὶ τῶν ἱρῶν κροκοδείλων. [6] οὕτω τῶν μὲν κάτω πέρι οἰκημάτων ἀκοῇ παραλαβόντες λέγομεν, τὰ δὲ ἄνω μέζονα ἀνθρωπηίων ἔργων αὐτοὶ ὡρῶμεν· αἵ τε γὰρ ἔξοδοι διὰ τῶν στεγέων καὶ οἱ εἱλιγμοὶ διὰ τῶν αὐλέων ἐόντες ποικιλώτατοι θῶμα μυρίον παρείχοντο ἐξ αὐλῆς τε ἐς τὰ οἰκήματα διεξιοῦσι καὶ ἐκ τῶν οἰκημάτων ἐς παστάδας, ἐς στέγας τε ἄλλας ἐκ τῶν παστάδων καὶ ἐς αὐλὰς ἄλλας ἐκ τῶν οἰκημάτων. [7] ὀροφὴ δὲ πάντων τούτων λιθίνη κατά περ οἱ τοῖχοι, οἱ δὲ τοῖχοι τύπων ἐγγεγλυμμένων πλέοι, αὐλὴ δὲ ἑκάστη περίστυλος λίθου λευκοῦ ἁρμοσμένου τὰ μάλιστα. τῆς δὲ γωνίης τελευτῶντος τοῦ λαβυρίνθου ἔχεται πυραμὶς τεσσερακοντόργυιος, ἐν τῇ ζῷα μεγάλα ἐγγέγλυπται ὁδὸς δ᾽ ἐς αὐτὴν ὑπὸ γῆν πεποίηται.

2.148.1

σφι Refers to the "Twelve," who supposedly shared power for a period of 15 years during the 7th century.

δόξαν Noun in apposition to λαβύρινθον.

ὑπὲρ τῆς λίμνης τῆς Μοίριος κατὰ Κροκοδείλων καλεομένην πόλιν μάλιστά κη κείμενον For locations, see map in Landmark *ad* 2.155.

κη = πη.

μέζω = μείζω (μείζονα).

2.148.2

ἔργων ἀπόδεξιν "Display of [mighty] works."

φανείη Aorist, optative, passive, 3rd, singular of φαίνω.

2.148.3

ἀνταξίη "Comparable to."

2.148.4

τετραμμέναι Literally, "having been turned." Here, "facing."

τὰ μὲν ὑπόγαια τὰ δὲ μετέωρα ἐπ᾽ ἐκείνοισι That is, there are two levels, one on top of the other.

ἀριθμόν Accusative of respect.

2.148.5

ἐπεστεῶτες τῶν Αἰγυπτίων "Those of the Egyptians in charge."

ἱρῶν = ἱερῶν.

2.148.6

ἀκοῇ παραλαβόντες "Obtaining by hearsay."

οἱ ἑλιγμοί. These labyrinthine passages must have given the building its name.

2.148.7

κατά περ = καθάπερ. "Just as."

ἁρμοσμένου τὰ μάλιστα "Fitted perfectly."

τεσσερακοντόργυιος "Of 40 fathoms," which is the equivalent of 240 feet (see note in Landmark *ad* 2.148.7).

ℭℬ

2.173.1-4 Too Much Work and Too Little Play

This delightful story of how the pharaoh Amasis (XXVI Dynasty, 6th century B.C.) found time for both kingly duties and playful activities apparently corresponds to native Egyptian accounts of his sometimes reckless ways, which included drunkenness (cf. ALC *ad* 2.173.1). In Herodotus' hands, the tale takes on Homeric characteristics, especially in the way Amasis and his advisors carry on a mini-debate. The metaphor of the strung bow does not appear to be Egyptian and offers further evidence of Greek influence (ALC *ad* 2.173.3). Centuries later, a similar metaphor will recur in Horace's beautiful *Ode* 1.10 (*Neque semper arcum tendit Apollo*).

τοιούτῳ μὲν τρόπῳ προσηγάγετο τοὺς Αἰγυπτίους ὥστε δικαιοῦν δουλεύειν. ἐχρᾶτο δὲ καταστάσι πρηγμάτων τοιῇδε· τὸ μὲν ὄρθριον μέχρι ὅτευ πληθούσης ἀγορῆς προθύμως ἔπρησσε τὰ προσφερόμενα πρήγματα, τὸ δὲ ἀπὸ τούτου ἔπινέ τε καὶ κατέσκωπτε τοὺς συμπότας καὶ ἦν μάταιός τε καὶ παιγνιήμων. [2] ἀχθεσθέντες δὲ τούτοισι οἱ φίλοι αὐτοῦ ἐνουθέτεον αὐτὸν τοιάδε λέγοντες· "ὦ βασιλεῦ, οὐκ ὀρθῶς σεωυτοῦ προέστηκας ἐς τὸ ἄγαν φαῦλον προάγων σεωυτόν· σὲ γὰρ ἐχρῆν ἐν θρόνῳ σεμνῷ σεμνὸν θωκέοντα δι' ἡμέρης πρήσσειν τὰ πρήγματα, καὶ οὕτω Αἰγύπτιοί τ' ἂν ἠπιστέατο ὡς ὑπ' ἀνδρὸς μεγάλου ἄρχονται καὶ σὺ ἄμεινον ἤκουες· νῦν δὲ ποιέεις οὐδαμῶς βασιλικά." [3] ὁ δ' ἀμείβετο τοισίδε αὐτούς· "τὰ τόξα οἱ ἐκτημένοι, ἐπεὰν μὲν δέωνται χρᾶσθαι, ἐντανύουσι· εἰ γὰρ δὴ τὸν πάντα χρόνον ἐντεταμένα εἴη, ἐκραγείη ἄν, ὥστε ἐς τὸ δέον οὐκ ἂν ἔχοιεν αὐτοῖσι χρᾶσθαι. [4] οὕτω δὲ καὶ ἀνθρώπου κατάστασις· εἰ ἐθέλοι κατεσπουδάσθαι αἰεὶ μηδὲ ἐς παιγνίην τὸ μέρος ἑωυτὸν ἀνιέναι, λάθοι ἂν ἤτοι μανεὶς ἢ ὅ γε ἀπόπληκτος γενόμενος· τὰ ἐγὼ ἐπιστάμενος μέρος ἑκατέρῳ νέμω." ταῦτα μὲν τοὺς φίλους ἀμείψατο.

2.173.1

τοιούτῳ μὲν τρόπῳ A reference to the previous chapter (2.172), where Amasis is said to have pleased the Egyptian people by comparing himself to a golden statue of a god which had once been a golden foot basin.

δικαιοῦν δουλεύειν Some irony here?

ἐχρᾶτο δὲ καταστάσι πρηγμάτων τοιῇδε "He established for himself the following routines for his daily activities."

μέχρι ὅτευ πληθούσης ἀγορῆς "Until whenever the marketplace was full."

ὅτευ = οὕτινος (ὅτου).

παιγνιήμων "Fond of joking around."

2.173.2

ἀχθεσθέντες Aorist, passive, masculine, nominative, plural participle of ἄχθομαι.

οὐκ ὀρθῶς σεωυτοῦ προέστηκας "You do not conduct yourself appropriately."

σεωυτοῦ = σεαυτοῦ.

θωκέοντα = θακέοντα.

ἠπιστέατο Imperfect, indicative, middle, 3rd, plural of ἐπίσταμαι.

ἄμεινον σὺ ἂν ἤκουες "Your reputation would improve."

2.173.3

ἀμείβετο τοισίδε αὐτούς Here, the verb ἀμείβω takes a dative and an accusative. Later in the passage (2.173.4), the same verb takes a double accusative.

ἐπεάν = ἐπειδάν.

ἐκραγείη Aorist, optative, passive, 3rd, singular of ἐκρήγνυμι.

ἐς τὸ δέον "When there was a need."

2.173.4

τὸ μέρος "In part."

γενόμενος Translate with λάθοι: "Without knowing it, he would become…."

☙

3.12.1-4 The Hardness of Egyptian Skulls

As a footnote to his description of the battle between the Persian army of Cambyses and the army of Psammenitos the new Egyptian king (c. 525 B.C.), Herodotus explains why Egyptian skulls are harder than Persian skulls. He tells us that the way he came to this conclusion was through "autopsy" (εἶδον) and "inquiry" (πυθόμενος). The opening word in this passage, θῶμα, lets us know right away that Herodotus has a fascinating tale in store for his readers.

θῶμα δὲ μέγα εἶδον πυθόμενος παρὰ τῶν ἐπιχωρίων· τῶν γὰρ ὀστέων κεχυμένων (χωρὶς ἑκατέρων τῶν ἐν τῇ μάχῃ ταύτῃ πεσόντων χωρὶς μὲν γὰρ τῶν Περσέων ἔκειτο τὰ ὀστέα, ὡς ἐχωρίσθη κατ᾽ ἀρχάς, ἑτέρωθι δὲ τῶν Αἰγυπτίων), αἱ μὲν τῶν Περσέων κεφαλαί εἰσι ἀσθενέες οὕτω ὥστε, εἰ θέλοις ψήφῳ μούνῃ βαλεῖν, διατετρανέεις, αἱ δὲ τῶν Αἰγυπτίων οὕτω δή τι ἰσχυραί, μόγις ἂν λίθῳ παίσας διαρρήξειας. [2] αἴτιον δὲ τούτου τόδε ἔλεγον, καὶ ἐμέ γ᾽ εὐπετέως ἔπειθον, ὅτι Αἰγύπτιοι μὲν αὐτίκα ἀπὸ παιδίων ἀρξάμενοι ξυρῶνται τὰς κεφαλὰς καὶ πρὸς τὸν ἥλιον παχύνεται τὸ ὀστέον. [3] τὠυτὸ δὲ τοῦτο καὶ τοῦ μὴ φαλακροῦσθαι αἴτιον ἐστί· Αἰγυπτίων γὰρ ἄν τις ἐλαχίστους ἴδοιτο φαλακροὺς πάντων ἀνθρώπων. [4] τούτοισι μὲν δὴ τοῦτό ἐστι αἴτιον ἰσχυρὰς φορέειν τὰς κεφαλάς, τοῖσι δὲ Πέρσῃσι, ὅτι

ἀσθενέας φορέουσι τὰς κεφαλάς, αἴτιον τόδε· σκιητροφέουσι ἐξ ἀρχῆς
πίλους τιάρας φορέοντες.

3.12.1

πυθόμενος Aorist, middle, masculine, nominative, singular participle of πυνθάνομαι.

κεχυμένων Perfect, passive, neuter, genitive, plural participle of χέω. Translate with χωρίς.

πεσόντων Aorist, active, masculine, genitive, plural participle of πίπτω.

ἐχωρίσθη Aorist, indicative, passive, 3rd, singular of χωρίζω.

κατ᾽ ἀρχάς "From the start."

παίσας Aorist, active, masculine, nominative, singular participle of παίω.

διαρρήξειας Aorist, optative, active, second, singular of διαρρήγνυμι.

3.12.2

ξυρῶνται Present, indicative, middle, 3rd, plural of ξυρέω.

3.12.3

τὠυτὸ Crasis (two words combined into one) for τὸ αὐτό.

τοῦ μὴ φαλακροῦσθαι The infinitive in this articular infinitive construction is present, middle of φαλακρόομαι.

3.12.4

φορέειν Here, the equivalent of ἔχειν.

σκιητροφέουσι Supply κεφαλάς.

τιάρας Persian head-dress. πίλους is in apposition.

☙

3.16.1-7 Cambyses Defiles the Body of Amasis

In this passage, and in many others like it throughout the Histories, Herodotus shows his great interest and, some might say, his expertise in the ethnography of non-Greeks, specifically, of Egyptians and Persians. He tells here the story of how Cambyses, the Persian king who conquered Egypt, went to Sais, a town on the Canopic branch of the Nile, and defiled the corpse of Amasis, the recently deceased Egyptian king. The story affords Herodotus the opportunity to delve into the burial customs of the Egyptians and Persians, and it helps him delineate further the deranged personality of Cambyses. This account has come under criticism for the way Herodotus portrays Persians as having no respect for the customs of the peoples they conquered. The very fact that Herodotus offers, at the end of this passage, a variant to the story suggests that his own level of confidence in the veracity of this tale may have been low.

Καμβύσης δὲ ἐκ Μέμφιος ἀπίκετο ἐς Σάϊν πόλιν, βουλόμενος ποιῆσαι τὰ δὴ
καὶ ἐποίησε. ἐπείτε γὰρ ἐσῆλθε ἐς τὰ τοῦ Ἀμάσιος οἰκία, αὐτίκα ἐκέλευε ἐκ

τῆς ταφῆς τὸν Ἀμάσιος νέκυν ἐκφέρειν ἔξω· ὡς δὲ ταῦτα οἱ ἐπιτελέα ἐγένετο, μαστιγοῦν ἐκέλευε καὶ τὰς τρίχας ἀποτίλλειν καὶ κεντοῦν τε καὶ τἆλλα πάντα λυμαίνεσθαι. [2] ἐπείτε δὲ καὶ ταῦτα ἔκαμον ποιεῦντες (ὁ γὰρ δὴ νεκρὸς ἅτε τεταριχευμένος ἀντεῖχέ τε καὶ οὐδὲν διεχέετο), ἐκέλευσέ μιν ὁ Καμβύσης κατακαῦσαι, ἐντελλόμενος οὐκ ὅσια· Πέρσαι γὰρ θεὸν νομίζουσι εἶναι τὸ πῦρ. [3] τὸ ὦν κατακαίειν γε τοὺς νεκροὺς οὐδαμῶς ἐν νόμῳ οὐδετέροισί ἐστι, Πέρσῃσι μὲν δι' ὅ περ εἴρηται, θεῷ οὐ δίκαιον εἶναι λέγοντες νέμειν νεκρὸν ἀνθρώπου· Αἰγυπτίοισι δὲ νενόμισται πῦρ θηρίον εἶναι ἔμψυχον, πάντα δὲ αὐτὸ κατεσθίειν τά περ ἂν λάβῃ, πλησθὲν δὲ αὐτὸ τῆς βορῆς συναποθνῄσκειν τῷ κατεσθιομένῳ. [4] οὐκ ὦν θηρίοισι νόμος οὐδαμῶς σφι ἐστι τὸν νέκυν διδόναι· καὶ διὰ ταῦτα ταριχεύουσι, ἵνα μὴ κείμενος ὑπὸ εὐλέων καταβρωθῇ. οὕτω οὐδετέροισι νομιζόμενα ἐνετέλλετο ποιέειν ὁ Καμβύσης. [5] ὡς μέντοι Αἰγύπτιοι λέγουσι, οὐκ Ἄμασις ἦν ὁ ταῦτα παθών, ἀλλὰ ἄλλος τις τῶν Αἰγυπτίων ἔχων τὴν αὐτὴν ἡλικίην Ἀμάσι, τῷ λυμαινόμενοι Πέρσαι ἐδόκεον Ἀμάσι λυμαίνεσθαι. [6] λέγουσι γὰρ ὡς πυθόμενος ἐκ μαντηίου ὁ Ἄμασις τὰ περὶ ἑωυτὸν ἀποθανόντα μέλλοι γίνεσθαι, οὕτω δὴ ἀκεόμενος τὰ ἐπιφερόμενα τὸν μὲν ἄνθρωπον τοῦτον τὸν μαστιγωθέντα ἀποθανόντα ἔθαψε ἐπὶ τῇσι θύρῃσι ἐντὸς τῆς ἑωυτοῦ θήκης, ἑωυτὸν δὲ ἐνετείλατο τῷ παιδὶ ἐν μυχῷ τῆς θήκης ὡς μάλιστα θεῖναι. [7] αἱ μέν νυν ἐκ τοῦ Ἀμάσιος ἐντολαὶ αὗται αἱ ἐς τὴν ταφήν τε καὶ τὸν ἄνθρωπον ἔχουσαι οὔ μοι δοκέουσι ἀρχὴν γενέσθαι, ἄλλως δ' αὐτὰ Αἰγύπτιοι σεμνοῦν.

3.16.1

ἀπίκετο Aorist, indicative, middle, 3rd, singular of ἀπικνέομαι (= ἀφικνέομαι).
ἐσῆλθε Aorist, indicative, active, 3rd, singular of εἰσέρχομαι.
ἐκφέρειν Supply "soldiers" as subject.
μαστιγοῦν, ἀποτίλλειν, κεντοῦν, λυμαίνεσθαι All are present infinitives.
τἆλλα Crasis (when two words are combined into one) for τὰ ἄλλα.
τἆλλα πάντα Internal accusative with λυμαίνεσθαι.

3.16.2

τεταριχευμένος Perfect, passive, masculine, nominative, singular participle of ταριχεύω.
διεχέετο Imperfect, indicative, passive, 3rd, singular of διαχέω. "Break into pieces."

3.16.3

τὸ...κατακαίειν Articular infinitive construction.
οὐδετέροισι That is, to neither Egyptians nor Persians.

εἴρηται Perfect, indicative, passive, 3rd, singular of ἐρῶ.

νενόμισται Perfect, indicative, passive, 3rd, singular of νομίζω. Here, used impersonally: "It is believed."

τά Used as a relative with πάντα as its antecedent.

πλησθὲν Aorist, passive, neuter, accusative, singular participle of πίμπλημι.

συναποθνήσκειν Takes the dative.

3.16.4

οὔκων = οὔκουν.

καταβρωθῇ Aorist, subjunctive, passive, 3rd, singular of καταβιβρώσκω.

ποιέειν Supply "soldiers" as the (accusative) subject.

3.16.5

τὴν αὐτὴν ἡλικίην "The same stature as." Takes the dative in Ἀμάσι.

3.16.6

πυθόμενος Aorist, middle, masculine, nominative, singular participle of πυνθάνομαι.

γίνεσθαι = γίγνεσθαι.

τὸν μὲν ἄνθρωπον τοῦτον τὸν μαστιγωθέντα "The one who was flogged."

μαστιγωθέντα Aorist, passive, masculine, accusative, singular participle of μαστιγόω.

ἀποθανόντα Aorist, active, masculine, accusative, singular participle of ἀποθνήσκω. "When he was dead."

ἐνετείλατο Aorist, indicative, middle, 3rd, singular of ἐντέλλω

3.16.7

ἔχουσαι "Having to do with."

ἀρχὴν Adverbial meaning: "In the first place."

σεμνοῦν Present, active infinitive of σεμνόω. Translate with δοκέουσι.

☙

3.32.1-4 A Deranged Cambyses Murders His Sister/Wife

Cambyses is clearly one of Herodotus' favorite topics. In an earlier passage (3.29.1), he labeled Cambyses a madman; in this passage, we see a most compelling manifestation of the King's madness. Meroe, the sister of Cambyses, also became his wife when the King's "seven judges" ruled that the King of Persia could do whatever he wished, including marrying his sister (3.31.8). Two versions (a Greek and an Egyptian one) of Meroe's death are reported by Herodotus; both are equally damning to the reputation of the King. That Herodotus tapped into hostile sources in his account of Cambyses' reign seems indisputable.

ἀμφὶ δὲ τῷ θανάτῳ αὐτῆς διξὸς ὥσπερ περὶ Σμέρδιος λέγεται λόγος. Ἕλληνες μὲν λέγουσι Καμβύσεα συμβαλεῖν σκύμνον λέοντος σκύλακι κυνός, θεωρέειν δὲ καὶ τὴν γυναῖκα ταύτην, νικωμένου δὲ τοῦ σκύλακος ἀδελφεὸν αὐτοῦ ἄλλον σκύλακα ἀπορρήξαντα τὸν δεσμὸν παραγενέσθαι οἱ, δύο δὲ γενομένους οὕτω δὴ τοὺς σκύλακας ἐπικρατῆσαι τοῦ σκύμνου. [2] καὶ τὸν μὲν Καμβύσεα ἥδεσθαι θεώμενον, τὴν δὲ παρημένην δακρύειν. Καμβύσεα δὲ μαθόντα τοῦτο ἐπειρέσθαι δι᾽ ὅ τι δακρύει, τὴν δὲ εἰπεῖν ὡς ἰδοῦσα τὸν σκύλακα τῷ ἀδελφεῷ τιμωρήσαντα δακρύσειε, μνησθεῖσά τε Σμέρδιος καὶ μαθοῦσα ὡς ἐκείνῳ οὐκ εἴη ὁ τιμωρήσων. [3] Ἕλληνες μὲν δὴ διὰ τοῦτο τὸ ἔπος φασὶ αὐτὴν ἀπολέσθαι ὑπὸ Καμβύσεω, Αἰγύπτιοι δὲ ὡς τραπέζῃ παρακατημένων λαβοῦσαν θρίδακα τὴν γυναῖκα περιτῖλαι καὶ ἐπανειρέσθαι τὸν ἄνδρα κότερον περιτετιλμένη ἢ θρίδαξ ἢ δασέα εἴη καλλίων, καὶ τὸν φάναι δασέαν, τὴν δ᾽ εἰπεῖν· [4] "ταύτην μέντοι κοτὲ σὺ τὴν θρίδακα ἐμιμήσαο, τὸν Κύρου οἶκον ἀποψιλώσας." τὸν δὲ θυμωθέντα ἐμπηδῆσαι αὐτῇ ἐχούσῃ ἐν γαστρί, καί μιν ἐκτρώσασαν ἀποθανεῖν.

3.32.1

αὐτῆς Referring to Cambyses' sister/wife.

συμβαλεῖν Supply ἐς μάχην.

κυνός Genitive of κύων.

ἀπορρήξαντα Aorist, active, masculine, accusative, singular participle of ἀπορρήγνυμι.

οἱ Dative case.

3.32.2

ἥδεσθαι Present, middle infinitive of ἥδομαι.

παρημένην Perfect, passive, feminine, accusative, singular participle of πάρημαι.

Καμβύσεα In the accusative, as the indirect statement continues.

ἐπειρέσθαι Aorist, middle infinitive of ἐπέρομαι (=ἐπείρομαι).

μνησθεῖσά Aorist, passive, feminine, nominative, singular participle of μιμνήσκω.

ὡς ἐκείνῳ οὐκ εἴη ὁ τιμωρήσων. A reference to Smerdis, Cambyses' brother. Cambyses had him murdered.

3.32.3

ἀπολέσθαι Aorist, middle infinitive of ἀπόλλυμι.

περιτῖλαι Aorist, active infinitive of περιτίλλω.

κότερον = πότερον

περιτετιλμένη Perfect, passive, feminine, nominative, singular participle of περιτίλλω

δασέα "Thick with leaves."

φάναι Present, active infinitive of φημί.

3.32.4

ἐμιμήσαο Aorist, indicative, middle, 2nd, singular of μιμέομαι

ἀποψιλώσας Aorist, active, masculine, nominative, singular participle of ἀποψιλόω.

θυμωθέντα Aorist, passive, masculine, accusative, singular participle of θυμόω. It is accusative, because the indirect statement continues.

ἐμπηδῆσαι Aorist, active infinitive of ἐμπηδάω (+ dative).

ἐχούσῃ ἐν γαστρί "Being pregnant."

ἐκτρώσασαν Aorist, active, feminine, accusative, singular participle of ἐκτιτρώσκω. "Having miscarried."

⊗

3.40.1-4 The Ring of Polycrates, Part I

Polycrates became tyrant of Samos (see map in Landmark *ad* 3.45) in c. 532 B.C. Thanks to a powerful navy—he is said (in 3.39) to have had a fleet of 100 pentaconters— he became one of the most powerful Greek tyrants in the first half of the sixth century. Herodotus devotes considerable portions of Book III to the story of Polycrates' great power, extraordinary wealth, and monumental construction projects. In this chapter, we learn that Amasis, the king of Egypt, had both a guest-friendship (ξενία) and a political alliance with Polycrates. Amasis, the story goes, was concerned that Polycrates' uninterrupted good fortune would incur the jealousy of the gods, and so he sent a message to his tyrant friend in which he recommended a way of averting this divine jealousy. Although the message was delivered in writing, we are not told in what language. Such details, vital from the standpoint of modern historiography, seem to have been of little or no concern to Herodotus. The Greek belief in *nemesis*, or a divine retribution upon humans who enjoy too much (and undeserved) success, is a major theme with Herodotus, who assumes that this belief is shared by Egyptians and other non-Greeks alike.

καί κως τὸν Ἄμασιν εὐτυχέων μεγάλως ὁ Πολυκράτης οὐκ ἐλάνθανε, ἀλλά οἱ τοῦτ᾽ ἦν ἐπιμελές. πολλῷ δὲ ἔτι πλεῦνός οἱ εὐτυχίης γινομένης γράψας ἐς βυβλίον τάδε ἐπέστειλε ἐς Σάμον· "Ἄμασις Πολυκράτεϊ ὧδε λέγει. [2] ἡδὺ μὲν πυνθάνεσθαι ἄνδρα φίλον καὶ ξεῖνον εὖ πρήσσοντα· ἐμοὶ δὲ αἱ σαὶ μεγάλαι εὐτυχίαι οὐκ ἀρέσκουσι, τὸ θεῖον ἐπισταμένῳ ὡς ἔστι φθονερόν. καί κως βούλομαι καὶ αὐτὸς καὶ τῶν ἂν κήδωμαι τὸ μέν τι εὐτυχέειν τῶν πρηγμάτων τὸ δὲ προσπταίειν, καὶ οὕτω διαφέρειν τὸν αἰῶνα ἐναλλὰξ πρήσσων ἢ εὐτυχέειν τὰ πάντα. [3] οὐδένα γάρ κω λόγῳ οἶδα ἀκούσας ὅστις ἐς τέλος οὐ κακῶς ἐτελεύτησε πρόρριζος, εὐτυχέων τὰ πάντα. σύ νυν ἐμοὶ πειθόμενος ποίησον πρὸς τὰς εὐτυχίας τοιάδε· [4] φροντίσας τὸ ἂν εὕρῃς ἐόν τοι πλείστου ἄξιον καὶ ἐπ᾽ ᾧ σὺ ἀπολομένῳ μάλιστα τὴν ψυχὴν ἀλγήσεις, τοῦτο ἀπόβαλε οὕτω ὅκως μηκέτι ἥξει ἐς ἀνθρώπους· ἤν τε μὴ ἐναλλὰξ ἤδη τὠπὸ τούτου αἱ εὐτυχίαι τοι τῇσι πάθῃσι προσπίπτωσι, τρόπῳ τῷ ἐξ ἐμεῦ ὑποκειμένῳ ἀκέο."

3.40.1

κῶς = πῶς

οἱ The form is dative.

πολλῷ δὲ ἔτι πλεῦνός οἱ εὐτυχίης γινομένης Genitive absolute construction.

ἐπέστειλε Aorist, indicative, active, 3rd, singular of ἐπιστέλλω.

3.40.2

ἡδὺ Supply ἐστί.

ἀρέσκουσι "Please" or "satisfy" (+ dative).

ἐπισταμένῳ Translate with the earlier ἐμοί.

καὶ αὐτὸς καὶ τῶν ἂν κήδωμαι "Both I myself and those I care for."

τῶν Used here as relative pronoun, with an implied antecedent.

ἐναλλὰξ πρήσσων Loosely, "Doing well some days and badly on others."

3.40.3

πρόρριζος Translate with ὅστις. "Thoroughly uprooted."

ποίησον Aorist, active, imperative, 2nd, singular of ποιέω.

3.40.4

εὕρης Aorist, active, subjunctive, 2nd, singular of εὑρίσκω.

ἐπ᾽ ᾧ...ἀπολομένῳ "For which, if lost."

ἀπολομένῳ Aorist, middle, neuter, dative, singular participle of ἀπόλλυμι.

τὴν ψυχήν Accusative of respect.

ὅκως = ὅπως.

τὠπό Crasis (when two words are combined into one) of τὸ ἀπό.

τὠπὸ τούτου "From this time forward."

ἐξ ἐμεῦ Here, the preposition ἐξ denotes agency.

ὑποκειμένῳ "Recommended."

ἀκέο Present, middle, imperative, 2nd, singular of ἀκέομαι. Supply τὰς εὐτυχίας as a direct object.

ଓଃ

3.41.1-2 The Ring of Polycrates, Part II

The story of the Ring of Polycrates has many of the trappings of a folktale, but Herodotus invests it with some credibility by specifying the name of the artist who made the ring. Since this Theodoros lived presumably two generations before Polycrates (cf. Pausanias 8.14.8), the ring which he crafted was truly irreplaceable. Note the subtle humor in the way Herodotus describes Polycrates' ritualized mourning over the loss of his ring.

ταῦτα ἐπιλεξάμενος ὁ Πολυκράτης καὶ νόῳ λαβὼν ὥς οἱ εὖ ὑπετίθετο Ἄμασις, ἐδίζητο ἐπ᾽ ᾧ ἂν μάλιστα τὴν ψυχὴν ἀσηθείη ἀπολομένῳ τῶν κειμηλίων, διζήμενος δὲ εὕρισκε τόδε· ἦν οἱ σφρηγὶς τὴν ἐφόρεε χρυσόδετος, σμαράγδου

μὲν λίθου ἐοῦσα, ἔργον δὲ ἦν Θεοδώρου τοῦ Τηλεκλέος Σαμίου. [2] ἐπεὶ
ὦν ταύτην οἱ ἐδόκεε ἀποβαλεῖν, ἐποίεε τοιάδε·πεντηκόντερον πληρώσας
ἀνδρῶν ἐσέβη ἐς αὐτήν, μετὰ δὲ ἀναγαγεῖν ἐκέλευε ἐς τὸ πέλαγος· ὡς δὲ
ἀπὸ τῆς νήσου ἑκὰς ἐγένετο, περιελόμενος τὴν σφρηγῖδα πάντων ὁρώντων
τῶν συμπλόων ῥίπτει ἐς τὸ πέλαγος. τοῦτο δὲ ποιήσας ἀπέπλεε, ἀπικόμενος
δὲ ἐς τὰ οἰκία συμφορῇ ἐχρᾶτο.

3.41.1

οἱ Dative of the personal pronoun.

ὑπετίθετο Imperfect, indicative, middle, 3rd, singular of ὑποτίθημι.

ἐδίζητο Imperfect, indicative, middle, 3rd, singular of δίζημαι

ἀσηθείη Aorist, optative, passive, 3rd, singular of ἀσάομαι.

σμαράγδου...λίθου Genitive of description construction. The stone was perhaps an emerald?

3.41.2

ἀνδρῶν Genitive after πληρώσας.

περιελόμενος Aorist, middle, masculine, nominative, singular participle of περιαιρέω.

συμφορῇ ἐχρᾶτο "He treated the loss as a calamity."

☙

3.42.1-4 The Ring of Polycrates, Part III

Herodotus continues the tale of the Ring of Polycrates with a demonstration of the
inevitability of fortune: no matter what Polycrates tries to do, he is destined for a catastrophic
fall. Note the almost Sophoclean irony in the way the servants, who are ignorant of the real
significance of their discovery of the ring inside the belly of the fish, rejoice (κεχαρηκότες)
over their tyrant's fortune. What Herodotus conveniently neglects to mention is that
Polycrates' demise, albeit a horrible one (cf. 3.125), doesn't happen until about 8 years after
the ring incident. Juvenal, the Roman satirist, parodied Herodotus with a story (4.45 ff.)
in which the emperor Domitian is presented with a huge fish (a turbot) while he was at his
villa in Alba Longa.

πέμπτῃ δὲ ἢ ἕκτῃ ἡμέρῃ ἀπὸ τούτων τάδε οἱ συνήνεικε γενέσθαι· ἀνὴρ
ἁλιεὺς λαβὼν ἰχθὺν μέγαν τε καὶ καλὸν ἠξίου μιν Πολυκράτεϊ δῶρον
δοθῆναι· φέρων δὴ ἐπὶ τὰς θύρας Πολυκράτεϊ ἔφη ἐθέλειν ἐλθεῖν ἐς ὄψιν,
χωρήσαντος δέ οἱ τούτου ἔλεγε διδοὺς τὸν ἰχθύν· [2] "ὦ βασιλεῦ, ἐγὼ τόνδε
ἑλὼν οὐκ ἐδικαίωσα φέρειν ἐς ἀγορήν, καίπερ γε ἐὼν ἀποχειροβίοτος, ἀλλά
μοι ἐδόκεε σεῦ τε εἶναι ἄξιος καὶ τῆς σῆς ἀρχῆς· σοὶ δή μιν φέρων δίδωμι."
ὁ δὲ ἡσθεὶς τοῖσι ἔπεσι ἀμείβεται τοισίδε· "κάρτα τε εὖ ἐποίησας καὶ χάρις

διπλῆ τῶν τε λόγων καὶ τοῦ δώρου· καί σε ἐπὶ δεῖπνον καλέομεν." [3] ὁ μὲν δὴ ἁλιεὺς μέγα ποιεύμενος ταῦτα ἤιε ἐς τὰ οἰκία, τὸν δὲ ἰχθὺν τάμνοντες οἱ θεράποντες εὑρίσκουσι ἐν τῇ νηδύι αὐτοῦ ἐνεοῦσαν τὴν Πολυκράτεος σφρηγῖδα. [4] ὡς δὲ εἶδόν τε καὶ ἔλαβον τάχιστα, ἔφερον κεχαρηκότες παρὰ τὸν Πολυκράτεα, διδόντες δέ οἱ τὴν σφρηγῖδα ἔλεγον ὅτεῳ τρόπῳ εὑρέθη. τὸν δὲ ὡς ἐσῆλθε θεῖον εἶναι τὸ πρῆγμα, γράφει ἐς βυβλίον πάντα τὰ ποιήσαντά μιν οἷα καταλελάβηκε, γράψας δὲ ἐς Αἴγυπτον ἐπέθηκε.

3.42.1

πέμπτη δὲ ἢ ἕκτη ἡμέρῃ Herodotus' quibbling over the exact day gives an air of authenticity to this story.

οἱ Dative of the personal pronoun.

συνήνεικε Aorist, indicative, active, 3rd, singular of συμφέρω. Triggers the infinitive in γενέσθαι.

ἠξίου Imperfect, indicative, active, 3rd, singular of ἀξιόω.

δοθῆναι Aorist, passive infinitive of δίδωμι.

χωρήσαντος δέ οἱ τούτου Genitive absolute construction. "When this [opportunity] came to pass for him."

3.42.2

ἀποχειροβίοτος Literally, "A person who works with his hands for a living."

ἡσθεὶς Aorist, passive, masculine, nominative, singular participle of ἥδομαι.

3.42.3

μέγα ποιεύμενος ταῦτα "Making a huge deal of this."

ποιεύμενος = ποιούμενος.

ἤιε Imperfect, indicative, active, 3rd, singular of εἶμι.

3.42.4

κεχαρηκότες Perfect, active, masculine, nominative, plural participle of χαίρω.

ὅτεῳ = ὅτῳ

εὑρέθη Aorist, indicative, passive, 3rd, singular of εὑρίσκω

τὸν δὲ ὡς ἐσῆλθε θεῖον εἶναι τὸ πρῆγμα "As it occurred to him that what happened was from a god."

καταλελάβηκε Perfect, indicative, active, 3rd, singular of καταλαμβάνω.

附

3.80.1-6 The Constitutional Debate, Part I

The so-called Constitutional Debate between the Seven Persians who overthrew the tyranny (or theocracy) of the Magi (cf. 3.67 ff.) is one of the most celebrated passages of the *Histories*. It is arguably the earliest extant document from the Greek world which delves into political philosophy. Otanes, the first participant, holds out for the elimination of the monarchy and for the creation of a kind of democracy. That a Persian should advocate even *isonomia* (never mind democracy) may have left Herodotus' audiences incredulous, and he acknowledges this by strongly affirming that this debate did in fact take place. In a later passage (6.43), he will cite the way Mardonios set up democracies in Ionia following the failure of the Ionian Revolt as further evidence that the Persians could in fact be supportive of democratic-style governments. As might be expected in a work that is occasionally tinged with ethnocentric views, Herodotus has his Persian debaters use terms of Greek (Athenian) political life, e.g., ἰσονομίην and ἀνευθύνῳ. The harshness of Otanes' views on monarchy or tyranny may reflect Herodotus' own distaste for a type of government which expelled him from his native Halicarnassus. An echo of this passage, specifically of the part where monarchs (tyrants) are said to abhor both those who stand up to them and those who are mere toadies, may be seen in Tacitus' description of the Julio-Claudian Emperor Tiberius and his attitude towards the Senate (*Annals* 1.12.2).

ἐπείτε δὲ κατέστη ὁ θόρυβος καὶ ἐκτὸς πέντε ἡμερέων ἐγένετο, ἐβουλεύοντο οἱ ἐπαναστάντες τοῖσι Μάγοισι περὶ τῶν πάντων πρηγμάτων, καὶ ἐλέχθησαν λόγοι ἄπιστοι μὲν ἐνίοισι Ἑλλήνων, ἐλέχθησαν δ' ὦν. [2] Ὀτάνης μὲν ἐκέλευε ἐς μέσον Πέρσῃσι καταθεῖναι τὰ πρήγματα, λέγων τάδε· "ἐμοὶ δοκέει ἕνα μὲν ἡμέων μούναρχον μηκέτι γενέσθαι· οὔτε γὰρ ἡδὺ οὔτε ἀγαθόν. εἴδετε μὲν γὰρ τὴν Καμβύσεω ὕβριν ἐπ' ὅσον ἐπεξῆλθε, μετεσχήκατε δὲ καὶ τῆς τοῦ Μάγου ὕβριος. [3] κῶς δ' ἂν εἴη χρῆμα κατηρτημένον μουναρχίη, τῇ ἔξεστι ἀνευθύνῳ ποιέειν τὰ βούλεται; καὶ γὰρ ἂν τὸν ἄριστον ἀνδρῶν πάντων στάντα ἐς ταύτην τὴν ἀρχὴν ἐκτὸς τῶν ἐωθότων νοημάτων στήσειε. ἐγγίνεται μὲν γάρ οἱ ὕβρις ὑπὸ τῶν παρεόντων ἀγαθῶν, φθόνος δὲ ἀρχῆθεν ἐμφύεται ἀνθρώπῳ. [4] δύο δ' ἔχων ταῦτα ἔχει πᾶσαν κακότητα· τὰ μὲν γὰρ ὕβρι κεκορημένος ἔρδει πολλὰ καὶ ἀτάσθαλα, τὰ δὲ φθόνῳ. καίτοι ἄνδρα γε τύραννον ἄφθονον ἔδει εἶναι, ἔχοντά γε πάντα τὰ ἀγαθά· τὸ δὲ ὑπεναντίον τούτου ἐς τοὺς πολιήτας πέφυκε· φθονέει γὰρ τοῖσι ἀρίστοισι περιεοῦσί τε καὶ ζώουσι, χαίρει δὲ τοῖσι κακίστοισι τῶν ἀστῶν, διαβολὰς δὲ ἄριστος ἐνδέκεσθαι. [5] ἀναρμοστότατον δὲ πάντων· ἤν τε γὰρ αὐτὸν μετρίως θωμάζῃς, ἄχθεται ὅτι οὐ κάρτα θεραπεύεται, ἤν τε θεραπεύῃ τις κάρτα, ἄχθεται ἄτε θωπί. τὰ δὲ δὴ μέγιστα ἔρχομαι ἐρέων· νόμαιά τε κινέει πάτρια καὶ βιᾶται γυναῖκας κτείνει τε ἀκρίτους. [6] πλῆθος δὲ ἄρχον πρῶτα

μὲν οὔνομα πάντων κάλλιστον ἔχει, ἰσονομίην, δεύτερα δὲ τούτων τῶν ὁ
μούναρχος ποιέει οὐδέν· πάλῳ μὲν ἀρχὰς ἄρχει, ὑπεύθυνον δὲ ἀρχὴν ἔχει,
βουλεύματα δὲ πάντα ἐς τὸ κοινὸν ἀναφέρει. τίθεμαι ὦν γνώμην μετέντας
ἡμέας μουναρχίην τὸ πλῆθος ἀέξειν· ἐν γὰρ τῷ πολλῷ ἔνι τὰ πάντα."

3.80.1

ἐκτὸς "Beyond."

οἱ ἐπαναστάντες "Those who had revolted."

ἐλέχθησαν Aorist, indicative, passive, 3rd, plural of λέγω.

λόγοι Here, "speeches."

ὦν = οὖν.

3.80.2

ἐς μέσον Πέρσῃσι καταθεῖναι τὰ πρήγματα Literally, "To put the affairs for the Persians into
the middle [of the Persians]." Idiomatically, "To establish popular government for the
Persians."

μετεσχήκατε Perfect, indicative, active, 2nd, plural of μετέχω (+ genitive). "You have
experience of."

3.80.3

κῶς = πῶς

χρῆμα κατηρτημένον "A well-ordered thing."

ἀνευθύνῳ Take with "monarchy" (understood).

στήσειε Aorist, optative, active, 3rd, singular of ἵστημι. "It [monarchy] would place."

ἐμφύεται "Is implanted in."

3.80.4

κακότητα Accusative of κακότης

κεκορημένος Perfect, passive, masculine, nominative, singular participle of κορέννυμι

τὸ δὲ ὑπεναντίον τούτου ἐς τοὺς πολιήτας πέφυκε "[The monarch] is by nature the opposite
of this towards his citizens."

πέφυκε Perfect, indicative, active, 3rd, singular of φύω.

περιεοῦσί τε καὶ ζώουσι "Who survive and live."

ἄριστος "[The monarch] is best at."

ἐνδέκεσθαι Present, middle, infinitive of ἐνδέκομαι (= ἐνδέχομαι).

3.80.5

ἀναρμοστότατον δὲ πάντων "The monarch is the most incongruous thing of all."

ἅτε θωπί "Just as with a flatterer."

3.80.6

πλῆθος...ἄρχον "Rule by the majority."

τῶν The relative is attracted into the case of its antecedent, τούτων.

ἀρχὰς ἄρχει Subject is "majority rule." "Assigns offices."

ὦν = οὖν.

μετέντας Aorist, active, masculine, accusative, plural participle of μετίημι (= μεθίημι).

ἀέξειν Present, active infinitive of ἀέξω. "Spread."

ἔνι = ἔνεστι.

൞

3.81.1-3 The Constitutional Debate, Part II

Megabyzos, another of the "Seven" who overthrew the Magi (cf. 3.67 ff.), makes his case for an oligarchic system of government. Except for the bromide which appears at the end of the passage ("the best counsels likely come from the best men"), most of the speech is taken up with the alleged evils of popular rule. (Curiously, *demos* is used here, but not in Otanes' speech.) Herodotus' putative sojourn in Athens might have given him ample opportunity to experience the shortcomings of an Athenian-style democracy.

Ὀτάνης μὲν δὴ ταύτην γνώμην ἐσέφερε· Μεγάβυζος δὲ ὀλιγαρχίῃ ἐκέλευε ἐπιτράπειν, λέγων τάδε·"τὰ μὲν Ὀτάνης εἶπε τυραννίδα παύων, λελέχθω κἀμοὶ ταῦτα, τὰ δ᾽ ἐς τὸ πλῆθος ἄνωγε φέρειν τὸ κράτος, γνώμης τῆς ἀρίστης ἡμάρτηκε· ὁμίλου γὰρ ἀχρηίου οὐδέν ἐστι ἀξυνετώτερον οὐδὲ ὑβριστότερον. [2] καίτοι τυράννου ὕβριν φεύγοντας ἄνδρας ἐς δήμου ἀκολάστου ὕβριν πεσεῖν ἐστὶ οὐδαμῶς ἀνασχετόν. ὁ μὲν γὰρ εἴ τι ποιέει, γινώσκων ποιέει, τῷ δὲ οὐδὲ γινώσκειν ἔνι· κῶς γὰρ ἂν γινώσκοι ὃς οὔτ᾽ ἐδιδάχθη οὔτε εἶδε καλὸν οὐδὲν οἰκήιον, ὠθέει τε ἐμπεσὼν τὰ πρήγματα ἄνευ νόου, χειμάρρῳ ποταμῷ ἴκελος; [3] δήμῳ μέν νυν, οἳ Πέρσῃσι κακὸν νοέουσι, οὗτοι χράσθων, ἡμεῖς δὲ ἀνδρῶν τῶν ἀρίστων ἐπιλέξαντες ὁμιλίην τούτοισι περιθέωμεν τὸ κράτος· ἐν γὰρ δὴ τούτοισι καὶ αὐτοὶ ἐνεσόμεθα·ἀρίστων δὲ ἀνδρῶν οἰκὸς ἄριστα βουλεύματα γίνεσθαι."

3.81.1

ἐπιτρέπειν Supply ἀρχήν as object.

παύων "Opposing."

λελέχθω Perfect, imperative, passive, 3rd, singular of λέγω.

κἀμοὶ Crasis (two words combined into one) of καί and ἐμοί. ἐμοί here is used as a dative of agent.

γνώμης τῆς ἀρίστης ἡμάρτηκε Literally, "He has missed the mark in terms of the best opinion."

3.81.2

ἐς δήμου ἀκολάστου ὕβριν πεσεῖν "To fall under the arrogance of the undisciplined demos." πεσεῖν is the aorist, active infinitive of πίπτω.

ὁ Referring to the tyrant.

ἔνι = ἔνεστι.

γινώσκων = γιγνώσκων.

κῶς = πῶς.

ἐδιδάχθη Aorist, indicative, passive, 3rd, singular of διδάσκω.

ὠθέει...ἐμπεσὼν Both the verb and the participle signify "to rush forward [blindly]."

3.81.3

χράσθων Present, imperative, middle, 3rd, plural of χράομαι (+ dative).

περιθέωμεν Aorist, subjunctive, active, 1st, plural of περιτίθημι.

οἰκός = εἰκός . "It is likely."

γίνεσθαι = γίγνεσθαι.

ଓଷ

3.82.1-5 The Constitutional Debate, Part III

Finally, it devolves on Darius to presents some arguments for monarchy. He begins his speech the way Megabyzos did…by acknowledging something that the previous speaker had said correctly. Darius' speech meanders some, and the logic of his arguments is difficult to follow. Two of the arguments employ a kind of ascending list which, while logically questionable, are rhetorically effective. Once again, terms from Greek (or Athenian) politics, such as στάσιες or "factional disputes" (a political phenomenon which the historian Thucydides treats extensively in Book III of his *Histories*) creep into the speech. Even a term from Athenian drama, κορυφαῖος or "head of the chorus," is woven into the Persian's arguments. Darius' punch line is delivered at the end, where he reminds his listeners that it was Cyrus the Great who as King rescued the Persians from the rule of the Medes. Besides, Darius adds, it is always a bad idea to violate πατρίους νόμους or "ancestral rules."

Μεγάβυζος μὲν δὴ ταύτην γνώμην ἐσέφερε· τρίτος δὲ Δαρεῖος ἀπεδείκνυτο γνώμην, λέγων· "ἐμοὶ δὲ τὰ μὲν εἶπε Μεγάβυζος ἐς τὸ πλῆθος ἔχοντα δοκέει ὀρθῶς λέξαι, τὰ δὲ ἐς ὀλιγαρχίην οὐκ ὀρθῶς. τριῶν γὰρ προκειμένων καὶ πάντων τῷ λόγῳ ἀρίστων ἐόντων, δήμου τε ἀρίστου καὶ ὀλιγαρχίης καὶ μουνάρχου, πολλῷ τοῦτο προέχειν λέγω. [2] ἀνδρὸς γὰρ ἑνὸς τοῦ ἀρίστου οὐδὲν ἄμεινον ἂν φανείη· γνώμῃ γὰρ τοιαύτῃ χρεώμενος ἐπιτροπεύοι ἂν ἀμωμήτως τοῦ πλήθεος, σιγῷτό τε ἂν βουλεύματα ἐπὶ δυσμενέας ἄνδρας οὕτω μάλιστα. [3] ἐν δὲ ὀλιγαρχίῃ πολλοῖσι ἀρετὴν ἐπασκέουσι ἐς τὸ κοινὸν ἔχθεα ἴδια ἰσχυρὰ φιλέει ἐγγίνεσθαι· αὐτὸς γὰρ ἕκαστος βουλόμενος κορυφαῖος εἶναι γνώμῃσί τε νικᾶν ἐς ἔχθεα μεγάλα ἀλλήλοισι ἀπικνέονται, ἐξ ὧν στάσιες ἐγγίνονται, ἐκ δὲ τῶν στασίων φόνος· ἐκ δὲ τοῦ φόνου ἀπέβη ἐς μουναρχίην, καὶ ἐν τούτῳ διέδεξε ὅσῳ ἐστὶ τοῦτο ἄριστον. [4] δήμου

τε αὖ ἄρχοντος ἀδύνατα μὴ οὐ κακότητα ἐγγίνεσθαι· κακότητος τοίνυν
ἐγγινομένης ἐς τὰ κοινὰ ἔχθεα μὲν οὐκ ἐγγίνεται τοῖσι κακοῖσι, φιλίαι
δὲ ἰσχυραί· οἱ γὰρ κακοῦντες τὰ κοινὰ συγκύψαντες ποιεῦσι. τοῦτο δὲ
τοιοῦτο γίνεται ἐς ὃ ἂν προστάς τις τοῦ δήμου τοὺς τοιούτους παύσῃ· ἐκ δὲ
αὐτῶν θωμάζεται οὗτος δὴ ὑπὸ τοῦ δήμου, θωμαζόμενος δὲ ἀν᾽ ὦν ἐφάνη
μούναρχος ἐών· καὶ ἐν τούτῳ δηλοῖ καὶ οὗτος ὡς ἡ μουναρχίη κράτιστον.
[5] ἑνὶ δὲ ἔπεϊ πάντα συλλαβόντα εἰπεῖν, κόθεν ἡμῖν ἡ ἐλευθερίη ἐγένετο καὶ
τεῦ δόντος; κότερα παρὰ τοῦ δήμου ἢ ὀλιγαρχίης ἢ μουνάρχου; ἔχω τοίνυν
γνώμην ἡμέας ἐλευθερωθέντας διὰ ἕνα ἄνδρα τὸ τοιοῦτο περιστέλλειν,
χωρίς τε τούτου πατρίους νόμους μὴ λύειν ἔχοντας εὖ· οὐ γὰρ ἄμεινον."

3.82.1

τριῶν γὰρ προκειμένων καὶ πάντων τῷ λόγῳ ἀρίστων ἐόντων Genitive absolute
   constructions.

τῷ λόγῳ "In theory," or "for the sake of an argument." In other words, Darius wants
   his listeners to conceive of the best possible representations of the three types of
   government.

τοῦτο Referring to monarchy.

προέχειν "To stand out."

3.82.2

ἀνδρὸς γὰρ ἑνὸς τοῦ ἀρίστου οὐδὲν ἄμεινον ἂν φανείη "Nothing would seem better than the
   rule of the one best man." The argument seems to be this: if you concede that a certain
   man is the "best," then the government of this best man is also best.

σιγῷτό Present, optative, middle, 3rd, singular of σιγάω.

3.82.3

πολλοῖσι ἀρετὴν ἐπασκέουσι "For the many who strive for excellence."

φιλέει "Tend to" (+ infinitive).

ἐγγίνεσθαι = ἐγγίγνεσθαι.

ἕκαστος Takes a plural verb (ἀπικνέονται).

στάσιες = στάσεις.

ἀπέβη Greek uses the gnomic aorist when γνῶμαι or proverbs are cited. Translate as if it were
   a present: "There is a transition to."

διέδεξε Another gnomic aorist, from διαδείκνυμι. Used intransitively, "It is clear."

3.82.4

δήμου…ἄρχοντος Genitive absolute construction.

κακότητα "Evil, baseness, cowardice, corruption."

κακότητος …ἐγγινομένης Another genitive absolute construction.

συγκύψαντες "Putting their heads together" or "conspiring."

ἐς ὅ "Until."

ἐκ δὲ αὐτῶν "As a result of all this."

ὦν = οὖν

3.82.5

ἑνὶ δὲ ἔπεϊ πάντα συλλαβόντα εἰπεῖν "To speak while wrapping things up in a single word."

κόθεν = πόθεν

ἡ ἐλευθερίη "Freedom," but only in the sense of not being subject to a foreign power.

τεῦ = τίνος.

κότερα = πότερα.

χωρίς …τούτου "Aside from this."

 C3

3.85.1-3 How Darius Was Chosen as King of Persia, Part I

This passage, and several others like it, show Herodotus' familiarity with animal husbandry. It also displays his admiration for the kind of trickery that Darius' groomsman was able to concoct. The real story of Darius' accession to the Persian throne was probably quite different from the one Herodotus tells, but it was probably not nearly as interesting. In any case, Darius enjoyed an amazingly long reign, from 521 to 485 B.C.

Δαρείῳ δὲ ἦν ἱπποκόμος ἀνὴρ σοφός, τῷ οὔνομα ἦν Οἰβάρης· πρὸς τοῦτον τὸν ἄνδρα, ἐπείτε διελύθησαν, ἔλεξε Δαρεῖος τάδε·" Οἴβαρες, ἡμῖν δέδοκται περὶ τῆς βασιληίης ποιέειν κατὰ τάδε· ὅτευ ἂν ὁ ἵππος πρῶτος φθέγξηται ἅμα τῷ ἡλίῳ ἀνιόντι αὐτῶν ἐπαναβεβηκότων, τοῦτον ἔχειν τὴν βασιληίην. νῦν ὦν εἴ τινα ἔχεις σοφίην, μηχανῶ ὡς ἂν ἡμεῖς σχῶμεν τοῦτο τὸ γέρας καὶ μὴ ἄλλος τις." [2] ἀμείβεται Οἰβάρης τοισίδε·"εἰ μὲν δή, ὦ δέσποτα, ἐν τούτῳ τοί ἐστι ἢ βασιλέα εἶναι ἢ μή, θάρσεε τούτου εἴνεκεν καὶ θυμὸν ἔχε ἀγαθόν, ὡς βασιλεὺς οὐδεὶς ἄλλος πρὸ σεῦ ἔσται· τοιαῦτα ἔχω φάρμακα." λέγει Δαρεῖος· "εἰ τοίνυν τι τοιοῦτον ἔχεις σόφισμα, ὥρη μηχανᾶσθαι καὶ μὴ ἀναβάλλεσθαι, ὡς τῆς ἐπιούσης ἡμέρης ὁ ἀγὼν ἡμῖν ἔσται." [3] ἀκούσας ταῦτα ὁ Οἰβάρης ποιέει τοιόνδε· ὡς ἐγίνετο ἡ νύξ, τῶν θηλέων ἵππων μίαν, τὴν ὁ Δαρείου ἵππος ἔστεργε μάλιστα, ταύτην ἀγαγὼν ἐς τὸ προάστιον κατέδησε καὶ ἐπήγαγε τὸν Δαρείου ἵππον, καὶ τὰ μὲν πολλὰ περιῆγε ἀγχοῦ τῇ ἵππῳ, ἐγχρίμπτων τῇ θηλέῃ, τέλος δὲ ἐπῆκε ὀχεῦσαι τὸν ἵππον.

3.85.1

διελύθησαν Aorist, indicative, passive, 3rd, plural of διαλύω. "After the assembly had been dissolved."

δέδοκται Perfect, indicative, passive, 3rd, singular of δοκέω. "It has seemed good for us...." Idiomatically, "we have decided."

ὅτευ = οὗτινος.

φθέγξηται Aorist, subjunctive, middle, 3rd, singular of φθέγγομαι. "Neighs."

ὦν = οὖν.

μηχανῶ Present, imperative, middle, 2nd, singular of μηχανάομαι.

3.85.2

εἵνεκεν = ἕνεκα.

ὥρη "Now is the time."

τῆς ἐπιούσης ἡμέρης Genitive absolute construction.

3.85.3

τῶν θηλέων ἵππων μίαν "One of the mares."

τήν Here, a relative pronoun.

τὸ προάστειον "The suburb of the town."

ἐγχρίμπτων "Bringing it close to."

τέλος Used as an adverb.

ἐπῆκε Aorist, indicative, active, 3rd, singular of ἐφίημι. "He permitted."

ὀχεῦσαι "To mount."

ॐ

3.86.1-2 How Darius Was Chosen as King of Persia, Part II

The horse omen is confirmed by thunder and lightning from a clear, blue sky. The reaction of the Persians who were competing with Darius was to dismount from their horses and kiss the ground (προσεκύνεον: literally, "they were like dogs") in front of him. This type of self-abasement among the Persians is regularly highlighted by Herodotus to emphasize the contrast between Persians and Greeks. (For a different and somewhat inelegant version of this horse strategem, see 3.87.)

ἅμ' ἡμέρη δὲ διαφωσκούσῃ οἱ ἓξ κατὰ συνεθήκαντο παρῆσαν ἐπὶ τῶν ἵππων· διεξελαυνόντων δὲ κατὰ τὸ προάστιον, ὡς κατὰ τοῦτο τὸ χωρίον ἐγίνοντο ἵνα τῆς παροιχομένης νυκτὸς κατεδέδετο ἡ θήλεα ἵππος, ἐνθαῦτα ὁ Δαρείου ἵππος προσδραμὼν ἐχρεμέτισε· [2] ἅμα δὲ τῷ ἵππῳ τοῦτο ποιήσαντι ἀστραπὴ ἐξ αἰθρίης καὶ βροντὴ ἐγένετο. ἐπιγενόμενα δὲ ταῦτα τῷ Δαρείῳ ἐτελέωσέ μιν ὥσπερ ἐκ συνθέτου τευ γενόμενα· οἱ δὲ καταθορόντες ἀπὸ τῶν ἵππων προσεκύνεον τὸν Δαρεῖον.

3.86.1

ἅμ᾽ ἡμέρῃ δὲ διαφωσκούσῃ "When day began to dawn."

κατά "According as."

συνεθήκαντο Aorist, indicative, middle, 3rd, plural of συντίθημι.

ἐγίνονται = ἐγίγνονται.

τῆς παροιχομένης νυκτὸς "The night before."

προσδραμὼν Aorist, active, masculine, nominative, singular participle of προστρέχω.

3.86.2

ἐξ αἰθρίης "From the clear, blue sky."

ἐτελέωσέ Aorist, indicative, active, 3rd, singular of τελεόω (= τελειόω).

τευ = τινός.

προσεκύνεον "Prostrated themselves in front of…."

☙

4.3.1-4 Scythians Are Kept from Returning to their Native Land

About half of Book IV of the *Histories* is taken up with the story of Darius' attempts to subdue Scythia, a vast region north and west of the Euxine (Black Sea). This story, while not directly associated with Herodotus' over-arching theme of the Greek-Persian conflict, nevertheless allows him to preview the kind of military tactics that the Persians will employ in their wars with the Greeks. Perhaps more importantly, Book IV gives Herodotus the opportunity to showcase his limitless interest in ethnography and his fondness for telling numerous "believe it or not" type tales concerning the tribal customs of remote tribes. Herodotus' knowledge of the geography of distant lands like Scythia also comes to the fore in this chapter. Given the vastness and the remoteness of Scythia, it is amazing that Herodotus was able to get even some of his facts right. Here he narrates the story of how the Scythian horde, which had been driven out of Asia by the Medes, were kept from returning to their original homeland by a new generation of Scythians, who had been born of slave fathers and Scythian mothers.

ἐκ τούτων δὴ ὦν σφι τῶν δούλων καὶ τῶν γυναικῶν ἐτράφη νεότης· οἳ ἐπείτε ἔμαθον τὴν σφετέρην γένεσιν, ἠντιοῦντο αὐτοῖσι κατιοῦσι ἐκ τῶν Μήδων. [2] καὶ πρῶτα μὲν τὴν χώρην ἀπετάμοντο, τάφρον ὀρυξάμενοι εὐρέαν κατατείνουσαν ἐκ τῶν Ταυρικῶν ὀρέων ἐς τὴν Μαιῆτιν λίμνην, τῇ πέρ ἐστι μεγίστη· μετὰ δὲ πειρωμένοισι ἐσβάλλειν τοῖσι Σκύθῃσι ἀντικατιζόμενοι ἐμάχοντο. [3] γινομένης δὲ μάχης πολλάκις καὶ οὐ δυναμένων οὐδὲν πλέον ἔχειν τῶν Σκυθέων τῇ μάχῃ, εἷς αὐτῶν ἔλεξε τάδε· "οἷα ποιεῦμεν, ἄνδρες Σκύθαι. δούλοισι τοῖσι ἡμετέροισι μαχόμενοι αὐτοί τε κτεινόμενοι ἐλάσσονες

γινόμεθα καὶ ἐκείνους κτείνοντες ἐλασσόνων τὸ λοιπὸν ἄρξομεν. [4] νῦν ὦν
μοι δοκέει αἰχμὰς μὲν καὶ τόξα μετεῖναι, λαβόντα δὲ ἕκαστον τοῦ ἵππου τὴν
μάστιγα ἰέναι ἆσσον αὐτῶν. μέχρι μὲν γὰρ ὥρων ἡμέας ὅπλα ἔχοντας, οἱ δὲ
ἐνόμιζον ὅμοιοί τε καί ἐξ ὁμοίων ἡμῖν εἶναι· ἐπεὰν δὲ ἴδωνται μάστιγας ἀντὶ
ὅπλων ἔχοντας, μαθόντες ὡς εἰσὶ ἡμέτεροι δοῦλοι καὶ συγγνόντες τοῦτο
οὐκ ὑπομενέουσι."

4.3.1

ὦν = οὖν

ἐτράφη Aorist, indicative, passive, 3rd, singular of τρέφω. Translate with νεότης as subject:
"A new generation was brought up."

4.3.2

ἀπετάμοντο Aorist, indicative, middle, 3rd, plural of ἀποτέμνω. "They marked off for
themselves."

ὀρυξάμενοι "Having excavated."

κατατείνουσαν ἐκ τῶν Ταυρικῶν ὀρέων ἐς τὴν Μαιῆτιν λίμνην See the map in Landmark
ad 4.7. Presumably, this trench extended from the northern end of the Tauric Mountain
range to the southern shores of Lake Maeotis (Sea of Azov), and it effectively blocked
the invading Scythians from re-entering their native land by way of the so-called
Cimmerian Bosporus.

τῇ πέρ ἐστι μεγίστη "Where it [Lake Maeotis] is widest."

ἀντικατιζόμενοι "Settling in (in a military sense)."

4.3.3

κτεινόμενοι Passive voice. "As we are being killed."

γινόμεθα = γιγνόμεθα.

4.3.4

ὥρων Imperfect, indicative, active, 3rd, plural of εἶδον.

καί ἐξ ὁμοίων ἡμῖν εἶναι "And that they come from people equal to us."

ἴδωνται Aorist, subjunctive, middle, 3rd, plural of ὁράω. The strategem of the whips
apparently worked, or so we are told in the next chapter (4.4).

☙

4.23.1-5 The Ways of the Argippaioi (or Bald Men)

We have here one in a series of remarkably interesting accounts of the peoples who
inhabited ancient Scythia. The Argippaioi were a peaceful tribe who cultivated a single
crop, something called *pontikon*, a cherry-like fruit which, when strained, could be drunk
or made into *palathai* or "cakes." That Herodotus may have tapped into some reliable
information for this passage can be inferred from the fact that the Tartars who lived in this

region in the early 20th century still cultivated this kind of cherry (HW *ad* 4.23.3). Apart from emphasizing the monoculture of the Argippaioi, Herodotus highlights the way these remarkable people carried no weapons and offered asylum to anyone who sought it.

μέχρι μὲν δὴ τῆς τούτων τῶν Σκυθέων χώρης ἐστὶ ἡ καταλεχθεῖσα πᾶσα πεδιάς τε γῆ καὶ βαθύγαιος, τὸ δ' ἀπὸ τούτου λιθώδης τ' ἐστὶ καὶ τρηχέα. [2] διεξελθόντι δὲ καὶ τῆς τρηχέης χώρης πολλὸν οἰκέουσι ὑπώρεαν ὀρέων ὑψηλῶν ἄνθρωποι λεγόμενοι εἶναι πάντες φαλακροὶ ἐκ γενετῆς γινόμενοι, καὶ ἔρσενες καὶ θήλεαι ὁμοίως, καὶ σιμοὶ καὶ γένεια ἔχοντες μεγάλα, φωνὴν δὲ ἰδίην ἱέντες, ἐσθῆτι δὲ χρεώμενοι Σκυθικῇ, ζῶντες δὲ ἀπὸ δενδρέων. [3] ποντικὸν μὲν οὔνομα τῷ δενδρέῳ ἀπ' οὗ ζῶσι, μέγαθος δὲ κατὰ συκέην μάλιστά κη· καρπὸν δὲ φορέει κυάμῳ ἴσον, πυρῆνα δὲ ἔχει. τοῦτο ἐπεὰν γένηται πέπον, σακκέουσι ἱματίοισι, ἀπορρέει δὲ ἀπ' αὐτοῦ παχὺ καὶ μέλαν· οὔνομα δὲ τῷ ἀπορρέοντί ἐστι ἄσχυ· τοῦτο καὶ λείχουσι καὶ γάλακτι συμμίσγοντες πίνουσι, καὶ ἀπὸ τῆς παχύτητος αὐτοῦ τῆς τρυγὸς παλάθας συντιθεῖσι καὶ ταύτας σιτέονται. [4] πρόβατα γάρ σφι οὐ πολλά ἐστι. οὐ γάρ τι σπουδαῖαι αἱ νομαὶ αὐτόθι εἰσί. ὑπὸ δενδρέῳ δὲ ἕκαστος κατοίκηται, τὸν μὲν χειμῶνα ἐπεὰν τὸ δένδρεον περικαλύψῃ πίλῳ στεγνῷ λευκῷ, τὸ δὲ θέρος ἄνευ πίλου. [5] τούτους οὐδεὶς ἀδικέει ἀνθρώπων (ἱροὶ γὰρ λέγονται εἶναι), οὐδέ τι ἀρήιον ὅπλον ἐκτέαται. καὶ τοῦτο μὲν τοῖσι περιοικέουσι οὗτοί εἰσι οἱ τὰς διαφορὰς διαιρέοντες, τοῦτο δέ, ὃς ἂν φεύγων καταφύγῃ ἐς τούτους, ὑπ' οὐδενὸς ἀδικέεται·οὔνομα δέ σφί ἐστι Ἀργιππαῖοι.

4.23.1

καταλεχθεῖσα Aorist, passive, feminine, nominative, singular participle of καταλέγω. "Having been described."

τὸ δ' ἀπὸ τούτου An adverbial expression. "But from this point forward."

4.23.2

γίνομαι = γίγνομαι.

ἔρσενες = ἄρσενες.

φωνὴν δὲ ἰδίην ἱέντες "Speaking [emitting] the same language."

ζῶντες δὲ ἀπὸ "Living off [the fruit]...."

4.23.3

οὔνομα = ὄνομα.

ποντικὸν A kind of cherry tree. See HW, *ad* 4.23.

μέγαθος = μέγεθος. Accusative of respect construction.

μάλιστά κη "Closest to."
ἐπεάν = ἐπειδάν.

4.23.4

κατοίκηται Perfect, indicative, middle, 3rd, singular of κατοικέω.
τὸν μὲν χειμῶνα "During the winter."

4.23.5

ἱροί = ἱεροί.
ἐκτέαται = κέκτηνται. Perfect, indicative, active, 3rd, plural of κτάομαι.
τοῦτο μὲν...τοῦτο δὲ "On the one hand...on the other."
τοῖσι περιοικέουσι οὗτοί εἰσι οἱ τὰς διαφορὰς διαιρέοντες "These are the ones who settle
disputes for those living around them."

☙

4.25.1-2 Herodotus Draws the Line

Herodotus display two levels of disbelief here. He describes the story of the goat-
footed men as "incredible" (οὐ πιστά), but he totally (τὴν ἀρχήν) rejects a report that some
Scythians sleep, uninterrupted, for half a year. Regardless of his skepticism, Herodotus
reports both stories.

μέχρι μὲν δὴ τούτων γινώσκεται, τὸ δὲ τῶν φαλακρῶν κατύπερθε οὐδεὶς
ἀτρεκέως οἶδε φράσαι· ὄρεα γὰρ ὑψηλὰ ἀποτάμνει ἄβατα καὶ οὐδείς σφεα
ὑπερβαίνει· οἱ δὲ φαλακροὶ οὗτοι λέγουσι, ἐμοὶ μὲν οὐ πιστὰ λέγοντες,
οἰκέειν τὰ ὄρεα αἰγίποδας ἄνδρας, ὑπερβάντι δὲ τούτους ἀνθρώπους
ἄλλους οἳ τὴν ἐξάμηνον κατεύδουσι· τοῦτο δὲ οὐκ ἐνδέκομαι τὴν ἀρχήν. [2]
ἀλλὰ τὸ μὲν πρὸς ἠῶ τῶν φαλακρῶν γινώσκεται ἀτρεκέως ὑπὸ Ἰσσηδόνων
οἰκεόμενη, τὸ μέντοι κατύπερθε πρὸς βορέην ἄνεμον οὐ γινώσκεται οὔτε
τῶν φαλακρῶν οὔτε τῶν Ἰσσηδόνων, εἰ μὴ ὅσα αὐτῶν τούτων λεγόντων.

4.25.1

τούτων Referring to the Argippaioi of chapter 23.
γινώσκεται Supply χώρη.
ὑπερβάντι δὲ τούτους "To someone traveling beyond these."
ἐνδέκομαι = ἐνδέχομαι.
τὴν ἀρχήν "Totally." Translate with the preceding negative.

4.25.2

εἰ μὴ ὅσα αὐτῶν τούτων λεγόντων "Except for whatever these tribes themselves have to say."

CB

4.26.1-2 The Funeral Rites of the Issedones

Like so many similar passages, 4.26 shows a Herodotus who remains non-judgmental even when describing a custom which probably seemed abhorrent to him. What is more, he takes this opportunity to demonstrate his skills as an ethnographer by adducing a comparison with the festival of the Genesia, where Greeks commemorated the anniversary of a parent's death. We see an echo of this chapter in Livy 23.24: here the Gallic Boii are said to have made a drinking cup from the head of the Roman Postumius.

νόμοισι δὲ Ἰσσηδόνες τοισίδε λέγονται χρᾶσθαι· ἐπεὰν ἀνδρὶ ἀποθάνῃ πατήρ, οἱ προσήκοντες πάντες προσάγουσι πρόβατα καὶ ἔπειτα ταῦτα θύσαντες καὶ καταταμόντες τὰ κρέα κατατάμνουσι καὶ τὸν τοῦ δεκομένου τεθνεῶτα γονέα, ἀναμίξαντες δὲ πάντα τὰ κρέα δαῖτα προτίθενται· [2] τὴν δὲ κεφαλὴν αὐτοῦ ψιλώσαντες καὶ ἐκκαθήραντες καταχρυσοῦσι καὶ ἔπειτα ἅτε ἀγάλματι χρέωνται, θυσίας μεγάλας ἐπετείους ἐπιτελέοντες. παῖς δὲ πατρὶ τοῦτο ποιέει, κατά περ Ἕλληνες τὰ γενέσια. ἄλλως δὲ δίκαιοι καὶ οὗτοι λέγονται εἶναι, ἰσοκρατέες δὲ ὁμοίως αἱ γυναῖκες τοῖσι ἀνδράσι.

4.26.1

ἐπεάν = ἐπειδάν.
ἀποθάνῃ Aorist, subjunctive, active, 3rd, singular of ἀποθνήσκω.
τοῦ δεκομένου "Of the one receiving," that is "of the host."
τεθνεῶτα Perfect, active, masculine, accusative, singular participle of θνήσκω.
δαῖτα Accusative of δαίς.

4.26.2

τὰ γενέσια The Genesia was a celebration on the anniversary of a parent's death.

CB

4.61.1-2 The Scythian Way of Cooking

A short passage that underscores Herodotus' keen eye for detail and his unbounded interest in the customs of non-Greeks. When reading his account of the cooking methods of the Scythians, one is left with the impression that Herodotus admired the ingenuity of a people who could substitute bones for firewood. That Herodotus would know about the special shape of Lesbian cauldrons helps support the often-held theory that his "other" occupation was that of a merchant, who would have been well-versed in the jargon of commerce. Whatever doubts a reader may have about the suitability of bones in place of firewood, or the suitability of an animal's stomach in place of a cauldron, are dispelled by Herodotus' charming conclusion that, in this way, the "ox cooks itself" (οὕτω βοῦς τε ἑωυτὸν ἐξέψει).

τῆς δὲ γῆς τῆς Σκυθικῆς αἰνῶς ἀξύλου ἐούσης ὧδέ σφι ἐς τὴν ἕψησιν τῶν κρεῶν ἐξεύρηται. ἐπειδὰν ἀποδείρωσι τὰ ἱρήια, γυμνοῦσι τὰ ὀστέα τῶν κρεῶν· ἔπειτα ἐσβάλλουσι, ἢν μὲν τύχωσι ἔχοντες, ἐς λέβητας ἐπιχωρίους, μάλιστα Λεσβίοισι κρητῆρσι προσεικέλους, χωρὶς ἢ ὅτι πολλῷ μέζονας· ἐς τούτους ἐσβάλλοντες ἕψουσι ὑποκαίοντες τὰ ὀστέα τῶν ἱρηίων· ἢν δὲ μή σφι παρῇ λέβης, οἱ δὲ ἐς τὰς γαστέρας τῶν ἱρηίων ἐμβάλοντες τὰ κρέα πάντα καὶ παραμείξαντες ὕδωρ ὑποκαίουσι τὰ ὀστέα· [2] τὰ δὲ αἴθεται κάλλιστα, αἱ δὲ γαστέρες χωρέουσι εὐπετέως τὰ κρέα ἐψιλωμένα τῶν ὀστέων· καὶ οὕτω βοῦς τε ἑωυτὸν ἐξέψει καὶ τἆλλα ἱρήια ἑωυτὸ ἕκαστον. ἐπεὰν δὲ ἑψηθῇ τὰ κρέα, ὁ θύσας τῶν κρεῶν καὶ τῶν σπλάγχνων ἀπαρξάμενος ῥίπτει ἐς τὸ ἔμπροσθε. θύουσι δὲ καὶ τὰ ἄλλα πρόβατα καὶ ἵππους μάλιστα.

4.61.1

τῆς δὲ γῆς τῆς Σκυθικῆς αἰνῶς ἀξύλου ἐούσης Genitive absolute construction.

ἐξεύρηται Used impersonally. "An invention was made."

ἱρήια = ἱερεῖα.

ἢν μὲν τύχωσι ἔχοντες = "If they happen to have one."

προσεικέλους Takes the dative.

χωρὶς ἢ ὅτι "Outside of the fact that."

4.61.2

τά Referring to the bones.

τὰ δὲ αἴθεται κάλλιστα "And they [the bones] burn splendidly."

ἑωυτόν = ἑαυτόν.

ἐπεὰν = ἐπειδάν.

τῶν κρεῶν καὶ τῶν σπλάγχνων ἀπαρξάμενος "After saving a portion of the meat and the entrails."

 CS

4.62.1-4 The Sword Worship of the Scythians

Herodotus would be very much at home in a modern academic setting where Comparative Religion is a branch of knowledge and the subject of research. Chapter 62 gives us a glimpse into the Scythian worship of an ancient iron sword, which supposedly represented the god of war (Ares, to Herodotus). It must be admitted that the reference to the giant mountain of branches, which the Scythians built for this sacred sword, discredits the claim from the previous chapter (4.61), that Scythia was bereft of wood. Herodotus follows this account with a terse description of the human sacrifice that is part of the sword worship. While there is no overt comment from Herodotus on this practice, he may have left behind a subtle editorial in the understated and haunting ending to this chapter. It is worth noting that the 4th century A.D. Roman historian Ammianus describes the Scythian sword worship in much the same way as Herodotus.

τοῖσι μὲν δὴ ἄλλοισι τῶν θεῶν οὕτω θύουσι καὶ ταῦτα τῶν κτηνέων, τῷ δὲ Ἄρεϊ ὧδε· κατὰ νομοὺς ἑκάστοισι τῶν ἀρχέων ἵδρυταί σφι Ἄρεος ἱρὸν τοιόνδε· φρυγάνων φάκελοι συννενέαται ὅσον τ' ἐπὶ σταδίους τρεῖς μῆκος καὶ εὖρος, ὕψος δὲ ἔλασσον. ἄνω δὲ τούτου τετράγωνον ἄπεδον πεποίηται, καὶ τὰ μὲν τρία τῶν κώλων ἐστὶ ἀπότομα, κατὰ δὲ τὸ ἓν ἐπιβατόν. [2] ἔτεος δὲ ἑκάστου ἁμάξας πεντήκοντα καὶ ἑκατὸν ἐπινέουσι φρυγάνων· ὑπονοστέει γὰρ δὴ αἰεὶ ὑπὸ τῶν χειμώνων. ἐπὶ τούτου δὴ τοῦ σηκοῦ ἀκινάκης σιδήρεος ἵδρυται ἀρχαῖος ἑκάστοισι, καὶ τοῦτ' ἐστι τοῦ Ἄρεος τὸ ἄγαλμα. τούτῳ δὲ τῷ ἀκινάκῃ θυσίας ἐπετείους προσάγουσι προβάτων καὶ ἵππων, καὶ δὴ καὶ τοισίδ' ἔτι πλέω θύουσι ἢ τοῖσι ἄλλοισι θεοῖσι. [3] ὅσους ἂν τῶν πολεμίων ζωγρήσωσι, ἀπὸ τῶν ἑκατὸν ἀνδρῶν ἄνδρα θύουσι τρόπῳ οὐ τῷ αὐτῷ καὶ τὰ πρόβατα, ἀλλ' ἑτεροίῳ· ἐπεὰν γὰρ οἶνον ἐπισπείσωσι κατὰ τῶν κεφαλέων, ἀποσφάζουσι τοὺς ἀνθρώπους ἐς ἄγγος καὶ ἔπειτα ἀνενείκαντες ἄνω ἐπὶ τὸν ὄγκον τῶν φρυγάνων καταχέουσι τὸ αἷμα τοῦ ἀκινάκεος. [4] ἄνω μὲν δὴ φορέουσι τοῦτο, κάτω δὲ παρὰ τὸ ἱρὸν ποιεῦσι τάδε· τῶν ἀποσφαγέντων ἀνδρῶν τοὺς δεξιοὺς ὤμους πάντας ἀποταμόντες σὺν τῇσι χερσὶ ἐς τὸν ἠέρα ἱεῖσι καὶ ἔπειτα καὶ τὰ ἄλλα ἀπέρξαντες ἱρήια ἀπαλλάσσονται· χεὶρ δὲ τῇ ἂν πέσῃ κέεται καὶ χωρὶς ὁ νεκρός.

4.62.1

ἵδρυται Perfect, indicative, passive, 3rd, singular of ἐσιδρύω (= εἰσιδρύω).

συννενέαται = συννενήνται. Perfect, indicative, passive, 3rd, plural of συννέω.

ἐπὶ σταδίους τρεῖς In a note in Landmark *ad* 4.62.1, this is converted to 580 yards.

μῆκος, εὖρος, ὕψος Accusatives of respect.

τῶν κώλων "Sides."

ἐπιβατόν Supply ἐστί.

4.62.2

φρυγάνων Genitive case after ἐπινέουσι.

ὑπονοστέει "[The mound] shrinks."

4.62.3

τρόπῳ οὐ τῷ αὐτῷ καὶ τὰ πρόβατα "Not in the same way that they sacrifice cattle."

ἐπεάν = ἐπειδάν.

ἐπισπείσωσι Aorist, subjunctive, active, 3rd, plural of ἐπισπένδω.

ἀνενείκαντες "Having poured." Aorist, active, masculine, nominative, plural participle of ἀναφέρω.

τοῦ ἀκινάκεω Genitive case after καταχέουσι.

4.62.4

ἀποσφαγέντων Aorist, passive, masculine, genitive, plural participle of ἀποσφάζω.

ἀπέρξαντες "Having completed."

 CB

4.71.1-5 The Burial Ceremonies for Scythian Kings

Nowhere in this passage does Herodotus state that he actually witnessed the funeral ceremonies he describes here, and so it would be fair to surmise that the entire description was based on the reports of his informants. Even so, modern writers agree that this account is mostly accurate: "There are many large burial mounds in the former Scythian territory whose interiors, as exposed by archaeologists, support Herodotus' description, including the remains of animals and servants which were slain and buried with the king" (note in Landmark *ad* 4.71.5). The characteristic reporting style of Herodotus is also on display here: note the way he refrains from making any comment about customs which were surely alien to his Greek cultural sensibilities.

ταφαὶ δὲ τῶν βασιλέων ἐν Γέρροισί εἰσι ἐς ὃ ὁ Βορυσθένης ἐστὶ προσπλωτός. ἐνθαῦτα, ἐπεὰν σφι ἀποθάνῃ ὁ βασιλεύς, ὄρυγμα γῆς μέγα ὀρύσσουσι τετράγωνον, ἕτοιμον δὲ τοῦτο ποιήσαντες ἀναλαμβάνουσι τὸν νεκρόν, κατακεκηρωμένον μὲν τὸ σῶμα, τὴν δὲ νηδὺν ἀνασχισθεῖσαν καὶ καθαρθεῖσαν, πλέην κυπέρου κεκομμένου καὶ θυμιήματος καὶ σελίνου σπέρματος καὶ ἀννήσου, συνερραμμένην ὀπίσω, καὶ κομίζουσι ἐν ἁμάξῃ ἐς ἄλλο ἔθνος. [2] οἳ δὲ ἂν παραδέξωνται κομισθέντα τὸν νεκρόν, ποιεῦσι τά περ οἱ βασιλήιοι Σκύθαι· τοῦ ὠτὸς ἀποτάμνονται, τρίχας περικείρονται, βραχίονας περιτάμνονται, μέτωπον καὶ ῥῖνα καταμύσσονται, διὰ τῆς ἀριστερῆς χειρὸς ὀιστοὺς διαβυνέονται. [3] ἐνθεῦτεν δὲ κομίζουσι ἐν τῇ ἁμάξῃ τοῦ βασιλέος τὸν νέκυν ἐς ἄλλο ἔθνος τῶν ἄρχουσι· οἱ δέ σφι ἕπονται ἐς τοὺς πρότερον ἦλθον. ἐπεὰν δὲ πάντας περιέλθωσι τὸν νέκυν κομίζοντες, ἐν Γέρροισι ἔσχατα κατοικημένοισί εἰσι τῶν ἐθνέων τῶν ἄρχουσι καὶ ἐν τῇσι ταφῇσι. [4] καὶ ἔπειτα, ἐπεὰν θέωσι τὸν νέκυν ἐν τῇσι θήκῃσι ἐπὶ στιβάδος, παραπήξαντες αἰχμὰς ἔνθεν καὶ ἔνθεν τοῦ νεκροῦ ξύλα ὑπερτείνουσι καὶ ἔπειτα ῥιψὶ καταστεγάζουσι, ἐν δὲ τῇ λοιπῇ εὐρυχωρίῃ τῆς θήκης τῶν παλλακέων τε μίαν ἀποπνίξαντες θάπτουσι καὶ τὸν οἰνοχόον καὶ μάγειρον καὶ ἱπποκόμον καὶ διήκονον καὶ ἀγγελιηφόρον καὶ ἵππους καὶ τῶν ἄλλων πάντων ἀπαρχὰς καὶ φιάλας χρυσέας· ἀργύρῳ δὲ οὐδὲν οὐδὲ χαλκῷ χρέωνται. [5] ταῦτα δὲ ποιήσαντες χοῦσι πάντες χῶμα μέγα, ἁμιλλώμενοι καὶ προθυμεόμενοι ὡς μέγιστον ποιῆσαι.

4.71.1

ἐν Γέρροισί εἰσι ἐς ὃ ὁ Βορυσθένης ἐστὶ προσπλωτός The location of the territory of the Gerroi is not known; the Borysthenes is the Dnieper River (cf. the maps in Landmark *ad* 4.53)

ἐπεάν = ἐπειδάν.

κατακεκηρωμένον "Covered with wax."

ἀνασχισθεῖσαν Aorist, passive, feminine, accusative, singular participle of ἀνασχίζω. "Having been opened up."

πλέην = πλέαν.

κυπέρου κεκομμένου "Crushed galingale," which is a kind of ginger. The other three ingredients are incense, seed of celery, and seed of anise. Cf. note in Landmark *ad* 4.71.1

συνερραμμένην Perfect, passive, feminine, accusative, singular participle of συρράπτω.

4.71.2

οἱ βασιλήιοι Σκύθαι These "Royal Scythians" seem to have had special status and privileges.

ἀποτάμνονται = ἀποτέμνονται.

βραχίονας περιτάμνονται "They make cuts all over their arms."

4.71.3

οἱ δέ σφι ἕπονται ἐς τοὺς πρότερον ἦλθον "Those to whom the procession came earlier follow along."

ἔσχατα κατοικημένοισι…τῶν ἐθνέων τῶν ἄρχουσι "Who live the furthest away of the people whom they [the Scythians] rule."

4.71.4

θέωσι = θῶσι.

παραπήξαντες Aorist, active, masculine, nominative, plural participle of παραπήγνυμι.

ὑπερτείνουσι Takes the genitive and the accusative (τοῦ νεκροῦ ξύλα).

μάγειρον "Cook."

τῶν ἄλλων πάντων ἀπαρχὰς "The first-fruit offerings of all the others."

☙

4.94.1-4 The Religion of the Thracian Getai ("Kill the Messenger")

In telling the story of Darius' march through Thrace, Herodotus takes a detour from the main narrative and describes the religion of the Thracian Getai. In the preceding chapter (4.93), the Getai were described as being the "most brave and the most just of all the people of Thrace," whose aggressive behavior towards the Persians led to their enslavement. The tale of Salmoxis, the "daimon" (an intermediary between gods and humans) is told with a touch of irony, but, as usual, without any overt comments. Herodotus dismisses the rationalizing story of the Hellespontine Greeks (4.95), whereby Salmoxis was but a mere mortal who had disappeared for three years in an underground chamber, only to reappear in the fourth year, thereby convincing his fellow Thracians that he was indeed immortal. The concluding section of this chapter should be of particular interest to students of Comparative Religion.

ἀθανατίζουσι δὲ τόνδε τὸν τρόπον· οὔτε ἀποθνήσκειν ἑωυτοὺς νομίζουσι ἰέναι τε τὸν ἀπολλύμενον παρὰ Σάλμοξιν δαίμονα· οἱ δὲ αὐτῶν τὸν αὐτὸν τοῦτον ὀνομάζουσι Γεβελέϊζιν.[2] διὰ πεντετηρίδος τε τὸν πάλῳ λαχόντα αἰεὶ σφέων αὐτῶν ἀποπέμπουσι ἄγγελον παρὰ τὸν Σάλμοξιν, ἐντελλόμενοι τῶν ἂν ἑκάστοτε δέωνται. πέμπουσι δὲ ὧδε· οἱ μὲν αὐτῶν ταχθέντες ἀκόντια τρία ἔχουσι, ἄλλοι δὲ διαλαβόντες τοῦ ἀποπεμπομένου παρὰ τὸν Σάλμοξιν τὰς χεῖρας καὶ τοὺς πόδας, ἀνακινήσαντες αὐτὸν μετέωρον ῥίπτουσι ἐς τὰς λόγχας. ἢν μὲν δὴ ἀποθάνῃ ἀναπαρείς, τοῖσι δὲ ἵλεος ὁ θεὸς δοκέει εἶναι· [3] ἢν δὲ μὴ ἀποθάνῃ, αἰτιῶνται αὐτὸν τὸν ἄγγελον, φάμενοί μιν ἄνδρα κακὸν εἶναι, αἰτιησάμενοι δὲ τοῦτον ἄλλον ἀποπέμπουσι· ἐντέλλονται δὲ ἔτι ζῶντι. [4] οὗτοι οἱ αὐτοὶ Θρήικες καὶ πρὸς βροντήν τε καὶ ἀστραπὴν τοξεύοντες ἄνω πρὸς τὸν οὐρανὸν ἀπειλέουσι τῷ θεῷ, οὐδένα ἄλλον θεὸν νομίζοντες εἶναι εἰ μὴ τὸν σφέτερον.

4.94.1

ἀθανατίζουσι "They [the Getai] think themselves to be immortal."

Οὔτε...τε Here, the equivalent of οὐ...ἀλλά.

τὸν ἀπολλύμενον "Once he has departed from this world."

4.94.2

διὰ πεντετηρίδος "Every fifth year."

ἐντελλόμενοι τῶν ἂν ἑκάστοτε δέωνται "Giving instructions on each occasion as to what they required."

ταχθέντες Aorist, passive, masculine, nominative, plural participle of τάσσω.

ἀναπαρείς Aorist, passive, masculine, nominative, singular participle of ἀναπείρω.

4.94.3

ἐντέλλονται δὲ ἔτι ζῶντι "They give their instructions to him while he is still alive."

4.94.4

ἀπειλέουσι "Speak threateningly."

C8

4.111.1-2 Scythians Encounter Amazons, Part I

The storyteller Herodotus takes center stage here. Charmingly told, the tale is about the Scythians meeting the Amazons in battle and trying their best to learn more about their mysterious opponents.

οἱ δὲ Σκύθαι οὐκ εἶχον συμβαλέσθαι τὸ πρῆγμα· οὔτε γὰρ φωνὴν οὔτε ἐσθῆτα οὔτε τὸ ἔθνος ἐγίνωσκον, ἀλλ' ἐν θώματι ἦσαν ὁκόθεν ἔλθοιεν, ἐδόκεον δ' αὐτὰς εἶναι ἄνδρας τὴν πρώτην ἡλικίην ἔχοντας, μάχην τε δὴ πρὸς αὐτὰς ἐποιεῦντο. ἐκ δὲ τῆς μάχης τῶν νεκρῶν ἐκράτησαν οἱ Σκύθαι καὶ οὕτως ἔγνωσαν ἐούσας γυναῖκας. [2] βουλευομένοισι ὦν αὐτοῖσι ἔδοξε κτείνειν μὲν οὐδενὶ τρόπῳ ἔτι αὐτάς, ἑωυτῶν δὲ τοὺς νεωτάτους ἀποπέμψαι ἐς αὐτάς, πλῆθος εἰκάσαντας ὅσαι περ ἐκεῖναι ἦσαν· τούτους δὲ στρατοπεδεύεσθαι πλησίον ἐκεινέων καὶ ποιεῖν τὰ περ ἂν καὶ ἐκεῖναι ποιέωσι· ἢν δὲ αὐτοὺς διώκωσι, μάχεσθαι μὲν μή, ὑποφεύγειν δέ· ἐπεὰν δὲ παύσωνται, ἐλθόντας αὐτοὺς πλησίον στρατοπεδεύεσθαι. ταῦτα ἐβουλεύσαντο οἱ Σκύθαι βουλόμενοι ἐξ αὐτέων παῖδας ἐκγενήσεσθαι. ἀποπεμφθέντες δὲ οἱ νεηνίσκοι ἐποίευν τὰ ἐντεταλμένα.

4.111.1

οὐκ εἶχον συμβαλέσθαι "Were not able to understand ."

τὸ πρῆγμα That is, the behavior of the Amazons, whom the Scythians had encountered only for the first time.

ὁκόθεν = ὁπόθεν.

τὴν πρώτην ἡλικίην ἔχοντας "Being in the prime of their lives."

4.111.2

ὦν = οὖν.

ἑωυτῶν = ἑαυτῶν.

μάχεσθαι μὲν μή "[They were told] not to fight."

νεηνίσκοι = νεανίσκοι.

ἐντεταλμένα Perfect, passive, neuter, accusative, plural participle of ἐντέλλω.

C8

4.112.1, 4.113.1-3 Scythians Encounter Amazons, Part II

The tale of the Scythian-Amazon encounter takes a strange twist and becomes a kind of a love story. Here and elsewhere, we see how Herodotus can be both a writer of consummate skill, as well as a dispassionate scientist who carefully collects field data for his inquiries.

ἐπεὶ δὲ ἔμαθον αὐτοὺς αἱ Ἀμαζόνες ἐπ' οὐδεμιῇ δηλήσι ἀπιγμένους, ἔων χαίρειν· προσεχώρεον δὲ πλησιαιτέρω τὸ στρατόπεδον τῷ στρατοπέδῳ ἐπ' ἡμέρῃ ἑκάστῃ. εἶχον δὲ οὐδὲν οὐδ' οἱ νεηνίσκοι, ὥσπερ αἱ Ἀμαζόνες, εἰ μὴ τὰ ὅπλα καὶ τοὺς ἵππους· ἀλλὰ ζόην ἔζωον τὴν αὐτὴν ἐκείνῃσι, θηρεύοντές τε καὶ ληιζόμενοι.

113.1-3

ἐποίευν δὲ αἱ Ἀμαζόνες ἐς τὴν μεσαμβρίην τοιόνδε· ἐγίνοντο σποράδες κατὰ μίαν τε καὶ δύο, πρόσω δὴ ἀπ' ἀλλήλεων ἐς εὐμαρείην ἀποσκιδνάμεναι. μαθόντες δὲ καὶ οἱ Σκύθαι ἐποίευν τὠυτὸ τοῦτο. καί τις μουνωθεισέων τινὶ αὐτέων ἐνεχρίμπτετο, [2] καὶ ἡ Ἀμαζὼν οὐκ ἀπωθέετο ἀλλὰ περιεῖδε χρήσασθαι. καὶ φωνῆσαι μὲν οὐκ εἶχε (οὐ γὰρ συνίεσαν ἀλλήλων), τῇ δὲ χειρὶ ἔφραζε ἐς τὴν ὑστεραίην ἐλθεῖν ἐς τὠυτὸ χωρίον καὶ ἕτερον ἄγειν, σημαίνουσα δύο γενέσθαι καὶ αὐτὴ ἑτέρην ἄξειν. [3] ὁ δὲ νεηνίσκος ἐπεὶ ἀπῆλθε, ἔλεξε ταῦτα πρὸς τοὺς λοιπούς· τῇ δὲ δευτεραίῃ ἦλθε ἐς τὸ χωρίον αὐτός τε οὗτος καὶ ἕτερον ἦγε, καὶ τὴν Ἀμαζόνα εὗρε δευτέρην αὐτὴν ὑπομένουσαν. οἱ δὲ λοιποὶ νεηνίσκοι ὡς ἐπύθοντο ταῦτα, καὶ αὐτοὶ ἐκτιλώσαντο τὰς λοιπὰς τῶν Ἀμαζόνων.

4.112.1

ἐπ' οὐδεμιῇ δηλήσι "With no harmful intent."

ἀπιγμένους = ἀφιγμένους Perfect, middle, masculine, accusative, plural participle of ἀπικνέομαι (= ἀφικνέομαι).

ἔων χαίρειν "They let them be."

ἔων Imperfect, indicative, active, 3rd, plural of ἐάω.

προσεχώρεον...τὸ στρατόπεδον "Those in the camp kept approaching." The verb takes here the dative case.

νεηνίσκοι = νεανίσκοι.

ἐκείνῃσι = ἐκείναις.

4.113.1

μεσαμβρίην = μεσημβρίαν.

τοιόνδε "In the following way."

ἐγίνοντο = ἐγίγνοντο.

ἐς εὐμαρείην "For the purpose of relieving themselves."

τὠυτό Crasis (two words combined into one) for τὸ αὐτό.

ἐποίευν = ἐποίεον.

αὐτέων = αὐτῶν.

4.113.2

περιεῖδε Aorist, indicative, active, 3rd, singular of περιοράω.

χρήσασθαι "To enjoy [to have sex with]." Aorist, middle infinitive of χράομαι.

οὐ γὰρ συνίεσαν ἀλλήλων "For they did not understand one another."

ἐς τὴν ὑστεραίην "On the next day."

4.113.3

ἐπύθοντο Aorist, indicative, middle, 3rd, plural of πυνθάνομαι.

ἐκτιλώσαντο Aorist, indicative, middle, 3rd, plural of κτιλόω.

ℭℨ

4.114.1-4 Scythians Encounter Amazons, Part III

The Scythian and Amazon alliance takes hold. Herodotus invents a dialogue in which the Scythian men and the Amazon women agree to have the men bring their "dowry" and join the Amazons, since Amazon women could never adapt to the Scythian way of life. (That men, and not women, should bring a dowry to a marriage is, of course, in stark contrast to the Greek way.) In the next two chapters (4.115, 4.116), Herodotus explains that, through this arrangement between the Scythians and the Amazons, the tribe of the Sauromatai was formed. (Cf. ALC *ad* 4.114, where the origins of the Amazon myth are explored.)

μετὰ δὲ συμμίξαντες τὰ στρατόπεδα οἴκεον ὁμοῦ, γυναῖκα ἔχων ἕκαστος ταύτην τῇ τὸ πρῶτον συνεμίχθη. τὴν δὲ φωνὴν τὴν μὲν τῶν γυναικῶν οἱ ἄνδρες οὐκ ἐδυνέατο μαθεῖν, τὴν δὲ τῶν ἀνδρῶν αἱ γυναῖκες συνέλαβον. [2] ἐπεὶ δὲ συνῆκαν ἀλλήλων, ἔλεξαν πρὸς τὰς Ἀμαζόνας τάδε οἱ ἄνδρες· "ἡμῖν εἰσὶ μὲν τοκέες, εἰσὶ δὲ κτήσιες. νῦν ὦν μηκέτι πλεῦνα χρόνον ζόην τοιήνδε ἔχωμεν, ἀλλ' ἀπελθόντες ἐς τὸ πλῆθος διαιτώμεθα· γυναῖκας δὲ ἕξομεν ὑμέας καὶ οὐδαμὰς ἄλλας." αἱ δὲ πρὸς ταῦτα ἔλεξαν τάδε· [3] "ἡμεῖς οὐκ ἂν δυναίμεθα οἰκεῖν μετὰ τῶν ὑμετέρων γυναικῶν· οὐ γὰρ τὰ αὐτὰ νόμαια ἡμῖν τε κἀκείνῃσί ἐστι. ἡμεῖς μὲν τοξεύομέν τε καὶ ἀκοντίζομεν καὶ ἱππαζόμεθα, ἔργα δὲ γυναικήια οὐκ ἐμάθομεν· αἱ δὲ ὑμέτεραι γυναῖκες τούτων μὲν οὐδὲν τῶν ἡμεῖς κατελέξαμεν ποιεῦσι, ἔργα δὲ γυναικήια ἐργάζονται μένουσαι ἐν τῇσι ἁμάξῃσι, οὔτ᾽ ἐπὶ θήρην ἰοῦσαι οὔτε ἄλλῃ οὐδαμῇ. [4] οὐκ ἂν ὦν δυναίμεθα ἐκείνῃσι συμφέρεσθαι. ἀλλ᾽ εἰ βούλεσθε γυναῖκας ἔχειν ἡμέας καὶ δοκέειν εἶναι δίκαιοι, ἐλθόντες παρὰ τοὺς τοκέας ἀπολάχετε τῶν κτημάτων τὸ μέρος, καὶ ἔπειτα ἐλθόντες οἰκέωμεν ἐπὶ ἡμέων αὐτῶν.” ἐπείθοντο καὶ ἐποίησαν ταῦτα οἱ νεηνίσκοι.

4.114.1

μετά Adverbial.

συμμίξαντες Aorist, active, masculine, nominative, plural participle of συμμίγνυμι.

ὁμοῦ “Together.”

τήν Supply φωνήν.

4.114.2

συνῆκαν Aorist, indicative, active, 3rd, plural of συνίημι. “They understood.”

κτήσιες = κτήσεις. “Possessions.”

ὦν = οὖν.

μηκέτι πλεῦνα χρόνον “Any longer.”

πλεῦνα = πλείωνα (πλέονα).

ἐς τὸ πλῆθος “Unto the greater part [of our people].”

4.114.3

κἀκείνῃσι Crasis (two words combined into one) of καὶ ἐκείνῃσι (= ἐκείναις).

οὐδὲν τῶν ἡμεῖς κατελέξαμεν “None of the things we have mentioned.”

4.114.4

συμφέρεσθαι “To co-exist.”

ἀπολάχετε Aorist, imperative, active, 2nd, plural of ἀπολαγχάνω.

ἐπὶ ἡμέων αὐτῶν “By ourselves [apart from the rest].”

νεηνίσκοι = νεανίσκοι.

☙

4.126.1, 4.127.1-4 A Scythian Tribe Defies Darius

A stirring tale of Scythian resistance to Persian oppression. The two speeches in this passage, both of which are, of course, made up, help to solidify and finalize the positions of the Persians and Scythians in their ongoing conflict. The speech of the Persian delegate perfectly captures the imperious nature of the Persians, especially when he demands that water and earth (the tokens of submission to Persian power) be offered even before any talks could take place. The Scythian reply puts into focus the Scythian way of (nomadic) life, in which freedom was non-negotiable. Later in Book IV (especially 4.137), Herodotus will place the Scythian devotion to freedom into sharp contrast with the way certain Ionian Greeks dealt with Persian intimidation.

4.126.1

ὡς δὲ πολλὸν τοῦτο ἐγίνετο καὶ οὐκ ἐπαύετο, πέμψας Δαρεῖος ἱππέα παρὰ τὸν Σκυθέων βασιλέα Ἰδάνθυρσον ἔλεγε τάδε· "δαιμόνιε ἀνδρῶν, τί φεύγεις αἰεί, ἐξεόν τοι τῶνδε τὰ ἕτερα ποιέειν; εἰ μὲν γὰρ ἀξιόχρεος δοκέεις εἶναι σεωυτῷ τοῖσι ἐμοῖσι πρήγμασι ἀντιωθῆναι, σὺ δὲ στάς τε καὶ παυσάμενος πλάνης μάχεσθαι· εἰ δὲ συγγινώσκεαι εἶναι ἥσσων, σὺ δὲ καὶ οὕτω παυσάμενος τοῦ δρόμου δεσπότῃ τῷ σῷ δῶρα φέρων γῆν τε καὶ ὕδωρ ἐλθὲ ἐς λόγους."

4.127.1-4

πρὸς ταῦτα ὁ Σκυθέων βασιλεὺς Ἰδάνθυρσος λέγει τάδε· "οὕτω τὸ ἐμὸν ἔχει, ὦ Πέρσα· ἐγὼ οὐδένα κω ἀνθρώπων δείσας ἔφυγον οὔτε πρότερον οὔτε νῦν σὲ φεύγω· οὐδέ τι νεώτερόν εἰμι ποιήσας νῦν ἢ καὶ ἐν εἰρήνῃ ἐώθεα ποιέειν. [2] ὅ τι δὲ οὐκ αὐτίκα μάχομαί τοι, ἐγὼ καὶ τοῦτο σημανέω· ἡμῖν οὔτε ἄστεα οὔτε γῆ πεφυτευμένη ἔστι, τῶν πέρι δείσαντες μὴ ἁλῷ, ἢ καρῇ ταχύτερον ἂν ὑμῖν συμμίσγοιμεν ἐς μάχην· εἰ δὲ δέοι πάντως ἐς τοῦτο κατὰ τάχος ἀπικνέεσθαι, τυγχάνουσι ἡμῖν ἐόντες τάφοι πατρώιοι. [3] φέρετε, τούτους ἀνευρόντες συγχέειν πειρᾶσθε αὐτούς, καὶ γνώσεσθε τότε εἴτε ὑμῖν μαχησόμεθα περὶ τῶν τάφων εἴτε καὶ οὐ μαχησόμεθα. πρότερον δέ, ἢν μὴ ἡμέας λόγος αἱρῇ, οὐ συμμίξομέν τοι. [4] ἀμφὶ μὲν μάχῃ τοσαῦτα εἰρήσθω, δεσπότας δὲ ἐμοὺς ἐγὼ Δία τε νομίζω τὸν ἐμὸν πρόγονον καὶ Ἱστίην τὴν Σκυθέων βασίλειαν μούνους εἶναι. σοὶ δὲ ἀντὶ μὲν δώρων γῆς τε καὶ ὕδατος δῶρα πέμψω τοιαῦτα οἷα σοὶ πρέπει ἐλθεῖν, ἀντὶ δὲ τοῦ ὅτι δεσπότης ἔφησας εἶναι ἐμός, κλαίειν λέγω." τοῦτό ἐστι ἡ ἀπὸ Σκυθέων ῥῆσις.

4.126.1

τοῦτο The Scythian tactic of fleeing the enemy and then attacking them.
ἐγίνετο = ἐγίγνετο.
δαιμόνιε ἀνδρῶν "Sir."
ἐξεόν "Since it was possible."
ἀξιόχρεος = ἀξιόχρεως.
ἀντιωθῆναι Aorist, passive infinitive of ἀντιόομαι.
συγγινώσκεαι εἶναι "Are aware that you are…."

4.127.1

οὕτω τὸ ἐμὸν ἔχει "This is the way things are with me."
ἐώθεα Pluperfect, indicative, active, 1st, singular of ἔθω.

4.127.2

περὶ Preposition follows its object (τῶν). Note the position of the accent.

ἁλῷ Aorist, subjunctive, active, 3rd, singular of ἁλίσκομαι.

καρῇ Aorist, subjunctive, passive, 3rd, singular of κείρω. "Be ravaged."

συμμίσγοιμεν Present, optative, active, 1st, plural of συμμίγνυμι.

δέοι Present, optative, active, 3rd, singular of δέω.

4.127.3

συγχέειν "To demolish." Present, active, infinitive of συγχέω.

ἢν μὴ ἡμέας λόγος αἱρῇ "Unless we think it reasonable."

4.127.4

ἀμφὶ μὲν μάχῃ τοσαῦτα εἰρήσθω "That's all that needs to be said about joining in battle."

τοιαῦτα οἷα σοὶ πρέπει ἐλθεῖν "Such as are fitting to come to you."

ἀντὶ δὲ τοῦ ὅτι δεσπότης ἔφησας εἶναι ἐμός "In answer to your claim that you are my master."

ἔφησας Aorist, indicative, active, 2nd, singular of φημί.

☙

4.137.1-3 The Ionian Tyrants at the Bridge over the Danube, Part I

Even if for no other reason, this passage is important as it introduces Miltiades, best known as the general who led the Athenian infantry to victory at Marathon in 490 B.C. (cf. 6.109). In his earlier career as tyrant of the Hellespontine Chersonese (cf. map in Landmark *ad* 4.138), he was part of the Ionian force which accompanied Darius on his march to Scythia and which stayed behind to safeguard a bridge which they (the Ionians) had constructed across the Danube (Ister). In the view of some scholars (cf. HW *ad* 4.137), Herodotus' description of the events leading up to and following the building of this Danube bridge is historically suspect.

πρὸς ταῦτα Ἴωνες ἐβουλεύοντο. Μιλτιάδεω μὲν τοῦ Ἀθηναίου, στρατηγέοντος καὶ τυραννεύοντος Χερσονησιτέων τῶν ἐν Ἑλλησπόντῳ, ἦν γνώμη πείθεσθαι Σκύθῃσι καὶ ἐλευθεροῦν Ἰωνίην, [2] Ἱστιαίου δὲ τοῦ Μιλησίου ἐναντίη ταύτῃ, λέγοντος ὡς νῦν μὲν διὰ Δαρεῖον ἕκαστος αὐτῶν τυραννεύει πόλιος, τῆς Δαρείου δὲ δυνάμιος καταιρεθείσης οὔτε αὐτὸς Μιλησίων οἷός τε ἔσεσθαι ἄρχειν οὔτε ἄλλον οὐδένα οὐδαμῶν· βουλήσεσθαι γὰρ ἑκάστην τῶν πολίων δημοκρατέεσθαι μᾶλλον ἢ τυραννεύεσθαι. [3] Ἱστιαίου δὲ γνώμην ταύτην ἀποδεικνυμένου αὐτίκα πάντες ἦσαν τετραμμένοι πρὸς ταύτην τὴν γνώμην, πρότερον τὴν Μιλτιάδεω αἱρεόμενοι.

4.137.1

πρὸς ταῦτα "In response to these things." That is, in response to the pleas of the Scythians that the Ionian tyrants, who had been left behind by Darius to guard the bridge over the Ister, destroy the bridge and leave the Persians in the lurch.

Μιλτιάδεω μὲν τοῦ Ἀθηναίου For the story of the family of Miltiades and their power base in the Chersonese (the long peninsula on the northern side of the Hellespont), see 6.34-39.

ἐλευθεροῦν Present, active, infinitive of ἐλευθερόω.

4.137.2

Ἱστιαίου δὲ τοῦ Μιλησίου Histiaios was the father-in-law of Aristagoras of Miletus, who began the Ionian Revolt. Histiaios was comfortable cooperating with Darius throughout much of his public life.

ἐναντίη Modifies γνώμη.

τῆς Δαρείου δὲ δυνάμιος καταιρεθείσης Genitive absolute construction.

δυνάμιος Genitive case.

οἷός τε ἔσεσθαι ἄρχειν "Would be able to rule."

4.137.3

Ἱστιαίου δὲ γνώμην ταύτην ἀποδεικνυμένου Genitive absolute construction.

πρότερον τὴν Μιλτιάδεω αἱρεόμενοι "Though initially they had favored Miltiades' view."

☙

4.139.1-3 Ionian Tyrants at the Danube Bridge, Part II

In 4.138, Herodotus mentions by name all of the Ionian tyrants who agreed with Histiaios' proposal that the Danube Bridge NOT be destroyed. Even worse from the standpoint of their medizing (i.e., yielding to the Persians), these tyrants are described as men who were respected by the Persian King. The speech that Herodotus puts into the mouth of Histiaios in this chapter underscores the treachery of the Ionians towards the Scythians, who had placed their trust in them. It also shows that the Ionians were very much aware of what was at stake when they were deciding whether to destroy or save the Danube Bridge.

οὗτοι ὦν ἐπείτε τὴν Ἱστιαίου αἱρέοντο γνώμην, ἔδοξέ σφι πρὸς ταύτῃ τάδε ἔργα τε καὶ ἔπεα προσθεῖναι, τῆς μὲν γεφύρης λύειν τὰ κατὰ τοὺς Σκύθας ἐόντα, λύειν δὲ ὅσον τόξευμα ἐξικνέεται, ἵνα καὶ ποιεῖν τι δοκέωσι ποιεῦντες μηδὲν καὶ οἱ Σκύθαι μὴ πειρῷατο βιώμενοι καὶ βουλόμενοι διαβῆναι τὸν Ἴστρον κατὰ τὴν γέφυραν, εἰπεῖν τε λύοντας τῆς γεφύρης τὸ ἐς τὴν Σκυθικὴν ἔχον ὡς πάντα ποιήσουσι τὰ Σκύθησί ἐστι ἐν ἡδονῇ. [2] ταῦτα μὲν προσέθηκαν τῇ γνώμῃ, μετὰ δὲ ἐκ πάντων ὑπεκρίνατο Ἱστιαῖος τάδε λέγων· Ἄνδρες Σκύθαι, χρηστὰ ἥκετε φέροντες καὶ ἐς καιρὸν ἐπείγεσθε· καὶ τά τε ἀπ᾽ ὑμέων ἡμῖν, χρηστῶς ὁδοῦται καὶ τὰ ἀπ᾽ ἡμέων ἐς ὑμέας ἐπιτηδέως

ὑπηρετέεται. ὡς γὰρ ὁρᾶτε, καὶ λύομεν τὸν πόρον καὶ προθυμίην πᾶσαν
ἔξομεν, θέλοντες εἶναι ἐλεύθεροι. [3] ἐν ᾧ δὲ ἡμεῖς τάδε λύομεν, ὑμέας
καιρός ἐστι δίζησθαι ἐκείνους, εὑρόντας δὲ ὑπέρ τε ἡμέων καὶ ὑμέων αὐτῶν
τείσασθαι οὕτως ὡς κείνους πρέπει."

4.139.1

ὦν = οὖν.

πρὸς ταύτῃ τάδε ἔργα τε καὶ ἔπεα προσθεῖναι "To add deeds and words to this [resolution]."

τῆς μὲν γεφύρης λύειν τὰ κατὰ τοὺς Σκύθας ἐόντα "To destroy the Scythian side of the bridge."

λύειν δὲ ὅσον τόξευμα ἐξικνέεται "To destroy as far as an arrow travels."

πειρῷατο = πειρῷντο. Present, optative, middle, 3rd, plural of πειράω.

τὰ Σκύθῃσί ἐστι ἐν ἡδονῇ "Things that are to the advantage of the Scythians."

4.139.2

ἐκ πάντων "From among all [the tyrants]."

χρηστὰ ἥκετε φέροντες "You have come bearing useful advice."

ὁδοῦται Literally, "are being put on the road." Idiomatically, "are being put to use."

4.139.3

τίσασθαι Aorist, middle infinitive of τίνω.

ꙮ

4.141, 4.142 Ionian Tyrants at the Danube Bridge, Part III

These two brief chapters are noteworthy for the haunting and evocative scene in which an Egyptian, endowed with a very loud voice, saves the Persians from imminent destruction, and for the strong indictment of the Ionian tyrants who betrayed the trust of the Scythians.

4.141.

ἦν δὲ περὶ Δαρεῖον ἀνὴρ Αἰγύπτιος φωνέων μέγιστον ἀνθρώπων· τοῦτον
τὸν ἄνδρα καταστάντα ἐπὶ τοῦ χείλεος τοῦ Ἴστρου ἐκέλευε Δαρεῖος καλέειν
Ἱστιαῖον Μιλήσιον. ὁ μὲν δὴ ἐποίεε ταῦτα, Ἱστιαῖος δὲ ἐπακούσας τῷ πρώτῳ
κελεύσματι τάς τε νέας ἁπάσας παρεῖχε διαπορθμεύειν τὴν στρατιὴν καὶ
τὴν γέφυραν ἔζευξε.

4.142.

Πέρσαι μὲν ὦν οὕτω ἐκφεύγουσι, Σκύθαι δὲ διζήμενοι καὶ τὸ δεύτερον ἥμαρτον τῶν Περσέων, καὶ τοῦτο μέν, ὡς ἐόντας Ἴωνας ἐλευθέρους, κακίστους τε καὶ ἀνανδροτάτους κρίνουσι εἶναι ἁπάντων ἀνθρώπων, τοῦτο δέ, ὡς δούλων Ἰώνων τὸν λόγον ποιεύμενοι, ἀνδράποδα φιλοδέσποτά φασι εἶναι καὶ ἄδρηστα μάλιστα. ταῦτα μὲν δὴ Σκύθησι ἐς Ἴωνας ἀπέρριπται.

4.141

χείλεος Genitive, singular of χεῖλος. "Shore."

ἐποίεε = ἐποίει.

ἐπακούσας τῷ πρώτῳ κελεύσματι The participle ἐπακούσας takes the dative in τῷ πρώτῳ κελεύσματι, as Histiaios both "heard" and "obeyed" the order.

τάς τε νέας ἁπάσας παρεῖχε διαπορθμεύειν τὴν στρατιὴν καὶ τὴν γέφυραν ἔζευξε Apparently, some Ionian ships were immediately available to ferry Darius and his personal guards across the river, while other ships were put in place to complete the chain of boats that had constituted the bridge and had earlier been disassembled.

4.142

ὦν = οὖν

διζήμενοι καὶ τὸ δεύτερον ἥμαρτον τῶν Περσέων "Failed for a second time to find the Persians."

καὶ τοῦτο μέν, ὡς ἐόντας Ἴωνας ἐλευθέρους,... "And, to begin with, they consider the Ionians, who are supposed to be free, to be the most base and cowardly of human beings. Then, when it comes to the Ionians as slaves, they [the Scythians] say that they are the most devoted of slaves and the least likely to run away."

ଓଃ

4.172.1-4 Some Libyan Customs

Starting with 4.148, Herodotus' inquiries take him to North Africa and the various Libyan tribes who lived there. The theme of Persian conquest is not quite as dominant as it was in the Scythian section of Book 4, but as digressions in the *Histories* go, this one has much to recommend it. The stories come very fast, are rarely developed, and often strain the reader's credulity, but they are never dull. As usual, Herodotus refrains from commenting on customs which probably seemed totally un-Greek and even bizarre to him.

Αὐσχισέων δὲ τούτων τὸ πρὸς ἑσπέρης ἔχονται Νασαμῶνες, ἔθνος ἐὸν πολλόν, οἳ τὸ θέρος καταλιπόντες ἐπὶ τῇ θαλάσσῃ τὰ πρόβατα ἀναβαίνουσι ἐς Αὔγιλα χῶρον ὀπωριεῦντες τοὺς φοίνικας· οἱ δὲ πολλοὶ καὶ ἀμφιλαφέες πεφύκασι, πάντες ἐόντες καρποφόροι. τοὺς δὲ ἀττελέβους ἐπεὰν θηρεύσωσι,

αὐήναντες πρὸς τὸν ἥλιον καταλέουσι καὶ ἔπειτα ἐπὶ γάλα ἐπιπάσσοντες
πίνουσι. [2] γυναῖκας δὲ νομίζοντες πολλὰς ἔχειν ἕκαστος ἐπίκοινον αὐτέων
τὴν μεῖξιν ποιεῦνται τρόπῳ παραπλησίῳ τῷ καὶ Μασσαγέται· ἐπεὰν σκίπωνα
προστήσωνται, μίσγονται. πρῶτον δὲ γαμέοντος Νασαμῶνος ἀνδρὸς νόμος
ἐστὶ τὴν νύμφην νυκτὶ τῇ πρώτῃ διὰ πάντων διεξελθεῖν τῶν δαιτυμόνων
μισγομένην· τῶν δὲ ὡς ἕκαστος οἱ μειχθῇ, διδοῖ δῶρον τὸ ἂν ἔχῃ φερόμενος
ἐξ οἴκου. [3] ὁρκίοισι δὲ καὶ μαντικῇ χρέωνται τοιῇδε· ὀμνύουσι μὲν τοὺς
παρὰ σφίσι ἄνδρας δικαιοτάτους καὶ ἀρίστους λεγομένους γενέσθαι, τούτους
τῶν τύμβων ἁπτόμενοι, μαντεύονται δὲ ἐπὶ τῶν προγόνων φοιτέοντες τὰ
σήματα καὶ κατευξάμενοι ἐπικατακοιμῶνται· τὸ δ᾽ ἂν ἴδῃ ἐν τῇ ὄψι ἐνύπνιον,
τούτῳ χρᾶται. [4] πίστισι δὲ τοιῇσίδε χρέωνται· ἐκ τῆς χειρὸς διδοῖ πιεῖν
καὶ αὐτὸς ἐκ τῆς τοῦ ἑτέρου πίνει· ἢν δὲ μὴ ἔχωσι ὑγρὸν μηδέν, οἱ δὲ τῆς
χαμᾶθεν σποδοῦ λαβόντες λείχουσι.

4.172.1

For the putative locations of the tribes mentioned in this section, see the map in Landmark
    ad 4.165.

ὀπωριεῦντες τοὺς φοίνικας The future participle (from ὀπωρίζω) indicates purpose. "To
    harvest dates."

ἐπεάν = ἐπειδάν.

αὐήναντες Aorist, active, masculine, nominative, plural participle of αὐαίνω.

4.172.2

ἐπίκοινον αὐτέων τὴν μεῖξιν ποιεῦνται "They regard intercourse [with their wives] as
    something to be shared [with others]."

προστήσωνται Aorist, subjunctive, passive, 3rd, plural of προΐστημι.

μίσγονται Present, indicative, passive, 3rd, plural of μίγνυμι. "They have intercourse."

πρῶτον δὲ γαμέοντος Νασαμῶνος ἀνδρὸς Genitive absolute construction.

οἱ μιχθῇ "With whom she had intercourse."

4.172.3

ὀμνύουσι μὲν τοὺς παρὰ σφίσι ἄνδρας δικαιοτάτους καὶ ἀρίστους λεγομένους γενέσθαι
    "They swear by the men who are reputed to be the most just and the best among them."

σήματα "Tombs."

κατευξάμενοι Aorist, middle, masculine, nominative, plural participle of κατεύχομαι.

τὸ δ᾽ ἂν ἴδῃ ἐν τῇ ὄψι ἐνύπνιον, τούτῳ χρᾶται "Whatever dream he sees in his sleep, this he
    regards as an oracle."

☙

4.180.1-6 The Interesting Customs of the Auseans of Libya

In a rapid-fire way, Herodotus describes the customs of the Auseans, a people who, despite their contact with the Greeks settlers of North Africa, had some very un-Greek customs. It should be noted that the "theology" that underlies this story of the Ausean maidens is typical, since it assumes that certain types of gods were universally worshipped and that only their names vary from place to place. Also worth pointing out is Herodotus' admission that he does not know something (οὐκ ἔχω εἰπεῖν). Paradoxically, this type of an admission confers added credibility on those passages where, in contrast, he claims to be in the know. Although there is a hint of criticism in Herodotus' description of the promiscuous sex practices of the Auseans (he calls them κτηνηδόν or "animal-like"), the passage is still mostly free of editorial comment. While Herodotus' notion that the Greek panoply was originally borrowed from Egyptian armor was ostensibly a mistaken one (see HW *ad* 4.180), it nevertheless lets us see a Herodotus who is quite willing to give credit to the Egyptians for their having transmitted to the Greeks a rather important feature of their civilization.

τούτων δὲ ἔχονται τῶν Μαχλύων Αὐσέες. οὗτοι δὲ καὶ οἱ Μάχλυες πέριξ τὴν Τριτωνίδα λίμνην οἰκέουσι, τὸ μέσον δέ σφι οὐρίζει ὁ Τρίτων. καὶ οἱ μὲν Μάχλυες τὰ ὀπίσω κομῶσι τῆς κεφαλῆς, οἱ δὲ Αὐσέες τὰ ἔμπροσθε. [2] ὁρτῇ δὲ ἐνιαυσίῃ Ἀθηναίης αἱ παρθένοι αὐτῶν δίχα διαστᾶσαι μάχονται πρὸς ἀλλήλας λίθοισί τε καὶ ξύλοισι, τῷ αὐθιγενέϊ θεῷ λέγουσαι τὰ πάτρια ἀποτελέειν, τὴν Ἀθηναίην καλέομεν. τὰς δὲ ἀποθνησκούσας τῶν παρθένων ἐκ τῶν τρωμάτων ψευδοπαρθένους καλέουσι. [3] πρὶν δὲ ἀνεῖναι αὐτὰς μάχεσθαι, τάδε ποιεῦσι· κοινῇ παρθένον τὴν καλλιστεύουσαν ἑκάστοτε κοσμήσαντες κυνέῃ τε Κορινθίῃ καὶ πανοπλίῃ Ἑλληνικῇ καὶ ἐπ᾽ ἅρμα ἀναβιβάσαντες περιάγουσι τὴν λίμνην κύκλῳ. [4] ὁτέοισι δὲ τὸ πάλαι ἐκόσμεον τὰς παρθένους πρὶν ἤ σφι Ἕλληνας παροικισθῆναι, οὐκ ἔχω εἰπεῖν, δοκέω δ᾽ ὦν Αἰγυπτίοισι ὅπλοισι κοσμέεσθαι αὐτάς· ἀπὸ γὰρ Αἰγύπτου καὶ τὴν ἀσπίδα καὶ τὸ κράνος φημὶ ἀπῖχθαι ἐς τοὺς Ἕλληνας. [5] τὴν δὲ Ἀθηναίην φασὶ Ποσειδέωνος εἶναι θυγατέρα καὶ τῆς Τριτωνίδος λίμνης, καί μιν μεμφθεῖσάν τι τῷ πατρὶ δοῦναι ἑωυτὴν τῷ Διί, τὸν δὲ Δία ἑωυτοῦ μιν ποιήσασθαι θυγατέρα. ταῦτα μὲν λέγουσι, μεῖξιν δὲ ἐπίκοινον τῶν γυναικῶν ποιέονται, οὔτε συνοικέοντες κτηνηδόν τε μισγόμενοι. [6] ἐπεὰν δὲ γυναικὶ τὸ παιδίον ἁδρὸν γένηται, συμφοιτῶσι ἐς τὠυτὸ οἱ ἄνδρες τρίτου μηνός, καὶ τῷ ἂν οἴκῃ τῶν ἀνδρῶν τὸ παιδίον, τούτου παῖς νομίζεται.

4.180.1

For the locations of the tribal regions and places mentioned in the opening sentence, see the map in Landmark *ad* 4.175.

ἔχονται "Border on" or "live next to" (+ genitive).

κομῶσι "Let their hair grow long."

4.180.2

αὐτῶν δίχα διαστᾶσαι "Having split into two groups."

τὴν Ἀθηναίην καλέομεν "Whom we [Hellenes] call Athena."

4.180.3

ποιεῦσι = ποιοῦσι.

περιάγουσι τὴν λίμνην "They bring her around the lake." τὴν λίμνην is in the accusative case, because of the force of the prepositional prefix in περιάγουσι.

4.180.4

ὁτέοισι = ὅτοις.

πρὶν ἢ σφιἝλληνας παροικισθῆναι "Before the Hellenes had settled next to them."

ἀπῖχθαι Perfect, middle infinitive of ἀπικνέομαι (= ἀφικνέομαι).

4.180.5

μεμφθεῖσάν τι τῷ πατρὶ "Having faulted her father for something."

μῖξιν δὲ ἐπίκοινον τῶν γυναικῶν ποιέονται A polite way of saying that the Ausean men have indiscriminate sex with their women.

4.180.6

ἐπεάν = ἐπειδάν.

ἁδρόν "Adequately developed."

τώυτό Crasis (two words combined into one) for τὸ αὐτό.

Ↄঽ

5.4.1-2 Thracian Customs, Part I

Herodotus resumes his narrative of the Persian conquests in Europe, but the march of Megabazus through Thrace prompts a fascinating excursus into the customs and beliefs of the various tribes of Thrace. Evidence that Herodotus was in control of his material can be seen in the first sentence of this chapter, where he reminds us that he has already mentioned, albeit very briefly (cf. 4.94), the beliefs of the Getai (one of the tribes of Thrace). The description here of the melancholy outlook on life of the Trausi (another of the Thracian tribes) is reminiscent of the Solon-Croesus episode in Book I, where a similarly pessimistic view was ascribed to Solon.

τούτων δὲ τὰ μὲν Γέται οἱ ἀθανατίζοντες ποιεῦσι, εἴρηταί μοι· Τραυσοὶ δὲ τὰ μὲν ἄλλα πάντα κατὰ ταὐτὰ τοῖσι ἄλλοισι Θρήιξι ἐπιτελέουσι, κατὰ δὲ τὸν γινόμενόν σφι καὶ ἀπογινόμενον ποιεῦσι τοιάδε· [2] τὸν μὲν

γενόμενον περιιζόμενοι οἱ προσήκοντες ὀλοφύρονται, ὅσα μιν δεῖ ἐπείτε
ἐγένετο ἀναπλῆσαι κακά, ἀνηγεόμενοι τὰ ἀνθρωπήια πάντα πάθεα·τὸν δ᾽
ἀπογενόμενον παίζοντές τε καὶ ἡδόμενοι γῇ κρύπτουσι, ἐπιλέγοντες ὅσων
κακῶν ἐξαπαλλαχθεὶς ἐστι ἐν πάσῃ εὐδαιμονίῃ.

5.4.1

τά Here, a relative pronoun.

Γέται See map in Landmark *ad* 5.5.

ἀθανατίζοντες "Claiming to be immortal."

εἴρηταί μοι In 4.94.

τὰ μὲν ἄλλα πάντα "In respect to all other things."

ταὐτά Crasis (two words combined into one) for τὰ αὐτά.

5.4.2

ἀναπλῆσαι Aorist, active infinitive of ἀναπίμπλημι.

παίζοντές "Celebrating."

ἐξαπαλλαχθεὶς Aorist, passive, masculine, nominative, singular participle of ἐξαπαλλάσσω.

ℭ

5.5.1 Thracian Customs, Part II

The Thracian tribe whose customs are described here do not even have a name but
are referred to merely as "those who live above the Crestonians." Their custom of having
multiple wives and of sacrificing the favorite wife to the shade of the deceased husband
elicits no comment from Herodotus, who is in his full ethnographic mode and displays the
admirable reserve of a field scientist.

οἱ δὲ κατύπερθε Κρηστωναίων ποιεῦσι τοιάδε. ἔχει γυναῖκας ἕκαστος
πολλάς· ἐπεὰν ὦν τις αὐτῶν ἀποθάνῃ, κρίσις γίνεται μεγάλη τῶν γυναικῶν
καὶ φίλων σπουδαὶ ἰσχυραὶ περὶ τοῦδε, ἥτις αὐτέων ἐφιλέετο μάλιστα ὑπὸ
τοῦ ἀνδρός· ἣ δ᾽ ἂν κριθῇ καὶ τιμηθῇ, ἐγκωμιασθεῖσα ὑπό τε ἀνδρῶν καὶ
γυναικῶν σφάζεται ἐς τὸν τάφον ὑπὸ τοῦ οἰκηιοτάτου ἑωυτῆς, σφαχθεῖσα
δὲ συνθάπτεται τῷ ἀνδρί. αἱ δὲ ἄλλαι συμφορὴν μεγάλην ποιεῦνται· ὄνειδος
γάρ σφι τοῦτο μέγιστον γίνεται.

5.5.1

Κρηστωναίων See map in Landmark *ad* 5.5.

ἐπεάν = ἐπειδάν.

ὦν = οὖν.

γίνεται = γίγνεται.

ἥτις αὐτέων ἐφιλέετο μάλιστα ὑπὸ τοῦ ἀνδρός Indirect question triggered by κρίσις and σπουδαὶ.

ἐγκωμιασθεῖσα Aorist, passive, feminine, nominative, singular participle of ἐγκωμιάζω.

ἑωυτῆς = ἑαυτῆς.

☙

5.6.1-2 Thracian Customs, Part III

When Herodotus writes in a rapid-fire mode, the results of his inquiries are often presented with little or no context. The opening part of this passage seems to pose a paradox: if it is true that among certain tribes of Thracians children were sold into slavery overseas, how could these same tribes have stayed in existence? Centuries later, the Roman historian Tacitus may have been following Herodotus' lead when he observed (*Germania* 14) that among the tribes of Germany farming and manual labor were considered a disgrace.

τῶν δὲ δὴ ἄλλων Θρηίκων ἐστὶ ὅδε νόμος· πωλεῦσι τὰ τέκνα ἐπ' ἐξαγωγῇ, τὰς δὲ παρθένους οὐ φυλάσσουσι, ἀλλ' ἐῶσι τοῖσι αὐταὶ βούλονται ἀνδράσι μίσγεσθαι· τὰς δὲ γυναῖκας ἰσχυρῶς φυλάσσουσι καὶ ὠνέονται τὰς γυναῖκας παρὰ τῶν γονέων χρημάτων μεγάλων. [2] καὶ τὸ μὲν ἐστίχθαι εὐγενὲς κέκριται, τὸ δὲ ἄστικτον ἀγεννές. ἀργὸν εἶναι κάλλιστον, γῆς δὲ ἐργάτην ἀτιμότατον· τὸ ζῆν ἀπὸ πολέμου καὶ ληιστύος κάλλιστον.

5.6.1
τοῖσι Relative pronoun, with its antecedent understood. "With those whom."
χρημάτων μεγάλων Genitive of value.

5.6.1
τὸ μὲν ἐστίχθαι Articular infinitive. "To be tattooed."
τὸ ζῆν Articular infinitive.

☙

5.18.1-5 Persians Party in Macedon, Part I

Just when it seems that Herodotus is ready to describe the Persian conquest of Macedon, he inserts into his narrative a story that shows the Persians in a very poor light. The tale has little to recommend it as history, and it even seems to contradict Herodotus' earlier claim that Persians do not lie (1.136, 1.138), but it has much going for it as a story of debauchery, intrigue, and murder. One can well imagine this chapter, and the next two, as having constituted a "performance piece," which Herodotus could have recited to appreciative audiences in festive settings like the Panathenaia.

οἱ ὦν Πέρσαι οἱ πεμφθέντες οὗτοι παρὰ τὸν Ἀμύντην ὡς ἀπίκοντο, αἴτεον ἐλθόντες ἐς ὄψιν τὴν Ἀμύντεω Δαρείῳ βασιλέι γῆν τε καὶ ὕδωρ. ὁ δὲ ταῦτά τε ἐδίδου καὶ σφεας ἐπὶ ξείνια καλέει, παρασκευασάμενος δὲ δεῖπνον μεγαλοπρεπὲς ἐδέκετο τοὺς Πέρσας φιλοφρόνως. [2] ὡς δὲ ἀπὸ δείπνου ἐγένοντο, διαπίνοντες εἶπαν οἱ Πέρσαι τάδε· "ξεῖνε Μακεδών, ἡμῖν νόμος ἐστὶ τοῖσι Πέρσῃσι, ἐπεὰν δεῖπνον προτιθώμεθα μέγα, τότε καὶ τὰς παλλακὰς καὶ τὰς κουριδίας γυναῖκας ἐσάγεσθαι παρέδρους. σύ νυν, ἐπεί περ προθύμως μὲν ἐδέξαο, μεγάλως δὲ ξεινίζεις, διδοῖς δὲ βασιλέι Δαρείῳ γῆν τε καὶ ὕδωρ, ἕπεο νόμῳ τῷ ἡμετέρῳ." [3] εἶπε πρὸς ταῦτα Ἀμύντης·"ὦ Πέρσαι, νόμος μὲν ἡμῖν γέ ἐστι οὐκ οὗτος, ἀλλὰ κεχωρίσθαι ἄνδρας γυναικῶν· ἐπείτε δὲ ὑμεῖς ἐόντες δεσπόται προσχρηίζετε τούτων, παρέσται ὑμῖν καὶ ταῦτα." εἴπας τοσαῦτα ὁ Ἀμύντης μετεπέμπετο τὰς γυναῖκας· αἳ δ' ἐπείτε καλεόμεναι ἦλθον, ἐπεξῆς ἀντίαι ἵζοντο τοῖσι Πέρσῃσι. [4] ἐνθαῦτα οἱ Πέρσαι ἰδόμενοι γυναῖκας εὐμόρφους ἔλεγον πρὸς Ἀμύντην φάμενοι τὸ ποιηθὲν τοῦτο οὐδὲν εἶναι σοφόν· κρέσσον γὰρ εἶναι ἀρχῆθεν μὴ ἐλθεῖν τὰς γυναῖκας ἢ ἐλθούσας καὶ μὴ παριζομένας ἀντίας ἵζεσθαι ἀλγηδόνας σφίσι ὀφθαλμῶν. [5] ἀναγκαζόμενος δὲ ὁ Ἀμύντης ἐκέλευε παρίζειν· πειθομενέων δὲ τῶν γυναικῶν αὐτίκα οἱ Πέρσαι μαστῶν τε ἅπτοντο οἷα πλεόνως οἰνωμένοι, καί κού τις καὶ φιλέειν ἐπειρᾶτο.

5.18.1

ὦν = οὖν.

ἀπίκοντο = ἀφίκοντο.

Δαρείῳ βασιλέι "In the name of Darius the King."

γῆν τε καὶ ὕδωρ The usual symbols of submission to the Persian king.

ξεινία = ξενία.

ἐδέκετο = ἐδέχετο.

5.18.2

εἶπαν Herodotus occasionally uses a first aorist form of this verb.

ἐπεάν = ἐπειδάν.

παλλακὰς "Concubines."

παρέδρους "As table companions."

ἐδέξαο Aorist, indicative, middle, 2nd, singular of δέκομαι (= δέχομαι).

5.18.3

κεχωρίσθαι Perfect, passive infinitive of χωρίζω. Supply "it is our custom."

5.18.4

τὸ ποιηθὲν τοῦτο "That which was done."

κρέσσον = κρείσσον.

μὴ παριζομένας ἀντίας ἵζεσθαι "Not sitting by their side but sitting opposite to them."

ἀλγηδόνας In apposition to τὰς γυναῖκας. "As a source of pain."

5.18.5

πειθομενέων δὲ τῶν γυναικῶν Genitive absolute construction.

οἷα "Seeing how."

κού = πού.

☙

5.19.1-2 Persians Party in Macedon, Part II

Herodotus presents here a study of how the old and the young react differently to the same crisis. The mature Amyntas (king of Macedon) wanted to look the other way and tolerated the outrageous behavior of his Persian guests. His son Alexandros, on the other hand, filled with the rashness of youth, wanted to respond to the Persian outrage in whatever way he could. Note how Herodotus, the psychological historian, seems to understand the way fathers and sons can communicate with one another in telepathic ways.

Ἀμύντης μὲν δὴ ταῦτα ὁρέων ἀτρέμας εἶχε, καίπερ δυσφορέων, οἷα ὑπερδειμαίνων τοὺς Πέρσας· Ἀλέξανδρος δὲ ὁ Ἀμύντεω παρεών τε καὶ ὁρέων ταῦτα, ἅτε νέος τε ἐὼν καὶ κακῶν ἀπαθής, οὐδαμῶς ἔτι κατέχειν οἷος τε ἦν, ὥστε δὲ βαρέως φέρων εἶπε πρὸς Ἀμύντην τάδε· "ὦ πάτερ, σὺ μὲν εἶκε τῇ ἡλικίῃ ἀπιών τε ἀναπαύεο, μηδὲ λιπάρεε τῇ πόσι· ἐγὼ δὲ προσμένων αὐτοῦ τῇδε πάντα τὰ ἐπιτήδεα παρέξω τοῖσι ξείνοισι." [2] πρὸς ταῦτα συνιεὶς Ἀμύντης ὅτι νεώτερα πρήγματα πρήσσειν μέλλοι ὁ Ἀλέξανδρος, λέγει· "ὦ παῖ, σχεδὸν γάρ σευ ἀνακαιομένου συνίημι τοὺς λόγους, ὅτι ἐθέλεις ἐμὲ ἐκπέμψας ποιέειν τι νεώτερον· ἐγὼ ὦν σευ χρηίζω μηδὲν νεοχμῶσαι κατ᾽ ἄνδρας τούτους, ἵνα μὴ ἐξεργάσῃ ἡμέας, ἀλλὰ ἀνέχευ ὁρέων τὰ ποιεύμενα: ἀμφὶ δὲ ἀπόδῳ τῇ ἐμῇ πείσομαί τοι."

5.19.1

ἀτρέμας εἶχε "Kept quiet."

οἷα "Seeing how."

κακῶν ἀπαθής "Inexperienced with evil."

οἷος τε ἦν "Was [not] able."

σὺ μὲν εἶκε τῇ ἡλικίῃ ἀπιών τε ἀναπαύεο "Act age-appropriate and, going away, take a break."

μηδὲ λιπάρεε τῇ πόσι "Do not keep on drinking."

ξείνοισι = ξένοισι.

5.19.2

συνιεὶς Present, active, masculine, nominative, singular participle of συνίημι. "Understanding."

νεώτερα πρήγματα "Rather radical things."

σχεδὸν γάρ σευ ἀνακαιομένου Genitive absolute construction.

ὦν = οὖν.

μηδὲν νεοχμῶσαι "Do nothing rash."

෨

5.20.1-5 Persians Party in Macedon, Part III

As befits a great storyteller, Herodotus deftly manipulates his readers (and possibly his listeners), who might have been anxious by now to see the evil Persians get their comeuppance. The words of Alexandros, directly quoted (but of course fictitious), help enhance the sense of anticipation. When Herodotus makes Alexandros refer to himself as a Hellene (1.20.4), he is letting us know what his position is concerning the eternal controversy over the ethnicity of the ancient Macedonians. The actual denouement is only briefly described, perhaps because Herodotus felt that any elaboration of the murder scene would have been anti-climactic.

ὡς δὲ ὁ Ἀμύντης χρήσας τούτων οἰχώκεε, λέγει ὁ Ἀλέξανδρος πρὸς τοὺς Πέρσας "γυναικῶν τουτέων, ὦ ξεῖνοι, ἔστι ὑμῖν πολλὴ εὐπετείη, καὶ εἰ πάσῃσι βούλεσθε μίσγεσθαι καὶ ὁκόσῃσι ὦν αὐτέων. [2] τούτου μὲν πέρι αὐτοὶ ἀποσημανέετε· νῦν δέ, σχεδὸν γὰρ ἤδη τῆς κοίτης ὥρη προσέρχεται ὑμῖν καὶ καλῶς ἔχοντας ὑμέας ὁρῶ μέθης, γυναῖκας ταύτας, εἰ ὑμῖν φίλον ἐστί, ἄπετε λούσασθαι, λουσαμένας δὲ ὀπίσω προσδέκεσθε." [3] εἴπας ταῦτα, συνέπαινοι γὰρ ἦσαν οἱ Πέρσαι, γυναῖκας μὲν ἐξελθούσας ἀπέπεμπε ἐς τὴν γυναικηίην, αὐτὸς δὲ ὁ Ἀλέξανδρος ἴσους τῇσι γυναιξὶ ἀριθμὸν ἄνδρας λειογενείους τῇ τῶν γυναικῶν ἐσθῆτι σκευάσας καὶ ἐγχειρίδια δοὺς ἦγε ἔσω, παράγων δὲ τούτους ἔλεγε τοῖσι Πέρσῃσι τάδε· [4] "ὦ Πέρσαι, οἴκατε πανδαισίῃ τελέῃ ἱστιῆσθαι· τά τε γὰρ ἄλλα ὅσα εἴχομεν, καὶ πρὸς τὰ οἷά τε ἦν ἐξευρόντας παρέχειν, πάντα ὑμῖν πάρεστι, καὶ δὴ καὶ τόδε τὸ πάντων μέγιστον, τάς τε ἑωυτῶν μητέρας καὶ τὰς ἀδελφεὰς ἐπιδαψιλευόμεθα ὑμῖν, ὡς παντελέως μάθητε τιμώμενοι πρὸς ἡμέων τῶν πέρ ἐστε ἄξιοι, πρὸς δὲ καὶ βασιλέι τῷ πέμψαντι ἀπαγγείλητε ὡς ἀνὴρ Ἕλλην Μακεδόνων ὕπαρχος εὖ ὑμέας ἐδέξατο καὶ τραπέζῃ καὶ κοίτῃ." [5] ταῦτα εἴπας ὁ Ἀλέξανδρος παρίζει

Πέρσῃ ἀνδρὶ ἄνδρα Μακεδόνα ὡς γυναῖκα τῷ λόγῳ· οἱ δέ, ἐπείτε σφέων οἱ
Πέρσαι ψαύειν ἐπειρῶντο, διεργάζοντο αὐτούς.

5.20.1

πάσῃσι = πάσαις.

ὁκόσῃσι = ὁπόσαις.

ὦν = οὖν.

5.20.2

πέρι An instance of anastrophe, where the preposition governs the preceding word (note the
position of the accent).

τῆς κοίτης ὥρη "Bed time."

φίλον "Agreeable."

5.20.3

εἴπας The participle has the first aorist form (rare in Attic Greek).

ἀριθμὸν "In respect to their number."

λειογενείους "Beardless."

ἐγχειρίδια "Hand-held weapons," or "Daggers."

5.20.4

οἴκατε πανδαισίῃ τελέῃ ἱστιῆσθαι "You seem to have been entertained with a complete
banquet."

καὶ πρὸς τὰ οἶά τε ἦν ἐξευρόντας παρέχειν "And, in addition, whatever it was possible for us
to find and offer."

ἑωυτῶν = ἑαυτῶν.

ὡς παντελέως μάθητε τιμώμενοι πρὸς ἡμέων τῶν περ ἐστὲ ἄξιοι "That you may fully know
how you, honored by us, are indeed worthy of these things."

τραπέζῃ καὶ κοίτῃ "With board and bed."

5.20.5

Πέρσῃ ἀνδρὶ ἄνδρα Μακεδόνα Note the chiasmatic arrangement.

τῷ λόγῳ "By [their] estimation."

ଊ

5.22.1-2 Are Macedonians Greeks?

Herodotus again deals with the question of the ethnic identity of the ancient Macedonians,
or more specifically, of Alexandros, the king of Macedon, and of his predecessors. In a later
section of the *Histories* (8.137-39), he will follow through on the promise which he makes
in this chapter, that is, to tell the story of Perdiccas, Alexandros' ancestor seven generations
earlier, and of his emigration from Argos to Macedon. This type of a cross-reference shows
that Herodotus was in control of his material and could follow up on promises he made
three books earlier. The argument that is made here in support of the Greek ethnicity of

Alexander and his ancestors is not all that compelling, as the Elean judges at the Olympic Games may have had political reasons for making their determination.

ὁ μέν νυν τῶν Περσέων τούτων θάνατος οὕτω καταλαμφθεὶς ἐσιγήθη. Ἕλληνας δὲ εἶναι τούτους τοὺς ἀπὸ Περδίκκεω γεγονότας, κατά περ αὐτοὶ λέγουσι, αὐτός τε οὕτω τυγχάνω ἐπιστάμενος καὶ δὴ καὶ ἐν τοῖσι ὄπισθε λόγοισι ἀποδέξω ὡς εἰσὶ Ἕλληνες, πρὸς δὲ καὶ οἱ τὸν ἐν Ὀλυμπίῃ διέποντες ἀγῶνα Ἑλληνοδίκαι οὕτω ἔγνωσαν εἶναι. [2] Ἀλεξάνδρου γὰρ ἀεθλεύειν ἑλομένου καὶ καταβάντος ἐπ᾽ αὐτὸ τοῦτο, οἱ ἀντιθευσόμενοι Ἑλλήνων ἐξεῖργόν μιν, φάμενοι οὐ βαρβάρων ἀγωνιστέων εἶναι τὸν ἀγῶνα ἀλλὰ Ἑλλήνων· Ἀλέξανδρος δὲ ἐπειδὴ ἀπέδεξε ὡς εἴη Ἀργεῖος, ἐκρίθη τε εἶναι Ἕλλην καὶ ἀγωνιζόμενος στάδιον συνεξέπιπτε τῷ πρώτῳ.

5.22.1

ὁ μέν νυν τῶν Περσέων τούτων θάνατος A reference to the story in 5.20-21, where Persian heralds, who had attempted to debauch royal Macedonian women, were secretly killed.

καταλαμφθεὶς Aorist, passive, masculine, nominative, singular participle of καταλαμβάνω. "Suppressed."

τοὺς ἀπὸ Περδίκκεω γεγονότας Perdiccas is said to have been the founder of the royal dynasty in Macedon. His story is told in 8.137-39.

κατά περ "Just as."

5.22.2

Ἀλεξάνδρου γὰρ ἀεθλεύειν ἑλομένου καὶ καταβάντος.... Genitive absolute constructions.

ἑλομένου Aorist, middle, masculine, genitive, singular participle of αἱρέω. "Having decided."

ἐξεῖργόν Imperfect, indicative, active, 3rd, plural of ἐξέργω.

συνεξέπιπτε "Tied for...."

☙

5.35.1-4 The Story of the Tattooed Head

The prelude to this episode is found in Book IV, where Herodotus narrates the events surrounding the bridge which Darius ordered built across the Ister (Danube) during his campaign against the Scythians (513 B.C.). The Ionian tyrants who accompanied the King had been left in charge of this bridge (4.98). On the advice of Miltiades, the tyrant of the Chersonese, they at first decided to destroy the bridge but were later dissuaded from doing so by Histiaios, the tyrant of Miletus (4.137). As a supposed reward for his help, Histiaios was sent to Susa, one of the two royal capitals of the Persian Empire, where for over a decade he endured an enforced stay. Meanwhile, his son-in-law Aristagoras ruled as a deputy tyrant of Miletus and was involved in any number of intrigues with Artaphrenes, the Persian satrap (governor) of Ionia. One of these was to re-install, with Persian help (in the person of Megabates), some oligarchs who had been exiled from their native Naxos, the largest and most prosperous (at the time) of the Greek islands in the Aegean (see map in Landmark *ad* 5.31). When this plan went awry, Aristagoras feared that his Persian overlords would depose him and decided to instigate a revolt. His decision was affirmed by a message which Histiaios had tattooed on the head of slave, who was dispatched from Susa to Miletus. This, at least, is the way Herodotus presents the story of the beginnings of the Ionian Revolt (499-94), the first of the Greco-Persian wars of the 5th century. Commentators often emphasize (and lament) that Herodotus is really our only source for this important event in Greek history. Not surprisingly, they have challenged the historicity of this episode involving the "tattooed head."

Ἀρισταγόρης δὲ οὐκ εἶχε τὴν ὑπόσχεσιν τῷ Ἀρταφρένεϊ ἐκτελέσαι· ἅμα δὲ ἐπίεζέ μιν ἡ δαπάνη τῆς στρατιῆς ἀπαιτεομένη, ἀρρώδεέ τε τοῦ στρατοῦ πρήξαντος κακῶς καὶ Μεγαβάτῃ διαβεβλημένος, ἐδόκεέ τε τὴν βασιληίην τῆς Μιλήτου ἀπαιρεθήσεσθαι. [2] ἀρρωδέων δὲ τούτων ἕκαστα ἐβουλεύετο ἀπόστασιν· συνέπιπτε γὰρ καὶ τὸν ἐστιγμένον τὴν κεφαλὴν ἀπῖχθαι ἐκ Σούσων παρὰ Ἱστιαίου, σημαίνοντα ἀπίστασθαι Ἀρισταγόρην ἀπὸ βασιλέος. [3] ὁ γὰρ Ἱστιαῖος βουλόμενος τῷ Ἀρισταγόρῃ σημῆναι ἀποστῆναι ἄλλως μὲν οὐδαμῶς εἶχε ἀσφαλέως σημῆναι ὥστε φυλασσομένέων τῶν ὁδῶν, ὁ δὲ τῶν δούλων τὸν πιστότατον ἀποξυρήσας τὴν κεφαλὴν ἔστιξε καὶ ἀνέμεινε ἀναφῦναι τὰς τρίχας, ὡς δὲ ἀνέφυσαν τάχιστα, ἀπέπεμπε ἐς Μίλητον ἐντειλάμενος αὐτῷ ἄλλο μὲν οὐδέν, ἐπεὰν δὲ ἀπίκηται ἐς Μίλητον, κελεύειν Ἀρισταγόρην ξυρήσαντά μιν τὰς τρίχας κατιδέσθαι ἐς τὴν κεφαλήν. τὰ δὲ στίγματα ἐσήμαινε, ὡς καὶ πρότερόν μοι εἴρηται, ἀπόστασιν. [4] ταῦτα δὲ ὁ Ἱστιαῖος ἐποίεε συμφορὴν ποιεύμενος μεγάλην τὴν ἑωυτοῦ κατοχὴν τὴν ἐν Σούσοισι· ἀποστάσιος ὢν γινομένης πολλὰς εἶχε ἐλπίδας μετήσεσθαι ἐπὶ θάλασσαν, μὴ δὲ νεώτερόν τι ποιεύσης τῆς Μιλήτου οὐδαμὰ ἐς αὐτὴν ἥξειν ἔτι ἐλογίζετο.

5.35.1

ὑπόσχεσιν The "promise" to capture the island of Naxos (see map in Landmark *ad* 5.31).

ἀπαιτεομένη "That was demanded as payment."

ἀρρώδεέ Imperfect, indicative, active, 3rd, singular of ἀρρωδέω (= ὀρρωδέω). Takes a genitive of the thing feared.

διαβεβλημένος Perfect, passive, masculine, nominative, singular participle of διαβάλλω. "Filled with resentment against...."

ἀπαιρεθήσεσθαι Future, passive infinitive of ἀπαιρέω (= ἀφαιρέω).

5.35.2

συνέπιπτε "It came to pass that…."

ἀπῖχθαι Perfect, middle infinitive of ἀπικνέομαι (= ἀφικνέομαι).

Σούσων Susa was one of the capital cities of the Persian Empire. See map in Landmark *ad* 5.14.

ἀπίστασθαι Present, middle infinitive of ἀπίστημι (= ἀφίστημι).

5.35.3

ὥστε "Insofar as."

φυλασσομενέων τῶν ὁδῶν Genitive absolute construction.

ἐπεάν = ἐπειδάν.

κατιδέσθαι "Look down upon."

5.35.4

ποιεύμενος "Considering." Takes a double accusative.

ἑωυτοῦ = ἑαυτοῦ.

ἀποστάσιος ὢν γινομένης Genitive absolute construction.

ὦν = οὖν.

μετήσεσθαι Future, middle infinitive of μετίημι (= μεθίημι). The middle infinitive has a passive sense: "He would be released."

μὴ δὲ νεώτερόν τι ποιεύσης τῆς Μιλήτου Another genitive absolute construction. "With Miletus doing nothing revolutionary."

◌

5.49.1-4 They Wear Trousers!

After Aristagoras receives assurances from his father-in-law Histiaios that a revolt from the Persians was the right thing to do (5.35), he sets out to mainland Greece to convince the Spartans and the Athenians to join the revolt of their fellow Greeks in Ionia. Aristagoras first travels to Sparta, where we get to eavesdrop on a conversation between him and Cleomenes, one of the most famous kings of Sparta. While Aristagoras' visit was almost certainly an event that really took place, we can be absolutely confident that his sales-pitch to the Spartan king was crafted by Herodotus. In his speech, Aristagoras belittles the military capabilities of the Persians, who, by his estimation, fight with arrows and short spears. (Cf. HW *ad* 5.49.3: "Compared with the Dorian hoplite, with his brazen helmet, cuirass and greaves, great shield, his sword and 8-foot spear, the Persians might rightly be called light-armed bowmen….") Aristagoras even makes fun of Persian trousers and tiaras, and yet, as part of his list of the treasures which Spartans would be able to have for themselves if they conquered Persia, he comically mentions "painted clothes" (5.49.4). The rest of this chapter (omitted here) consists of a survey of the regions of the East controlled by the Persians. It is the kind of geographical tour de force which we have come to expect from Herodotus.

ἀπικνέεται δὲ ὦν ὁ Ἀρισταγόρης ὁ Μιλήτου τύραννος ἐς τὴν Σπάρτην Κλεομένεος ἔχοντος τὴν ἀρχήν· τῷ δὴ ἐς λόγους ἤιε, ὡς Λακεδαιμόνιοι

λέγουσι, ἔχων χάλκεον πίνακα ἐν τῷ γῆς ἀπάσης περίοδος ἐνετέτμητο καὶ
θάλασσά τε πᾶσα καὶ ποταμοὶ πάντες. [2] ἀπικνεόμενος δὲ ἐς λόγους ὁ
Ἀρισταγόρης ἔλεγε πρὸς αὐτὸν τάδε· "Κλεόμενες, σπουδὴν μὲν τὴν ἐμὴν μὴ
θωμάσῃς τῆς ἐνθαῦτα ἀπίξιος· τὰ γὰρ κατήκοντά ἐστι τοιαῦτα· Ἰώνων παῖδας
δούλους εἶναι ἀντ᾽ ἐλευθέρων ὄνειδος καὶ ἄλγος μέγιστον μὲν αὐτοῖσι ἡμῖν,
ἔτι δὲ τῶν λοιπῶν ὑμῖν, ὅσῳ προέστατε τῆς Ἑλλάδος. [3] νῦν ὦν πρὸς θεῶν
τῶν Ἑλληνίων ῥύσασθε Ἴωνας ἐκ δουλοσύνης ἄνδρας ὁμαίμονας. εὐπετέως
δὲ ὑμῖν ταῦτα οἷά τε χωρέειν ἐστί· οὔτε γὰρ οἱ βάρβαροι ἄλκιμοί εἰσι, ὑμεῖς τε
τὰ ἐς τὸν πόλεμον ἐς τὰ μέγιστα ἀνήκετε ἀρετῆς πέρι, ἥ τε μάχη αὐτῶν ἐστι
τοιήδε, τόξα καὶ αἰχμὴ βραχέα· ἀναξυρίδας δὲ ἔχοντες ἔρχονται ἐς τὰς μάχας
καὶ κυρβασίας ἐπὶ τῇσι κεφαλῇσι. [4] οὕτω εὐπετέες χειρωθῆναι εἰσί. ἔστι δὲ
καὶ ἀγαθὰ τοῖσι τὴν ἤπειρον ἐκείνην νεμομένοισι ὅσα οὐδὲ τοῖσι συνάπασι
ἄλλοισι, ἀπὸ χρυσοῦ ἀρξαμένοισι, ἄργυρος καὶ χαλκὸς καὶ ἐσθὴς ποικίλη
καὶ ὑποζύγιά τε καὶ ἀνδράποδα· τὰ θυμῷ βουλόμενοι αὐτοὶ ἂν ἔχοιτε.

5.49.1

ἀπικνέεται = ἀφικνεῖται.

ὦν = οὖν.

Κλεομένεος Cleomenes was one of the most long-lived kings of Sparta. He died in 490 B.C. after a reign of c. 30 years.

τῷ δὴ ἐς λόγους ἤιε "He entered into conversation with him."

ἐνετέτμητο Pluperfect, indicative, passive, 3rd, plural of ἐντέμνω.

5.49.2

θωμάσῃς Aorist, subjunctive, active, 2nd, singular of θωμάζω (= θαυμάζω).

ἀπίξιος = ἀφίξιος.

κατήκοντα = καθήκοντα.

ὄνειδος καὶ ἄλγος μέγιστον Triggers the accusative/infinitive construction in Ἰώνων παῖδας δούλους εἶναι.

τῶν λοιπῶν ὑμῖν "To you of the rest [of the Greek world]."

ὅσῳ "Insofar as."

5.49.3

εὐπετέως δὲ ὑμῖν ταῦτα οἷά τε χωρέειν ἐστί "These are things which are easy for you to achieve."

τὰ ἐς τὸν πόλεμον "In matters pertaining to war."

πέρι An instance of anastrophe, where the preposition governs the preceding word (note the position of the accent).

5.49.4

χειρωθῆναι Aorist, passive infinitive of χειρόω.

τὰ θυμῷ βουλόμενοι This participial phrase functions like the protasis of a conditional sentence. "If you wish for these things in your heart [of hearts]."

☙

5.50.1-3 Aristagoras Slips Up

Herodotus portrays Aristagoras, the tyrant of Miletus, as a bit of a con-artist who, in trying to convince King Cleomenes of Sparta to render assistance to the revolt of the Ionians, inadvertently tells the truth about the number of days (months, actually) it would take for a hoplite army, setting out from the coast of Ionia, to reach the Persian capital of Susa. Presumably, the map that Aristagoras had earlier (5.49) shown to Cleomenes—this is the earliest reference to a "map of the earth" in our ancient sources—was still on display, but it apparently could not be deciphered by the Spartan. In the follow-up to this passage (5.51), Aristagoras attempts to bribe Cleomenes and offers a reward of 50 talents (the equivalent of 300,000 days' wages) if he complied with the Milesian's request. Gorgo, Cleomenes' virtuous daughter, rises to the occasion and tells her father to send Aristagoras away.

τότε μὲν ἐς τοσοῦτον ἤλασαν· ἐπείτε δὲ ἡ κυρίη ἡμέρη ἐγένετο τῆς ὑποκρίσιος καὶ ἦλθον ἐς τὸ συγκείμενον, εἴρετο ὁ Κλεομένης τὸν Ἀρισταγόρην ὁκοσέων ἡμερέων ἀπὸ θαλάσσης τῆς Ἰώνων ὁδὸς εἴη παρὰ βασιλέα. [2] ὁ δὲ Ἀρισταγόρης τἆλλα ἐὼν σοφὸς καὶ διαβάλλων ἐκεῖνον εὖ ἐν τούτῳ ἐσφάλη· χρεὸν γάρ μιν μὴ λέγειν τὸ ἐόν, βουλόμενόν γε Σπαρτιήτας ἐξαγαγεῖν ἐς τὴν Ἀσίην, λέγει δ᾽ ὦν τριῶν μηνῶν φὰς εἶναι τὴν ἄνοδον. ὁ δὲ ὑπαρπάσας τὸν ἐπίλοιπον λόγον τὸν ὁ Ἀρισταγόρης ὥρμητο λέγειν περὶ τῆς ὁδοῦ, εἶπε· [3] "ὦ ξεῖνε Μιλήσιε, ἀπαλλάσσεο ἐκ Σπάρτης πρὸ δύντος ἡλίου· οὐδένα γὰρ λόγον εὐεπέα λέγεις Λακεδαιμονίοισι, ἐθέλων σφέας ἀπὸ θαλάσσης τριῶν μηνῶν ὁδὸν ἀγαγεῖν."

5.50.1

τότε μὲν ἐς τοσοῦτον ἤλασαν "At that meeting (τότε), they got this far [in their deliberations]."

ἡ κυρίη ἡμέρη "The appointed day."

ἐς τὸ συγκείμενον "To the agreed-upon [place]."

ὁκοσέων = ὁποσῶν.

5.50.2

τἆλλα Crasis (two words combined into one) for τὰ ἄλλα.

διαβάλλων "Misleading."

ἐσφάλη Aorist, indicative, passive, 3rd, singular of σφάλλω.

τὸ ἐόν "The truth."

ὦν = οὖν.

τριῶν μηνῶν Genitive of time within which.

ὑπαρπάσας = ὑφαρπάσας.

5.50.3

ἀπαλλάσσεο Present, imperative, middle, 2nd, singular of ἀπαλλάσσω.

εὐεπέα "Acceptable."

CB

5.58.1-3 Herodotus' Theory on the Origin of the Greek Alphabet

Various theories were floated in antiquity concerning the origin of the Greek alphabet. Aeschylus, for example, attributed its discovery to the legendary Prometheus (*Prometheus Bound* 460 f.). In an excursus to an excursus, Herodotus takes up the subject here. Although his explanation is tied in with the myth of Cadmus settling in Thebes, most scholars think it has some merit (cf. note in Landmark *ad* 5.58.3a). Of course, there is much that Herodotus does not know regarding the history of Greek writing (he knew nothing, for example, of the Linear B syllabary that was used during the Mycenaean era), but he deserves kudos for his theory of the Phoenician origins of the Greek alphabet. This particular theory shows us (once again) a Herodotus who, for the most part, is not ethnocentric and who is quite willing to give credit to non-Greeks for their having made important "discoveries," like that of the alphabet.

οἱ δὲ Φοίνικες οὗτοι οἱ σὺν Κάδμῳ ἀπικόμενοι, τῶν ἦσαν οἱ Γεφυραῖοι, ἄλλα τε πολλὰ οἰκήσαντες ταύτην τὴν χώρην ἐσήγαγον διδασκάλια ἐς τοὺς Ἕλληνας καὶ δὴ καὶ γράμματα, οὐκ ἐόντα πρὶν Ἕλλησι ὡς ἐμοὶ δοκέειν, πρῶτα μὲν τοῖσι καὶ ἅπαντες χρέωνται Φοίνικες· μετὰ δὲ χρόνου προβαίνοντος ἅμα τῇ φωνῇ μετέβαλλον καὶ τὸν ῥυθμὸν τῶν γραμμάτων. [2] περιοίκεον δὲ σφέας τὰ πολλὰ τῶν χώρων τοῦτον τὸν χρόνον Ἑλλήνων Ἴωνες, οἳ παραλαβόντες διδαχῇ παρὰ τῶν Φοινίκων τὰ γράμματα, μεταρρυθμίσαντες σφέων ὀλίγα ἐχρέωντο, χρεώμενοι δὲ ἐφάτισαν, ὥσπερ καὶ τὸ δίκαιον ἔφερε, ἐσαγαγόντων Φοινίκων ἐς τὴν Ἑλλάδα, Φοινικήια κεκλῆσθαι. [3] καὶ τὰς βύβλους διφθέρας καλέουσι ἀπὸ τοῦ παλαιοῦ οἱ Ἴωνες, ὅτι κοτὲ ἐν σπάνι βύβλων ἐχρέωντο διφθέρῃσι αἰγέῃσί τε καὶ οἰέῃσι· ἔτι δὲ καὶ τὸ κατ᾽ ἐμὲ πολλοὶ τῶν βαρβάρων ἐς τοιαύτας διφθέρας γράφουσι.

5.58.1

Κάδμῳ In Greek tradition, the Phoenician Cadmus was the founder of Thebes.

ἀπικόμενοι = ἀφικόμενοι.

Γεφυραῖοι For an explanation as to who these Gephyrians were, see note in Landmark *ad*
5.51d.

δοκέειν The infinitive functions "absolutely," that is, like a finite verb.

πρῶτα "First."

τοῖσι Here, a relative pronoun.

μετέβαλλον Subject is the "Hellenes."

ῥυθμὸν "Shape[s]."

5.58.2

τοῦτον τὸν χρόνον Accusative of duration of time.

περιοίκεον δὲ σφέας τὰ πολλὰ τῶν χώρων "They [the Hellenes] inhabited many of the places
around them [the Boeotians]."

ἐφάτισαν…Φοινικήια κεκλῆσθαι "They spoke of them [the letters] by the name 'Phoenician'."

ὥσπερ καὶ τὸ δίκαιον ἔφερε "As is only right."

ἐσαγαγόντων Φοινίκων Genitive absolute construction.

5.58.3

κοτέ = ποτέ.

καὶ τὸ κατ᾿ ἐμὲ "Even in my time."

☙

5.73.1-3 Athenians Offer Earth and Water to the Persian King

After failing to get King Cleomenes of Sparta to lend his support to the fledgling
Ionian Revolt (cf. 5.50), Aristagoras of Miletus journeys to Athens to try his luck there. But
before Herodotus can get down to the business of telling us what Aristagoras said to the
Athenians and how he was received there, he launches into a long narrative (5.62-96) on
the constitutional history of 6th century Athens, specifically, on how the Athenians were
able to safeguard the democratic reforms instituted in 508/7 B.C. by their great lawgiver
Cleisthenes. This narrative formed the basis for later works on Athenian constitutional
history, like the Aristotelian *Constitution of Athens*. (The historian Thucydides [1.126]
presumed to correct portions of Herodotus' account.) The passage presented below is a
curious one: it celebrates the overthrow of a Spartan-sponsored oligarchy in Athens, but
it also tells the story of how the Athenians, feeling insecure in the wake of their hostile
dealings with Sparta, immediately went to Susa (the Persian capital) and asked for an
alliance, symbolized by the Athenians' offering of earth and water to the Persian King.
This latter episode, which shows Athenians in a poor light, demonstrates that Herodotus
was in fact capable of writing critically about Athens.

οὗτοι μέν νυν δεδεμένοι ἐτελεύτησαν. Ἀθηναῖοι δὲ μετὰ ταῦτα Κλεισθένεα
καὶ τὰ ἑπτακόσια ἐπίστια τὰ διωχθέντα ὑπὸ Κλεομένεος μεταπεμψάμενοι
πέμπουσι ἀγγέλους ἐς Σάρδις, συμμαχίην βουλόμενοι ποιήσασθαι

πρὸς Πέρσας· ἠπιστέατο γὰρ σφίσι Λακεδαιμονίους τε καὶ Κλεομένεα ἐκπεπολεμῶσθαι. [2] ἀπικομένων δὲ τῶν ἀγγέλων ἐς τὰς Σάρδις καὶ λεγόντων τὰ ἐντεταλμένα, Ἀρταφρένης ὁ Ὑστάσπεος Σαρδίων ὕπαρχος ἐπειρώτα τίνες ἐόντες ἄνθρωποι καὶ κοῦ γῆς οἰκημένοι δεοίατο Περσέων σύμμαχοι γενέσθαι, πυθόμενος δὲ πρὸς τῶν ἀγγέλων ἀπεκορύφου σφι τάδε· εἰ μὲν διδοῦσι βασιλέι Δαρείῳ Ἀθηναῖοι γῆν τε καὶ ὕδωρ, ὁ δὲ συμμαχίην σφι συνετίθετο, εἰ δὲ μὴ διδοῦσι, ἀπαλλάσσεσθαι αὐτοὺς ἐκέλευε. [3] οἱ δὲ ἄγγελοι ἐπὶ σφέων αὐτῶν βαλόμενοι διδόναι ἔφασαν, βουλόμενοι τὴν συμμαχίην ποιήσασθαι. οὗτοι μὲν δὴ ἀπελθόντες ἐς τὴν ἑωυτῶν αἰτίας μεγάλας εἶχον.

5.73.1

οὗτοι μέν νυν δεδεμένοι ἐτελεύτησαν The Athenians who were "bound and put to death" were supporters of Isagoras, an Athenian politician with oligarchic tendencies, who, with Spartan help, attempted to thwart the democratic reforms of Cleisthenes. According to Herodotus (5.72), a popular revolt in 507 B.C. sent the Spartan king and his hoplites packing and reinstalled the democratic faction of Cleisthenes.

ἐπίστια = ἐφέστια. "[Extended] families."

διωχθέντα Aorist, passive, neuter, accusative, plural participle of διώκω.

ἠπιστέατο Imperfect, indicative, middle, 3rd, plural of ἐπίσταμαι.

ἐκπεπολεμῶσθαι Perfect, middle infinitve of ἐκπολεμόω.

5.73.2

ἀπικομένων = ἀφικομένων.

ἀπικομένων δὲ τῶν ἀγγέλων... καὶ λεγόντων Genitive absolute constructions.

ἐντεταλμένα Perfect, passive, neuter, accusative, plural participle of ἐντέλλω. As a substantive, it means "commands."

Ἀρταφρένης ὁ Ὑστάσπεος Σαρδίων ὕπαρχος Artaphrenes governed the district surrounding the Lydian city of Sardis. His title was most likely that of satrap, although Herodotus does not use this word.

κοῦ = ποῦ. With γῆς, "where of a place," or "what place."

δεοίατο Present, optative, middle, 3rd, plural of δέω.

5.73.3

ἐπὶ σφέων αὐτῶν βαλόμενοι "Having deliberated among themselves."

ἐς τὴν ἑωυτῶν Supply γήν.

ἑωυτῶν = ἑαυτῶν.

☙

5.78.1 Herodotus Endorses Freedom

We see in this passage an emphatic statement from Herodotus that the freedom(s) which the Athenians enjoyed made them a stronger people. The specific word that he uses to describe this freedom is ἰσηγορίη, or "freedom of speech," a privilege which all Athenian male citizens could, in theory, exercise in their popular assembly. This is a notion that Herodotus revisits in 5.91, where he concludes that a free Athenian people were a match for the military might of Sparta. By contrast, he sees the despotism of the Persian King as a deterrent to any courageous behavior on the part of his subjects, a point that he will make on more than one occasion when narrating Xerxes' invasion of mainland Greece.

Ἀθηναῖοι μέν νυν ηὔξηντο. δηλοῖ δὲ οὐ κατ᾽ ἓν μοῦνον ἀλλὰ πανταχῇ ἡ ἰσηγορίη ὡς ἐστὶ χρῆμα σπουδαῖον, εἰ καὶ Ἀθηναῖοι τυραννευόμενοι μὲν οὐδαμῶν τῶν σφέας περιοικεόντων ἦσαν τὰ πολέμια ἀμείνους, ἀπαλλαχθέντες δὲ τυράννων μακρῷ πρῶτοι ἐγένοντο. δηλοῖ ὦν ταῦτα ὅτι κατεχόμενοι μὲν ἐθελοκάκεον ὡς δεσπότῃ ἐργαζόμενοι, ἐλευθερωθέντων δὲ αὐτὸς ἕκαστος ἑωυτῷ προεθυμέετο κατεργάζεσθαι.

5.78.1

ηὔξηντο Pluperfect, indicative, active, 3rd, plural of αὐξάνω.
οὐ κατ᾽ ἓν μοῦνον ἀλλὰ πανταχῇ "Not merely in one way, but in every way."
τὰ πολέμια Accusative of respect.
ὦν = οὖν.
ὡς "Insofar as."
ἑωυτῷ = ἑαυτῷ.

 C3

5.97.1-3 "The Beginning of Evils"

The above heading is a translation of a phrase from the last sentence of this chapter (5.97.3), where Herodotus expresses a rather critical view of the Ionian Revolt and of the role that Athens played in it. His portrait of Aristagoras, the Milesian tyrant who instigated the revolt, continues to be negative, just as it was back in 5.50, where Aristagoras was shown trying to convince the Spartans to come to the aid of the Ionians. Herodotus clearly sees Aristagoras as an opportunist whose primary motive in instigating the revolt was so he could stay in power. It is not surprising, therefore, that Herodotus would also take a dim view of the revolt which Aristagoras instigated. What is really surprising—indeed, shocking—is the remark that Herodotus makes about how much easier it was for Aristagoras to fool 30,000 people in the Athenian Assembly than to dupe the one king of Sparta (5.79.2). This cynical and even hostile comment stands in stark contrast to the very positive statements which Herodotus makes elsewhere in the *Histories* (for example, in 5.78) about democracy and its effects on the Athenian people.

νομίζουσι δὲ ταῦτα καὶ διαβεβλημένοισι ἐς τοὺς Πέρσας, ἐν τούτῳ δὴ τῷ καιρῷ ὁ Μιλήσιος Ἀρισταγόρης, ὑπὸ Κλεομένεος τοῦ Λακεδαιμονίου ἐξελασθεὶς ἐκ τῆς Σπάρτης, ἀπίκετο ἐς Ἀθήνας· αὕτη γὰρ ἡ πόλις τῶν λοιπέων ἐδυνάστευε μέγιστον. ἐπελθὼν δὲ ἐπὶ τὸν δῆμον ὁ Ἀρισταγόρης ταὐτὰ ἔλεγε τὰ καὶ ἐν τῇ Σπάρτῃ περὶ τῶν ἀγαθῶν τῶν ἐν τῇ Ἀσίῃ καὶ τοῦ πολέμου τοῦ Περσικοῦ, ὡς οὔτε ἀσπίδα οὔτε δόρυ νομίζουσι εὐπετέες τε χειρωθῆναι εἴησαν. [2] ταῦτά τε δὴ ἔλεγε καὶ πρὸς τοῖσι τάδε, ὡς οἱ Μιλήσιοι τῶν Ἀθηναίων εἰσὶ ἄποικοι, καὶ οἰκός σφεας εἴη ῥύεσθαι δυναμένους μέγα· καὶ οὐδὲν ὅ τι οὐκ ὑπίσχετο οἷα κάρτα δεόμενος, ἐς ὃ ἀνέπεισε σφέας. πολλοὺς γὰρ οἶκε εἶναι εὐπετέστερον διαβάλλειν ἢ ἕνα, εἰ Κλεομένεα μὲν τὸν Λακεδαιμόνιον μοῦνον οὐκ οἷός τε ἐγένετο διαβάλλειν, τρεῖς δὲ μυριάδας Ἀθηναίων ἐποίησε τοῦτο. [3] Ἀθηναῖοι μὲν δὴ ἀναπεισθέντες ἐψηφίσαντο εἴκοσι νέας ἀποστεῖλαι βοηθοὺς Ἴωσι, στρατηγὸν ἀποδέξαντες αὐτῶν εἶναι Μελάνθιον ἄνδρα τῶν ἀστῶν ἐόντα τὰ πάντα δόκιμον· αὗται δὲ αἱ νέες ἀρχὴ κακῶν ἐγένοντο Ἕλλησί τε καὶ βαρβάροισι.

5.97.1

νομίζουσι δὲ ταῦτα καὶ διαβεβλημένοισι ἐς τοὺς Πέρσας This phrase looks back to the previous chapter (5.96), where the Athenians are said to have rejected the orders of Artaphrenes (the Persian governor or satrap of the region surrounding the Lydian city of Sardis) to receive Hippias, their former tyrant, back into the city.

νομίζουσι Dative participle.

διαβεβλημένοισι ἐς τοὺς Πέρσας "Being at variance with the Persians."

ἐξελασθεὶς Aorist, passive, masculine, nominative, singular participle of ἐξελαύνω.

ἀπίκετο = ἀφίκετο.

τὰ καὶ ἐν τῇ Σπάρτῃ "Things which he had also said in Sparta."

νομίζουσι "Employ."

χειρωθῆναι Aorist, passive infinitive of χειρόω.

5.97.2

οἰκός...εἴη "It would be fitting."

δυναμένους Modifies "Athenians" (understood).

οἷα "Insofar as."

ἐς ὃ "Until."

οἶκε = ἔοικε.

οὐκ οἷός τε ἐγένετο "He was not able."

ἐποίησε When ποεῖν means "to do something to someone," it takes a double accusative.

5.97.3

τὰ πάντα Accusative of respect.

⋘

5.105.1-2 Master, Remember the Athenians

In the chapters preceding this one, we learn about the successes and failures of the Ionian Revolt. The forecasts of Aristagoras notwithstanding, the light-armed Persians proved quite capable of defeating Greek hoplites, and the Phoenician navy rendered invaluable assistance to the Persian cause. The Ionians and their allies, including the Athenians, did have their share of successful battles, however, and managed to take and burn the Lydian capital of Sardis (5.101), only to suffer a setback at nearby Ephesus. For reasons that are still the subject of much scholarly debate, the Athenians withdrew their forces from Asia Minor after the debacles at Sardis and Ephesus and returned to Athens (HW *ad* 5.103.1 speculate that the Athenians retreated because of concerns over the belligerent moves of Aegina, the island city-state in the Saronic Gulf). The passage below takes us into a fantasy world, where we get to witness the Persian King's reactions to the news from Sardis. His initial response, according to Herodotus, was to ask who these Athenians were. This question, if indeed it was ever really asked, may have indicated Persian ignorance of Greek geography (so HW *ad* 5.105.1) or, as is more likely, Darius' contempt for a people who, to him, must have seemed quite insignificant.

Ὀνήσιλος μέν νυν ἐπολιόρκεε Ἀμαθοῦντα. βασιλέι δὲ Δαρείῳ ὡς ἐξαγγέλθη Σάρδις ἁλούσας ἐμπεπρῆσθαι ὑπό τε Ἀθηναίων καὶ Ἰώνων, τὸν δὲ ἡγεμόνα γενέσθαι τῆς συλλογῆς ὥστε ταῦτα συνυφανθῆναι τὸν Μιλήσιον Ἀρισταγόρην, πρῶτα μὲν λέγεται αὐτόν, ὡς ἐπύθετο ταῦτα, Ἰώνων οὐδένα λόγον ποιησάμενον, εὖ εἰδότα ὡς οὗτοί γε οὐ καταπροΐξονται ἀποστάντες, εἰρέσθαι οἵτινες εἶεν οἱ Ἀθηναῖοι, μετὰ δὲ πυθόμενον αἰτῆσαι τὸ τόξον, λαβόντα δὲ καὶ ἐπιθέντα δὲ ὀιστὸν ἄνω πρὸς τὸν οὐρανὸν ἀπεῖναι, καί μιν ἐς τὸν ἠέρα βάλλοντα εἰπεῖν· [2] "ὦ Ζεῦ, ἐκγενέσθαι μοι Ἀθηναίους τίσασθαι," εἴπαντα δὲ ταῦτα προστάξαι ἑνὶ τῶν θεραπόντων δείπνου προκειμένου αὐτῷ ἐς τρὶς ἑκάστοτε εἰπεῖν· "δέσποτα, μέμνεο τῶν Ἀθηναίων."

5.105.1

Ὀνήσιλος μέν νυν ἐπολιόρκεε Ἀμαθοῦντα Quite often, a chapter in the *Histories* begins with a sentence (or phrase) that refers to the previous chapter. Onesilos was a Cypriot who took advantage of the distractions provided by the Ionian Revolt and launched his own rebellion. For the location of Amathous, a Cypriot city which Onesilos placed under siege, see map in Landmark *ad* 5.108.

ἁλούσας Aorist, active, masculine, nominative, singular participle of ἁλίσκομαι, a defective
   passive.

ἐμπεπρῆσθαι Perfect, passive infinitve of ἐμπίπρημι.

ὥστε ταῦτα συνυφανθῆναι "So as to weave together these things."

ἀποστάντες "For rebelling."

πυθόμενον "Having learned."

5.105.2

δείπνου προκειμένου Genitive absolute construction.

μέμνεο Perfect, imperative, middle, 2nd singular of μιμνήσκω.

☙

6.9.3-4 Persians Threaten the Ionian Tyrants

The year is 494 B.C. and the Ionian Revolt is well underway. The Persians in charge
of the suppression of the revolt have gathered those Ionian tyrants who had medized and
exhort them to convince the citizens of their respective cities to end their rebellion. That
the punishments which the Persians mention were not mere idle threats can be seen in
6.32. Clearly, a lot was at stake with the success or failure of the revolt.

[3] "ἄνδρες Ἴωνες, νῦν τις ὑμέων εὖ ποιήσας φανήτω τὸν βασιλέος οἶκον· τοὺς
γὰρ ἑωυτοῦ ἕκαστος ὑμέων πολιήτας πειράσθω ἀποσχίζων ἀπὸ τοῦ λοιποῦ
συμμαχικοῦ. προϊσχόμενοι δὲ ἐπαγγείλασθε τάδε, ὡς πείσονταί τε ἄχαρι
οὐδὲν διὰ τὴν ἀπόστασιν, οὐδέ σφι οὔτε τὰ ἱρὰ οὔτε τὰ ἴδια ἐμπεπρήσεται, οὐδὲ
βιαιότερον ἕξουσι οὐδὲν ἢ πρότερον εἶχον. [4] εἰ δὲ ταῦτα μὲν οὐ ποιήσουσι,
οἱ δὲ πάντως διὰ μάχης ἐλεύσονται, τάδε ἤδη σφι λέγετε ἐπηρεάζοντες,
τά περ σφέας κατέξει, ὡς ἑσσωθέντες τῇ μάχῃ ἐξανδραποδιεῦνται, καὶ ὡς
σφεων τοὺς παῖδας ἐκτομίας ποιήσομεν, τὰς δὲ παρθένους ἀνασπάστους ἐς
Βάκτρα, καὶ ὡς τὴν χώρην ἄλλοισι παραδώσομεν."

6.9.3

τις = ἕκαστος.

τις ὑμέων εὖ ποιήσας φανήτω "Let each one of you show yourselves as a benefactor [to the
   house of the King]."

φανήτω Aorist, imperative, passive, 3rd, singular of φαίνω.

πειράσθω ἀποσχίζων "Let [each one of you] attempt to separate." Note that Herodotus often
   uses a participle where Attic Greek would normally have an infinitive.

πειράσθω Present, imperative, middle, 3rd, singular of πειράω.

ἐμπεπρήσεται Future perfect, indicative, middle, 3rd, singular of ἐμπίμπρημι.

6.9.4

διὰ μάχης ἐλεύσονται A periphrasis for μαχήσονται.

ἐπηρεάζοντες "In a threatening way."

τά περ σφέας κατέξει "The very things which will overtake them."

ἑσσωθέντες Aorist, passive, masculine, nominative, plural participle of ἑσσόομαι (= ἡσσάομαι).

ἐκτομίας "Eunuchs."

Βάκτρα For the location of Bactria, see map in Landmark *ad* 4.195. It was the Persian province furthest away from Ionia.

ℭℨ

6.15.1-2 The Fog of War, Part I

The Chians (for the location of Chios, see map in Landmark *ad* 6.8) receive high praise from Herodotus for their persistent courage during the Battle of Lade (494 B.C.), the decisive naval engagement of the Ionian Revolt. Despite the defection of most of the other Ionian naval contingents, the Chians apparently continued the fight.

τῶν δὲ παραμεινάντων ἐν τῇ ναυμαχίῃ περιέφθησαν τρηχύτατα Χῖοι ὡς ἀποδεικνύμενοί τε ἔργα λαμπρὰ καὶ οὐκ ἐθελοκακέοντες. παρείχοντο μὲν γάρ, ὥσπερ καὶ πρότερον εἰρέθη, νέας ἑκατόν, καὶ ἐπ᾿ ἑκάστης αὐτέων ἄνδρας τεσσεράκοντα τῶν ἀστῶν λογάδας ἐπιβατεύοντας. [2] ὁρέοντες δὲ τοὺς πολλοὺς τῶν συμμάχων προδιδόντας οὐκ ἐδικαίευν γίνεσθαι τοῖσι κακοῖσι αὐτῶν ὅμοιοι, ἀλλὰ μετ᾿ ὀλίγων συμμάχων μεμουνωμένοι διεκπλέοντες ἐναυμάχεον, ἐς ὃ τῶν πολεμίων ἑλόντες νέας συχνὰς ἀπέβαλον τῶν σφετερέων τὰς πλεῦνας.

6.15.1

περιέφθησαν τρηχύτατα "Were treated very badly."

περιέφθησαν Aorist, indicative, passive, 3rd, plural of περιέπω.

εἰρέθη "Was mentioned."

ἐπιβατεύοντας "Marines."

6.15.2

μεμουνωμένοι Perfect, passive, masculine, nominative, plural participle of μονόω.

διεκπλέοντες A naval maneuver whereby a trireme would break through the enemy lines only to make a sudden turn and attack the stern or the undefended side (flank) of an enemy ship.

ℭℨ

6.16.1-2 Fog of War, Part II

Some of the Chians who survived the Battle of Lade (494 B.C.) are mistaken for marauders by the people of Ephesus (for the location of Ephesus, see map in Landmark *ad* 6.8). How the Ephesians could have remained ignorant about the events at nearby Lade and the approach of the Chians is not something that Herodotus cares to explain.

Χῖοι μὲν δὴ τῇσι λοιπῇσι τῶν νεῶν ἀποφεύγουσι ἐς τὴν ἑωυτῶν ὅσοισι δὲ τῶν Χίων ἀδύνατοι ἦσαν αἱ νέες ὑπὸ τρωμάτων, οὗτοι δὲ ὡς ἐδιώκοντο καταφυγγάνουσι πρὸς τὴν Μυκάλην. νέας μὲν δὴ αὐτοῦ ταύτῃ ἐποκείλαντες κατέλιπον, οἱ δὲ πεζῇ ἐκομίζοντο διὰ τῆς ἠπείρου. [2] ἐπειδὴ δὲ ἐσέβαλον ἐς τὴν Ἐφεσίην κομιζόμενοι οἱ Χῖοι, νυκτός τε γὰρ ἀπίκατο ἐς αὐτὴν καὶ ἐόντων τῇσι γυναιξὶ αὐτόθι θεσμοφορίων, ἐνθαῦτα δὴ οἱ Ἐφέσιοι, οὔτε προακηκοότες ὡς εἶχε περὶ τῶν Χίων ἰδόντες τε στρατὸν ἐς τὴν χώρην ἐσβεβληκότα, πάγχυ σφέας καταδόξαντες εἶναι κλῶπας καὶ ἰέναι ἐπὶ τὰς γυναῖκας, ἐξεβοήθεον πανδημεὶ καὶ ἔκτεινον τοὺς Χίους.

6.16.1

ἐς τὴν ἑωυτῶν Supply γῆν: "To their own land."

Μυκάλην For the location of Mykale, see map in Landmark *ad* 6.8.

ἐκομίζοντο "They traveled."

6.16.2

ἐόντων...θεσμοφορίων Genitive absolute construction.

θεσμοφορίων A pan-Hellenic celebration of the goddess Demeter in which only women could participate.

προακηκοότες Perfect, active, masculine, nominative, plural participle of προακούω.

ὡς εἶχε περὶ τῶν Χίων "How things turned out with the Chians."

ἐσβεβληκότα Perfect, active, masculine, accusative, singular participle of εἰσβάλλω.

πάγχυ...καταδόξαντες "Having become thoroughly convinced."

ⓒⓈ

6.21.1-2 The "Fall of Miletus"

The actual capture and fall of the city of Miletus is only briefly described in 6.18. Herodotus prefers to concentrate instead on the aftermath of the fall and shows us how news of the capture of Miletus was received in Athens, a city which considered itself to be the metropolis or "mother city" of Ionian Miletus. The chapter below opens with a fascinating glimpse into events from the late 6th century B.C. in Magna Graecia (the Greek part of S. Italy and Sicily), where, in 510 B.C., the proverbially rich city of Sybaris was destroyed by nearby Croton. Herodotus then turns his attention to Athens and the reaction there to the fall of Miletus. The fine imposed by the Athenian state on the playwright Phrynicus, a near-contemporary of Aeschylus, provides powerful evidence for the profound effect that plays could have on Athenian audiences, even in the early phases of the development of Athenian tragedy.

παθοῦσι δὲ ταῦτα Μιλησίοισι πρὸς Περσέων οὐκ ἀπέδοσαν τὴν ὁμοίην Συβαρῖται, οἳ Λαόν τε καὶ Σκίδρον οἴκεον τῆς πόλιος ἀπεστερημένοι. Συβάριος γὰρ ἁλούσης ὑπὸ Κροτωνιητέων Μιλήσιοι πάντες ἡβηδὸν ἀπεκείραντο τὰς κεφαλὰς καὶ πένθος μέγα προσεθήκαντο· πόλιες γὰρ αὗται μάλιστα δὴ τῶν ἡμεῖς ἴδμεν ἀλλήλῃσι ἐξεινώθησαν· [2] οὐδὲν ὁμοίως καὶ Ἀθηναῖοι. Ἀθηναῖοι μὲν γὰρ δῆλον ἐποίησαν ὑπεραχθεσθέντες τῇ Μιλήτου ἁλώσι τῇ τε ἄλλῃ πολλαχῇ, καὶ δὴ καὶ ποιήσαντι Φρυνίχῳ δρᾶμα Μιλήτου ἅλωσιν καὶ διδάξαντι ἐς δάκρυά τε ἔπεσε τὸ θέητρον, καὶ ἐζημίωσάν μιν ὡς ἀναμνήσαντα οἰκήϊα κακὰ χιλίῃσι δραχμῇσι, καὶ ἐπέταξαν μηδένα χρᾶσθαι τούτῳ τῷ δράματι.

6.21.1

παθοῦσι This participle (from πάσχω) is in the dative case.

τὴν ὁμοίην A word like χάριν needs to be supplied.

Συβαρῖται, Λαόν For the locations of Sybaris and Laos, towns in Magna Graecia (S. Italy), see map in Landmark *ad* 6.20. The location of Skidros is not attested.

Κροτωνιητέων For the location of Croton, yet another town in Magna Graecia, see map in Landmark *ad* 6.20.

ἡβηδόν An adverb: "Of all ages [from the very young on up]."

τῶν ἡμεῖς ἴδμεν "Of all [the cities] we know."

6.21.2

δῆλον ἐποίησαν The equivalent of ἐδήλωσαν. The nominative participle, ὑπεραχθεσθέντες, is used as a supplementary participle.

διδάξαντι Playwrights would "teach" their plays to the actors and the chorus.

ὡς "On the ground that."

δραχμῇσι A drachma would roughly be the equivalent of a day's wage.

☙

6.27.1-3 Signs From the Gods

After the failure of the Ionian Revolt, Histiaios, the tyrant who instigated the Revolt and who seems to have been incapable of remaining idle, captured the island city-state of Chios (see map in Landmark *ad* 6.8) with the help of Lesbian forces (494 B.C.) In telling this story, Herodotus weaves into his narrative a strong statement about the importance of humans' paying heed to portents or signs from the gods. Coupled with an earlier statement (in 6.19), where Herodotus resolutely claims that Delphi did in fact predict the fall of Miletus—these were the Oracle's words:"Your wives will wash the feet of long-haired Persians"—his position on portents and oracles, at least in this part of the *Histories*, seems well defined.

φιλέει δέ κως προσημαίνειν, εὖτ' ἂν μέλλη μεγάλα κακὰ ἢ πόλι ἢ ἔθνεϊ ἔσεσθαι· καὶ γὰρ Χίοισι πρὸ τούτων σημήια μεγάλα ἐγένετο· [2] τοῦτο μέν σφι πέμψασι ἐς Δελφοὺς χορὸν νεηνιέων ἑκατὸν δύο μοῦνοι τούτων ἀπενόστησαν, τοὺς δὲ ὀκτώ τε καὶ ἐνενήκοντα αὐτῶν λοιμὸς ὑπολαβὼν ἀπήνεικε· τοῦτο δὲ ἐν τῇ πόλι τὸν αὐτὸν τοῦτον χρόνον, ὀλίγον πρὸ τῆς ναυμαχίης, παισὶ γράμματα διδασκομένοισι ἐνέπεσέ ἡ στέγη, ὥστε ἀπ' ἑκατὸν καὶ εἴκοσι παίδων εἷς μοῦνος ἀπέφυγε. [3] ταῦτα μέν σφι σημήια ὁ θεὸς προέδεξε, μετὰ δὲ ταῦτα ἡ ναυμαχίη ὑπολαβοῦσα ἐς γόνυ τὴν πόλιν ἔβαλε, ἐπὶ δὲ τῇ ναυμαχίῃ ἐπεγένετο Ἱστιαῖος Λεσβίους ἄγων· κεκακωμένων δὲ τῶν Χίων, καταστροφὴν εὐπετέως αὐτῶν ἐποιήσατο.

6.27.1

φιλέει A subject like ὁ θεός needs to be supplied. "A god is likely…."

κως = πως.

εὖτ' ἂν The equivalent of ὅταν.

6.27.2

τοῦτο μέν Translate with τοῦτο δὲ. "For one thing…for another."

πέμψασι Participle in the dative case.

ἀπήνεικε = ἀπήνεγκε. Aorist, indicative, active, 3rd, singular of ἀποφέρω.

6.27.3

προέδεξε = προέδειξε. Aorist, indicative, active, 3rd, singular of προδείκνυμι.

ἐς γόνυ τὴν πόλιν ἔβαλε A sports metaphor: "Brought the city to its knees."

κεκακωμένων δὲ τῶν Χίων Genitive absolute construction.

ଔ

6.31.1-2 The Persian Dragnet

Herodotus describes a Persian version of a dragnet, whereby Persian soldiers would lock hands and sweep an entire Aegean island in order to capture those who had resisted the King. This kind of a search over an island the size of Chios or Lesbos (see map in Landmark *ad* 6.8) would seem impractical, especially in view of the mountainous terrain.

Perhaps Herodotus was too ready to believe such stories which exaggerate the plight of Ionia and the islands lying off the coast of Asia Minor (cf. HW *ad* 6.31.2).

τὰ μὲν περὶ Ἱστιαῖον οὕτω ἔσχε. ὁ δὲ ναυτικὸς στρατὸς ὁ Περσέων χειμερίσας περὶ Μίλητον, τῷ δευτέρῳ ἔτεϊ ὡς ἀνέπλωσε, αἱρέει εὐπετέως τὰς νήσους τὰς πρὸς τῇ ἠπείρῳ κειμένας, Χίον καὶ Λέσβον καὶ Τένεδον. ὅκως δὲ λάβοι τινὰ τῶν νήσων, ὡς ἑκάστην αἱρέοντες οἱ βάρβαροι ἐσαγήνευον τοὺς ἀνθρώπους. [2] σαγηνεύουσι δὲ τόνδε τὸν τρόπον· ἀνὴρ ἀνδρὸς ἁψάμενος τῆς χειρὸς ἐκ θαλάσσης τῆς βορηΐης ἐπὶ τὴν νοτίην διήκουσι, καὶ ἔπειτα διὰ πάσης τῆς νήσου διέρχονται ἐκθηρεύοντες τοὺς ἀνθρώπους. αἵρεον δὲ καὶ τὰς ἐν τῇ ἠπείρῳ πόλιας τὰς Ἰάδας κατὰ ταὐτά, πλὴν οὐκ ἐσαγήνευον τοὺς ἀνθρώπους· οὐ γὰρ οἷά τ᾽ ἦν.

6.31.1

δευτέρῳ "Following."

Χίον καὶ Λέσβον καὶ Τένεδον For the locations of Chios, Lesbos, and Tenedos, see map in Landmark *ad* 6.30.

ἐσαγήνευον "They caught with a fish net."

6.31.2

Ἰάδας "Ionian."

οὐ γὰρ οἷά τ᾽ ἦν. "It was not possible."

 conclusion

6.105.1-3 The Run of Pheidippides

A large part of Book VI (50-86) deals with the internal affairs of Sparta in the early part of the 5th century B.C. and the struggles between the various claimants to Spartan kingship. The result of all this turmoil was a weakened Sparta which was even more susceptible than usual to revolts from the helots (Sparta's serf population) and to challenges from other city states within the Peloponnese. To make matters worse for the Spartans, Demaratos, the exiled Spartan king, took up residence in the court of Darius and served as his trusted counsel (6.70). This, then, was the setting in 490 B.C. for the Persian expedition against Eretria and Athens, cities which had participated in the ill-fated attack on Sardis during the Ionian Revolt. In this chapter, we hear about Pheidippides, the famous runner, who was sent by the Athenians on a 150-mile journey to Sparta in order to secure Spartan help in face of the impending Persian attack at Marathon. Later additions to the story have Pheidippides returning to Attica in time to fight at the Battle of Marathon and then running the more than 26 miles from Marathon to Athens in order to report the news of the victory.

καὶ πρῶτα μὲν ἐόντες ἔτι ἐν τῷ ἄστεϊ οἱ στρατηγοὶ ἀποπέμπουσι ἐς Σπάρτην κήρυκα Φειδιππίδην Ἀθηναῖον μὲν ἄνδρα, ἄλλως δὲ ἡμεροδρόμην τε καὶ τοῦτο μελετῶντα· τῷ δή, ὡς αὐτός τε ἔλεγε Φειδιππίδης καὶ Ἀθηναίοισι ἀπήγγελλε, περὶ τὸ Παρθένιον ὄρος τὸ ὑπὲρ Τεγέης ὁ Πὰν περιπίπτει: [2] βώσαντα δὲ τὸ οὔνομα τοῦ Φειδιππίδεω τὸν Πᾶνα Ἀθηναίοισι κελεῦσαι ἀπαγγεῖλαι, δι’ ὅ τι ἑωυτοῦ οὐδεμίαν ἐπιμελείην ποιεῦνται ἐόντος εὐνόου Ἀθηναίοισι καὶ πολλαχῇ γενομένου σφι ἤδη χρησίμου, τὰ δ’ ἔτι καὶ ἐσομένου. [3] καὶ ταῦτα μὲν Ἀθηναῖοι, καταστάντων σφι εὖ ἤδη τῶν πρηγμάτων, πιστεύσαντες εἶναι ἀληθέα ἱδρύσαντο ὑπὸ τῇ ἀκροπόλι Πανὸς ἱρόν, καὶ αὐτὸν ἀπὸ ταύτης τῆς ἀγγελίης θυσίῃσι ἐπετείοισι καὶ λαμπάδι ἱλάσκονται.

6.105.1

ἡμεροδρόμην A runner who would deliver his message within a day.

τοῦτο μελετῶντα “Specially trained for this.”

Παρθένιον ὄρος τὸ ὑπὲρ Τεγέης For the location of this mountain, see map in Landmark *ad* 6.105.

περιπίπτει Comparable to the English expression “Fell in with.”

6.105.2

βώσαντα Starting with this word, which is in the accusative case and modifies τὸν Πᾶνα, Herodotus switches to indirect discourse.

οὐδεμίαν ἐπιμελείην ποιεῦνται “Pay no respect.”

τὰ δ’ Accusative of respect: “And in other matters.”

6.105.3

καταστάντων σφι εὖ ἤδη τῶν πρηγμάτων Genitive absolute construction: “Once their situation returned to normal.”

☙

6.106.1-3 Pheidippides Delivers His Urgent Message

Herodotus seems to accept the reason offered by the Spartans for why they could not immediately send their hoplites to Marathon to help the Athenians. In contrast, Plato (*Laws* 693) claims that the Spartans did not want to commit their hoplites to the battle at Marathon because of the situation in Messenia, where a revolt of the Messenian helots required the immediate attention of the Spartan army. Plutarch (*de Malignitate Herodoti* 26) also doubts the validity of the Spartan excuse and maintains that the Spartans could have reached Marathon in plenty of time without violating their sacred laws.

τότε δὲ πεμφθεὶς ὑπὸ τῶν στρατηγῶν ὁ Φειδιππίδης οὗτος, ὅτε πέρ οἱ ἔφη
καὶ τὸν Πᾶνα φανῆναι, δευτεραῖος ἐκ τοῦ Ἀθηναίων ἄστεος ἦν ἐν Σπάρτῃ,
ἀπικόμενος δὲ ἐπὶ τοὺς ἄρχοντας ἔλεγε· [2] "ὦ Λακεδαιμόνιοι, Ἀθηναῖοι
ὑμέων δέονται σφίσι βοηθῆσαι καὶ μὴ περιιδεῖν πόλιν ἀρχαιοτάτην ἐν τοῖσι
Ἕλλησι δουλοσύνῃ περιπεσοῦσαν πρὸς ἀνδρῶν βαρβάρων· καὶ γὰρ νῦν
Ἐρέτριά τε ἠνδραπόδισται καὶ πόλι λογίμῳ ἡ Ἑλλὰς γέγονε ἀσθενεστέρη."
[3] "ὁ μὲν δή σφι τὰ ἐντεταλμένα ἀπήγγελλε, τοῖσι δὲ ἕαδε μὲν βοηθέειν
Ἀθηναίοισι, ἀδύνατα δέ σφι ἦν τὸ παραυτίκα ποιέειν ταῦτα, οὐ βουλομένοισι
λύειν τὸν νόμον· ἦν γὰρ ἱσταμένου τοῦ μηνὸς εἰνάτη, εἰνάτη δὲ οὐκ
ἐξελεύσεσθαι ἔφασαν μὴ οὐ πλήρεος ἐόντος τοῦ κύκλου.

6.106.1

φανῆναι Aorist, passive infinitive of φαίνω.

τοὺς ἄρχοντας Probably, the Ephors.

6.106.2

γέγονε ἀσθενεστέρη "Has been made weaker."

6.106.3

τοῖσι The Spartan magistrates.

ἕαδε Aorist, indicative, active, 3rd, singular of ἁνδάνω. Herodotus uses this verb to refer to
    the decisions of a group of individuals.

τὸ παραυτίκα "Right away."

ἦν γὰρ ἱσταμένου τοῦ μηνὸς εἰνάτη "It was the ninth of the month."

οὐ πλήρεος ἐόντος τοῦ κύκλου "Until the moon was full."

☙

✳ 6.107.1-4 Hippias Loses a Tooth at Marathon

Just when all the players and events of the Battle of Marathon seem to be coming into
focus, Herodotus interrupts his narrative for this amusing and memorable story of how
Hippias, the exiled tyrant of Athens who was guiding the Persian forces to Marathon,
had a bizarre dream which he interpreted with the help of a lost tooth. The story is, of
course, hardly credible, but it does highlight, once more, the important role that dreams
and portents play in the world of the Herodotus.

οὗτοι μέν νυν τὴν πανσέληνον ἔμενον. τοῖσι δὲ βαρβάροισι κατηγέετο Ἱππίης
ὁ Πεισιστράτου ἐς τὸν Μαραθῶνα, τῆς παροιχομένης νυκτὸς ὄψιν ἰδὼν
τοιήνδε· ἐδόκεε ὁ Ἱππίης τῇ μητρὶ τῇ ἑωυτοῦ συνευνηθῆναι. [2] συνεβάλετο

ὧν ἐκ τοῦ ὀνείρου κατελθὼν ἐς τὰς Ἀθήνας καὶ ἀνασωσάμενος τὴν ἀρχὴν τελευτήσειν ἐν τῇ ἑωυτοῦ γηραιός. ἐκ μὲν δὴ τῆς ὄψιος συνεβάλετο ταῦτα, τότε δὲ κατηγεόμενος τοῦτο μὲν τὰ ἀνδράποδα τὰ ἐξ Ἐρετρίης ἀπέβησε ἐς τὴν νῆσον τὴν Στυρέων, καλεομένην δὲ Αἰγλείην, τοῦτο δὲ καταγομένας ἐς τὸν Μαραθῶνα τὰς νέας ὅρμιζε οὗτος, ἐκβάντας τε ἐς γῆν τοὺς βαρβάρους διέτασσε. [3] καὶ οἱ ταῦτα διέποντι ἐπῆλθε πταρεῖν τε καὶ βῆξαι μεζόνως ἢ ὡς ἐώθεε· οἷα δέ οἱ πρεσβυτέρῳ ἐόντι τῶν ὀδόντων οἱ πλεῦνες ἐσείοντο· τούτων ὧν ἕνα τῶν ὀδόντων ἐκβάλλει ὑπὸ βίης βήξας· ἐκπεσόντος δὲ ἐς τὴν ψάμμον αὐτοῦ ἐποιέετο σπουδὴν πολλὴν ἐξευρεῖν. [4] ὡς δὲ οὐκ ἐφαίνετό οἱ ὁ ὀδών, ἀναστενάξας εἶπε πρὸς τοὺς παραστάτας "ἡ γῆ ἥδε οὐκ ἡμετέρη ἐστί, οὐδέ μιν δυνησόμεθα ὑποχειρίην ποιήσασθαι· ὁκόσον δέ τι μοι μέρος μετῆν, ὁ ὀδὼν μετέχει."

6.107.1

οὗτοι The Spartans, whose dilatoriness is described in the previous chapter.

τῆς παροιχομένης νυκτὸς Genitive absolute construction.

συνευνηθῆναι "To have slept."

6.107.2

ὧν = οὖν.

ἀνασωσάμενος "Having recovered."

ἐν τῇ Supply γῇ.

τοῦτο μὲν...τοῦτο δέ "In the first place...in the second place."

Αἰγλείην For the putative location of this island, see map in Landmark *ad* 6.15.

6.107.3

μεζόνως ἢ ὡς ἐώθεε "More than he had been accustomed."

οἷα δέ οἱ πρεσβυτέρῳ ἐόντι "The sort of thing that was likely to happen to him, being rather old."

πλεῦνες = πλείονες.

ὑπὸ βίης βήξας "From the force of the cough." Note the alliteration.

ἐξευρεῖν Aorist, active infinitive of ἐξευρίσκω.

6.107.4

ὁκόσον = ὁπόσον.

☙

6.112.1-3 The Battle of Marathon, Part I: Charge!

As soon as the Athenian hoplites were properly positioned and the omens were declared propitious, the Athenian generals at Marathon decided to attack the Persian forces. The distance between the two armies was about a mile, and yet the heavily armed Athenians are said to have attacked "on the run" (δρόμῳ). There may have been a couple of reasons for this particular strategy: (1) the Athenian generals wanted to take advantage of the element of surprise and attacked before the Persian commanders had a chance to line up their infantry; (2) by attacking "on the run," the Athenian hoplites were able to minimize the effect of the Persian archers. In any case, one can easily imagine how exhausted the heavily-armored Athenians must have been after their mile-long run. Another noteworthy feature to the Battle of Marathon was the absence of cavalry on the Persian side. (For a possible explanation, see Landmark note *ad* 6.112.2.)

ὡς δέ σφι διετέτακτο καὶ τὰ σφάγια ἐγίνετο καλά, ἐνθαῦτα ὡς ἀπείθησαν οἱ Ἀθηναῖοι δρόμῳ ἵεντο ἐς τοὺς βαρβάρους. ἦσαν δὲ στάδιοι οὐκ ἐλάσσονες τὸ μεταίχμιον αὐτῶν ἢ ὀκτώ. [2] οἱ δὲ Πέρσαι ὁρέοντες δρόμῳ ἐπιόντας παρεσκευάζοντο ὡς δεξόμενοι, μανίην τε τοῖσι Ἀθηναίοισι ἐπέφερον καὶ πάγχυ ὀλεθρίην, ὁρέοντες αὐτοὺς ὀλίγους καὶ τούτους δρόμῳ ἐπειγομένους, οὔτε ἵππου ὑπαρχούσης σφι οὔτε τοξευμάτων. [3] ταῦτα μέν νυν οἱ βάρβαροι κατείκαζον· Ἀθηναῖοι δὲ ἐπείτε ἀθρόοι προσέμειξαν τοῖσι βαρβάροισι, ἐμάχοντο ἀξίως λόγου. πρῶτοι μὲν γὰρ Ἑλλήνων πάντων τῶν ἡμεῖς ἴδμεν δρόμῳ ἐς πολεμίους ἐχρήσαντο, πρῶτοι δὲ ἀνέσχοντο ἐσθῆτά τε Μηδικὴν ὁρέοντες καὶ τοὺς ἄνδρας ταύτην ἐσθημένους· τέως δὲ ἦν τοῖσι Ἕλλησι καὶ τὸ οὔνομα τὸ Μήδων φόβος ἀκοῦσαι.

6.112.1

διετέτακτο Pluperfect, indicative, passive, 3rd, singular of διατάσσω. Used impersonally.

ἀπείθησαν Aorist, indicative, passive, 3rd, plural of ἀπίημι (= ἀφίημι): "They [the Athenians] were sent forth." That is, they were given permission by their officers to attack.

6.112.2

ὡς δεξόμενοι The future participle is used here to indicate purpose.

ὀλεθρίην Supply μανίην.

οὔτε ἵππου ὑπαρχούσης σφι οὔτε τοξευμάτων Genitive absolute construction.

6.112.3

τῶν ἡμεῖς ἴδμεν "Of whom we know."

6.113.1-2 The Battle of Marathon, Part II: Athenian Victory!

Herodotus tells the actual story of the Battle of Marathon in a very succinct way, but we can turn to other sources for additional information. According to Pausanias (1.14), scenes from the battle were later painted on the walls of the Stoa Poikile ("Painted Porch") in the Athenian Agora: Miltiades, the Athenian general, was depicted in the murals exhorting his men, and so was Cynegiros, the brother of the great tragedian Aeschylus (who also took part in the Battle).

μαχομένων δὲ ἐν τῷ Μαραθῶνι χρόνος ἐγίνετο πολλός, καὶ τὸ μὲν μέσον τοῦ στρατοπέδου ἐνίκων οἱ βάρβαροι, τῇ Πέρσαι τε αὐτοὶ καὶ Σάκαι ἐτετάχατο· κατὰ τοῦτο μὲν δὴ ἐνίκων οἱ βάρβαροι καὶ ῥήξαντες ἐδίωκον ἐς τὴν μεσόγαιαν, τὸ δὲ κέρας ἑκάτερον ἐνίκων Ἀθηναῖοί τε καὶ Πλαταιέες· [2] νικῶντες δὲ τὸ μὲν τετραμμένον τῶν βαρβάρων φεύγειν ἔων, τοῖσι δὲ τὸ μέσον ῥήξασι αὐτῶν συναγαγόντες τὰ κέρεα ἀμφότερα ἐμάχοντο, καὶ ἐνίκων Ἀθηναῖοι. φεύγουσι δὲ τοῖσι Πέρσῃσι εἵποντο κόπτοντες, ἐς ὃ ἐς τὴν θάλασσαν ἀπικόμενοι πῦρ τε αἴτεον καὶ ἐπελαμβάνοντο τῶν νεῶν.

6.113.1

μαχομένων δὲ ἐν τῷ Μαραθῶνι Genitive absolute construction.

ἐγίνετο = ἐγίγνετο.

τῇ An adverb.

Σάκαι For the location of the land of the Sakai, see map in Landmark *ad* 6.125.

ἐτετάχατο = τεταγμένοι ἦσαν.

Πλαταιέες The Plataeans—for the location of Plataea, see map in Landmark *ad* 9.80—were frequent allies of the Athenians, much to the displeasure of the Thebans, their fellow Boeotians.

6.113.2

τετραμμένον Perfect, passive, neuter, accusative, singular participle of τρέπω.

ἔων = εἴων. Imperfect, indicative, active, 3rd, plural of ἐάω.

τοῖσι δὲ τὸ μέσον ῥήξασι "Those [Persians] who had broken through the center."

ῥήξασι Aorist, active, masculine, dative, plural participle of ῥήγνυμι.

τὰ κέρεα = τὰ κέρατα.

☙

6.120.1 Spartans Finally Arrive at Marathon

In a rather understated way, Herodotus reports on the late arrival at Marathon of two thousand Spartan hoplites. (Plato [*Laws* 698e] specifies that the Spartans arrived on the day after the battle.) The dilatoriness of the Spartans—who, it should be stipulated, had to travel some 180 miles from Sparta to Marathon—becomes almost a theme in the *Histories*…one that is handled delicately by its author.

Λακεδαιμονίων δὲ ἦκον ἐς τὰς Ἀθήνας δισχίλιοι μετὰ τὴν πανσέληνον, ἔχοντες σπουδὴν πολλὴν καταλαβεῖν, οὕτω ὥστε τριταῖοι ἐκ Σπάρτης ἐγένοντο ἐν τῇ Ἀττικῇ. ὕστεροι δὲ ἀπικόμενοι τῆς συμβολῆς ἱμείροντο ὅμως θεήσασθαι τοὺς Μήδους· ἐλθόντες δὲ ἐς τὸν Μαραθῶνα ἐθεήσαντο. μετὰ δὲ αἰνέοντες Ἀθηναίους καὶ τὸ ἔργον αὐτῶν ἀπαλλάσσοντο ὀπίσω.

6.120.1

μετὰ τὴν πανσέληνον A reference to the religious scruple which kept the Spartans from doing anything to help the Athenians until the arrival of the full moon (cf. 6.106).

καταλαβεῖν The meaning here is not altogether clear. As an explanatory infinitive (to ἔχοντες σπουδὴν πολλὴν), καταλαβεῖν may mean "to take part [in the battle]."

ὕστεροι "Too late for…."

ఆ

6.125.1-5 How Alcmaeon Became Rich

Herodotus devotes quite a bit of his narrative (cf. 6.123) to an exoneration of the Alcmaeonid family, an Athenian *genos* whose members had been accused of medizing (collaborating with the Persians) around the time of the Battle of Marathon. In the chapter below, Herodotus tells the story of Alcmaeon, the eponymous founder of the Alcmaeonid family, and how he became wealthy, thanks to the generosity of Croesus. Chronological problems (cf. HW *ad* 6.125) make the tale of Alcmaeon and Croesus historically suspect (Alcmaeon most likely lived a generation before Croesus) and leave us with little more than an entertaining anecdote, one which demonstrates anew Herodotus' great talent for telling stories, especially the kind which have a moral lesson to impart.

οἱ δὲ Ἀλκμεωνίδαι ἦσαν μὲν καὶ τὰ ἀνέκαθεν λαμπροὶ ἐν τῇσι Ἀθήνησι, ἀπὸ δὲ Ἀλκμέωνος καὶ αὖτις Μεγακλέος ἐγένοντο καὶ κάρτα λαμπροί. [2] τοῦτο μὲν γὰρ Ἀλκμέων ὁ Μεγακλέος τοῖσι ἐκ Σαρδίων Λυδοῖσι παρὰ Κροίσου ἀπικνεομένοισι ἐπὶ τὸ χρηστήριον τὸ ἐν Δελφοῖσι συμπρήκτωρ τε ἐγίνετο καὶ συνελάμβανε προθύμως, καί μιν Κροῖσος πυθόμενος τῶν Λυδῶν τῶν ἐς τὰ χρηστήρια φοιτεόντων ἑωυτὸν εὖ ποιέειν μεταπέμπεται ἐς Σάρδις, ἀπικόμενον δὲ δωρέεται χρυσῷ τὸν ἂν δύνηται τῷ ἑωυτοῦ σώματι ἐξενείκασθαι ἐσάπαξ. [3] ὁ δὲ Ἀλκμέων πρὸς τὴν δωρεὴν ἐοῦσαν τοιαύτην τοιάδε ἐπιτηδεύσας προσέφερε· ἐνδὺς κιθῶνα μέγαν καὶ κόλπον βαθὺν καταλιπόμενος τοῦ κιθῶνος, κοθόρνους τε τοὺς εὕρισκε εὐρυτάτους ἐόντας ὑποδησάμενος, ἤιε ἐς τὸν θησαυρὸν ἐς τόν οἱ κατηγέοντο. [4] ἐσπεσὼν δὲ ἐς σωρὸν ψήγματος πρῶτα μὲν παρέσαξε παρὰ τὰς κνήμας τοῦ χρυσοῦ ὅσον ἐχώρεον οἱ κόθορνοι, μετὰ δὲ τὸν κόλπον πάντα πλησάμενος τοῦ χρυσοῦ καὶ ἐς τὰς τρίχας τῆς κεφαλῆς διαπάσας τοῦ ψήγματος καὶ ἄλλο λαβὼν ἐς τὸ στόμα, ἐξήιε ἐκ τοῦ θησαυροῦ ἕλκων μὲν μόγις τοὺς κοθόρνους, παντὶ δὲ τεῷ οἰκὼς μᾶλλον ἢ ἀνθρώπῳ· τοῦ τό τε στόμα ἐβέβυστο καὶ πάντα ἐξώγκωτο. [5] ἰδόντα δὲ τὸν Κροῖσον γέλως ἐσῆλθε, καί οἱ πάντα τε ἐκεῖνα διδοῖ καὶ πρὸς ἕτερα δωρέεται οὐκ ἐλάσσω ἐκείνων. οὕτω μὲν ἐπλούτησε ἡ οἰκίη αὕτη μεγάλως, καὶ ὁ Ἀλκμέων οὗτος οὕτω τεθριπποτροφήσας Ὀλυμπιάδα ἀναιρέεται.

6.125.1

τὰ ἀνέκαθεν An adverbial expression: "From a long time ago."

6.125.2

ἐγίνετο = ἐγίγνετο.
πυθόμενος Takes the genitive (τῶν Λυδῶν τῶν...φοιτεόντων).
ἑωυτόν = ἑαυτόν. The reference is to Croesus.
ἐξενείκασθαι Aorist, middle, infinitive of ἐκφέρω.

6.125.3

πρὸς τὴν δωρεὴν ἐοῦσαν τοιαύτην τοιάδε ἐπιτηδεύσας προσέφερε "In view of the fact that the gift was so large, he gave it much thought and put into play the following [scheme]."
κοθόρνους The kothornos was a high boot. The word is often associated with the boot or buskin worn by actors in the Theater of Dionysus in Athens.

6.125.4

ἐσπεσὼν "Diving."
ψήγματος "Gold dust."
ὅσον ἐχώρεον οἱ κόθορνοι "As much as his kothornoi [boots] could hold."
μετὰ δέ "Next" (cf. πρῶτα μέν).
παντὶ δὲ τεῷ οἰκὼς μᾶλλον ἢ ἀνθρώπῳ "Looking like anything rather than a human being."
ἐβέβυστο Pluperfect, indicative, passive, 3rd, singular of βύω.

6.125.5

γέλως ἐσῆλθε "Laughter overcame him."
Ὀλυμπιάδα ἀναιρέεται "He was victorious at the Olympic Games."

6.128.1-2 The Dance of Hippokleides, Part I

While still on the subject of the Alcmaeonid family, Herodotus branches off to yet another tangent and tells the myth-laden story of Cleisthenes, a 6th century B.C. tyrant of Sicyon (cf. map in Landmark *ad* 6.125) and a friend of the Alcmaeonids of Athens. This Cleisthenes' main claim to fame was the huge banquet he once gave in order to find a suitable husband for his daughter Agariste. In 6.127, Herodotus lists the names of the many famous suitors who came to Sicyon to compete in a variety of contests. These included athletic games, as well as certain competitions which were meant to test the character and social grace of the competitors. The story has all the earmarks of a folktale (cf. the courtship of Helen of Troy), but it does at the same time preserve important information about the social values which may have mattered most in the Archaic period of Greek history.

τοσοῦτοι μὲν ἐγένοντο οἱ μνηστῆρες. ἀπικομένων δὲ τούτων ἐς τὴν προειρημένην ἡμέρην, ὁ Κλεισθένης πρῶτα μὲν τὰς πάτρας τε αὐτῶν ἀνεπύθετο καὶ γένος ἑκάστου, μετὰ δὲ κατέχων ἐνιαυτὸν διεπειρᾶτο αὐτῶν τῆς τε ἀνδραγαθίης καὶ τῆς ὀργῆς καὶ παιδεύσιός τε καὶ τρόπου, καὶ ἑνὶ ἑκάστῳ ἰὼν ἐς συνουσίην καὶ συνάπασι, καὶ ἐς γυμνάσιά τε ἐξαγινέων ὅσοι ἦσαν αὐτῶν νεώτεροι, καὶ τό γε μέγιστον, ἐν τῇ συνεστίῃ διεπειρᾶτο· ὅσον γὰρ κατεῖχε χρόνον αὐτούς, τοῦτον πάντα ἐποίεε καὶ ἅμα ἐξείνιζε μεγαλοπρεπέως. [2] καὶ δή κου μάλιστα τῶν μνηστήρων ἠρέσκοντο οἱ ἀπ᾿ Ἀθηνέων ἀπιγμένοι, καὶ τούτων μᾶλλον Ἱπποκλείδης ὁ Τισάνδρου καὶ κατ᾿ ἀνδραγαθίην ἐκρίνετο καὶ ὅτι τὸ ἀνέκαθεν τοῖσι ἐν Κορίνθῳ Κυψελίδῃσι ἦν προσήκων.

6.128.1

ἀπικομένων δὲ τούτων ἐς τὴν προειρημένην ἡμέρην Genitive absolute construction.
τὴν προειρημένην ἡμέρην "The appointed day."
πρῶτα μὲν...μετὰ δὲ "First...next."
ἰὼν ἐς συνουσίην "Keeping company with...."
ἐν τῇ συνεστίῃ "In a social setting."

6.128.2

καὶ δή κου "And truly, on more than one occasion."
τὸ ἀνέκαθεν "From a long time ago."

☙

6.129.1-4 The Dance of Hippokleides, Part II

The story of the Dance of Hippokleides, sandwiched between the narratives of the Battle of Marathon and Xerxes' invasion (in Book 7), may be out of place in a work that purports to describe the great clash between East and West. Even so, the story is a delight, as it exudes that charm we enjoy in so many of the other ahistorical tales of the *Histories*. It is also perfectly told: it has just enough detail; it appeals to multiple senses (one can hear the music and see the flailing legs of Hippokleides); and it has the ability to evoke at least a smile, if not outright laughter, from all but the most severe reader.

ὡς δὲ ἡ κυρίη ἐγένετο τῶν ἡμερέων τῆς τε κατακλίσιος τοῦ γάμου καὶ ἐκφάσιος αὐτοῦ Κλεισθένεος τὸν κρίνοι ἐκ πάντων, θύσας βοῦς ἑκατὸν ὁ Κλεισθένης εὐώχεε αὐτούς τε τοὺς μνηστῆρας καὶ Σικυωνίους πάντας. [2] ὡς δὲ ἀπὸ δείπνου ἐγίνοντο, οἱ μνηστῆρες ἔριν εἶχον ἀμφί τε μουσικῇ καὶ τῷ λεγομένῳ ἐς τὸ μέσον. προϊούσης δὲ τῆς πόσιος κατέχων πολλὸν τοὺς ἄλλους ὁ Ἱπποκλείδης ἐκέλευσέ οἱ τὸν αὐλητὴν αὐλῆσαι ἐμμελείην, πειθομένου δὲ τοῦ αὐλητέω ὀρχήσατο. καί κως ἑωυτῷ μὲν ἀρεστῶς ὀρχέετο, ὁ Κλεισθένης δὲ ὁρέων ὅλον τὸ πρῆγμα ὑπώπτευε. [3] μετὰ δὲ ἐπισχὼν ὁ Ἱπποκλείδης χρόνον ἐκέλευσε τινὰ τράπεζαν ἐσενεῖκαι, ἐσελθούσης δὲ τῆς τραπέζης πρῶτα μὲν ἐπ' αὐτῆς ὀρχήσατο Λακωνικὰ σχημάτια, μετὰ δὲ ἄλλα Ἀττικά, τὸ τρίτον δὲ τὴν κεφαλὴν ἐρείσας ἐπὶ τὴν τράπεζαν τοῖσι σκέλεσι ἐχειρονόμησε. [4] Κλεισθένης δὲ τὰ μὲν πρῶτα καὶ τὰ δεύτερα ὀρχεομένου, ἀποστυγέων γαμβρὸν ἄν οἱ ἔτι γενέσθαι Ἱπποκλείδεα διὰ τήν τε ὄρχησιν καὶ τὴν ἀναιδείην, κατεῖχε ἑωυτόν, οὐ βουλόμενος ἐκραγῆναι ἐς αὐτόν· ὡς δὲ εἶδε τοῖσι σκέλεσι χειρονομήσαντα, οὐκέτι κατέχειν δυνάμενος εἶπε· "ὦ παῖ Τισάνδρου, ἀπορχήσαό γε μὲν τὸν γάμον." ὁ δὲ Ἱπποκλείδης ὑπολαβὼν εἶπε· "οὐ φροντὶς Ἱπποκλείδη." ἀπὸ τούτου μὲν τοῦτο ὀνομάζεται.

6.129.1

ἡ κυρίη...τῶν ἡμερέων "The appointed one of the days."
τὸν Here, a relative pronoun.

6.129.2

ἐγίνοντο = ἐγίγνοντο.
τῷ λεγομένῳ ἐς τὸ μέσον "In carrying on a public conversation."
προϊούσης δὲ τῆς πόσιος Genitive absolute construction.
κατέχων πολλὸν τοὺς ἄλλους "[Hippokleides] outdoing, by a whole lot, the others."
πειθομένου δὲ τοῦ αὐλητέω Genitive absolute construction.

ἐμμελείην A kind of tune that came to accompany the choral dances of Athenian tragedy.
κως = πως.

6.129.3

ἐσελθούσης δὲ τῆς τραπέζης Genitive absolute construction.

πρῶτα μὲν...μετὰ δὲ... τὸ τρίτον "First...next...finally."

τοῖσι σκέλεσι ἐχειρονόμησε "He gesticulated with his legs." That is, he moved his legs in the
    way he would normally have moved his arms.

6.129.4

τὰ μὲν πρῶτα καὶ τὰ δεύτερα ὀρχεομένου Genitive absolute construction with
    "Hippokleides" understood as its subject.

ἐκραγῆναι Aorist, passive infinitive of ἐκρήγνυμι. "Burst out in anger."

ἀπορχήσαό "You have danced away."

τοῦτο Supply a word like "maxim."

☙

7.5.1-3 Mardonios Urges Xerxes to Punish the Athenians

In the prologue to the *Histories*, Herodotus stated that he will inquire into the causes
of the great conflict between East and West. In this early chapter of Book VII, he tries to
discover the specific causes underlying Xerxes' invasion of Greece. He offers the view that
Mardonios, Xerxes' cousin and the disgraced commander of the Persian fleet which was
destroyed off Mt. Athos (cf.6.44), may have played a key role in convincing the King that
an attack on mainland Greece was absolutely necessary. The speech which Herodotus puts
into the mouth of Mardonios is, of course, fiction.

ἀποθανόντος δὲ Δαρείου ἡ βασιληίη ἀνεχώρησε ἐς τὸν παῖδα τὸν ἐκείνου
Ξέρξην. ὁ τοίνυν Ξέρξης ἐπὶ μὲν τὴν Ἑλλάδα οὐδαμῶς πρόθυμος ἦν κατ᾽
ἀρχὰς στρατεύεσθαι, ἐπὶ δὲ Αἴγυπτον ἐποιέετο στρατιῆς ἄγερσιν. παρεὼν
δὲ καὶ δυνάμενος παρ᾽ αὐτῷ μέγιστον Περσέων Μαρδόνιος ὁ Γοβρύεω, ὃς
ἦν Ξέρξῃ μὲν ἀνεψιὸς Δαρείου δὲ ἀδελφεῆς παῖς, τοιούτου λόγου εἴχετο,
λέγων· [2] "δέσποτα, οὐκ οἰκός ἐστι Ἀθηναίους ἐργασαμένους πολλὰ δὴ
κακὰ Πέρσας μὴ οὐ δοῦναι δίκην τῶν ἐποίησαν. ἀλλ᾽ εἰ τὸ μὲν νῦν ταῦτα
πρήσσοις τά περ ἐν χερσὶ ἔχεις· ἡμερώσας δὲ Αἴγυπτον τὴν ἐξυβρίσασαν
στρατηλάτεε ἐπὶ τὰς Ἀθήνας, ἵνα λόγος τέ σε ἔχῃ πρὸς ἀνθρώπων ἀγαθός,
καί τις ὕστερον φυλάσσηται ἐπὶ γῆν τὴν σὴν στρατεύεσθαι." [3] οὗτος μέν
οἱ ὁ λόγος ἦν τιμωρός· τοῦδε δὲ τοῦ λόγου παρενθήκην ποιεέσκετο τήνδε,
ὡς ἡ Εὐρώπη περικαλλὴς εἴη χώρη, καὶ δένδρεα παντοῖα φέρει τὰ ἥμερα,
ἀρετήν τε ἄκρη, βασιλέι τε μούνῳ θνητῶν ἀξίη ἐκτῆσθαι.

7.5.1

τοιούτου λόγου εἴχετο "He adhered to such talk." In other words, Mardonios kept saying the same things over and over.

7.5.2

οἰκός = εἰκός.

ἐργασαμένους Takes a double accusative.

μὴ οὐ The second of the negatives is redundant.

τῶν As often happens in Herodotus, the relative and its antecedent are combined into one word.

πρήσσοις = πράσσοις.

ἵνα λόγος τέ σε ἔχῃ πρὸς ἀνθρώπων ἀγαθός "So that a good report may prevail for you among men." That is, "so that men may speak favorably of you."

7.5.3

ποιεέσκετο Iterative imperfect, with -εσκ- as the infix.

ἀρετήν Accusative of respect. "In terms of its fertility."

CB

7.8a.1-2 Xerxes in Conference, Part I

Xerxes, convinced that an invasion of Greece will bring even greater glory for himself and will pay back the Athenians for what they did during the Ionian Revolt, calls for a meeting with his chief advisors. We are not in a position to know whether the Achaemenid kings of Persia did in fact regularly consult with a kind of high council when making important decisions. Such meetings are, however, a regular feature of the *Iliad*, and Herodotus may have merely assumed that this was also the way Persians conducted their affairs. The speech which Herodotus has Xerxes deliver in this passage contains a Herodotean law of history: where possible, Persians (being Persians) will conquer. This is a generalization which Herodotus will formulate on more than one occasion in the *Histories*.

"ἄνδρες Πέρσαι, οὔτ' αὐτὸς κατηγήσομαι νόμον τόνδε ἐν ὑμῖν τιθείς, παραδεξάμενός τε αὐτῷ χρήσομαι. ὡς γὰρ ἐγὼ πυνθάνομαι τῶν πρεσβυτέρων, οὐδαμά κω ἠτρεμίσαμεν, ἐπείτε παρελάβομεν τὴν ἡγεμονίην τήνδε παρὰ Μήδων, Κύρου κατελόντος Ἀστυάγεα· ἀλλὰ θεός τε οὕτω ἄγει καὶ αὐτοῖσι ἡμῖν πολλὰ ἐπέπουσι συμφέρεται ἐπὶ τὸ ἄμεινον. τὰ μέν νυν Κῦρός τε καὶ Καμβύσης πατήρ τε ἐμὸς Δαρεῖος κατεργάσαντο καὶ προσεκτήσαντο ἔθνεα, ἐπισταμένοισι εὖ οὐκ ἄν τις λέγοι. [2] ἐγὼ δὲ ἐπείτε παρέλαβον τὸν θρόνον τοῦτον, ἐφρόντιζον ὅκως μὴ λείψομαι τῶν πρότερον γενομένων ἐν τιμῇ τῇδε μηδὲ ἐλάσσω προσκτήσομαι δύναμιν Πέρσῃσι· φροντίζων δὲ εὑρίσκω ἅμα μὲν κῦδός τε ἡμῖν προσγινόμενον χώρην τε τῆς νῦν ἐκτήμεθα οὐκ ἐλάσσονα οὐδὲ φλαυροτέρην παμφορωτέρην τε, ἅμα δὲ τιμωρίην τε καὶ τίσιν γινομένην. διὸ ὑμέας νῦν ἐγὼ συνέλεξα, ἵνα τὸ νοέω πρήσσειν ὑπερθέωμαι ὑμῖν.

7.8a.1

οὔτε...τε In Herodotus, the equivalent of οὔτε...ἀλλά.

Κύρου κατελόντος Ἀστυάγεα The story of Cyrus's victory over the Mede Astyages is told in 1.123ff.

ἐπέπουσι = ἐφέπουσι.

τά Relative and antecedent combined into one word.

ἐπισταμένοισι εὖ οὐκ ἄν τις λέγοι "No one would need to say to those who know all too well."

7.8a.2

λείψομαι "I am inferior." Takes the genitive of comparison in τῶν πρότερον γενομένων.

πρήσσειν = πράσσειν.

ὑπερθέωμαι "Let me explain."

ℭℨ

7.8b.1-3 Xerxes in Conference, Part II

This continuation of Xerxes' purported speech is redolent with tragic irony. Herodotus' ancient audience would have been quite aware of the folly of the King's words, which were clearly spoken in ignorance. The modern reader might question the way Herodotus gives away too much information too soon by having Xerxes state that he will "yoke the Hellespont," an event which is one of the highlights of Book VII.

μέλλω ζεύξας τὸν Ἑλλήσποντον ἐλᾶν στρατὸν διὰ τῆς Εὐρώπης ἐπὶ τὴν Ἑλλάδα, ἵνα Ἀθηναίους τιμωρήσωμαι ὅσα δὴ πεποιήκασι Πέρσας τε καὶ πατέρα τὸν ἐμόν. [2] ὡρᾶτε μέν νυν καὶ πατέρα τὸν ἐμὸν Δαρεῖον ἰθύοντα στρατεύεσθαι ἐπὶ τοὺς ἄνδρας τούτους. ἀλλ' ὃ μὲν τετελεύτηκε καὶ οὐκ ἐξεγένετο αὐτῷ τιμωρήσασθαι· ἐγὼ δὲ ὑπέρ τε ἐκείνου καὶ τῶν ἄλλων Περσέων οὐ πρότερον παύσομαι πρὶν ἢ ἕλω τε καὶ πυρώσω τὰς Ἀθήνας, οἵ γε ἐμὲ καὶ πατέρα τὸν ἐμὸν ὑπῆρξαν ἄδικα ποιεῦντες. [3] πρῶτα μὲν ἐς Σάρδις ἐλθόντες, ἅμα Ἀρισταγόρῃ τῷ Μιλησίῳ δούλῳ δὲ ἡμετέρῳ ἀπικόμενοι, ἐνέπρησαν τά τε ἄλσεα καὶ τὰ ἱρά· δεύτερα δὲ ἡμέας οἷα ἔρξαν ἐς τὴν σφετέρην ἀποβάντας, ὅτε Δᾶτίς τε καὶ Ἀρταφρένης ἐστρατήγεον, τὰ ἐπίστασθέ κου πάντες.

7.8b.1

μέλλω "I propose."

ἐλᾶν Future, active infinitive of ἐλαύνω.

τιμωρήσωμαι Takes a double accusative.

7.8b.2

οὐκ ἐξεγένετο "It was not possible." Takes a dative and an infinitive.

ἕλω Aorist, subjunctive, active, 1st, singular of αἱρέω.

οἵ The antecedent is implied in τὰς Ἀθήνας.

ὑπῆρξαν "Were first to" (+ participle).

7.8b.3

πρῶτα μὲν Translate with δεύτερα δέ.

ἐνέπρησαν Aorist, indicative, active, 3rd, plural of ἐμπίπρημι.

ἱρά = ἱερά.

ὅτε Δᾶτίς τε καὶ Ἀρταφρένης ἐστρατήγεον The reference here is to the Battle of Marathon.

☙

7.9b.1-2 Xerxes in Conference, Part III

Mardonios, Xerxes' cousin, argues for an invasion of mainland Greece. In so doing, he belittles the Greek way of fighting wars, particularly when Greeks fight among themselves. It may be that the views Mardonios expresses here are those of Herodotus, who will occasionally show disdain for the Greek penchant for internecine warfare. Speeches in the *Histories* tend to be persuasive, and Mardonios' speech is no exception. It may be noted that Mardonios conveniently leaves out of his speech the catastrophic shipwreck his fleet endured at Mt. Athos during his earlier expedition to Greece (6.43-45).

καίτοι γε ἐώθασι Ἕλληνες, ὡς πυνθάνομαι, ἀβουλότατα πολέμους ἵστασθαι ὑπό τε ἀγνωμοσύνης καὶ σκαιότητος. ἐπεὰν γὰρ ἀλλήλοισι πόλεμον προείπωσι, ἐξευρόντες τὸ κάλλιστον χωρίον καὶ λειότατον, ἐς τοῦτο κατιόντες μάχονται, ὥστε σὺν κακῷ μεγάλῳ οἱ νικῶντες ἀπαλλάσσονται· περὶ δὲ τῶν ἑσσουμένων οὐδὲ λέγω ἀρχήν· ἐξώλεες γὰρ δὴ γίνονται· [2] τοὺς χρῆν ἐόντας ὁμογλώσσους κήρυξί τε διαχρεωμένους καὶ ἀγγέλοισι καταλαμβάνειν τὰς διαφορὰς καὶ παντὶ μᾶλλον ἢ μάχῃσι· εἰ δὲ πάντως ἔδεε πολεμέειν πρὸς ἀλλήλους, ἐξευρίσκειν χρῆν τῇ ἑκάτεροί εἰσι δυσχειρωτότατοι καὶ ταύτῃ πειρᾶν. τρόπῳ τοίνυν οὐ χρηστῷ Ἕλληνες διαχρεώμενοι, ἐμέο ἐλάσαντος μέχρι Μακεδονίης γῆς, οὐκ ἦλθον ἐς τούτου λόγον ὥστε μάχεσθαι.

7.9b.1

ἀβουλότατα "In the most ill-advised way."

ἐπεάν = ἐπειδάν.

ἐσσουμένων Present, passive, masculine, genitive, plural participle of ἔσσοομαι (= ἡσσάομαι).

οὐδὲ λέγω ἀρχήν "I say nothing at all."

γίνονται = γίγνονται.

7.9b.2

παντὶ μᾶλλον ἤ "With anything other than…."

ἐμέο ἐλάσαντος μέχρι Μακεδονίης γῆς Genitive absolute construction.

ἐς τούτου λόγον ὥστε μάχεσθαι "To a consideration of this, namely, to fight."

ೞ

7.10b.1-2 Xerxes in Conference, Part IV

Artabanos, Xerxes' uncle (and brother to King Darius), argues against the war plans which Mardonios had so strongly recommended (cf. 7.8a, 7.8b). Although Artabanos has to speak carefully lest he offend his nephew (note the hemming and hawing at the beginning of his speech), he somehow feels free to praise the Athenians and the way they destroyed the Persian army at the Battle of Marathon. Herodotus, of course, creates the speech of Artabanos and can make him say the sorts of things which would have pleased an Athenian audience. Artabanos' remarkable prescience, which allows him to anticipate what might happen if the Athenians had the opportunity to destroy the Hellespontine bridge, is further evidence of the free hand which Herodotus had in constructing the speeches of his characters.

ζεύξας φῆς τὸν Ἑλλήσποντον ἐλᾶν στρατὸν διὰ τῆς Εὐρώπης ἐς τὴν Ἑλλάδα. καὶ δὴ καὶ συνήνεικέ σε ἤτοι κατὰ γῆν ἢ καὶ κατὰ θάλασσαν ἑσσωθῆναι, ἢ καὶ κατ' ἀμφότερα· οἱ γὰρ ἄνδρες λέγονται εἶναι ἄλκιμοι, πάρεστι δὲ καὶ σταθμώσασθαι, εἰ στρατιήν γε τοσαύτην σὺν Δάτι καὶ Ἀρταφρένεϊ ἐλθοῦσαν ἐς τὴν Ἀττικὴν χώρην μοῦνοι Ἀθηναῖοι διέφθειραν. [2] οὔκων ἀμφοτέρη σφι ἐχώρησε. ἀλλ' ἢν τῇσι νηυσὶ ἐμβάλωσι καὶ νικήσαντες ναυμαχίῃ πλέωσι ἐς τὸν Ἑλλήσποντον καὶ ἔπειτα λύσωσι τὴν γέφυραν, τοῦτο δὴ βασιλεῦ γίνεται δεινόν.

7.10b.1

καὶ δὴ καὶ συνήνεικέ "And now [suppose] it really happened that…"

ἑσσωθῆναι Aorist, passive infinitive of ἔσσοομαι (= ἡσσάομαι).

σταθμώσασθαι "To infer [this fact]."

στρατιήν γε τοσαύτην σὺν Δάτι καὶ Ἀρταφρένεϊ Referring to the Persian army at Marathon.

7.10b.2

οὔκων ἀμφοτέρη σφι ἐχώρησε "[Consider what would happen if] things did not go their way on both land and sea."

οὔκων = οὔκουν.

γίνεται = γίγνεται.

❦

7.10e.1 Xerxes in Conference, Part V

The Persian Artabanos is made to formulate here a Greek philosophical doctrine, which also happens to be one of the running themes of the *Histories*. The Roman poet Horace explores a similar outlook on life in *Odes* 2.10, where he writes about the vulnerability of tall pine trees, lofty towers, and the highest mountain tops.

ὁρᾷς τὰ ὑπερέχοντα ζῷα ὡς κεραυνοῖ ὁ θεὸς οὐδὲ ἐᾷ φαντάζεσθαι, τὰ δὲ σμικρὰ οὐδέν μιν κνίζει· ὁρᾷς δὲ ὡς ἐς οἰκήματα τὰ μέγιστα αἰεὶ καὶ δένδρεα τὰ τοιαῦτα ἀποσκήπτει τὰ βέλεα· φιλέει γὰρ ὁ θεὸς τὰ ὑπερέχοντα πάντα κολούειν. οὕτω δὲ καὶ στρατὸς πολλὸς ὑπὸ ὀλίγου διαφθείρεται κατὰ τοιόνδε· ἐπεάν σφι ὁ θεὸς φθονήσας φόβον ἐμβάλῃ ἢ βροντήν, δι' ὧν ἐφθάρησαν ἀναξίως ἑωυτῶν. οὐ γὰρ ἐᾷ φρονέειν μέγα ὁ θεὸς ἄλλον ἢ ἑωυτόν.

7.10e.1

φαντάζεσθαι "Be ostentatious."

κνίζει "Scratch" or "touch."

φιλέει "Is wont to...."

ἐπεάν = ἐπειδάν.

δι'… ἐφθάρησαν An instance of tmesis (where the prepositional prefix is separated from its verb).

ὧν = οὖν.

ἀναξίως ἑωυτῶν "Through no fault of their own."

❦

7.12.1-2 Xerxes' Dream, Part I

The story of Xerxes' Dream may have been one of those "performance pieces" which Herodotus would have recited to audiences. Two and a half millennia later, it would still makes for a wonderful ghost story around a campfire. Despite the tale's obvious charm and great entertainment value, even Herodotus must have thought it prudent to distance himself from this story by specifying that it was something he had heard from his Persian sources. Dreams and their meanings play a large part in the *Histories*, but it is not always possible to tell what Herodotus really thought about them or to make them fit into a systematic, Herodotean theology.

ταῦτα μὲν ἐπὶ τοσοῦτο ἐλέγετο. μετὰ δὲ εὐφρόνη τε ἐγίνετο καὶ Ξέρξην ἔκνιζε ἡ Ἀρταβάνου γνώμη· νυκτὶ δὲ βουλὴν διδοὺς πάγχυ εὕρισκέ οἱ οὐ πρῆγμα εἶναι στρατεύεσθαι ἐπὶ τὴν Ἑλλάδα. δεδογμένων δέ οἱ αὖτις τούτων κατύπνωσε, καὶ δή κου ἐν τῇ νυκτὶ εἶδε ὄψιν τοιήνδε, ὡς λέγεται ὑπὸ Περσέων· ἐδόκεε ὁ Ξέρξης ἄνδρα οἱ ἐπιστάντα μέγαν τε καὶ εὐειδέα εἰπεῖν· [2] "μετὰ δὴ βουλεύεαι, ὦ Πέρσα, στράτευμα μὴ ἄγειν ἐπὶ τὴν Ἑλλάδα, προείπας ἁλίζειν Πέρσας στρατόν; οὔτε ὦν μεταβουλευόμενος ποιέεις εὖ οὔτε ὁ συγγνωσόμενός τοι πάρα· ἀλλ' ὥσπερ τῆς ἡμέρης ἐβουλεύσαο ποιέειν, ταύτην ἴθι τῶν ὁδῶν."

7.12.1

ταῦτα μὲν ἐπὶ τοσοῦτο ἐλέγετο A transitional sentence which refers to the response that Xerxes gave to Artabanos.

μετά Here, an adverb.

ἐγίνετο = ἐγίγνετο.

νυκτὶ δὲ βουλὴν διδοὺς "Confiding his plan[s] to the night."

πρῆγμα = πρᾶγμα. "Obligation."

δεδογμένων δέ οἱ αὖτις τούτων Genitive absolute construction.

κου = που.

7.12.2

μετὰ δὴ βουλεύεαι An instance of tmesis, where a prepositional prefix (μετά) is separated from its verb (βουλεύεαι).

ὦν = οὖν.

πάρα = πάρεστι.

ταύτην ἴθι τῶν ὁδῶν "Travel on this one of the roads."

☙

7.15.1-3 The Dream of Xerxes, Part II

In 7.13, we are told that Xerxes publicly apologized to his uncle Artabanos and revoked his earlier decision to launch an invasion of Greece…this to the great joy of the Persians, who proceeded to prostrate themselves in front of the King. We then learn (7.14) that Xerxes was again visited by a ghost and threatened with violence if he did not return to his original plan. In this chapter, Xerxes again summons his uncle to tell him about his apparitions and to propose a scheme—one that involved exchanging pajamas—to find out whether or not his visions were from a god.

Ξέρξης μὲν περιδεὴς γενόμενος τῇ ὄψι ἀνά τε ἔδραμε ἐκ τῆς κοίτης καὶ πέμπει
ἄγγελον ἐπὶ Ἀρτάβανον καλέοντα· ἀπικομένῳ δέ οἱ ἔλεγε Ξέρξης τάδε·
"Ἀρτάβανε, ἐγὼ τὸ παραυτίκα μὲν οὐκ ἐσωφρόνεον εἴπας ἐς σὲ μάταια ἔπεα
χρηστῆς εἵνεκα συμβουλίης· [2] μετὰ μέντοι οὐ πολλὸν χρόνον μετέγνων,
ἔγνων δὲ ταῦτα μοι ποιητέα ἐόντα τὰ σὺ ὑπεθήκαο. οὔκων δυνατός τοι εἰμὶ
ταῦτα βουλόμενος ποιέειν· τετραμμένῳ γὰρ δὴ καὶ μετεγνωκότι ἐπιφοιτέον
ὄνειρον φαντάζεταί μοι οὐδαμῶς συνεπαινέον ποιέειν με ταῦτα· νῦν δὲ καὶ
διαπειλῆσαν οἴχεται. [3] εἰ ὦν θεός ἐστι ὁ ἐπιπέμπων καί οἱ πάντως ἐν ἡδονῇ
ἐστι γενέσθαι στρατηλασίην ἐπὶ Ἑλλάδα, ἐπιπτήσεται καὶ σοὶ τὠυτὸ τοῦτο
ὄνειρον, ὁμοίως καὶ ἐμοὶ ἐντελλόμενον. εὑρίσκω δὲ ὧδ' ἂν γινόμενα ταῦτα,
εἰ λάβοις τὴν ἐμὴν σκευὴν πᾶσαν καὶ ἐνδὺς μετὰ τοῦτο ἵζοιο ἐς τὸν ἐμὸν
θρόνον, καὶ ἔπειτα ἐν κοίτῃ τῇ ἐμῇ κατυπνώσειας."

7.15.1

ἔδραμε ἐκ τῆς κοίτης καὶ πέμπει Herodotus often mixes tenses.
εἵνεκα = ἕνεκα.

7.15.2

ταῦτα μοι ποιητέα ἐόντα "I should do these things." More literally, "these things are to be
   done by me."
ὑπεθήκαο Aorist, indicative, middle, 2nd, singular of ὑποτίθημι. The first aorist form is rare.
οὔκων = οὔκουν.
τετραμμένῳ Perfect, passive, masculine, dative, singular participle of τρέπω.
μετεγνωκότι Perfect, active, masculine, dative, singular participle of μεταγιγνώσκω.
διαπειλῆσαν "He made violent threats."

7.15.3

ὦν = οὖν.
ἐπιπτήσεται Future, indicative, middle, 3rd, singular of ἐπιπέτομαι.
γινόμενα = γιγνόμενα.

☙

7.16b.1-2. The Dream of Xerxes, Part III

In 7.16 and 7.16a, Herodotus describes how Artabanos graciously accepted Xerxes'
apology for his recent outburst and then suggested that his nephew's ill-behavior had been
caused by the bad company he kept. To drive home this point, Artabanos observed that
it is not the sea itself that can cause great harm, but the winds that stir up the sea. In the
present passage, Herodotus has Artabanos explain the true nature of dreams in ways that

seem remarkably modern. (Cicero [*de Divinatione* 1.45] offers a similar explanation for what causes dreams.)

νῦν ὦν, ἐπειδὴ τέτραψαι ἐπὶ τὴν ἀμείνω, φής τοι μετιέντι τὸν ἐπ᾽Ἕλληνας στόλον ἐπιφοιτᾶν ὄνειρον θεοῦ τινος πομπῇ, οὐκ ἐῶντά σε καταλύειν τὸν στόλον. [2] ἀλλ᾽ οὐδὲ ταῦτα ἐστι, ὦ παῖ, θεῖα. ἐνύπνια γὰρ τὰ ἐς ἀνθρώπους πεπλανημένα τοιαῦτα ἐστὶ οἷά σε ἐγὼ διδάξω, ἔτεσι σεῦ πολλοῖσι πρεσβύτερος ἐών· πεπλανῆσθαι αὗται μάλιστα ἐώθασι αἱ ὄψιες τῶν ὀνειράτων, τά τις ἡμέρης φροντίζει. ἡμεῖς δὲ τὰς πρὸ τοῦ ἡμέρας ταύτην τὴν στρατηλασίην καὶ τὸ κάρτα εἴχομεν μετὰ χεῖρας.

7.16.b.1

ὦν = οὖν.

τέτραψαι Perfect, indicative, passive, 2nd, singular of τρέπω.

ἐπὶ τὴν ἀμείνω "To the better [advice]."

θεοῦ τινος πομπῇ "With the escort of some god." That is, "sent by some god."

7.16b.2

πεπλανημένα Perfect, passive, neuter, nominative, plural participle of πλανάω.

τὰς πρὸ τοῦ ἡμέρας "During the days before this [dream]."

☙

7.17.1-2 The Dream of Xerxes, Part IV

The phantom of Xerxes' dream cannot be easily duped and immediately recognizes the fraud that Xerxes and his uncle had so carefully planned. (For a description of the kind of elaborate clothes which Artabanos might have worn in order to pass himself off as Xerxes, see HW *ad* 7.15.3.)

τοσαῦτα εἴπας Ἀρτάβανος, ἐλπίζων Ξέρξην ἀποδέξειν λέγοντα οὐδέν, ἐποίεε τὸ κελευόμενον. ἐνδὺς δὲ τὴν Ξέρξεω ἐσθῆτα καὶ ἱζόμενος ἐς τὸν βασιλήιον θρόνον ὡς μετὰ ταῦτα κοῖτον ἐποιέετο, ἦλθέ οἱ κατυπνωμένῳ τὠυτὸ ὄνειρον τὸ καὶ παρὰ Ξέρξην ἐφοίτα, ὑπερστὰν δὲ τοῦ Ἀρταβάνου εἶπε· [2] "ἆρα σὺ δὴ κεῖνος εἷς ὁ ἀποσπεύδων Ξέρξην στρατεύεσθαι ἐπὶ τὴν Ἑλλάδα ὡς δὴ κηδόμενος αὐτοῦ; ἀλλ᾽ οὔτε ἐς τὸ μετέπειτα οὔτε ἐς τὸ παραυτίκα νῦν καταπροΐξεαι ἀποτρέπων τὸ χρεὸν γενέσθαι. Ξέρξην δὲ τὰ δεῖ ἀνηκουστέοντα παθεῖν, αὐτῷ ἐκείνῳ δεδήλωται."

7.17.1

λέγοντα οὐδέν "Was speaking nonsense."

τὠυτό An instance of crasis, when two words (τὸ αὐτό) are combined into one.

ὑπερστὰν Aorist, active, neuter, nominative, singular participle of ὑπερίσταμαι.

7.17.2

κεῖνος = ἐκεῖνος.

ὡς δὴ κηδόμενος αὐτοῦ "As though you worried for him"

καταπροΐξεαι "Will you go unpunished for…." This verb is usually followed by a participle (ἀποτρέπων).

ἀνηκουστέοντα The participle functions like the protasis to a conditional sentence: "If he does not obey."

ᛃ

7.18.1-4 The Dream of Xerxes, Part V

The Dream of Xerxes concludes very dramatically with Artabanos screaming and leaping out of bed as the specter approaches him in his sleep and threatens to put out his eyes with hot irons (cf. HW *ad* 7.18 for citations from the Bible and Xenophon concerning blinding as a form of punishment). Given that Xerxes will experience disastrous military defeats precisely because he followed the dictates of a specter, Herodotus' story may be seen as a cautionary tale, one where the main lesson is that dreams, with or without menacing ghosts, are often misleading and even destructive.

ταῦτά τε ἐδόκεε Ἀρτάβανος τὸ ὄνειρον ἀπειλέειν καὶ θερμοῖσι σιδηρίοισι ἐκκαίειν αὐτοῦ μέλλειν τοὺς ὀφθαλμούς. καὶ ὃς ἀμβώσας μέγα ἀναθρώσκει, καὶ παριζόμενος Ξέρξῃ, ὡς τὴν ὄψιν οἱ τοῦ ἐνυπνίου διεξῆλθε ἀπηγεόμενος, δεύτερά οἱ λέγει τάδε· [2] "ἐγὼ μέν, ὦ βασιλεῦ, οἷα ἄνθρωπος ἰδὼν ἤδη πολλά τε καὶ μεγάλα πεσόντα πρήγματα ὑπὸ ἡσσόνων, οὐκ ἔων σε τὰ πάντα τῇ ἡλικίῃ εἴκειν, ἐπιστάμενος ὡς κακὸν εἴη τὸ πολλῶν ἐπιθυμέειν, μεμνημένος μὲν τὸν ἐπὶ Μασσαγέτας Κύρου στόλον ὡς ἔπρηξε, μεμνημένος δὲ καὶ τὸν ἐπ' Αἰθίοπας τὸν Καμβύσεω, συστρατευόμενος δὲ καὶ Δαρείῳ ἐπὶ Σκύθας. [3] ἐπιστάμενος ταῦτα γνώμην εἶχον ἀτρεμίζοντά σε μακαριστὸν εἶναι πρὸς πάντων ἀνθρώπων. ἐπεὶ δὲ δαιμονίη τις γίνεται ὁρμή, καὶ Ἕλληνας, ὡς οἶκε, καταλαμβάνει τις φθορὴ θεήλατος, ἐγὼ μὲν καὶ αὐτὸς τρέπομαι καὶ τὴν γνώμην μετατίθεμαι, σὺ δὲ σήμηνον μὲν Πέρσῃσι τὰ ἐκ τοῦ θεοῦ πεμπόμενα, χρᾶσθαι δὲ κέλευε τοῖσι ἐκ σέο πρώτοισι προειρημένοισι ἐς τὴν παρασκευήν, ποίεε δὲ οὕτω ὅκως τοῦ θεοῦ παραδιδόντος τῶν σῶν ἐνδεήσει μηδέν." [4] τούτων δὲ λεχθέντων, ἐνθαῦτα ἐπαερθέντες τῇ ὄψι, ὡς ἡμέρη ἐγένετο τάχιστα, Ξέρξης τε ὑπερετίθετο ταῦτα Πέρσῃσι, καὶ Ἀρτάβανος, ὃς πρότερον ἀποσπεύδων μοῦνος ἐφαίνετο, τότε ἐπισπεύδων φανερὸς ἦν.

7.18.1

διεξῆλθε "Gave a detailed account."

δεύτερά "Next."

7.18.2

οἷα ἄνθρωπος ἰδὼν "As a man who has seen."

πεσόντα "Be ruined."

ἔων = εἴων. Imperfect, indicative, active, 3rd, plural of ἐάω. Herodotus does not augment this verb.

τὸ πολλῶν ἐπιθυμέειν Articular infinitive construction.

τὸν ἐπὶ Μασσαγέτας Κύρου στόλον This was the occasion of Cyrus' death in 529.

συστρατευόμενος δὲ καὶ Δαρείῳ ἐπὶ Σκύθας Recounted in 1.103, 4.1.

7.18.3

δαιμονίη τις...ὁρμή "Some divine impulse."

γίνεται = γίγνεται.

σήμηνον Aorist, imperative, active, 2nd, singular of σημαίνω.

τοῖσι ἐκ σέο πρώτοισι προειρημένοισι "The instructions they initially received from you."

ὅκως = ὅπως.

τοῦ θεοῦ παραδιδόντος Genitive absolute construction. "So long as the god allows."

τῶν σῶν ἐνδεήσει μηδέν "Not one of your [undertakings] will be found wanting."

7.18.4

τούτων δὲ λεχθέντων Genitive absolute construction.

ἐπαερθέντες Aorist, passive, masculine, nominative, plural participle of ἐπαίρω. "Having been lifted," or "having become elated."

☙

7.21.1-2 Rivers Drunk Dry

In the previous section (7.20), Herodotus maintains that Xerxes' expedition against mainland Greece dwarfed all other previous military campaigns, including the one at Troy. In this paragraph, he underscores his point with a couple of rhetorical questions. Two observations are in order: one is that Herodotus appears to relish challenging Homer and asserting that "his" war is bigger than Homer's; the second is that Thucydides, the historian of the Peloponnesian War, who wrote less than one generation after Herodotus, makes a similar claim about the size of the war that he is about to relate (1.1.3), perhaps because of Herodotus' influence. In any case, Herodotus will return to the theme of the size of Xerxes' expedition on several occasions and leave himself open to the charge that he grossly exaggerated the numbers on the Persian side. (Cf. Landmark, Appendix R, "The Size of Xerxes' Expeditionary Force.")

αὗται αἱ πᾶσαι οὐδ᾽ εἰ ἔτεραι πρὸς ταύτῃσι προσγενόμεναι στρατηλασίαι μιῆς τῆσδε οὐκ ἄξιαι. τί γὰρ οὐκ ἤγαγε ἐκ τῆς Ἀσίης ἔθνος ἐπὶ τὴν Ἑλλάδα Ξέρξης; κοῖον δὲ πινόμενόν μιν ὕδωρ οὐκ ἐπέλιπε, πλὴν τῶν μεγάλων ποταμῶν; [2] οἱ μὲν γὰρ νέας παρείχοντο, οἱ δὲ ἐς πεζὸν ἐτετάχατο, τοῖσι δὲ ἵππος προσετέτακτο, τοῖσι δὲ ἱππαγωγὰ πλοῖα ἅμα στρατευομένοισι, τοῖσι δὲ ἐς τὰς γεφύρας μακρὰς νέας παρέχειν, τοῖσι δὲ σῖτά τε καὶ νέας.

7.21.1

προσγενόμεναι "Having been added."

κοῖον = ποῖον.

7.21.2

μακρὰς νέας These "long boats," which were used for the construction of the bridge at the Hellespont, were likely triremes.

 og

7.24.1 Cities Turned into Islands

In chapters 7.22-23, Herodotus described the construction of a canal through the northernmost of the three peninsulas that emanate from a region known as the Chalcidice (see map in Landmark *ad* 7.24). At the tip of this peninsula is Mt. Athos, which rises some 6,000 feet above sea level (and is today the site of a group of monasteries of the Greek Orthodox Church). Since Mardonios' fleet had earlier been destroyed by a storm off Mt. Athos in 493 B.C., Xerxes wanted to take precautions lest the same fate befall his fleet. His solution was to dig a waterway through the narrowest portion of the peninsula—the famous Canal of Mt. Athos (7.22). In this section, Herodotus questions Xerxes' motives in building this Canal and argues that the Persian ships could have been dragged across the peninsula. (This was the practice in antiquity at the Isthmus of Corinth, where a "diolkos" served as a slipway for ships). The very existence of a canal at Mt. Athos was questioned already in antiquity: cf. Juvenal 10.73ff., where the story of the Canal is attributed to *Graecia mendax*. Modern satellite photos, however, confirm its existence.

ὡς μὲν ἐμὲ συμβαλλόμενον εὑρίσκειν, μεγαλοφροσύνης εἵνεκεν αὐτὸ Ξέρξης ὀρύσσειν ἐκέλευε, ἐθέλων τε δύναμιν ἀποδείκνυσθαι καὶ μνημόσυνα λιπέσθαι· παρεὸν γὰρ μηδένα πόνον λαβόντας τὸν ἰσθμὸν τὰς νέας διειρύσαι, ὀρύσσειν ἐκέλευε διώρυχα τῇ θαλάσσῃ εὖρος ὡς δύο τριήρεας πλέειν ὁμοῦ ἐλαστρεομένας. τοῖσι δὲ αὐτοῖσι τούτοισι, τοῖσί περ καὶ τὸ ὄρυγμα, προσετέτακτο καὶ τὸν Στρυμόνα ποταμὸν ζεύξαντας γεφυρῶσαι.

7.24.1

ὡς μὲν ἐμὲ συμβαλλόμενον εὑρίσκειν The accusative/infinitive construction with ὡς is used to indicate conjecture. "As far as I can tell, after due consideration."

παρεὸν "Though it was possible."

εὖρος ὡς "Of such a width so that…."

Στρυμόνα The bridging of the Strymon River in Macedonia (see map in Landmark *ad* 7.24) is mentioned again in 7.114.

ॐ

7.29.1-3 The Good Xerxes

The great march of Xerxes' army is underway, and the first region it passes through is Lydia. Herodotus takes a detour from the narrative to tell the story of Pythios, a fabulously wealthy Lydian, who lavishly entertains Xerxes and offers him an incredibly large sum of money to support the expedition against Greece. Xerxes' reaction, which Herodotus fashions into a little speech, reveals—somewhat surprisingly—a different Xerxes from the one we have seen so far. This "new" Xerxes knows how to repay generosity with even greater generosity and is motivated by the same kind of code of conduct which ancient Greeks cherished, namely, that of *xenia*. (For a useful definition of this behavioral code, see note in Landmark *ad* 7.29.2a). This is not the last time we will hear about Pythios' dealings with Xerxes: in a later chapter (7.39), Herodotus will let us see, once again, the true character of Xerxes.

ὁ μὲν ταῦτα ἔλεγε, Ξέρξης δὲ ἡσθεὶς τοῖσι εἰρημένοισι εἶπε· "ξεῖνε Λυδέ, ἐγὼ ἐπείτε ἐξῆλθον τὴν Περσίδα χώρην, οὐδενὶ ἀνδρὶ συνέμιξα ἐς τόδε ὅστις ἠθέλησε ξείνια προθεῖναι στρατῷ τῷ ἐμῷ, οὐδὲ ὅστις ἐς ὄψιν τὴν ἐμὴν καταστὰς αὐτεπάγγελτος ἐς τὸν πόλεμον ἐμοὶ ἠθέλησε συμβαλέσθαι χρήματα, ἔξω σεῦ. σὺ δὲ καὶ ἐξείνισας μεγάλως στρατὸν τὸν ἐμὸν καὶ χρήματα μεγάλα ἐπαγγέλλεαι. [2] σοὶ ὦν ἐγὼ ἀντὶ αὐτῶν γέρεα τοιάδε δίδωμι· ξεῖνόν τέ σε ποιεῦμαι ἐμὸν καὶ τὰς τετρακοσίας μυριάδας τοι τῶν στατήρων ἀποπλήσω παρ᾽ ἐμεωυτοῦ δοὺς τὰς ἑπτὰ χιλιάδας, ἵνα μή τοι ἐπιδεέες ἔωσι αἱ τετρακόσιαι μυριάδες ἑπτὰ χιλιάδων, ἀλλὰ ᾖ τοι ἀπαρτιλογίη ὑπ᾽ ἐμέο πεπληρωμένη. [3] ἔκτησό τε αὐτὸς τά περ αὐτὸς ἐκτήσαο, ἐπίστασό τε εἶναι αἰεὶ τοιοῦτος· οὐ γάρ τοι ταῦτα ποιεῦντι οὔτε ἐς τὸ παρεὸν οὔτε ἐς χρόνον μεταμελήσει."

7.29.1

ὁ μὲν ταῦτα ἔλεγε The speaker referred to here is Pythios.

ἡσθεὶς Aorist, passive, masculine, nominative, singular participle of ἥδομαι.

ἐς τόδε "Up to the present moment."

7.29.2

ὦν = οὖν.

τετρακοσίας μυριάδας τοι τῶν στατήρων To get an idea of the value of 400 x 10,000 (= 4 million) staters, see Landmark, Appendix J, "Ancient Greek Units of Currency, Weight, and Distance."

παρ᾿ ἐμεωυτοῦ "From my own possessions."

ἑπτὰ χιλιάδων Pythios had said to Xerxes (cf. 7.28) that he was 7,000 staters short of having 4 million staters.

7.29.3

ἔκτησό Perfect, imperative, middle, 2nd, singular of κτέομαι (= κτάομαι).

ἐπίστασό τε εἶναι Present, imperative, middle, 2nd, singular of ἐπίσταμαι. "And know how to be…."

ἐς χρόνον "Unto [the future] time."

ೞ

7.35.1-3 Scourging the Hellespont

Chapters 7.33-34 describe the construction of the original bridge which Xerxes had built across the Hellespont (cf. map in Landmark *ad* 7.33) so that his vast army could cross over from Asia to Europe. After a storm wrecks this first bridge, Xerxes flies into a rage and orders his men to punish and degrade the waters of the "turbulent and briny river" (7.35.2). Many controversies attend Herodotus' descriptions of both the original bridge and the floating bridge which replaced it (see HW *ad* 7.36). The latter was supposedly constructed with pontoons, over which a causeway could be built once the boats had been fastened together.

ὡς δ᾿ ἐπύθετο Ξέρξης, δεινὰ ποιεύμενος τὸν Ἑλλήσποντον ἐκέλευσε τριηκοσίας ἐπικέσθαι μάστιγι πληγὰς καὶ κατεῖναι ἐς τὸ πέλαγος πεδέων ζεῦγος. ἤδη δὲ ἤκουσα ὡς καὶ στιγέας ἅμα τούτοισι ἀπέπεμψε στίξοντας τὸν Ἑλλήσποντον. [2] ἐνετέλλετο δὲ ὦν ῥαπίζοντας λέγειν βάρβαρά τε καὶ ἀτάσθαλα· "ὦ πικρὸν ὕδωρ, δεσπότης τοι δίκην ἐπιτιθεῖ τήνδε, ὅτι μιν ἠδίκησας οὐδὲν πρὸς ἐκείνου ἄδικον παθόν. καὶ βασιλεὺς μὲν Ξέρξης διαβήσεταί σε, ἤν τε σύ γε βούλῃ ἤν τε μή· σοὶ δὲ κατὰ δίκην ἄρα οὐδεὶς ἀνθρώπων θύει ὡς ἐόντι καὶ θολερῷ καὶ ἁλμυρῷ ποταμῷ." [3] τήν τε δὴ θάλασσαν ἐνετέλλετο τούτοισι ζημιοῦν καὶ τῶν ἐπεστεώτων τῇ ζεύξι τοῦ Ἑλλησπόντου ἀποταμεῖν τὰς κεφαλάς.

7.35.1

δεινὰ ποιεύμενος "Being terribly enraged."

ποιεύμενος = ποιούμενος.

ἐπικέσθαι Aorist, middle infinitive of ἐπικνέομαι (= ἐφικνέομαι); it takes a double accusative (τὸν Ἑλλήσποντον and πληγὰς). "To visit the Hellespont with blows."

πέλαγος The Hellespont is also referred to as a "river" (cf. 7.35.2), because of its strong currents.

τούτοισι Referring to the men who were instructed to whip the Hellespont.

7.35.2

ὦν = οὖν.

διαβήσεταί Future, indicative, middle, 3rd, singular of διαβαίνω.

7.35.3

τῶν ἐπεστεώτων "Those in charge." It takes the dative case in τῇ ζεύξι.

℘

7.39.1-3 Xerxes Shows His True Colors

We last saw Pythios in 7.29, where a gracious Xerxes repaid the generosity of his Lydian host with even greater generosity…all in the name of *xenia*, perhaps the single most important component of the code of conduct for ancient Greeks. We learn in 7.38 that this Pythios, frightened by what he thought was a bad omen for Xerxes' expedition (the eclipse of the sun), asked Xerxes to allow the oldest of his five sons to stay behind so he could care for his father. Xerxes' response to this seemingly reasonable request is the subject of the passage below. While Herodotus may occasionally grant Xerxes a few admirable qualities, equanimity or level-headedness is not one of them.

κάρτα τε ἐθυμώθη ὁ Ξέρξης καὶ ἀμείβετο τοισίδε· "ὦ κακὲ ἄνθρωπε, σὺ ἐτόλμησας, ἐμεῦ στρατευομένου αὐτοῦ ἐπὶ τὴν Ἑλλάδα καὶ ἄγοντος παῖδας ἐμοὺς καὶ ἀδελφεοὺς καὶ οἰκηίους καὶ φίλους, μνήσασθαι περὶ σέο παιδός, ἐὼν ἐμὸς δοῦλος, τὸν χρῆν πανοικίῃ αὐτῇ τῇ γυναικὶ συνέπεσθαι; εὖ νυν τόδ᾽ ἐξεπίστασο, ὡς ἐν τοῖσι ὠσὶ τῶν ἀνθρώπων οἰκέει ὁ θυμός, ὃς χρηστὰ μὲν ἀκούσας τέρψιος ἐμπιπλεῖ τὸ σῶμα, ὑπεναντία δὲ τούτοισι ἀκούσας ἀνοιδέει. [2] ὅτε μέν νυν χρηστὰ ποιήσας ἕτερα τοιαῦτα ἐπηγγέλλεο, εὐεργεσίῃσι βασιλέα οὐ καυχήσεαι ὑπερβαλέσθαι· ἐπείτε δὲ ἐς τὸ ἀναιδέστερον ἐτράπευ, τὴν μὲν ἀξίην οὐ λάμψεαι, ἐλάσσω δὲ τῆς ἀξίης. σὲ μὲν γὰρ καὶ τοὺς τέσσερας τῶν παίδων ῥύεται τὰ ξείνια· τοῦ δὲ ἑνός, τοῦ περιέχεαι μάλιστα, τῇ ψυχῇ ζημιώσεαι." [3] ὡς δὲ ταῦτα ὑπεκρίνατο, αὐτίκα ἐκέλευε τοῖσι προσετέτακτο ταῦτα πρήσσειν, τῶν Πυθίου παίδων ἐξευρόντας τὸν πρεσβύτατον μέσον διαταμεῖν, διαταμόντας δὲ τὰ ἡμίτομα διαθεῖναι τὸ μὲν ἐπὶ δεξιὰ τῆς ὁδοῦ τὸ δ᾽ ἐπ᾽ ἀριστερά, καὶ ταύτῃ διεξιέναι τὸν στρατόν.

7.39.1

ἐθυμώθη Aorist, indicative, passive, 3rd, singular of θυμόω.

ἐμεῦ στρατευομένου αὐτοῦ ἐπὶ τὴν Ἑλλάδα καὶ ἄγοντος παῖδας ἐμοὺς καὶ ἀδελφεοὺς καὶ οἰκηίους καὶ φίλους A long, genitive absolute construction.

μνήσασθαι Aorist, middle infinitive of μιμνήσκω.

τὸν χρῆν "For whom it is necessary."

πανοικίῃ Used adverbially: "With an entire household."

ἐξεπίστασο Present, imperative, middle, 2nd, singular of ἐξεπίσταμαι.

ἐμπιπλεῖ Present, indicative, active, 3rd, singular of ἐμπίπλημι.

ἀνοιδέει Supply "with rage."

7.39.2

ἕτερα τοιαῦτα "Other such favors."

οὐ καυχήσεαι ὑπερβαλέσθαι "You will not boast that you have surpassed."

ἐς τὸ ἀναιδέστερον "To rather shameful [conduct]."

τὴν μὲν ἀξίην "On the one hand, that which you deserve."

περιέχεαι "You cling." It takes the genitive case (τοῦ).

7.39.3

τοῖσι προσετέτακτο ταῦτα πρήσσειν "Those men who were entrusted to do these things."

πρήσσειν = πράσσειν.

ଓ3

7.44.1 Xerxes and His Portable Throne

On his march to Greece, Xerxes made several stops, including one at Ilium (the site of ancient Troy). According to our author (7.43), the Persians drank dry the Scamander, the river which is often mentioned in Homer's *Iliad*. This is yet another indication that Herodotus was ready to challenge Homer and show that his war was greater than Homer's. In the passage below, we see Xerxes following the example of Darius, who also had ordered a throne to be set up when he was reviewing his forces at the Thracian Bosporus (cf. 4.88).

ἐπεὶ δ᾽ ἐγένοντο ἐν Ἀβύδῳ, ἠθέλησε Ξέρξης ἰδέσθαι πάντα τὸν στρατόν· καὶ προεπεποίητο γὰρ ἐπὶ κολωνοῦ ἐπίτηδες αὐτῷ ταύτῃ προεξέδρη λίθου λευκοῦ, ἐποίησαν δὲ Ἀβυδηνοὶ ἐντειλαμένου πρότερον βασιλέος, ἐνθαῦτα ὡς ἵζετο, κατορῶν ἐπὶ τῆς ἠιόνος ἐθηεῖτο καὶ τὸν πεζὸν καὶ τὰς νέας, θηεύμενος δὲ ἱμέρθη τῶν νεῶν ἅμιλλαν γινομένην ἰδέσθαι. ἐπεὶ δὲ ἐγένετό τε καὶ ἐνίκων Φοίνικες Σιδώνιοι, ἥσθη τε τῇ ἁμίλλῃ καὶ τῇ στρατιῇ.

7.44.1

ἐγένοντο Subject is "the Persians."

Ἀβύδῳ Abydos is a city on the Asian side of the Hellespont; it was from here that the pontoon bridge extended to Sestos on the European side of the straits. See map in Landmark *ad* 7.42.

ἰδέσθαι "Review."

ταύτῃ Used as an adverb here.

λίθου λευκοῦ "White stone" indicates that the throne was made from marble.

ἐντειλαμένου πρότερον βασιλέος Genitive absolute construction.

ἐθηεῖτο Imperfect, indicative, middle, 3rd, singular of θεάομαι.

ἱμέρθη Aorist, indicative, passive, 3rd, singular of ἱμείρω.

Σιδώνιοι Sidon constituted one of the three kingdoms of ancient Phoenicia.

ἥσθη Aorist, indicative, passive, 3rd, singular of ἥδομαι.

ఠ

7.46.1-4 Xerxes and Artabanos Wax Pessimistic...Really Pessimistic

Hermogenes, the second century A.D. rhetorician, considered this section of the *Histories* to be "sublime," mostly because of the profound themes which Xerxes and Artabanos are made to discuss. At any rate, we have here another example of Herodotus' interest in a very pessimistic philosophy of life (and death), one which is explored on more than one occasion in the Histories, most notably in the story of Cleobis and Biton (1.32). The passage also reminds us of the several thematic similarities between the *Histories* and the plays of Sophocles, especially *Oedipus Tyrannus* (1186) and *Oedipus at Colonus* (1225). Lastly, there is a Homeric touch to the passage, as the picture of a melancholy Xerxes is reminiscent of the opening lines of *Iliad* X, where Homer shows us a similarly depressed (and sleepless) Agamemnon.

μαθὼν δέ μιν Ἀρτάβανος ὁ πάτρως, ὃς τὸ πρῶτον γνώμην ἀπεδέξατο ἐλευθέρως οὐ συμβουλεύων Ξέρξῃ στρατεύεσθαι ἐπὶ τὴν Ἑλλάδα, οὗτος ὡνὴρ φρασθεὶς Ξέρξην δακρύσαντα εἴρετο τάδε· "ὦ βασιλεῦ, ὡς πολλὸν ἀλλήλων κεχωρισμένα ἐργάσαο νῦν τε καὶ ὀλίγῳ πρότερον· μακαρίσας γὰρ σεωυτὸν δακρύεις." [2] ὁ δὲ εἶπε· "ἐσῆλθε γάρ με λογισάμενον κατοικτεῖραι ὡς βραχὺς εἴη ὁ πᾶς ἀνθρώπινος βίος, εἰ τούτων γε ἐόντων τοσούτων οὐδεὶς ἐς ἑκατοστὸν ἔτος περιέσται." ὁ δὲ ἀμείβετο λέγων· "ἕτερα τούτου παρὰ τὴν ζόην πεπόνθαμεν οἰκτρότερα. [3] ἐν γὰρ οὕτω βραχέι βίῳ οὐδεὶς οὕτω ἄνθρωπος ἐὼν εὐδαίμων πέφυκε οὔτε τούτων οὔτε τῶν ἄλλων, τῷ οὐ παραστήσεται πολλάκις καὶ οὐκὶ ἅπαξ τεθνάναι βούλεσθαι μᾶλλον ἢ ζώειν. αἵ τε γὰρ συμφοραὶ προσπίπτουσαι καὶ αἱ νοῦσοι συνταράσσουσαι καὶ βραχὺν ἐόντα μακρὸν δοκέειν εἶναι ποιεῦσι τὸν βίον. [4] οὕτω ὁ μὲν θάνατος μοχθηρῆς ἐούσης τῆς ζόης καταφυγὴ αἱρετωτάτη τῷ ἀνθρώπῳ γέγονε, ὁ δὲ θεὸς γλυκὺν γεύσας τὸν αἰῶνα φθονερὸς ἐν αὐτῷ εὑρίσκεται ἐών."

7.46.1

φρασθεὶς Aorist, passive, masculine, nominative, singular participle of φράζω. In the passive, it can mean "Having noticed."

ὡς πολλὸν ἀλλήλων κεχωρισμένα ἐργάσαο νῦν "Just now, you did things [that were] very much at variance with the other things."

7.46.2

ἐσῆλθε Impersonal: "it occurred."

κατοικτεῖραι ὡς "To lament how...."

τούτων γε ἐόντων τοσούτων οὐδεὶς Xerxes is referring to the countless soldiers he had just been reviewing (7.44).

πεπόνθαμεν Perfect, indicative, active, 1st, plural of πάσχω.

7.46.3

τεθνάναι Perfect, active infinitive of θνήσκω.

7.46.4

μοχθηρῆς ἐούσης τῆς ζόης Genitive absolute construction.

εὑρίσκεται ἐών "Is discovered to be."

☙

7.60.1-3 Counting by Myriads

More than perhaps any other feature of the *Histories*, the figures which Herodotus gives when estimating the size of Xerxes' expedition have damaged his credibility as a historian. HW *ad* 7.60 have this to say: "The enormous numbers, and the naïve and cumbrous method of counting, make this story as it stands incredible." (For a more recent and somewhat less censorious appraisal, see Landmark, Appendix R, "The Size of Xerxes' Expeditionary Force.") In Herodotus' defense, it may be argued that the method he describes for counting the Persian infantry has a certain visual and even theoretical appeal. Moreover, Herodotus' typical eye for detail—e.g., he specifies that the wall which was built after the first 10,000 men had been counted reached navel height—adds to the story's believability. It could also be argued that Herodotus arrived at his figures by using the Greek city-states as his model. In other words, he may have assumed that all men of fighting age from all of the 61 national contingents in Xerxes' army would have reported for duty in much the same way that all men of fighting age would normally have served in the citizen armies of Greek city-states such as Athens.

ὅσον μέν νυν ἕκαστοι παρεῖχον πλῆθος ἐς ἀριθμόν, οὐκ ἔχω εἰπεῖν τὸ ἀτρεκές· οὐ γὰρ λέγεται πρὸς οὐδαμῶν ἀνθρώπων· σύμπαντος δὲ τοῦ στρατοῦ τοῦ πεζοῦ τὸ πλῆθος ἐφάνη ἑβδομήκοντα καὶ ἑκατὸν μυριάδες. [2] ἐξηρίθμησαν δὲ τόνδε τὸν τρόπον· συνήγαγόν τε ἐς ἕνα χῶρον μυριάδα ἀνθρώπων, καὶ συννάξαντες ταύτην ὡς μάλιστα εἶχον περιέγραψαν ἔξωθεν κύκλον· περιγράψαντες δὲ καὶ ἀπέντες τοὺς μυρίους αἱμασιὴν περιέβαλον κατὰ τὸν κύκλον, ὕψος ἀνήκουσαν ἀνδρὶ ἐς τὸν ὀμφαλόν· [3] ταύτην δὲ ποιήσαντες ἄλλους ἐσεβίβαζον ἐς τὸ περιοικοδομημένον, μέχρι οὗ πάντας τούτῳ τῷ τρόπῳ ἐξηρίθμησαν. ἀριθμήσαντες δὲ κατὰ ἔθνεα διέτασσον.

7.60.1

ἕκαστοι Referring to the individual national contingents which had arrived at Doriskos (for the location of this Thracian town, see map in Landmark *ad* 7.58).

ἐς ἀριθμόν "For a counting."

πρὸς οὐδαμῶν ἀνθρώπων Genitive of source.

ἑβδομήκοντα καὶ ἑκατὸν μυριάδες 170 x 10,000 = 1,700,000.

7.60.2

συννάξαντες ταύτην ὡς μάλιστα εἶχον "Squeezing this [group of] 10,000 together as much as they could."

ἀνήκουσαν Modifies αἱμασιὴν: "That came up."

7.60.3

κατὰ ἔθνεα There were 61 nations represented in Xerxes' army.

∞

7.83.1-2 The 10,000 Immortals

Herodotus provides us with a fascinating look at the Immortals, the elite force of 10,000 soldiers who accompanied the Great King as his bodyguards. We are also introduced to the ordinary Persian soldier who, if Herodotus can be believed, was not so ordinary at all. A running theme in the *Histories* is that the Persians, unlike the Greeks who adhered to the notion of "nothing in excess," lived by the principle of "everything in excess."

οὗτοι ἦσαν στρατηγοὶ τοῦ σύμπαντος πεζοῦ χωρὶς τῶν μυρίων· τῶν δὲ μυρίων τούτων Περσέων τῶν ἀπολελεγμένων ἐστρατήγεε μὲν Ὑδάρνης ὁ Ὑδάρνεος, ἐκαλέοντο δὲ ἀθάνατοι οἱ Πέρσαι οὗτοι ἐπὶ τοῦδε· εἴ τις αὐτῶν ἐξέλιπε τὸν ἀριθμὸν ἢ θανάτῳ βιηθεὶς ἢ νούσῳ, ἄλλος ἀνὴρ ἀραίρητο, καὶ ἐγίνοντο οὐδαμὰ οὔτε πλεῦνες μυρίων οὔτε ἐλάσσονες. [2] κόσμον δὲ πλεῖστον παρείχοντο διὰ πάντων Πέρσαι, καὶ αὐτοὶ ἄριστοι ἦσαν· σκευὴν μὲν τοιαύτην εἶχον ἥ περ εἴρηται, χωρὶς δὲ χρυσόν τε πολλὸν καὶ ἄφθονον ἔχοντες ἐνέπρεπον, ἁρμαμάξας τε ἅμα ἤγοντο, ἐν δὲ παλλακὰς καὶ θεραπηίην πολλήν τε καὶ εὖ ἐσκευασμένην· σῖτα δέ σφι, χωρὶς τῶν ἄλλων στρατιωτέων, κάμηλοί τε καὶ ὑποζύγια ἦγον.

7.83.1

ἐστρατήγεε The verb takes the genitive case.

βιηθεὶς Aorist, passive, masculine, nominative, singular participle of βιάω.

ἀραίρητο Pluperfect, indicative, passive, 3rd, singular of αἱρέω. The replacements "had been chosen" and were, therefore, ready to be slotted into the unit as soon as there was a vacancy.

ἐγίνοντο = ἐγίγνοντο.

7.83.2

διὰ πάντων "Of all [the soldiers in the entire army]."

αὐτοὶ Apart from their uniforms and equipment, the Persians "themselves" were the best.

ἥ περ εἴρηται "The very thing which has been mentioned."

χωρὶς "Besides."

παλλακὰς "Concubines."

θεραπηίην Used as a collective noun, it means "retinue."

☙

7.102.1-3 Demaratos' Discourse on the Spartans, Part I

Demaratos, the exiled Spartan King—the reasons for his exile are described in 6.51, 6.63, 6.65-69—ultimately became Xerxes' trusted advisor (6.70) and even helped him succeed to the Persian throne (6.73). In the passage below, Xerxes asks Demaratos for information concerning the character of Greeks in general and of Spartans in particular. Demaratos' response ends up being a very compelling testament to Spartan ἀρετή or "excellence," one which should inform any discussion concerning the bias which Herodotus is often alleged to have shown in favor of Athens. As a side-note, it may be pointed out that Xerxes himself receives some praise in this passage for his demand that he be told only the truth. One last point: Herodotus' description of poverty as the "twin sister" of Greece is rightly regarded as one of his best formulations in the *Histories*.

ὡς δὲ ταῦτα ἤκουσε Δημάρητος, ἔλεγε τάδε·"βασιλεῦ, ἐπειδὴ ἀληθείη διαχρήσασθαι πάντως κελεύεις ταῦτα λέγοντα τὰ μὴ ψευδόμενός τις ὕστερον ὑπὸ σεῦ ἁλώσεται, τῇ Ἑλλάδι πενίη μὲν αἰεί κοτε σύντροφός ἐστι, ἀρετὴ δὲ ἔπακτός ἐστι, ἀπό τε σοφίης κατεργασμένη καὶ νόμου ἰσχυροῦ· τῇ διαχρεωμένη ἡ Ἑλλὰς τήν τε πενίην ἀπαμύνεται καὶ τὴν δεσποσύνην. [2] αἰνέω μέν νυν πάντας Ἕλληνας τοὺς περὶ ἐκείνους τοὺς Δωρικοὺς χώρους οἰκημένους, ἔρχομαι δὲ λέξων οὐ περὶ πάντων τούσδε τοὺς λόγους ἀλλὰ περὶ Λακεδαιμονίων μούνων, πρῶτα μὲν ὅτι οὐκ ἔστι ὅκως κοτὲ σοὺς δέξονται λόγους δουλοσύνην φέροντας τῇ Ἑλλάδι, αὖτις δὲ ὡς ἀντιώσονταί τοι ἐς μάχην καὶ ἢν οἱ ἄλλοι Ἕλληνες πάντες τὰ σὰ φρονέωσι. [3] ἀριθμοῦ δὲ πέρι, μή πύθῃ ὅσοι τινὲς ἐόντες ταῦτα ποιεῖν οἷοί τέ εἰσι· ἤν τε γὰρ τύχωσι ἐξεστρατευμένοι χίλιοι, οὗτοι μαχήσονταί τοι, ἤν τε ἐλάσσονες τούτων ἤν τε καὶ πλεῦνες."

7.102.1

ταῦτα λέγοντα τὰ μὴ ψευδόμενός τις ὕστερον ὑπὸ σεῦ ἁλώσεται The sense seems to be that Xerxes does not want Demaratos or anyone to be telling lies, which would ultimately be discovered as lies by him.

κοτε = ποτε.

σύντροφος Literally, "nursed together." Poverty is seen as a family member for the Greeks.

ἔπακτος "Acquired."

κατεργασμένη "Cultivated from."

τῇ Refers to ἀρετή.

7.102.2

ἔρχομαι Equivalent to the English expression "I am going to…," but in Greek it is followed by a participle (λέξων) instead of by an infinitive.

πρῶτα μὲν Paired with αὖτις δὲ.

ὅκως κοτέ = ὅπως ποτέ.

δουλοσύνην φέροντας "Offering slavery."

τὰ σὰ φρονέωσι Supply a word like φρονήματα: "They should agree with your proposals."

7.102.3

πέρι An instance of anastrophe, where the preposition governs the preceding word (note the position of the accent).

ἤν τε γὰρ τύχωσι ἐξεστρατευμένοι χίλιοι "If a thousand of them happen to march out."

☙

7.104.1-5 Demaratos' Discourse on the Spartans, Part II

Herodotus writes that, when Xerxes heard Demaratos' description of Spartan valor, he reacted by laughing and by questioning Demaratos' own courage (7.103). The passage below is a vigorous response from Demaratos to Xerxes' taunts, but its greater claim to fame comes from the section where Demaratos refutes Xerxes' notion that men will fight and die only when they have a master who wields a whip. According to Demaratos (Herodotus, really), the major component of the Spartan national character is an absolute adherence to the law, which compels the Spartans to fight, no matter the odds. This passage and others like it (cf. 7.209) offer a useful antidote to the descriptions of a seemingly bizarre Spartan life-style which one often finds in ancient sources (for example, Plutarch's *Life of Lycurgus*).

πρὸς ταῦτα Δημάρητος λέγει· "ὦ βασιλεῦ, ἀρχῆθεν ἠπιστάμην ὅτι ἀληθείῃ χρεώμενος οὐ φίλα τοι ἐρέω· σὺ δ' ἐπεὶ ἠνάγκασας λέγειν τῶν λόγων τοὺς ἀληθεστάτους, ἔλεγον τὰ κατήκοντα Σπαρτιήτῃσι. [2] καίτοι ὡς ἐγὼ τυγχάνω τὰ νῦν τάδε ἐστοργὼς ἐκείνους, αὐτὸς μάλιστα ἐξεπίστεαι, οἵ με τιμήν τε καὶ γέρεα ἀπελόμενοι πατρώια ἄπολίν τε καὶ φυγάδα πεποιήκασι, πατὴρ δὲ σὸς ὑποδεξάμενος βίον τέ μοι καὶ οἶκον ἔδωκε. οὔκων οἰκός ἐστι ἄνδρα τὸν σώφρονα εὐνοίην φαινομένην διωθέεσθαι, ἀλλὰ στέργειν μάλιστα. [3] ἐγὼ δὲ οὔτε δέκα ἀνδράσι ὑπίσχομαι οἷός τε εἶναι μάχεσθαι οὔτε δυοῖσι, ἑκών τε εἶναι οὐδ' ἂν μουνομαχέοιμι. εἰ δὲ ἀναγκαίη εἴη ἢ μέγας τις ὁ ἐποτρύνων ἀγών, μαχοίμην ἂν πάντων ἥδιστα ἑνὶ τούτων τῶν ἀνδρῶν οἳ Ἑλλήνων ἕκαστός φησι τριῶν ἄξιος εἶναι. [4] ὣς δὲ καὶ Λακεδαιμόνιοι κατὰ μὲν ἕνα μαχόμενοι οὐδαμῶν εἰσι κακίονες ἀνδρῶν, ἁλέες δὲ ἄριστοι ἀνδρῶν ἁπάντων. ἐλεύθεροι γὰρ ἐόντες οὐ πάντα ἐλεύθεροί εἰσι· ἔπεστι γάρ σφι δεσπότης νόμος, τὸν ὑποδειμαίνουσι πολλῷ ἔτι μᾶλλον ἢ οἱ σοὶ σέ. [5] ποιεῦσι γῶν τὰ ἂν ἐκεῖνος ἀνώγῃ· ἀνώγει δὲ τὼυτὸ αἰεί, οὐκ ἐῶν φεύγειν οὐδὲν πλῆθος ἀνθρώπων ἐκ μάχης, ἀλλὰ μένοντας ἐν τῇ τάξι ἐπικρατέειν ἢ ἀπόλλυσθαι. σοὶ δὲ εἰ φαίνομαι ταῦτα λέγων φλυηρέειν, τἆλλα σιγᾶν θέλω τὸ λοιπόν· νῦν τε ἀναγκασθεὶς ἔλεξα. γένοιτο μέντοι κατὰ νόον τοι, βασιλεῦ"

7.104.1

οὐ φίλα τοι "Not pleasing to you."

τὰ κατήκοντα "The things that pertain."

7.104.2

ἐγὼ τυγχάνω... ἐστοργὼς ἐκείνους Demaratos is speaking ironically.

τὰ νῦν τάδε "At this present time."

οἵ The antecedent is ἐκείνους.

ἀπελόμενοι Aorist, middle, masculine, nominative, plural participle of ἀπαιρέω (= ἀφαιρέω).

οὔκων οἰκός ἐστι "It is not at all likely."

οὔκων = οὔκουν.

7.104.3

ὑπίσχομαι οἷός τε εἶναι "I [do not] claim to be able."

ἑκών τε εἶναι "Given a choice."

ἥδιστα Superlative adverb.

ἕκαστος φησὶ The verb φησὶ is singular, because it is attracted to the singular ἕκαστος.

7.104.4

κατὰ μὲν ἕνα μαχόμενοι "Fighting one-on-one."

πάντα Accusative of respect.

7.104.5

γῶν = γοῦν.

τὠυτό Crasis (when two words are combined into one) for τὸ αὐτό.

οὐδὲν πλῆθος ἀνθρώπων "Not even a vast crowd of [enemy] men."

τἄλλα Crasis for τὰ ἄλλα.

γένοιτο The optative is used to express a wish.

☙

7.139.1-6 The Judgment of Herodotus

Arguably, Herodotus wrote this part of the *Histories* just before the outbreak of the Peloponnesian War (431-404 B.C.), that is, at a time when the Athenian-sponsored Delian League had come to be viewed by more than a few Greek states as an oppressively imperialistic enterprise. In view of the political climate of the late 430s, Herodotus' famous judgment, that the Athenians (and not the Spartans) were the "saviors of Greece," probably elicited a strong negative reaction from many of his readers. Herodotus maintains that his sense of what is true compels him to formulate this judgment.

ἐνθαῦτα ἀναγκαίῃ ἐξέργομαι γνώμην ἀποδέξασθαι ἐπίφθονον μὲν πρὸς τῶν πλεόνων ἀνθρώπων, ὅμως δὲ τῇ γέ μοι φαίνεται εἶναι ἀληθὲς οὐκ ἐπισχήσω. [2] εἰ Ἀθηναῖοι καταρρωδήσαντες τὸν ἐπιόντα κίνδυνον ἐξέλιπον τὴν σφετέρην, ἢ καὶ μὴ ἐκλιπόντες ἀλλὰ μείναντες ἔδοσαν σφέας αὐτοὺς Ξέρξῃ, κατὰ τὴν θάλασσαν οὐδαμοὶ ἂν ἐπειρῶντο ἀντιούμενοι βασιλέι. εἰ τοίνυν κατὰ τὴν θάλασσαν μηδεὶς ἠντιοῦτο Ξέρξῃ, κατά γε ἂν τὴν ἤπειρον τοιάδε ἐγίνετο·[3] εἰ καὶ πολλοὶ τειχέων κιθῶνες ἦσαν ἐληλαμένοι διὰ τοῦ Ἰσθμοῦ Πελοποννησίοισι, προδοθέντες ἂν Λακεδαιμόνιοι ὑπὸ τῶν συμμάχων οὐκ ἑκόντων ἀλλ᾽ ὑπ᾽ ἀναγκαίης, κατὰ πόλις ἁλισκομένων ὑπὸ τοῦ ναυτικοῦ στρατοῦ τοῦ βαρβάρου, ἐμουνώθησαν, μουνωθέντες δὲ ἂν καὶ ἀποδεξάμενοι ἔργα μεγάλα ἀπέθανον γενναίως. [4] ἢ ταῦτα ἂν ἔπαθον, ἢ πρὸ τοῦ ὁρῶντες ἂν καὶ τοὺς ἄλλους Ἕλληνας μηδίζοντας ὁμολογίῃ ἂν ἐχρήσαντο πρὸς Ξέρξην. καὶ οὕτω ἂν ἐπ᾽ ἀμφότερα ἡ Ἑλλὰς ἐγίνετο ὑπὸ Πέρσῃσι. τὴν γὰρ ὠφελίην τὴν τῶν τειχέων τῶν διὰ τοῦ Ἰσθμοῦ ἐληλαμένων οὐ δύναμαι πυθέσθαι ἥτις ἂν ἦν, βασιλέος ἐπικρατέοντος τῆς θαλάσσης. [5] νῦν δὲ Ἀθηναίους ἄν τις λέγων σωτῆρας γενέσθαι τῆς Ἑλλάδος οὐκ ἂν ἁμαρτάνοι τὸ ἀληθές. οὗτοι γὰρ ἐπὶ ὁκότερα τῶν πρηγμάτων ἐτράποντο, ταῦτα ῥέψειν ἔμελλε· ἑλόμενοι δὲ τὴν Ἑλλάδα περιεῖναι ἐλευθέρην, τοῦτο τὸ Ἑλληνικὸν πᾶν τὸ λοιπόν, ὅσον μὴ ἐμήδισε, αὐτοὶ οὗτοι ἦσαν οἱ ἐπεγείραντες καὶ βασιλέα μετά γε θεοὺς ἀνωσάμενοι. [6] οὐδὲ σφέας χρηστήρια φοβερὰ ἐλθόντα ἐκ Δελφῶν καὶ ἐς δεῖμα βαλόντα ἔπεισε ἐκλιπεῖν τὴν Ἑλλάδα, ἀλλὰ καταμείναντες ἀνέσχοντο τὸν ἐπιόντα ἐπὶ τὴν χώρην δέξασθαι.

7.139.1

ἐξέργομαι Literally, "I am excluded [from every other option]." Idiomatically, "I am compelled to."

οὐκ ἐπισχήσω Supply γνώμην ἀποδέξασθαι.

7.139.2

οὐδαμοὶ = οὐδένες.

ἂν ἐπειρῶντο ἀντιούμενοι βασιλέϊ "Would have tried to oppose the King."

τοιάδε ἐγίνετο "The following things would have happened."

ἐγίνετο = ἐγίγνετο.

7.139.3

τειχέων κιθῶνες Literally, "coats of walls," which is a poetic way of saying "walls."

ἑκόντων…ἁλισκομένων Both modify τῶν συμμάχων.

κατὰ πόλις "City by city."

7.139.4

πρὸ τοῦ "Beforehand."

ἐπ᾽ ἀμφότερα "In both cases."

τὴν…ὠφελίην "Advantage."

ἥτις ἂν ἦν "What it [the advantage of the wall across the Isthmus] would have been."

βασιλέος ἐπικρατέοντος τῆς θαλάσσης Genitive absolute construction.

7.139.5

τὸ ἀληθές Used adverbially: "In truth."

ἐπὶ ὁκότερα τῶν πρηγμάτων "To whichever of the two sides."

ὁκότερα = ὁπότερα.

ταῦτα ῥέψειν ἔμελλε "This side was going to dominate" (or "this side was going to tip the scales").

7.139.6

ἐς δεῖμα βαλόντα "Throwing [them] into panic."

τὸν ἐπιόντα "The one invading."

☙

7.152.1-3 Out of Fairness to the Argives…

The history of Argive medizing is a complicated one, and Herodotus recognizes this. To give some background, he writes about the recent battle between Sparta and Argos (494 B.C.) and about the abiding hatred the Argives had towards the Spartans (7.148-149). He also describes a post-war mission to Susa (7.151) in which Argive ambassadors were reported to have asked Artaxerxes, Xerxes' son and successor, for a renewal of the friendship treaty they had supposedly concluded, before the Persian Wars, with Xerxes. In the passage below, Herodotus applies an old Greek maxim (quoted in Valerius Maximus 7.2.2) to the matter at hand. What he seems to be suggesting is that the medizing of the Argives, however egregious it may have been, was not as bad as the medizing of other Greeks (like that of the Thebans, for example). Tucked away in this discourse on Argive medizing is a remarkable sentence (7.153.3), in which Herodotus formulates what appears to be his over-arching historiographical principle (cf. 2.123.1 and 4.195.2 for similar statements concerning his modus operandi).

εἰ μέν νυν Ξέρξης τε ἀπέπεμψε ταῦτα λέγοντα κήρυκα ἐς Ἄργος καὶ Ἀργείων ἄγγελοι ἀναβάντες ἐς Σοῦσα ἐπειρώτων Ἀρταξέρξεα περὶ φιλίης, οὐκ ἔχω ἀτρεκέως εἰπεῖν, οὐδέ τινα γνώμην περὶ αὐτῶν ἀποφαίνομαι ἄλλην γε ἢ τήν περ αὐτοὶ Ἀργεῖοι λέγουσι· [2] ἐπίσταμαι δὲ τοσοῦτο ὅτι εἰ πάντες ἄνθρωποι τὰ οἰκήια κακὰ ἐς μέσον συνενείκαιεν ἀλλάξασθαι βουλόμενοι τοῖσι πλησίοισι, ἐγκύψαντες ἂν ἐς τὰ τῶν πέλας κακὰ ἀσπασίως ἕκαστοι αὐτῶν ἀποφεροίατο ὀπίσω τὰ ἐσενεικαίατο. [3] οὕτω δὲ οὐδ᾽ Ἀργείοισι αἴσχιστα πεποίηται. ἐγὼ δὲ ὀφείλω λέγειν τὰ λεγόμενα, πείθεσθαί γε μὲν οὐ παντάπασι ὀφείλω, καί μοι τοῦτο τὸ ἔπος ἐχέτω ἐς πάντα λόγον· ἐπεὶ καὶ ταῦτα λέγεται, ὡς ἄρα Ἀργεῖοι ἦσαν οἱ ἐπικαλεσάμενοι τὸν Πέρσην ἐπὶ τὴν Ἑλλάδα, ἐπειδή σφι πρὸς τοὺς Λακεδαιμονίους κακῶς ἡ αἰχμὴ ἑστήκεε, πᾶν δὴ βουλόμενοι σφίσι εἶναι πρὸ τῆς παρεούσης λύπης.

7.152.1

ἐπειρώτων Imperfect, indicative, active, 3rd, plural of ἐπειρωτάω (= ἐπερωτάω).

οὐκ ἔχω "I am unable."

ἄλλην γε ἢ τήν "Other than the one which."

7.152.2

συνενείκαιεν Aorist, optative, active, 3rd, plural of συμφέρω.

7.152.3

τοῦτο τὸ ἔπος ἐχέτω "Let this principle apply."

ἐς πάντα λόγον Referring to the Histories.

ἦσαν οἱ "Were the ones who."

πᾶν Here, "Anything."

βουλόμενοι "Preferring."

CZ

7.208.1-3 Spartans Fix Their Hair

This is one of the "quiet" sections leading up to the Battle of Thermopylae. Herodotus writes that Xerxes, curious about the small Greek force holding the Pass at Thermopylae, sent a spy to check on their number and activities. What the spy saw astonished him and perplexed Xerxes. Perhaps the most telling part of Herodotus' narrative here is his observation that not only did the Spartans not give chase to the Persian spy but they ignored him with a studied indifference.

ταῦτα βουλευομένων σφέων, ἔπεμπε Ξέρξης κατάσκοπον ἱππέα ἰδέσθαι ὁκόσοι εἰσὶ καὶ ὅ τι ποιέοιεν. ἀκηκόεε δὲ ἔτι ἐὼν ἐν Θεσσαλίῃ ὡς ἁλισμένη εἴη ταύτῃ στρατιὴ ὀλίγη, καὶ τοὺς ἡγεμόνας ὡς εἴησαν Λακεδαιμόνιοί τε καὶ Λεωνίδης ἐὼν γένος Ἡρακλείδης. [2] ὡς δὲ προσήλασε ὁ ἱππεὺς πρὸς τὸ στρατόπεδον, ἐθηεῖτό τε καὶ κατώρα πᾶν μὲν οὒ τὸ στρατόπεδον· τοὺς γὰρ ἔσω τεταγμένους τοῦ τείχεος, τὸ ἀνορθώσαντες εἶχον ἐν φυλακῇ, οὐκ οἷά τε ἦν κατιδέσθαι· ὁ δὲ τοὺς ἔξω ἐμάνθανε, τοῖσι πρὸ τοῦ τείχεος τὰ ὅπλα ἔκειτο· ἔτυχον δὲ τοῦτον τὸν χρόνον Λακεδαιμόνιοι ἔξω τεταγμένοι. [3] τοὺς μὲν δὴ ὥρα γυμναζομένους τῶν ἀνδρῶν, τοὺς δὲ τὰς κόμας κτενιζομένους. ταῦτα δὴ θεώμενος ἐθώμαζε καὶ τὸ πλῆθος ἐμάνθανε. μαθὼν δὲ πάντα ἀτρεκέως ἀπήλαυνε ὀπίσω κατ᾽ ἡσυχίην· οὔτε γάρ τις ἐδίωκε ἀλογίης τε ἐνεκύρησε πολλῆς· ἀπελθών τε ἔλεγε πρὸς Ξέρξην τά περ ὀπώπεε πάντα.

7.208.1

ταῦτα βουλευομένων σφέων Genitive absolute construction. It refers to the Greek deliberations at Thermopylae.

ὁκόσοι = ὁπόσοι.

ἀκηκόεε Pluperfect, indicative, active, 3rd, singular of ἀκούω.

τοὺς ἡγεμόνας Direct object of ἀκηκόεε, which means "become aware of" when it takes the accusative.

ὡς εἴησαν Λακεδαιμόνιοί τε καὶ Λεωνίδης The clause follows ἀκηκόεε and expands on the information provided by τοὺς ἡγεμόνας: "How they were...."

7.208.2

ἔσω The preposition takes the genitive case.

τό A relative pronoun here; its antecedent is τείχεος.

οὐκ οἶά τε ἦν "And it was not possible."

7.208.3

τὸ πλῆθος ἐμάνθανε One of the two tasks of the spy was to learn the size of the Greek forces at Thermopylae (ἰδέσθαι ὁκόσοι εἰσί).

ἀλογίης "Indifference."

ὀπώπεε Pluperfect, indicative, active, 3rd, singular of ὁράω.

ை

7.209.1-5 Demaratos Talks About the Spartans...Again

Back in chapters 7.102 and 7.104, we saw how Demaratos, the exiled Spartan king and counselor to Xerxes, described the extraordinary valor and devotion to law which characterized his fellow Spartans. In the passage below, Herodotus shows Demaratos heaping even more praise on the Spartans, whom he now calls ἄνδρας ἀρίστους and whose city he refers to as καλλίστην πόλιν. To judge from the way Spartans are described in the battle narratives which follow, it seems clear that Herodotus himself held these views. Such championing of Sparta should give pause to the critics of Herodotus who malign him for his alleged pro-Athenian bias.

ἀκούων δὲ Ξέρξης οὐκ εἶχε συμβαλέσθαι τὸ ἐόν, ὅτι παρασκευάζοιντο ὡς ἀπολεόμενοί τε καὶ ἀπολέοντες κατὰ δύναμιν· ἀλλ' αὐτῷ γελοῖα γὰρ ἐφαίνοντο ποιέειν, μετεπέμψατο Δημάρητον τὸν Ἀρίστωνος ἐόντα ἐν τῷ στρατοπέδῳ· [2] ἀπικόμενον δέ μιν εἰρώτα Ξέρξης ἕκαστα τούτων, ἐθέλων μαθεῖν τὸ ποιεύμενον πρὸς τῶν Λακεδαιμονίων, ὁ δὲ εἶπε· "ἤκουσας μὲν καὶ πρότερόν μευ, εὖτε ὁρμῶμεν ἐπὶ τὴν Ἑλλάδα, περὶ τῶν ἀνδρῶν τούτων, ἀκούσας δὲ γέλωτά με ἔθευ λέγοντα τῇ περ ὥρων ἐκβησόμενα πρήγματα ταῦτα· ἐμοὶ γὰρ τὴν ἀληθείην ἀσκέειν ἀντία σεῦ βασιλεῦ ἀγὼν μέγιστός ἐστι.

[3] ἄκουσον δὲ καὶ νῦν: οἱ ἄνδρες οὗτοι ἀπίκαται μαχησόμενοι ἡμῖν περὶ τῆς ἐσόδου, καὶ ταῦτα παρασκευάζονται. νόμος γάρ σφι ἔχων οὕτω ἐστί· ἐπεὰν μέλλωσι κινδυνεύειν τῇ ψυχῇ, τότε τὰς κεφαλὰς κοσμέονται. [4] ἐπίστασο δέ, εἰ τούτους γε καὶ τὸ ὑπομένον ἐν Σπάρτῃ καταστρέψεαι, ἔστι οὐδὲν ἄλλο ἔθνος ἀνθρώπων τὸ σὲ βασιλεῦ ὑπομενέει χεῖρας ἀνταειρόμενον· νῦν γὰρ πρὸς βασιληίην τε καὶ καλλίστην πόλιν τῶν ἐν Ἕλλησι προσφέρεαι καὶ ἄνδρας ἀρίστους." [5] κάρτα τε δὴ Ξέρξῃ ἄπιστα ἐφαίνετο τὰ λεγόμενα εἶναι, καὶ δεύτερα ἐπειρώτα ὄντινα τρόπον τοσοῦτοι ἐόντες τῇ ἑωυτοῦ στρατιῇ μαχήσονται. ὁ δὲ εἶπε· "ὦ βασιλεῦ, ἐμοὶ χρᾶσθαι ὡς ἀνδρὶ ψεύστῃ, ἢν μὴ ταῦτά τοι ταύτῃ ἐκβῇ τῇ ἐγὼ λέγω."

7.209.1

οὐκ εἶχε "Was not able."

τὸ ἐόν "That which was." In other words, the truth.

κατὰ δύναμιν "To the full extent of their might."

7.209.2

ἀπικόμενον = ἀφικόμενον.

τὸ ποιεύμενον πρὸς τῶν Λακεδαιμονίων "That which was being done by the Lacedaemonians."

γέλωτά με ἔθευ "You made me a subject of derision."

λέγοντα "When I was telling you."

τῇ περ ὥρων ἐκβησόμενα πρήγματα ταῦτα "In what way I saw that these things would turn out."

ἀγὼν μέγιστος "Highest ambition."

7.209.3

ἀπίκαται Perfect, indicative, middle, 3rd, plural of ἀπικνέομαι (= ἀφικνέομαι).

μαχησόμενοι The future participle indicates purpose here.

ἔχων οὕτω ἐστί A variant to οὕτως ἔχει ("is thus").

7.209.4

τὸ ὑπομένον "That which is left behind." That is, "the remaining men."

χεῖρας ἀνταειρόμενον "Who would raise their hands against…."

τοσοῦτοι ἐόντες "Being so few [in number]."

7.209.5

χρᾶσθαι The infinitive functions as an imperative.

☙

View looking northeast from the mainland towards the northern tip of Euboea. The waterway in the foreground is the northern end of the Straights of Euboea where Xerxes' fleet engaged the Athenian navy in the battle of Artemision. (Photo and caption courtesy of Henry Bender)

7.210.1-2 The Battle of Thermopylae, Part I

With this chapter, the narrative for the Battle of Thermopylae commences. Xerxes waited for four days before ordering his troops to advance, as he fully expected the Greeks to give up their positions at the Pass. His decision to attack was actually prompted by a fit of anger (θυμωθείς), a rather common occurrence for the Herodotean Xerxes. The section closes with a memorable formulation which questions the "manliness" of Xerxes' soldiers. HW (ad 7.210.2) see this as an "inapposite remark," given that the Persians fought stubbornly and relentlessly, albeit without success.

ταῦτα λέγων οὐκ ἔπειθε τὸν Ξέρξην τέσσερας μὲν δὴ παρεξῆκε ἡμέρας, ἐλπίζων αἰεί σφεας ἀποδρήσεσθαι· πέμπτῃ δέ, ὡς οὐκ ἀπαλλάσσοντο ἀλλά οἱ ἐφαίνοντο ἀναιδείῃ τε καὶ ἀβουλίῃ διαχρεώμενοι μένειν, πέμπει ἐπ' αὐτοὺς Μήδους τε καὶ Κισσίους θυμωθείς, ἐντειλάμενος σφέας ζωγρήσαντας ἄγειν ἐς ὄψιν τὴν ἑωυτοῦ. [2] ὡς δ' ἐσέπεσον φερόμενοι ἐς τοὺς Ἕλληνας οἱ Μῆδοι, ἔπιπτον πολλοί, ἄλλοι δ' ἐπεσήισαν, καὶ οὐκ ἀπηλαύνοντο, καίπερ μεγάλως προσπταίοντες. δῆλον δ' ἐποίευν παντὶ τεῳ καὶ οὐκ ἥκιστα αὐτῷ βασιλέι, ὅτι πολλοὶ μὲν ἄνθρωποι εἶεν, ὀλίγοι δὲ ἄνδρες. ἐγίνετο δὲ ἡ συμβολὴ δι' ἡμέρης.

7.210.1

παρεξῆκε Aorist, indicative, active, 3rd, singular of παρεξίημι. "He let pass."

ἀποδρήσεσθαι Future, middle, infinitive of ἀποδιδράσκω.

ἀναιδείη τε καὶ ἀβουλίη διαχρεώμενοι "Displaying shamelessness and recklessness." (This was from Xerxes' point of view, of course.)

Κισσίους For the possible location of Kissia, see map in Landmark *ad* 7.186.

ἑωυτοῦ = ἑαυτοῦ.

7.210.2

φερόμενοι "Headlong."

ἐπεσήισαν Imperfect, indicative, active, 3rd, plural of ἐπέσειμι (= ἐπείσειμι).

τεῳ = τινι.

ℭ

7.211.1-3 The Battle of Thermopylae, Part II

In an earlier chapter (7.176), Herodotus described just how narrow the Pass at Thermopylae was: at some places, it was only wide enough to allow for the passage of a single wagon, while elsewhere it was no more than 50 feet wide. We see in this present chapter that the Spartans and their allies were able to take advantage of the narrow confines of the Pass, especially when executing a feigned retreat. We are also told that the long spears of the Greeks proved to be clearly superior to the shorter spears of the enemy. Diodorus Siculus, the 1st century B.C. historian, comments (9.7) that the Persians who fought at Thermopylae were also at a disadvantage because of their shields, which were made of wicker. (The Greeks fought, of course, with metallic shields.)

ἐπείτε δὲ οἱ Μῆδοι τρηχέως περιείποντο, ἐνθαῦτα οὗτοι μὲν ὑπεξήισαν, οἱ δὲ Πέρσαι ἐκδεξάμενοι ἐπήισαν, τοὺς ἀθανάτους ἐκάλεε βασιλεύς, τῶν ἦρχε Ὑδάρνης, ὡς δὴ οὗτοί γε εὐπετέως κατεργασόμενοι. [2] ὡς δὲ καὶ οὗτοι συνέμισγον τοῖσι Ἕλλησι, οὐδὲν πλέον ἐφέροντο τῆς στρατιῆς τῆς Μηδικῆς ἀλλὰ τὰ αὐτά, ἅτε ἐν στεινοπόρῳ τε χώρῳ μαχόμενοι καὶ δόρασι βραχυτέροισι χρεώμενοι ἤ περ οἱ Ἕλληνες, καὶ οὐκ ἔχοντες πλήθεϊ χρήσασθαι. [3] Λακεδαιμόνιοι δὲ ἐμάχοντο ἀξίως λόγου, ἄλλα τε ἀποδεικνύμενοι ἐν οὐκ ἐπισταμένοισι μάχεσθαι ἐξεπιστάμενοι, καὶ ὅκως ἐντρέψειαν τὰ νῶτα, ἀλέες φεύγεσκον δῆθεν, οἱ δὲ βάρβαροι ὁρῶντες φεύγοντας βοῇ τε καὶ πατάγῳ ἐπήισαν, οἱ δ' ἂν καταλαμβανόμενοι ὑπέστρεφον ἀντίοι εἶναι τοῖσι βαρβάροισι, μεταστρεφόμενοι δὲ κατέβαλλον πλήθεϊ ἀναριθμήτους τῶν Περσέων· ἔπιπτον δὲ καὶ αὐτῶν τῶν Σπαρτιητέων ἐνθαῦτα ὀλίγοι. ἐπεὶ δὲ οὐδὲν ἐδυνέατο παραλαβεῖν οἱ Πέρσαι τῆς ἐσόδου πειρώμενοι καὶ κατὰ τέλεα καὶ παντοίως προσβάλλοντες, ἀπήλαυνον ὀπίσω.

7.211.1

τρηχέως = τραχέως.

ἐκδεξάμενοι "Taking their place." *to take up*

τούς Here, a relative pronoun.

ὡς δὴ οὗτοί γε εὐπετέως κατεργασόμενοι The future participle with ὡς is used to express purpose.

7.211.2

οὐκ ἔχοντες πλήθεϊ χρήσασθαι "Being unable to take advantage of their number[s]."

7.211.3

ἄλλα "In other ways."

ὅκως = ὅπως.

φεύγεσκον The iterative infix -εσκ- emphasizes repeated action.

δῆθεν "Or so it seemed."

ἀντίοι εἶναι The infinitive expresses result. "With the result that they [the Greeks] were face-to-face…."

πλήθεϊ Dative of respect.

τῆς ἐσόδου The Thermopylae Pass.

πειρώμενοι καὶ κατὰ τέλεα καὶ παντοίως προσβάλλοντες The two participles are concessive. "Although…."

κατὰ τέλεα "By entire regiments."

☙

7.212.1-2 The Battle of Thermopylae, Part III

This passage is not the first in which Xerxes is shown sitting on a throne and taking an active interest in the progress of his assault on Greece. In 7.45, he is said to have reviewed the entire expeditionary force while seated on a marble throne which was positioned on the top of a hill. At that time, Xerxes was pleased with what he saw, but his reaction to the first day of engagements at the Battle of Thermopylae was one of fear, so much so that he jumped from his throne on three separate occasions. HW *ad* 7.212.1 point to a comparable scene in *Iliad* 20.62, where Hades, fearing that the commotion at Troy might cause a fissure which would expose his kingdom, "jumped in terror from his throne." Later in the *Histories*, we will see Xerxes once more sitting on a hilltop, this time to oversee the Battle of Salamis. He will not like what he sees in that battle as well.

ἐν ταύτῃσι τῇσι προσόδοισι τῆς μάχης λέγεται βασιλέα θηεύμενον τρὶς ἀναδραμεῖν ἐκ τοῦ θρόνου δείσαντα περὶ τῇ στρατιῇ. τότε μὲν οὕτω ἠγωνίσαντο, τῇ δ' ὑστεραίῃ οἱ βάρβαροι οὐδὲν ἄμεινον ἀέθλεον. ἅτε γὰρ ὀλίγων ἐόντων, ἐλπίσαντες σφέας κατατετρωματίσθαι τε καὶ οὐκ οἵους τε ἔσεσθαι ἔτι χεῖρας ἀνταείρασθαι συνέβαλλον. [2] οἱ δὲ Ἕλληνες κατὰ τάξις τε καὶ κατὰ ἔθνεα κεκοσμημένοι ἦσαν, καὶ ἐν μέρεϊ ἕκαστοι ἐμάχοντο, πλὴν Φωκέων· οὗτοι δὲ ἐς τὸ ὄρος ἐτάχθησαν φυλάξοντες τὴν ἀτραπόν. ὡς δὲ οὐδὲν εὕρισκον ἀλλοιότερον οἱ Πέρσαι ἢ τῇ προτεραίῃ ἐνώρων, ἀπήλαυνον.

7.212.1

προσόδοισι "Attacks."

θηεύμενον Present, middle, masculine, accusative, singular participle of θηέομαι (= θεάομαι).

ἀναδραμεῖν Aorist, active infinitive of ἀνατρέχω. "Leapt up."

οὐδὲν ἄμεινον "In no way better."

ὀλίγων ἐόντων Genitive absolute construction.

κατατετρωματίσθαι Perfect, passive infinitive of κατατραυματίζω.

καὶ οὐκ οἵους τε ἔσεσθαι "And that they would not be able."

7.212.2

ἐτάχθησαν Aorist, indicative, passive, 3rd, plural of τάσσω.

ೞ

7.218.1-3 The Battle of Thermopylae, Part IV

Chapters 7.213-215 tell the story of Ephialtes, a Greek from nearby Malis, who alerted the Persians to the existence of a mountain path, which went around the Pass at Thermopylae. In the chapter below, Herodotus describes the Persian ascent of this mountain path and their encounter with the Phocian soldiers who were stationed near the highest point. Few other passages in the *Histories* are as beautifully crafted as this one. Herodotus, at his poetic best, skillfully describes the stillness of dawn, the crunching of leaves under the feet of the Persians, and the confusion on the part of both the Persians and the Phocians when they finally meet. Some commentators (cf. HW *ad* 7.218) see this chapter as an attempt on the part of Herodotus to fashion a defense for the Phocians, who retreated to the mountain top as soon as they caught sight of the Persians.

ἔμαθον δὲ σφέας οἱ Φωκέες ὧδε ἀναβεβηκότας· ἀναβαίνοντες γὰρ ἐλάνθανον οἱ Πέρσαι τὸ ὄρος πᾶν ἐὸν δρυῶν ἐπίπλεον. ἦν μὲν δὴ νηνεμίη, ψόφου δὲ γινομένου πολλοῦ, ὡς οἰκὸς ἦν φύλλων ὑποκεχυμένων ὑπὸ τοῖσι ποσί, ἀνά τε ἔδραμον οἱ Φωκέες καὶ ἐνέδυνον τὰ ὅπλα, καὶ αὐτίκα οἱ βάρβαροι παρῆσαν. [2] ὡς δὲ εἶδον ἄνδρας ἐνδυομένους ὅπλα, ἐν θώματι ἐγένοντο· ἐλπόμενοι γὰρ οὐδένα σφι φανήσεσθαι ἀντίξοον ἐνεκύρησαν στρατῷ. ἐνθαῦτα Ὑδάρνης καταρρωδήσας μὴ οἱ Φωκέες ἔωσι Λακεδαιμόνιοι, εἴρετο Ἐπιάλτην

The line visible in the terrain from right to left actually marks the contour of the Pass at Thermopylae. The higher mountain peaks in the background are thought to be the ones which were occupied surreptitiously by Xerxes' men overnight and from which they hurled weapons upon the exposed back of the Spartan position while a frontal assault took place as well. (Photo and caption courtesy of Henry Bender)

ὁποδαπὸς εἴη ὁ στρατός, πυθόμενος δὲ ἀτρεκέως διέτασσε τοὺς Πέρσας ὡς ἐς μάχην. [3] οἱ δὲ Φωκέες ὡς ἐβάλλοντο τοῖσι τοξεύμασι πολλοῖσί τε καὶ πυκνοῖσι, οἴχοντο φεύγοντες ἐπὶ τοῦ ὄρεος τὸν κόρυμβον, ἐπιστάμενοι ὡς ἐπὶ σφέας ὁρμήθησαν ἀρχήν, καὶ παρεσκευάδατο ὡς ἀπολεόμενοι. οὗτοι μὲν δὴ ταῦτα ἐφρόνεον, οἱ δὲ ἀμφὶ Ἐπιάλτην καὶ Ὑδάρνεα Πέρσαι Φωκέων μὲν οὐδένα λόγον ἐποιεῦντο, οἱ δὲ κατέβαινον τὸ ὄρος κατὰ τάχος.

7.218.1

ἀναβεβηκότας Refers to the Persian ascent of the mountain where the path which the Phocians were guarding was located.

ψόφου δὲ γινομένου πολλοῦ Genitive absolute construction.

ὡς οἰκὸς ἦν "As was likely."

φύλλων ὑποκεχυμένων ὑπὸ τοῖσι ποσί Genitive absolute construction.

ὑποκεχυμένων Perfect, passive, genitive, neuter, plural participle of ὑποχέω.

7.218.2

ἐλπόμενοι "Expecting wrongly."

Ἐπιάλτην The Greek who showed the path over the mountain to the Persians. Also spelled Ἐφιάλτης.

7.218.3

ἐβάλλοντο In the passive, βάλλω means "they were hit" (and not "they were thrown").

ὡς ἐπὶ σφέας ὁρμήθησαν "That they [the Persians] were attacking them."

ἀρχήν "From the start."

ἀπολεόμενοι Future, middle, masculine, nominative, plural participle of ἀπόλλυμι.

οὐδένα λόγον ἐποιεῦντο "Paid no attention at all."

ぴ

7.220.1-3 The Battle of Thermopylae, Part V

It probably took the Persians about five hours to come down from the mountain path which brought them behind the Greek forces at Thermopylae. Facing certain death, the Greeks met in an emergency council to decide what to do next. Leonidas, sensing the dispiritedness and indecision of his Greek allies, sent them away and rejoined his 300 fellow Spartans. In this passage, Herodotus strongly suggests that Leonidas had long ago made up his mind to die at Thermopylae and, in so doing, to save Sparta. According to Plutarch (*de Malignitate Herodoti* 32), funeral games had already been celebrated for Leonidas at Sparta even before he had left for Thermopylae.

λέγεται δὲ καὶ ὡς αὐτός σφεας ἀπέπεμψε Λεωνίδης, μὴ ἀπόλωνται κηδόμενος· αὐτῷ δὲ καὶ Σπαρτιητέων τοῖσι παρεοῦσι οὐκ ἔχειν εὐπρεπέως ἐκλιπεῖν τὴν τάξιν ἐς τὴν ἦλθον φυλάξοντες ἀρχήν. [2] ταύτῃ καὶ μᾶλλον τὴν γνώμην πλεῖστός εἰμι, Λεωνίδην, ἐπείτε ᾔσθετο τοὺς συμμάχους ἐόντας ἀπροθύμους καὶ οὐκ ἐθέλοντας συνδιακινδυνεύειν, κελεῦσαι σφέας ἀπαλλάσσεσθαι, αὐτῷ δὲ ἀπιέναι οὐ καλῶς ἔχειν· μένοντι δὲ αὐτοῦ κλέος μέγα ἐλείπετο, καὶ ἡ Σπάρτης εὐδαιμονίη οὐκ ἐξηλείφετο. [3] ἐκέχρηστο γὰρ ὑπὸ τῆς Πυθίης τοῖσι Σπαρτιήτῃσι χρεωμένοισι περὶ τοῦ πολέμου τούτου αὐτίκα κατ' ἀρχὰς ἐγειρομένου, ἢ Λακεδαίμονα ἀνάστατον γενέσθαι ὑπὸ τῶν βαρβάρων ἢ τὴν βασιλέα σφέων ἀπολέσθαι.

7.220.1

σφεας Referring to the all the Greeks who had stood with the 300 Spartans at Thermopylae. In 7.202, Herodotus lists the city-states which had sent contingents to the battle.

οὐκ ἔχειν The infinitive depends on some word of mental action, which is implied by κηδόμενος.

7.220.2

ταύτῃ καὶ μᾶλλον τὴν γνώμην πλεῖστός εἰμι "I am mostly inclined to this in my judgment." In other words, "I am very much of this opinion that...."

ἀπιέναι The infinitive here depends on some word of "saying," which is implied by κελεῦσαι.

οὐ καλῶς ἔχειν "Was not honorable."

ἐξηλείφετο Imperfect, indicative, passive, 3rd, singular of ἐξαλείφω. A very effective metaphor!

7.220.3

ἐκέχρηστο Pluperfect, indicative, passive, 3rd, singular of χρέομαι (= χράομαι). "It had been prophesied."

κατ' ἀρχὰς "At its very beginning."

☙

7.223.1-4 The Battle of Thermopylae, Part VI

As the Persians descend from the mountain path and attack the Spartans from behind, the only recourse left to the 300 is to wade into the enemy forces and kill as many of the Persians as they can. Herodotus emphasizes in this passage, as he has done before (cf. 7.106), that the Persians had to be driven on to fight by the whips of their officers, whereas the Spartans rushed into certain death because of a sense of duty. Herodotus displays here (and elsewhere) a considerable knowledge of the topography of Thermopylae, so much so that a visitor today can still use the appropriate sections of the *Histories* as a guidebook. (Allowance has to be made, however, for the geological fact that the sea has receded by a few kilometers since Herodotus wrote the *Histories*.) Interestingly, there are in this passage a couple of instances of anacoluthon (where the syntax seems to break down). Could it be that Herodotus wanted his syntax to mimic the confusion of the battle? (Cf. Thucydides' account [7.42-44] of the Night Battle in Syracuse, where a confused syntax mirrors the very confusing events of a battle fought in near-darkness.)

Ξέρξης δὲ ἐπεὶ ἡλίου ἀνατείλαντος σπονδὰς ἐποιήσατο, ἐπισχὼν χρόνον ἐς ἀγορῆς κου μάλιστα πληθώρην πρόσοδον ἐποιέετο· καὶ γὰρ ἐπέσταλτο ἐξ Ἐπιάλτεω οὕτω. ἀπὸ γὰρ τοῦ ὄρεος ἡ κατάβασις συντομωτέρη τέ ἐστι καὶ βραχύτερος ὁ χῶρος πολλὸν ἤ περ ἡ περίοδός τε καὶ ἀνάβασις. [2] οἵ τε δὴ βάρβαροι οἱ ἀμφὶ Ξέρξην προσήισαν, καὶ οἱ ἀμφὶ Λεωνίδην Ἕλληνες, ὡς τὴν ἐπὶ θανάτῳ ἔξοδον ποιεύμενοι, ἤδη πολλῷ μᾶλλον ἤ κατ' ἀρχὰς ἐπεξήισαν ἐς τὸ εὐρύτερον τοῦ αὐχένος. τὸ μὲν γὰρ ἔρυμα τοῦ τείχεος ἐφυλάσσετο, οἱ δὲ ἀνὰ τὰς προτέρας ἡμέρας ὑπεξιόντες ἐς τὰ στεινόπορα ἐμάχοντο. [3] τότε δὲ συμμίσγοντες ἔξω τῶν στεινῶν ἔπιπτον πλήθεϊ πολλοὶ τῶν βαρβάρων· ὄπισθε γὰρ οἱ ἡγεμόνες τῶν τελέων ἔχοντες μάστιγας ἐρράπιζον πάντα ἄνδρα, αἰεὶ ἐς τὸ πρόσω ἐποτρύνοντες. πολλοὶ μὲν δὴ ἐσέπιπτον αὐτῶν ἐς τὴν θάλασσαν καὶ διεφθείροντο, πολλῷ δ' ἔτι πλεῦνες κατεπατέοντο ζωοὶ ὑπ' ἀλλήλων· ἦν δὲ λόγος οὐδεὶς τοῦ ἀπολλυμένου. [4] ἅτε γὰρ ἐπιστάμενοι τὸν μέλλοντα σφίσι ἔσεσθαι θάνατον ἐκ τῶν περιιόντων τὸ ὄρος, ἀπεδείκνυντο

ῥώμης ὅσον εἶχον μέγιστον ἐς τοὺς βαρβάρους, παραχρεώμενοί τε καὶ
ἀτέοντες.

(marginal notes: "might", "reckless", "being reckless")

7.223.1

ἡλίου ἀνατείλαντος Genitive absolute construction.

ἀνατείλαντος Aorist, active, masculine, genitive, singular participle of ἀνατέλλω.

ἐπισχὼν χρόνον "Pausing for a while."

ἐς ἀγορῆς κου μάλιστα πληθώρην Literally, "Until approximately the filling of the marketplace." That is, "Until late morning."

ἐπέσταλτο Pluperfect, indicative, passive, 3rd, singular of ἐπιστέλλω: "it had been enjoined."

ὁ χῶρος "The space [in between]."

πολλὸν Accusative of extent in degree: "By much." But cf. the dative πολλῷ in the next sentence.

7.223.2

τοῦ αὐχένος The Pass at Thermopylae.

ἐφυλάσσετο The imperfect is used here to emphasize habitual action.

7.223.3

συμμίσγοντες The participle modifies πολλοὶ τῶν βαρβάρων, the subject of ἔπιπτον.

τῶν τελέων "Regiments."

λόγος οὐδεὶς "No accounting."

τοῦ ἀπολλυμένου The equivalent of τῶν ἀπολλυμένων.

7.223.4

ῥώμης ὅσον εἶχον μέγιστον "The greatest of strength they could muster."

παραχρεώμενοί "Acting without forethought."

ɞ

7.225.1-3 The Battle of Thermopylae, Part VII

The present chapter, one of the best in the entire *Histories*, details the struggle over Leonidas' body and the final moments of the 300 Spartans, all of whose names Herodotus went on to learn (7.224.1) in a demonstration of historical inquiry at its best. The struggle over Patroklos' body in *Iliad* 17 is evoked by the narrative here: the use of Homeric words like νεῖκος, as well as the foray into dactylic hexameter (καὶ Λακεδαιμονίων...πολλός), suggest that Herodotus had Homer on his mind. Apart from any literary allusions, the passage is made especially memorable by the description of the Spartans fighting to the very end with their hands and teeth. Not surprisingly, Cicero picks up on this stirring image in his *Tusculan Disputations* (5.27), essays he wrote as a moral guide for his son.

Ξέρξεώ τε δὴ δύο ἀδελφεοὶ ἐνθαῦτα πίπτουσι μαχόμενοι, καὶ ὑπὲρ τοῦ νεκροῦ τοῦ Λεωνίδεω Περσέων τε καὶ Λακεδαιμονίων ὠθισμὸς ἐγίνετο πολλός, ἐς ὃ τοῦτόν τε ἀρετῇ οἱ Ἕλληνες ὑπεξείρυσαν καὶ ἐτρέψαντο τοὺς ἐναντίους τετράκις, τοῦτο δὲ συνεστήκεε μέχρι οὗ οἱ σὺν Ἐπιάλτῃ παρεγένοντο. [2] ὡς δὲ τούτους ἥκειν ἐπύθοντο οἱ Ἕλληνες, ἐνθεῦτεν ἤδη ἑτεροιοῦτο τὸ νεῖκος· ἔς τε γὰρ τὸ στεινὸν τῆς ὁδοῦ ἀνεχώρεον ὀπίσω, καὶ παραμειψάμενοι τὸ τεῖχος ἐλθόντες ἵζοντο ἐπὶ τὸν κολωνὸν πάντες ἁλέες οἱ ἄλλοι πλὴν Θηβαίων. ὁ δὲ κολωνός ἐστι ἐν τῇ ἐσόδῳ, ὅκου νῦν ὁ λίθινος λέων ἕστηκε ἐπὶ Λεωνίδῃ. [3] ἐν τούτῳ σφέας τῷ χώρῳ ἀλεξομένους μαχαίρῃσι, τοῖσι αὐτῶν ἐτύγχανον ἔτι περιεοῦσαι, καὶ χερσὶ καὶ στόμασι κατέχωσαν οἱ βάρβαροι βάλλοντες, οἱ μὲν ἐξ ἐναντίης ἐπισπόμενοι καὶ τὸ ἔρυμα τοῦ τείχεος συγχώσαντες, οἱ δὲ περιελθόντες πάντοθεν περισταδόν.

7.225.1

ἀρετῇ "By their courage."

τοῦτο δὲ συνεστήκεε "This [struggle] lasted."

7.225.2

ἐπύθοντο Aorist, indicative, middle, 3rd, plural of πυνθάνομαι.

ἑτεροιοῦτο "Took on a different complexion."

ἐλθόντες ἵζοντο "They came and stationed themselves."

ἐπὶ Λεωνίδῃ "In honor of Leonidas."

7.225.3

τοῖσι αὐτῶν ἐτύγχανον ἔτι περιεοῦσαι "Those who still happened to have daggers."

κατέχωσαν...βάλλοντες "Overwhelmed them with arrows."

7.226.1 We Shall Fight in the Shade

When we look back over the just-concluded narrative of the Battle of Thermopylae, it is striking to see that no individual Greek—not even Leonidas—is described performing some heroic deed. In this section, Herodotus presents a mere anecdote, albeit a very memorable one, about the clever pre-battle riposte of a Spartan named Dienekes. On the basis of this anecdote, Herodotus concludes that this Spartan may have been the bravest (ἄριστος) of them all. Plutarch, Herodotus' most severe ancient critic, found fault with the absence of any glorious exploits in the actual battle narrative and attributed it to Herodotus' lack of patriotism (*de Malignitate Herodoti* 32). HW *ad* 7.226, on the other hand, see it as "wise reticence."

Λακεδαιμονίων δὲ καὶ Θεσπιέων τοιούτων γενομένων ὅμως λέγεται ἀνὴρ ἄριστος γενέσθαι Σπαρτιήτης Διηνέκης· τὸν τόδε φασὶ εἰπεῖν τὸ ἔπος πρὶν ἢ

συμμῖξαι σφέας τοῖσι Μήδοισι, πυθόμενον πρός τευ τῶν Τρηχινίων ὡς ἐπεὰν
οἱ βάρβαροι ἀπίωσι τὰ τοξεύματα, τὸν ἥλιον ὑπὸ τοῦ πλήθεος τῶν ὀιστῶν
ἀποκρύπτουσι· τοσοῦτο πλῆθος αὐτῶν εἶναι. [2] τὸν δὲ οὐκ ἐκπλαγέντα
τούτοισι εἰπεῖν (ἐν ἀλογίη ποιεύμενον) τὸ Μήδων πλῆθος, ὡς πάντα σφι
ἀγαθὰ ὁ Τρηχίνιος ξεῖνος ἀγγέλλοι, εἰ ἀποκρυπτόντων τῶν Μήδων τὸν
ἥλιον ὑπὸ σκιῇ ἔσοιτο πρὸς αὐτοὺς ἡ μάχη καὶ οὐκ ἐν ἡλίῳ.

7.226.1

Λακεδαιμονίων δὲ καὶ Θεσπιέων τοιούτων γενομένων Genitive absolute construction.
    Translate as a concessive clause: "Although…."

συμμῖξαι Aorist, active infinitive of συμμίγνυμι.

πρός τευ "From someone."

τευ = τινός.

Τρηχινίων Trachis is a region in Thessaly, west of Thermopylae. See map in Landmark *ad*
    7.213.

ἐπεάν = ἐπειδάν.

7.226.2

τόν Referring to Dienekes.

ἐν ἀλογίη ποιεύμενον "Regarded as unimportant."

ἀποκρυπτόντων τῶν Μήδων τὸν ἥλιον Genitive absolute construction.

 appleⳫ

7.233.1-2 Thebans Get Branded

Theban conduct during the Persian War is regularly described by Herodotus as
traitorous towards the Greek cause, and this passage is no exception. The Thebans who
surrendered at Thermopylae (and who later professed that they had been loyal to the King
all along) are shown here being ignominiously branded with the royal seal by the orders
of Xerxes himself. Plutarch's animus towards Herodotus (displayed abundantly in *de
Malignitate Herodoti*) may well have been motivated by passages such as this: though not a
Theban, Plutarch, like the Thebans, was a Boeotian, as he was born in Chaeronea, a city in
Boeotia. Herodotus concludes this chapter with a reference to an event from just before the
start of the Peloponnesian War (431 B.C.), when 400 Thebans, along with Eurymachus (the
son of the Leontiades, the Theban who is said to have surrendered at Thermopylae), were
murdered in Plataea. (Herodotus may have gotten some of his facts wrong in this historical
footnote. Without naming Herodotus, Thucydides [2.2-6] stipulates that there were only
300 Thebans in Plataea at the time of this incident.) In any case, because of this reference
to an event from 431 B.C., we can be confident that Herodotus was still alive at the start of
the Peloponnesian War.

οἱ δὲ Θηβαῖοι, τῶν ὁ Λεοντιάδης ἐστρατήγεε, τέως μὲν μετὰ τῶν Ἑλλήνων ἐόντες ἐμάχοντο ὑπ' ἀναγκαίης ἐχόμενοι πρὸς τὴν βασιλέος στρατιήν· ὡς δὲ εἶδον κατυπέρτερα τῶν Περσέων γινόμενα τὰ πρήγματα, οὕτω δή, τῶν σὺν Λεωνίδῃ Ἑλλήνων ἐπειγομένων ἐπὶ τὸν κολωνόν, ἀποσχισθέντες τούτων χεῖράς τε προέτεινον καὶ ἤισαν ἆσσον τῶν βαρβάρων, λέγοντες τὸν ἀληθέστατον τῶν λόγων, ὡς καὶ μηδίζουσι καὶ γῆν τε καὶ ὕδωρ ἐν πρώτοισι ἔδοσαν βασιλέι, ὑπὸ δὲ ἀναγκαίης ἐχόμενοι ἐς Θερμοπύλας ἀπικοίατο καὶ ἀναίτιοι εἶεν τοῦ τρώματος τοῦ γεγονότος βασιλέι. [2] ὥστε ταῦτα λέγοντες περιεγίνοντο· εἶχον γὰρ καὶ Θεσσαλοὺς τούτων τῶν λόγων μάρτυρας· οὐ μέντοι τά γε πάντα εὐτύχησαν· ὡς γὰρ αὐτοὺς ἔλαβον οἱ βάρβαροι ἐλθόντας, τοὺς μὲν τινὰς καὶ ἀπέκτειναν προσιόντας, τοὺς δὲ πλέονας αὐτῶν κελεύσαντος Ξέρξεω ἔστιζον στίγματα βασιλήια, ἀρξάμενοι ἀπὸ τοῦ στρατηγοῦ Λεοντιάδεω· τοῦ τὸν παῖδα Εὐρύμαχον χρόνῳ μετέπειτα ἐφόνευσαν Πλαταιέες στρατηγήσαντα ἀνδρῶν Θηβαίων τετρακοσίων καὶ σχόντα τὸ ἄστυ τὸ Πλαταιέων.

7.233.1

ὑπ' ἀναγκαίης ἐχόμενοι "Constrained by necessity."

γινόμενα = γιγνόμενα.

τῶν σὺν Λεωνίδῃ Ἑλλήνων ἐπειγομένων ἐπὶ τὸν κολωνόν Genitive absolute construction. The event referred to is described in 7.225.

ἀποσχισθέντες Aorist, passive, masculine, nominative, plural participle of ἀποσχίζω.

λέγοντες τὸν ἀληθέστατον τῶν λόγων There appears to be a touch of cynicism here.

ἀπικοίατο Aorist, optative, middle, 3rd, plural of ἀπικνέομαι (= ἀφικνέομαι).

τρώματος = τραύματος.

7.233.2

τά...πάντα Accusative of respect.

ἔστιζον Takes a double accusative (τοὺς δὲ πλέονας and στίγματα βασιλήια).

κελεύσαντος Ξέρξεω Genitive absolute construction.

τοῦ Relative pronoun.

σχόντα "Having captured."

☙

7.238.1-2 Xerxes' Hatred for Leonidas

In this epilogue to his account of the Battle of Thermopylae, Herodotus describes the mistreatment of Leonidas' body, an outrage which was surely contrary to the Persian notion that warriors who fought bravely, even if they were enemy combatants, deserved respect. It may be relevant to note that Pausanias, the commander of the Greek forces at the Battle of Plataea (479 B.C.), was supposedly urged on by his soldiers to inflict the same kind of insults on Mardonios' corpse that Leonidas' body had endured. Pausanias rejected this idea outright (9.78).

ταῦτα εἴπας Ξέρξης διεξήιε διὰ τῶν νεκρῶν, καὶ Λεωνίδεω, ἀκηκοὼς ὅτι βασιλεύς τε ἦν καὶ στρατηγὸς Λακεδαιμονίων, ἐκέλευσε ἀποταμόντας τὴν κεφαλὴν ἀνασταυρῶσαι. [2] δῆλά μοι πολλοῖσι μὲν καὶ ἄλλοισι τεκμηρίοισι, ἐν δὲ καὶ τῷδε οὐκ ἥκιστα γέγονε, ὅτι βασιλεὺς Ξέρξης πάντων δὴ μάλιστα ἀνδρῶν ἐθυμώθη ζῶντι Λεωνίδῃ· οὐ γὰρ ἄν κοτε ἐς τὸν νεκρὸν ταῦτα παρενόμησε, ἐπεὶ τιμᾶν μάλιστα νομίζουσι τῶν ἐγὼ οἶδα ἀνθρώπων Πέρσαι ἄνδρας ἀγαθοὺς τὰ πολέμια. οἱ μὲν δὴ ταῦτα ἐποίευν, τοῖσι ἐπετέτακτο ποιέειν.

7.238.1

ταῦτα Refers to what Xerxes had said in support of Demaratos.

καὶ Λεωνίδεω "Including the body of Leonidas."

ἀκηκοὼς Perfect, active, masculine, nominative, singular participle of ἀκούω.

ἐκέλευσε Supply as direct object a word like "men."

τὴν κεφαλὴν ἀνασταυρῶσαι "To affix his head to a stake."

7.238.2

δῆλά μοι "It is clear to me."

ἐν δὲ καὶ τῷδε Supply τεκμηρίῳ.

κοτε = ποτε.

ταῦτα παρενόμησε "Committed these outrages."

νομίζουσι "Are accustomed to...."

τὰ πολέμια Accusative of respect.

τοῖσι Here, a relative pronoun.

ἐπετέτακτο Pluperfect, indicative, passive, 3rd, singular of ἐπιτάσσω. The verb is used impersonally here.

CB

View of the path leading into the Pass at Thermopylae as it appears today; the sense of its original width can still be perceived. Remains of a Greek defensive wall, although obscured greatly by the undergrowth, can be seen on the lower right side of the photo. (Photo and caption courtesy of Henry Bender)

8.3.1-2 Who's in Charge?

Even before the start of Xerxes' campaign against Greece, there had been numerous discussions among the Greek allies about whether the Athenians should be placed in command of the allied fleet (HW *ad* 8.3.1 date these discussions to autumn, 481 B.C.). According to Herodotus, the Athenians soon realized that they would have to give up on their claim to leadership, as there was significant opposition from the allies. The Athenians felt that preserving Greek freedom was more important than their taking control of the allied fleet. Herodotus, indulging in a bit of Realpolitik, quickly adds that the Athenian attitude changed, once Xerxes had been defeated and the Athenians no longer needed their Greek allies. As a side note, the last sentence in this chapter gives some indication that Herodotus never intended to cover events beyond 477 B.C., the year when the Athenians adopted a more aggressive foreign policy.

ἐγένετο γὰρ κατ' ἀρχὰς λόγος, πρὶν ἢ καὶ ἐς Σικελίην πέμπειν ἐπὶ συμμαχίην, ὡς τὸ ναυτικὸν Ἀθηναίοισι χρεὸν εἴη ἐπιτρέπειν. ἀντιβάντων δὲ τῶν συμμάχων εἶκον οἱ Ἀθηναῖοι μέγα πεποιημένοι περιεῖναι τὴν Ἑλλάδα καὶ γνόντες, εἰ στασιάσουσι περὶ τῆς ἡγεμονίης, ὡς ἀπολέεται ἡ Ἑλλάς, ὀρθὰ νοεῦντες· στάσις γὰρ ἔμφυλος πολέμου ὁμοφρονέοντος τοσούτῳ κάκιόν ἐστι ὅσῳ πόλεμος εἰρήνης. [2] ἐπιστάμενοι ὦν αὐτὸ τοῦτο οὐκ ἀντέτεινον ἀλλ' εἶκον, μέχρι ὅσου κάρτα ἐδέοντο αὐτῶν, ὡς διέδεξαν· ὡς γὰρ δὴ ὠσάμενοι τὸν Πέρσην περὶ τῆς ἐκείνου ἤδη τὸν ἀγῶνα ἐποιεῦντο, πρόφασιν τὴν Παυσανίεω ὕβριν προϊσχόμενοι ἀπείλοντο τὴν ἡγεμονίην τοὺς Λακεδαιμονίους. ἀλλὰ ταῦτα μὲν ὕστερον ἐγένετο.

8.3.1

ἐγένετο γὰρ κατ᾽ ἀρχὰς λόγος "From the beginning, there was talk."

ἀντιβάντων δὲ τῶν συμμάχων Genitive absolute construction.

στάσις γὰρ... Herodotus waxes poetic here and states a kind of universal truth: internal quarrels (στάσις γὰρ ἔμφυλος) are worse than foreign wars, during which all the people are at least of the same mind (πολέμου ὁμοφρονέοντος), in the same way that war is worse than peace.

8.3.2

ὦν = οὖν.

μέχρι ὅσου "Until such time as."

αὐτῶν Genitive object of ἐδέοντο, it refers to the Greek allies of the Athenians.

διέδεξαν Subject is "the Athenians."

ὠσάμενοι Aorist, middle, masculine, nominative, plural participle of ὠθέω.

περὶ τῆς Supply γῆς.

ἐκείνου Referring to τὸν Πέρσην.

προϊσχόμενοι Takes a double accusative (πρόφασιν and τὴν...ὕβριν).

ἀπείλοντο Aorist, indicative, middle, 3rd, plural of ἀπαιρέω (= ἀφαιρέω). It takes a double accusative (τὴν ἡγεμονίην and τοὺς Λακεδαιμονίους).

8.5.1-3 Bribery Can Go a Long Way

Themistokles, as the chief architect of Athenian naval power, is a major character in the *Histories* and in Greek history in general. Although he was introduced earlier in the *Histories* (7.143), it is in this section that he takes center stage. According to Herodotus, it was because of Themistokles' skills in vigorous, back-room diplomacy that the commanders of the Greek fleet finally agreed to stay at Aphetai (see map in Landmark *ad* 8.3) and defend Euboea. In this chapter, we see a very energetic Themistokles who accepts a bribe of 30 talents from the Euboeans (cf. 8.4) and then farms it out, first to Eurybiades, the Spartan admiral, and then to Adeimantos, the Corinthian commander. (What is usually overlooked is the damage done by this story to the reputations of the Spartan and Corinthian commanders.) Commentators have often accused Herodotus of displaying a strong bias against Themistokles by portraying him as a wily, conniving politician whose primary purpose was to advance his own cause(s) through some rather questionable schemes. Unfortunately, Plutarch's *Life of Themistokles* is of little help as a corrective, since it mostly agrees with Herodotus' negative portrayal.

ὁ δὲ Θεμιστοκλέης τοὺς Ἕλληνας ἐπισχεῖν ὧδε ποιέει· Εὐρυβιάδῃ τούτων τῶν χρημάτων μεταδιδοῖ πέντε τάλαντα ὡς παρ᾽ ἑωυτοῦ δῆθεν διδούς. ὡς δέ οἱ οὗτος ἀνεπέπειστο, Ἀδείμαντος γὰρ ὁ Ὠκύτου ὁ Κορίνθιος στρατηγὸς τῶν λοιπῶν ἤσπαιρε μοῦνος, φάμενος ἀποπλεύσεσθαί τε ἀπὸ τοῦ Ἀρτεμισίου καὶ οὐ παραμενέειν, πρὸς δὴ τοῦτον εἶπε ὁ Θεμιστοκλέης ἐπομόσας· [2] "οὐ σύ γε ἡμέας ἀπολείψεις, ἐπεί τοι ἐγὼ μέζω δῶρα δώσω ἢ βασιλεὺς ἄν τοι ὁ Μῆδων πέμψειε ἀπολιπόντι τοὺς συμμάχους." ταῦτά τε ἅμα ἠγόρευε καὶ πέμπει ἐπὶ τὴν νέα τὴν Ἀδειμάντου τάλαντα ἀργυρίου τρία· [3] οὗτοί τε δὴ πάντες δώροισι ἀναπεπεισμένοι ἦσαν καὶ τοῖσι Εὐβοεῦσι ἐκεχάριστο, αὐτός τε ὁ Θεμιστοκλέης ἐκέρδηνε, ἐλάνθανε δὲ τὰ λοιπὰ ἔχων, ἀλλ᾽ ἠπιστέατο οἱ μεταλαβόντες τούτων τῶν χρημάτων ἐκ τῶν Ἀθηνέων ἐλθεῖν ἐπὶ τῷ λόγῳ τούτῳ τὰ χρήματα.

8.5.1

ἐπισχεῖν ὧδε ποιέει "Did the following to hold back…."
δῆθεν "Supposedly [but not really]."
οἱ οὗτος οἱ refers to Eurybiades; οὗτος, to Themistokles.
ἤσπαιρε Literally, "Gasped." Idiomatically, "Resisted."
ἐπομόσας Aorist, active, masculine, nominative, singular participle of ἐπόμνυμι.

8.5.2

μέζω = μείζονα.

8.5.3

τοῖσι Εὐβοεῦσι ἐκεχάριστο "The Euboeans were pleased."
ἐκεχάριστο Pluperfect, indicative, passive, 3rd, singular of χαρίζομαι.
ἐκέρδηνε Aorist, indicative, active, 3rd, singular of κερδαίνω.
ἠπιστέατο Imperfect, indicative, middle, 3rd, plural of ἐπίσταμαι. "Thought [mistakenly]."
μεταλαβόντες Takes the genitive case.
ἐπὶ τῷ λόγῳ τούτῳ "For this purpose."

℘

8.12.1-2 An Unusual Storm, Part I

The sea battle off the coast of Artemision (see map in Landmark *ad* 8.16) was fought at about the same time as the Battle of Thermopylae. During the initial skirmish, the Greek fleet enjoyed some success, which is briefly described in 8.11. (Battle narratives are usually concise in the *Histories*.) A storm from Mt. Pelion, the subject matter of the chapter below, causes great distress to the Persians, since it caught them completely off guard.

ὡς δὲ εὐφρόνη ἐγεγόνεε, ἦν μὲν τῆς ὥρης μέσον θέρος, ἐγίνετο δὲ ὕδωρ
τε ἄπλετον διὰ πάσης τῆς νυκτὸς καὶ σκληραὶ βρονταὶ ἀπὸ τοῦ Πηλίου·
οἱ δὲ νεκροὶ καὶ τὰ ναυήγια ἐξεφέροντο ἐς τὰς Ἀφέτας, καὶ περί τε τὰς
πρῴρας τῶν νεῶν εἱλέοντο καὶ ἐτάρασσον τοὺς ταρσοὺς τῶν κωπέων. [2] οἱ
δὲ στρατιῶται οἱ ταύτῃ ἀκούοντες ταῦτα ἐς φόβον κατιστέατο, ἐλπίζοντες
πάγχυ ἀπολέεσθαι ἐς οἷα κακὰ ἧκον. πρὶν γὰρ ἢ καὶ ἀναπνεῦσαι σφέας ἔκ
τε τῆς ναυηγίης καὶ τοῦ χειμῶνος τοῦ γενομένου κατὰ Πήλιον, ὑπέλαβε
ναυμαχίη καρτερή, ἐκ δὲ τῆς ναυμαχίης ὄμβρος τε λάβρος καὶ ῥεύματα
ἰσχυρὰ ἐς θάλασσαν ὁρμημένα βρονταί τε σκληραί.

8.12.1

τῆς ὥρης Genitive of time when.

ἐγίνετο = ἐγίγνετο.

σκληραὶ "Fierce."

ἐς τὰς Ἀφέτας Aphetai is where part of the Persian fleet was moored. See map in Landmark
    ad 8.16.

νεκροὶ καὶ τὰ ναυήγια That is, the detritus from the first naval skirmish off the coast of
    Artemision (cf. 8.11).

εἱλέοντο Imperfect, indicative, middle, 3rd, plural of εἴλω. "Collected around."

τοὺς ταρσούς "The blades."

8.12.2

οἱ δὲ στρατιῶται οἱ ταύτῃ "The [Persian] soldiers who were here [at Aphetai]," as opposed to
    those Persians who were trying to sail around the island of Euboea (cf. 8.7).

ἐς οἷα κακὰ ἧκον "[Considering] into what kind of evils they had come."

ἐς θάλασσαν ὁρμημένα "Pouring into the sea."

☙

8.13.1 An Unusual Storm, Part II

We read in this chapter that the 200 Persian ships which had been sailing around the
island of Euboea (cf. 8.7) were shipwrecked near a place called the "Hollows of Euboea"
(for the possible location, see note in Landmark *ad* 8.13.1a). In a straightforward way,
Herodotus proclaims this Persian catastrophe to have been the work of "the god," who
wanted to level the playing field for the Greeks. Is our author displaying here a genuine
belief in the possibility of divine involvement in human affairs, or is he merely indulging
in some pious commonplace?

καὶ τούτοισι μὲν τοιαύτη ἡ νὺξ ἐγίνετο, τοῖσι δὲ ταχθεῖσι αὐτῶν περιπλέειν
Εὔβοιαν ἡ αὐτή περ ἐοῦσα νὺξ πολλὸν ἦν ἔτι ἀγριωτέρη, τοσούτῳ ὅσῳ ἐν
πελάγεϊ φερομένοισι ἐπέπιπτε, καὶ τὸ τέλος σφι ἐγίνετο ἄχαρι. ὡς γὰρ δὴ
πλέουσι αὐτοῖσι χειμών τε καὶ τὸ ὕδωρ ἐπεγίνετο ἐοῦσι κατὰ τὰ Κοῖλα τῆς
Εὐβοίης, φερόμενοι τῷ πνεύματι καὶ οὐκ εἰδότες τῇ ἐφέροντο ἐξέπιπτον
πρὸς τὰς πέτρας· ἐποιέετό τε πᾶν ὑπὸ τοῦ θεοῦ ὅκως ἂν ἐξισωθείη τῷ
Ἑλληνικῷ τὸ Περσικὸν μηδὲ πολλῷ πλέον εἴη.

8.13.1

τούτοισι Refers to the Persians whose ships were moored at Aphetai (see map in Landmark
   ad 8.16).

ταχθεῖσι Aorist, passive, masculine, dative, plural participle of τάσσω.

ἡ αὐτή περ ἐοῦσα νὺξ "The night, although it was the same [night]."

ἐν πελάγεϊ φερομένοισι ἐπέπιπτε The subject of the verb is νὺξ. The night that fell upon the
   men who were out at sea (ἐν πελάγεϊ φερομένοισι) was more difficult to endure.

ἐπεγίνετο = ἐπεγίγνετο.

ὅκως = ὅπως.

ἐξισωθείη Aorist, optative, passive, 3rd, singular of ἐξισόω.

☙

8.22.1-3 Themistokles the Trickster

Although Herodotus takes a mostly dim view of Themistokles' exploits, he allows that
his back-room dealings (8.5) and his style of diplomacy (or chicanery) did occasionally
get results. We see in this chapter that, soon after the naval engagements at Artemision,
Themistokles came ashore (the exact landfall isn't mentioned) and carved into the rocks
a message which he hoped the Ionian sailors serving with the Persians would read. The
message presumably gave the Ionians three choices: the first was that they defect; the
second, that they stay neutral; the third, that they exert as little combative energy as
possible when the fighting actually resumes. We have no way of knowing whether any of
this really happened, as no such inscription has ever been found. Moreover, Themistokles'
message, as it is cited in this passage, reads more like a letter or a speech than an actual
inscription. (For another story in the *Histories* that involves an unorthodox method of
communication, recall the story in 5.35, where Histiaios sends to Aristagoras a message
that was tattooed on the head of the courier.)

Ἀθηναίων δὲ νέας τὰς ἄριστα πλεούσας ἐπιλεξάμενος Θεμιστοκλέης
ἐπορεύετο περὶ τὰ πότιμα ὕδατα, ἐντάμνων ἐν τοῖσι λίθοισι γράμματα. τὰ
Ἴωνες ἐπελθόντες τῇ ὑστεραίῃ ἡμέρῃ ἐπὶ τὸ Ἀρτεμίσιον ἐπελέξαντο. τὰ δὲ

γράμματα τάδε ἔλεγε· "ἄνδρες Ἴωνες, οὐ ποιέετε δίκαια ἐπὶ τοὺς πατέρας στρατευόμενοι καὶ τὴν Ἑλλάδα καταδουλούμενοι. [2] ἀλλὰ μάλιστα μὲν πρὸς ἡμέων γίνεσθε· εἰ δὲ ὑμῖν ἐστι τοῦτο μὴ δυνατὸν ποιῆσαι, ὑμεῖς δὲ ἔτι καὶ νῦν ἐκ τοῦ μέσου ἡμῖν ἕζεσθε καὶ αὐτοὶ καὶ τῶν Καρῶν δέεσθε τὰ αὐτὰ ὑμῖν ποιεῖν. εἰ δὲ μηδέτερον τούτων οἷόν τε γίνεσθαι, ἀλλ' ὑπ' ἀναγκαίης μέζονος κατέζευχθε ἢ ὥστε ἀπίστασθαι, ὑμεῖς δὲ ἐν τῷ ἔργῳ, ἐπεὰν συμμίσγωμεν, ἐθελοκακέετε μεμνημένοι ὅτι ἀπ' ἡμέων γεγόνατε καὶ ὅτι ἀρχῆθεν ἡ ἔχθρη πρὸς τὸν βάρβαρον ἀπ' ὑμέων ἡμῖν γέγονε." [3] Θεμιστοκλέης δὲ ταῦτα ἔγραφε, δοκέειν ἐμοί, ἐπ' ἀμφότερα νοέων, ἵνα ἢ λαθόντα τὰ γράμματα βασιλέα Ἴωνας ποιήσῃ μεταβαλεῖν καὶ γενέσθαι πρὸς ἑωυτῶν, ἢ ἐπείτε ἀνενειχθῇ καὶ διαβληθῇ πρὸς Ξέρξην, ἀπίστους ποιήσῃ τοὺς Ἴωνας καὶ τῶν ναυμαχιέων αὐτοὺς ἀπόσχῃ.

8.22.1

νέας τὰς ἄριστα πλεούσας "The ships that sailed the best." In other words, the ships that were in the best condition, because their timbers had not become water-logged.

8.22.2

μάλιστα πρὸς ἡμέων γίνεσθε "First and foremost, come over to our side."
γίνεσθε = γίγνεσθε.
ἐκ τοῦ μέσου ἡμῖν ἕζεσθε "Position yourselves in the middle," or "stay neutral."
οἷόν τε γίνεσθαι "Is possible to happen."
κατέζευχθε Perfect, indicative, passive, 2nd, plural of καταζεύγνυμι.
ἐπεάν = ἐπειδάν.

8.22.3

δοκέειν ἐμοί The infinitive is used absolutely: "As far as I can tell."
λαθόντα τὰ γράμματα Nominative case.
ἀνενειχθῇ Aorist, subjunctive, passive, 3rd, singular of ἀναφέρω.
διαβληθῇ Aorist, subjunctive, passive, 3rd, singular of διαβάλλω. "Slandered."
ποιήσῃ Subject is still τὰ γράμματα.

☙

8.26.1-3 "Good Grief, Mardonios"

The passage below is famous for its indirect praise of the Greek outlook on what constitutes real worth; it is also useful for fixing the specific date of the Battle of Thermopylae. To judge from the conversation between certain Arcadian mercenaries and the Persians, the battle was fought at approximately the same time that the Olympic Games of 480 B.C.

were celebrated, that is, a month past the summer solstice of that year. An interesting side-note: Vitruvius, the Roman writer on architecture from the time of Augustus, claims (1.1.5) that the architectural term "caryatid" (a support column in the shape of a human, notably on the Erechtheum in Athens) was derived from the historical fact that residents of the Arcadian town of Caryai, who had medized during the Persian War, were punished after the war by being turned into slaves; as such, they had to bear the burden of slavery in the same way that the architectural caryatids have to bear the weight of a building. Could it be that these Arcadian mercenaries, who sought employment in Xerxes' army, were themselves residents of traitorous Caryai? Returning to the present passage, while the notion of Greeks competing for a crown made of olive leaves makes them seem like idealists, at least in their sporting events, there exists plenty of evidence to show that Olympic victors could also receive huge material rewards from their own city-states. (A modern reader might also want to know how it was possible for pan-Hellenic games to have been going on at a time when the army of Xerxes was about to enter central Greece.)

ἧκον δέ σφι αὐτόμολοι ἄνδρες ἀπ᾽ Ἀρκαδίης ὀλίγοι τινές, βίου τε δεόμενοι καὶ ἐνεργοὶ βουλόμενοι εἶναι. ἄγοντες δὲ τούτους ἐς ὄψιν τὴν βασιλέος ἐπυνθάνοντο οἱ Πέρσαι περὶ τῶν Ἑλλήνων τί ποιέοιεν· εἷς δέ τις πρὸ πάντων ἦν ὁ εἰρωτῶν αὐτοὺς ταῦτα. [2] οἳ δέ σφι ἔλεγον ὡς Ὀλύμπια ἄγουσι καὶ θεωρέοιεν ἀγῶνα γυμνικὸν καὶ ἱππικόν. ὁ δὲ ἐπείρετο ὅ τι τὸ ἄεθλον εἴη σφι κείμενον περὶ ὅτευ ἀγωνίζονται· οἱ δ᾽ εἶπον τῆς ἐλαίης τὸν διδόμενον στέφανον. ἐνθαῦτα εἴπας γνώμην γενναιοτάτην Τιγράνης ὁ Ἀρταβάνου δειλίην ὦφλε πρὸς βασιλέος. [3] πυνθανόμενος γὰρ τὸ ἄεθλον ἐὸν στέφανον ἀλλ᾽ οὐ χρήματα, οὔτε ἠνέσχετο σιγῶν εἶπέ τε ἐς πάντας τάδε· "παπαῖ Μαρδόνιε, κοίους ἐπ᾽ ἄνδρας ἤγαγες μαχησομένους ἡμέας, οἳ οὐ περὶ χρημάτων τὸν ἀγῶνα ποιεῦνται ἀλλὰ περὶ ἀρετῆς." τούτῳ μὲν δὴ ταῦτα εἴρητο.

8.26.1

ἀπ᾽ Ἀρκαδίης For Arcadia (a region in the Peloponnese), see map in Landmark *ad* 8.32.

βίου τε δεόμενοι καὶ ἐνεργοὶ βουλόμενοι εἶναι Simply put, the Arcadians asked for work.

8.26.2

ἄγουσι καὶ θεωρέοιεν For reasons that are not clear, the mood switches from the indicative to the optative.

δειλίην ὦφλε πρὸς βασιλέος "Incurred a charge of cowardice from the point of view of the King."

ὦφλε Aorist, indicative, active, 3rd, singular of ὀφλισκάνω.

8.26.3

οὔτε ἠνέσχετο σιγῶν "Was not able to keep silent."

ἠνέσχετο Aorist, indicative, middle, 3rd, singular of ἀνέχω.

παπαῖ "Good grief!"

κοίους = ποίους.

 C3

8.37.1-3 Miracles at Delphi

Herodotus recalls in this passage what happened when the Persian host approached Delphi on its march through central Greece. Leaving aside the miraculous events which Herodotus reports, commentators (cf. HW *ad* 8.39) have thought it unlikely that the Persians would have attacked Delphi, since it had all along been in support of the Persian invasion. In any case, miracles take up most of this current passage, as well as the next two (8.38-39), where the story is told of two local heroes who appear as giants and scare the Persians away. The question of whether Herodotus believed that these miracles actually happened has been variously answered in commentaries. It may be argued, however, that, when Herodotus writes (8.39) that he actually saw the rocks which fell from Mt. Parnassus lying near the temple of Athena Pronaia, he may have been signaling by means of autopsy, his most reliable method of inquiry, that he was a believer.

τούτῳ ὁ προφήτης, τῷ οὔνομα ἦν Ἀκήρατος, ὁρᾷ πρὸ τοῦ νηοῦ ὅπλα προκείμενα ἔσωθεν ἐκ τοῦ μεγάρου ἐξενηνειγμένα ἱρά, τῶν οὐκ ὅσιον ἦν ἅπτεσθαι ἀνθρώπων οὐδενί. [2] ὁ μὲν δὴ ἤιε Δελφῶν τοῖσι παρεοῦσι σημανέων τὸ τέρας· οἱ δὲ βάρβαροι ἐπειδὴ ἐγίνοντο ἐπειγόμενοι κατὰ τὸ ἱρὸν τῆς Προναίης Ἀθηναίης, ἐπιγίνεταί σφι τέρεα ἔτι μέζονα τοῦ πρὶν γενομένου τέρεος. θῶμα μὲν γὰρ καὶ τοῦτο κάρτα ἐστί, ὅπλα ἀρήια αὐτόματα φανῆναι ἔξω προκείμενα τοῦ νηοῦ· τὰ δὲ δὴ ἐπὶ τούτῳ δεύτερα ἐπιγενόμενα καὶ διὰ πάντων φασμάτων ἄξια θωμάσαι μάλιστα. [3] ἐπεὶ γὰρ δὴ ἦσαν ἐπιόντες οἱ βάρβαροι κατὰ τὸ ἱρὸν τῆς Προναίης Ἀθηναίης, ἐν τούτῳ ἐκ μὲν τοῦ οὐρανοῦ κεραυνοὶ αὐτοῖσι ἐνέπιπτον, ἀπὸ δὲ τοῦ Παρνησοῦ ἀπορραγεῖσαι δύο κορυφαὶ ἐφέροντο πολλῷ πατάγῳ ἐς αὐτοὺς καὶ κατέβαλον συχνοὺς σφεων, ἐκ δὲ τοῦ ἱροῦ τῆς Προναίης βοή τε καὶ ἀλαλαγμὸς ἐγίνετο.

8.37.1

τὸ ἱρόν = τὸ ἱερόν. The sanctuary complex at Delphi.

τῷ οὔνομα "Whose name."

ὁρᾷ Historic present.

ἐξενηνειγμένα Perfect, passive, neuter, accusative, plural participle of ἐκφέρω, modifying ὅπλα. "Having been carried out of."

ἱρά = ἱερά. This adjective also modifies ὅπλα.

τῶν Relative pronoun; antecedent is ὅπλα.

οὐκ ὅσιον ἦν "It was forbidden [by divine law]."

8.37.2

ἤιε Δελφῶν τοῖσι παρεοῦσι σημανέων "He went to report to those still in Delphi."

γίνοντο = γίγνοντο.

ἐγίνοντο ἐπειγόμενοι A roundabout (periphrastic) way of saying "They were moving [themselves] quickly."

τὸ ἱρὸν τῆς Προναίης Ἀθηναίης Near the eastern entrance to the town of Delphi.

φανῆναι Aorist, passive infinitve of φαίνω. It explains and expands on the claim that the movement of the sacred weapons was indeed a θῶμα.

8.37.3

ἐπεὶ Used co-relatively with ἐν τούτῳ.

ἀπορραγεῖσαι Aorist, passive, feminine, nominative, plural participle of ἀπορρήγνυμι.

ἐγίνετο = ἐγίγνετο.

βοή...ἀλαλαγμὸς "War whoop."

&

8.41.1-3 The Snake Abandons Athens

In what must have been a painfully traumatic experience, the Athenians, in obedience to the Delphic oracle (cf. 7.141) and for fear of the approaching Persian army, evacuated their city. One wonders how they managed to remove in such a short time the many sacred objects from their temples, including the wooden statue of Athena Polias, the most revered occupant of the Acropolis. In this chapter, Herodotus describes how the apparent disappearance of the "large snake" from the Acropolis, a snake which no one ever saw but which always consumed a honey cake which worshippers left as an offering, provided the Athenians with another compelling reason to abandon their city. (Plutarch, *Themistokles* 10.1, even entertained the possibility that Themistokles was in some way responsible for the disappearance of the snake!) It is interesting to note that the island of Aegina was one of the asylums for the Athenians...in spite of their long, drawn-out war against the island polis (cf. 5.80-5.89). That Troizen would also take in Athenian refugees may not be all that surprising in view of the tradition that Theseus' mother, Aithra, was a Troizenian. (For the locations of Aegina and Troizen, see map in Landmark *ad* 8.43.)

οἱ μὲν δὴ ἄλλοι κατέσχον ἐς τὴν Σαλαμῖνα, Ἀθηναῖοι δὲ ἐς τὴν ἑωυτῶν. μετὰ δὲ τὴν ἄπιξιν κήρυγμα ἐποιήσαντο, Ἀθηναίων τῇ τις δύναται σῴζειν τέκνα τε καὶ τοὺς οἰκέτας. ἐνθαῦτα οἱ μὲν πλεῖστοι ἐς Τροίζηνα ἀπέστειλαν, οἱ δὲ ἐς Αἴγιναν, οἳ δὲ ἐς Σαλαμῖνα. [2] ἔσπευσαν δὲ ταῦτα ὑπεκθέσθαι τῷ χρηστηρίῳ τε βουλόμενοι ὑπηρετέειν καὶ δὴ καὶ τοῦδε εἵνεκα οὐκ ἥκιστα. λέγουσι Ἀθηναῖοι ὄφιν μέγαν φύλακα τῆς ἀκροπόλιος ἐνδιαιτᾶσθαι ἐν τῷ ἱρῷ· λέγουσί τε ταῦτα καὶ δὴ ὡς ἐόντι ἐπιμήνια ἐπιτελέουσι προτιθέντες· τὰ δ᾽ ἐπιμήνια μελιτόεσσά ἐστι. [3] αὕτη δὴ ἡ μελιτόεσσα ἐν τῷ πρόσθε αἰεὶ χρόνῳ ἀναισιμουμένη τότε ἦν ἄψαυστος. σημηνάσης δὲ ταῦτα τῆς ἱρείης, μᾶλλόν τι οἱ Ἀθηναῖοι καὶ προθυμότερον ἐξέλιπον τὴν πόλιν, ὡς καὶ τῆς θεοῦ ἀπολελοιπυίης τὴν ἀκρόπολιν. ὡς δέ σφι πάντα ὑπεξέκειτο, ἔπλεον ἐς τὸ στρατόπεδον.

8.41.1

ἄλλοι The Greek allies.

ἐς τὴν Σαλαμῖνα See map in Landmark *ad* 8.43.

ἐς τὴν ἑωυτῶν "To their own [harbor]." The Piraeus, most likely.

Ἀθηναίων τῇ τις δύναται "In whatever way each of the Athenians could."

σώζειν τέκνα τε καὶ τοὺς οἰκέτας This was the content of the κήρυγμα.

8.41.2

ὑπεκθέσθαι Aorist, middle infinitive of ὑπεκτίθεμαι.

τῷ χρηστηρίῳ Probably, the second oracle (7.141), which told the Athenians to evacuate their city.

εἵνεκα = ἕνεκα.

φύλακα In apposition with ὄφιν μέγαν.

ὡς ἐόντι "As though it [the snake] really existed."

ἐπιμήνια ἐπιτελέουσι προτιθέντες "They continually set out offerings."

8.41.3

σημηνάσης δὲ ταῦτα τῆς ἱρείης Genitive absolute construction.

ὡς "On the grounds that…."

τῆς θεοῦ ἀπολελοιπυίης Genitive absolute construction.

ℂℬ

8.52.1-2 The Defense of the Acropolis

This is a very moving account of the courageous resistance of the Athenians who stayed behind to defend the Acropolis after the rest of the citizenry had been evacuated to Troizen, Aegina, or Salamis (cf. 8.37). By sheer determination, these hopelessly outnumbered Athenians managed to frustrate the Persians in much the same way that the Greek forces did at Thermopylae. (For the sad demise of these defenders, see 8.53.) This must have been a particularly gripping story for an Athenian audience to hear, as the specific locations mentioned in the narrative would have been all too familiar to them. Even a modern reader of the *Histories* may experience a slight shiver when reading about the Persian occupation of the Areiopagos, the altogether familiar site of Orestes' trial in Aeschylus' *Eumenides* and—in the 1st century B.C.—of St. Paul's discourse on the altar to the "unknown god."

οἱ δὲ Πέρσαι ἱζόμενοι ἐπὶ τὸν καταντίον τῆς ἀκροπόλιος ὄχθον, τὸν Ἀθηναῖοι καλέουσι Ἀρήιον πάγον, ἐπολιόρκεον τρόπον τοιόνδε· ὅκως στυππεῖον περὶ τοὺς ὀιστοὺς περιθέντες ἅψειαν, ἐτόξευον ἐς τὸ φράγμα. ἐνθαῦτα Ἀθηναίων οἱ πολιορκεόμενοι ὅμως ἠμύνοντο, καίπερ ἐς τὸ ἔσχατον κακοῦ ἀπιγμένοι καὶ τοῦ φράγματος προδεδωκότος· [2] οὐδὲ λόγους τῶν Πεισιστρατιδέων προσφερόντων περὶ ὁμολογίης ἐνεδέκοντο, ἀμυνόμενοι δὲ ἄλλα τε ἀντεμηχανῶντο καὶ δὴ καὶ προσιόντων τῶν βαρβάρων πρὸς τὰς πύλας ὀλοιτρόχους ἀπίεσαν, ὥστε Ξέρξην ἐπὶ χρόνον συχνὸν ἀπορίῃσι ἐνέχεσθαι οὐ δυνάμενον σφέας ἑλεῖν.

8.52.1

ἐπὶ τὸν καταντίον τῆς ἀκροπόλιος ὄχθον The hill (Areiopagos) lies "opposite"(καταντίον) the west end of the Acropolis. See inset map in Landmark *ad* 8.47.

ὅκως = ὅπως.

στυππεῖον περὶ τοὺς ὀιστοὺς περιθέντες ἅψειαν Although Herodotus does not say so, the inescapable implication is that the Persians set these arrows on fire.

ἀπιγμένοι Perfect, middle, masculine, nominative, plural participle of ἀπιγνέομαι (= ἀφικνέομαι).

τοῦ φράγματος προδεδωκότος Genitive absolute construction. Note that the participle is active: "The barricade having proved useless."

8.52.2

τῶν Πεισιστρατιδέων The last we heard of the Peisistratids was back at the court of Xerxes (7.6), where they were depicted trying to convince Xerxes to go ahead with his invasion of Greece.

προσιόντων τῶν βαρβάρων Genitive absolute construction.

ἀπορίῃσι ἐνέχεσθαι Xerxes was similarly frustrated at Thermopylae.

ἑλεῖν Aorist, active infinitive of αἱρέω.

ଓଃ

8.62.1-2 "In That Case, We'll Move to Siris"

Following the arrival of the news that Athens had been destroyed by the Persians, the Greek generals who had assembled their ships at Salamis decided to abandon the island and sail to the Isthmus of Corinth (6.56). The setting for this passage is a conference, where the Greek commanders gather to listen to the pleas of Themistokles that they not abandon Salamis. Clearly, it was Adeimantos, the Corinthian commander (cf. 8.5), who opposed most vigorously Themistokles' urgent request. At one point in the debate, he basically tells Themistokles to shut up, since he is now a man without a city, who should not even have a voice in a discussion like this (8.61). It is in response to this insult that Themistokles utters the ultimate threat, that the Athenians, ships and all, would emigrate to Siris, a city in southern Italy (see map in Landmark *ad* 8.47), if the Greeks refused to make a stand at Salamis. This threat may have had some credibility, as Themistokles had some close associations with Magna Graecia, the Greek part of Southern Italy (he even named his two daughters "Italia" and "Sybaris"). Moreover, a fairly recent precedent had been created for an entire population to emigrate westward, when the Phocaeans of Ionia left their homeland about 60 years earlier to escape Persian oppression (1.163). (They eventually founded the colony of Massalia in what is today Southern France.)

σημαίνων δὲ ταῦτα τῷ λόγῳ διέβαινε ἐς Εὐρυβιάδην, λέγων μᾶλλον ἐπεστραμμένα. "σὺ εἰ μενέεις αὐτοῦ καὶ μένων ἔσεαι ἀνὴρ ἀγαθός· εἰ δὲ μή, ἀνατρέψεις τὴν Ἑλλάδα· τὸ πᾶν γὰρ ἡμῖν τοῦ πολέμου φέρουσι αἱ νέες. ἀλλ' ἐμοὶ πείθεο. [2] εἰ δὲ ταῦτα μὴ ποιήσῃς, ἡμεῖς μὲν ὡς ἔχομεν ἀναλαβόντες τοὺς οἰκέτας κομιεύμεθα ἐς Σῖριν τὴν ἐν Ἰταλίῃ, ἥ περ ἡμετέρη τε ἐστὶ ἐκ παλαιοῦ ἔτι, καὶ τὰ λόγια λέγει ὑπ' ἡμέων αὐτὴν δέειν κτισθῆναι· ὑμεῖς δὲ συμμάχων τοιῶνδε μουνωθέντες μεμνήσεσθε τῶν ἐμῶν λόγων."

8.62.1

μᾶλλον ἐπεστραμμένα "More vehemently." The participle (perfect, passive, neuter, accusative, plural of ἐπιστρέφω) functions like an adverb.

καὶ μένων "Just because of the fact that you are remaining."

8.62.2

ὡς ἔχομεν "Just as we are." That is, in their present situation, as evacuees from a city that had been destroyed.

κομιεύμεθα Future, indicative, middle, 1st, plural of κομίζω.

ἥ περ ἡμετέρη τε ἐστὶ ἐκ παλαιοῦ ἔτι The claim to Siris seems to anticipate the eventual foundation of Thurii (446 B.C.), an Athenian colony near to Siris.

κτισθῆναι Aorist, passive infinitive of κτίζω.

☙

8.75.1-3 The Biggest Ruse of All

Earlier in the *Histories* (8.5, 8.22), we saw what an enterprising and clever individual Themistokles really was, especially when it came to back-room diplomacy. In this passage, we see him concocting a ruse which, if we can believe Herodotus, made the eventual Greek victory at Salamis possible. Despite Themistokles' threats to re-settle all of the Athenians (and their ships) to Southern Italy (8.62), he was apparently losing ground in his efforts to keep the Greek fleet at Salamis. Never at a loss for tricks, Themistokles sprang into action and sent a trusted messenger to the Persians. His task was to lie to them and say that the

Greeks were trying to get away from Salamis and that a golden opportunity awaited the Persians if only they would block the Greek escape route (see the outstanding maps in Landmark *ad* 8.65). This crucial event in the history of the Persian Wars happens to be the back-story to the *Persae*, a play written by the great Athenian dramatist Aeschylus, who was himself a participant in the wars. Although there are some differences between the accounts in the *Persae* and the *Histories* (cf. HW Appendix 21), both testimonia agree that it was this message that made Xerxes decide to attack the Greek fleet at Salamis. According to the Herodotus account, the success of Themistokles' ruse was ensured by the cooperation of Aristeides, an old political rival of Themistokles (cf. Plutarch, *Aristeides*, for details of their quarrels). Aristeides, it seems, had just returned from exile (engineered in part by Themistokles) when he noticed that Persian ships were already blocking every entrance to and exit from the Bay of Salamis, this as a result of Themistokles' message to the Persians. Herodotus writes (8.79-81) that Themistokles told Aristeides about the ruse and then convinced him to report the news of the Persian blockade to the Greek commanders. Aristeides "The Just" was thus co-opted into going along with Themistokles' trick!

ἐνθαῦτα Θεμιστοκλέης ὡς ἑσσοῦτο τῇ γνώμῃ ὑπὸ τῶν Πελοποννησίων, λαθὼν ἐξέρχεται ἐκ τοῦ συνεδρίου, ἐξελθὼν δὲ πέμπει ἐς τὸ στρατόπεδον τὸ Μήδων ἄνδρα πλοίῳ ἐντειλάμενος τὰ λέγειν χρεόν, τῷ οὔνομα μὲν ἦν Σίκιννος, οἰκέτης δὲ καὶ παιδαγωγὸς ἦν τῶν Θεμιστοκλέος παίδων· τὸν δὴ ὕστερον τούτων τῶν πρηγμάτων Θεμιστοκλέης Θεσπιέα τε ἐποίησε, ὡς ἐπεδέκοντο οἱ Θεσπιέες πολιήτας, καὶ χρήμασι ὄλβιον. [2] ὃς τότε πλοίῳ ἀπικόμενος ἔλεγε πρὸς τοὺς στρατηγοὺς τῶν βαρβάρων τάδε· "ἔπεμψέ με στρατηγὸς ὁ Ἀθηναίων λάθρη τῶν ἄλλων Ἑλλήνων (τυγχάνει γὰρ φρονέων τὰ βασιλέος καὶ βουλόμενος μᾶλλον τὰ ὑμέτερα κατύπερθε γίνεσθαι ἢ τὰ τῶν Ἑλλήνων πρήγματα) φράσοντα ὅτι οἱ Ἕλληνες δρησμὸν βουλεύονται καταρρωδηκότες, καὶ νῦν παρέχει κάλλιστον ὑμέας ἔργων ἁπάντων ἐξεργάσασθαι, ἢν μὴ περιίδητε διαδράντας αὐτούς. [3] οὔτε γὰρ ἀλλήλοισι ὁμοφρονέουσι οὔτε ἀντιστήσονται ὑμῖν, πρὸς ἑωυτούς τε σφέας ὄψεσθε ναυμαχέοντας τοὺς τὰ ὑμέτερα φρονέοντας καὶ τοὺς μή."

8.75.1

ἑσσοῦτο Imperfect, indicative, passive, 3rd, singular of ἑσσόομαι (= ἡσσάομαι). "He was being defeated."

τῷ Relative pronoun.

τὸν δὴ ὕστερον τούτων τῶν πρηγμάτων "At a later time than these matters."

Θεσπιέα For the location of Thespis (Thespiai), a polis in Boeotia, see reference map # 5 in Landmark. It was re-populated with new citizens at some point after the Battle of Plataea (479 B.C.).

8.75.2

ἀπικόμενος = ἀφικόμενος.

λάθρῃ "Without the knowledge." Verb takes the genitive.

τυγχάνει γὰρ φρονέων "He happens to support."

τὰ βασιλέος Literally, "The things of the King."

φράσοντα This future participle modifies the με that appears earlier in the sentence (before the parentheses).

καταρρωδηκότες Perfect, active, masculine, nominative, plural participle of κατορρωδέω.

παρέχει Used impersonally. "It is in your power."

ἢν μὴ περιίδητε διαδράντας αὐτούς "Unless you look the other way while they escape."

περιίδητε Aorist, subjunctive, active, 2nd, plural of περιοράω.

8.75.3

τοὺς τὰ ὑμέτερα φρονέοντας καὶ τοὺς μή In apposition to σφέας.

☙

8.86.1 The Battle of Salamis

Battle narratives in Herodotus tend to be episodic and brief (cf. the account of the Battle of Marathon in 6.112-113), as Herodotus pays more attention to the events leading up to and following a battle than the battle itself. The chapter here comes closest to being the kind of narrative where the larger movements of a battle are described. It also contains another Herodotean judgment, this time about the reason(s) why the Greek ships, but especially those of the Athenians and Aeginetans, proved to be superior to those of the Persian fleet. Note the back-handed compliment which Herodotus pays to the Persians who were involved in the Battle of Salamis: apparently, they fought better than they had at Euboea, but only because they were afraid that Xerxes might be watching.

περὶ μὲν νυν τούτους οὕτω εἶχε· τὸ δὲ πλῆθος τῶν νεῶν ἐν τῇ Σαλαμῖνι ἐκεραΐζετο, αἱ μὲν ὑπ᾽ Ἀθηναίων διαφθειρόμεναι αἱ δὲ ὑπ᾽ Αἰγινητέων. ἅτε γὰρ τῶν μὲν Ἑλλήνων σὺν κόσμῳ ναυμαχεόντων καὶ κατὰ τάξιν, τῶν δὲ βαρβάρων οὔτε τεταγμένων ἔτι οὔτε σὺν νόῳ ποιεόντων οὐδέν, ἔμελλε τοιοῦτό σφι συνοίσεσθαι οἷόν περ ἀπέβη. καίτοι ἦσάν γε καὶ ἐγένοντο ταύτην τὴν ἡμέρην μακρῷ ἀμείνονες αὐτοὶ ἑωυτῶν ἢ πρὸς Εὐβοίῃ, πᾶς τις προθυμεόμενος καὶ δειμαίνων Ξέρξην, ἐδόκεέ τε ἕκαστος ἑωυτὸν θεήσασθαι βασιλέα.

═══════════

8.86.1

ἐκεραΐζετο Observe the force of the imperfect in this verb.

ἅτε Introduces three genitive absolute constructions.

τεταγμένων Perfect, passive, masculine, genitive, plural of τάσσω.

οὔτε σὺν νόῳ ποιεόντων οὐδέν "Doing nothing with a purpose in mind."

θεήσασθαι Aorist, middle infinitive of θεάομαι.

8.88.1-3 The Clever Exploits of Artemisia

Artemisia figures prominently in the *Histories* (cf. 8.68-69), perhaps because of the home-grown pride which Herodotus may have felt for a fellow native of Halicarnassus. In the previous chapter, she is said to have rammed one of the allied ships from the Persian fleet in order to confuse the Athenian trierarch, who was in hot pursuit of her ship. She did this, according to Herodotus, in order to escape from Salamis, as the Greek victory seemed all but certain. In this chapter, we learn that Artemisia was especially fortunate, since Xerxes, who was indeed watching the battle (cf. 8.86), thought that Artemisia had sunk an enemy ship. In a display of what might be described as black humor, Herodotus adds that Artemisia owed her good fortune to the fact that none of the crew from the ship she had sunk had survived to testify against her. How much of this Artemisia episode is historically accurate can be estimated by the several qualifiers in the text (λέγεται, εἴρηται, φασὶ), which may indicate that Herodotus was not entirely willing to vouch for the story. The passage concludes with a saying of Xerxes which calls to mind 2.35, where Herodotus muses over the gender-based role reversals in Egyptian society.

τοῦτο μὲν τοιοῦτο αὐτῇ συνήνεικε γενέσθαι διαφυγεῖν τε καὶ μὴ ἀπολέσθαι, τοῦτο δὲ συνέβη ὥστε κακὸν ἐργασαμένην ἀπὸ τούτων αὐτὴν μάλιστα εὐδοκιμῆσαι παρὰ Ξέρξῃ. [2] λέγεται γὰρ βασιλέα θηεύμενον μαθεῖν τὴν νέα ἐμβαλοῦσαν, καὶ δή τινα εἰπεῖν τῶν παρεόντων· "δέσποτα, ὁρᾷς Ἀρτεμισίην ὡς εὖ ἀγωνίζεται καὶ νέα τῶν πολεμίων κατέδυσε;" καὶ τὸν ἐπειρέσθαι εἰ ἀληθέως ἐστὶ Ἀρτεμισίης τὸ ἔργον, καὶ τοὺς φάναι, σαφέως τὸ ἐπίσημον τῆς νεὸς ἐπισταμένους· τὴν δὲ διαφθαρεῖσαν ἠπιστέατο εἶναι πολεμίην. [3] τά τε γὰρ ἄλλα, ὡς εἴρηται, αὐτῇ συνήνεικε ἐς εὐτυχίην γενόμενα, καὶ τὸ τῶν ἐκ τῆς Καλυνδικῆς νεὸς μηδένα ἀποσωθέντα κατήγορον γενέσθαι. Ξέρξην δὲ εἰπεῖν λέγεται πρὸς τὰ φραζόμενα· "οἱ μὲν ἄνδρες γεγόνασί μοι γυναῖκες, αἱ δὲ γυναῖκες ἄνδρες." ταῦτα μὲν Ξέρξην φασὶ εἰπεῖν.

8.88.1

τοῦτο μὲν Translate with its correlative τοῦτο δὲ.

τοιοῦτο Referring to the ramming incident in 8.87.

αὐτῇ συνήνεικε γενέσθαι Cf. the fuller expression in 8.88.3 (αὐτῇ συνήνεικε ἐς εὐτυχίην γενόμενα).

συνήνεικε Aorist, indicative, active, 3rd, singular of συμφέρω.

διαφυγεῖν τε καὶ μὴ ἀπολέσθαι The two infinitives are epexegetic. In other words, they "explain" the τοιοῦτο.

8.88.2

θηεύμενον Present, middle, masculine, accusative, singular participle of θεάομαι.

μαθεῖν "Noticed."

καὶ τοὺς φάναι "And they said 'Yes.'"

τὸ ἐπίσημον τῆς νεὸς Most likely, the figurehead of a ship. A late source (Polyaenus, fl. late 2nd century A.D.) does, however, indicate that ships flew flags already by c. 500 B.C.

8.88.3

Καλυνδικῆς For the location of Kalynda, see map in Landmark *ad* 8.86.

CB

8.90.1-4 An Episode From the Sea Battle

Herodotus' battle narratives focus more on individual episodes than on larger movements or maneuvers. Even in his battle vignettes, he is sometimes sparing with the details and can almost seem to be in a hurry. For example, in the present passage, he sums up the actions of the Samothracian marines, who took over an Aeginetan ship, in a kind of staccato fashion (ἀπήραξαν καὶ ἐπέβησάν τε καὶ ἔσχον αὐτήν). He then quickly moves on to the topic which appears to be of greater interest to him, namely, Xerxes' personality. And we are in for a treat, as we have an opportunity to see Xerxes sitting on a hill overlooking the Bay of Salamis, watching everything, and, true to his tyrannical ways, dispensing draconian judgments. (This part of Herodotus' narrative is corroborated by the account in Aeschylus' *Persae*.)

ἐγένετο δὲ καὶ τόδε ἐν τῷ θορύβῳ τούτῳ. τῶν τινες Φοινίκων, τῶν αἱ νέες διεφθάρατο, ἐλθόντες παρὰ βασιλέα διέβαλλον τοὺς Ἴωνας, ὡς δι' ἐκείνους ἀπολοίατο αἱ νέες, ὡς προδόντων. συνήνεικε ὦν οὕτω ὥστε Ἰώνων τε τοὺς στρατηγοὺς μὴ ἀπολέσθαι Φοινίκων τε τοὺς διαβάλλοντας λαβεῖν τοιόνδε μισθόν. [2] ἔτι τούτων ταῦτα λεγόντων ἐνέβαλε νηὶ Ἀττικῇ Σαμοθρηικίη νηῦς. ἥ τε δὴ Ἀττικὴ κατέδυετο καὶ ἐπιφερομένη Αἰγιναίη νηῦς κατέδυσε τῶν Σαμοθρηίκων τὴν νέα. ἅτε δὲ ἐόντες ἀκοντισταὶ οἱ Σαμοθρήικες τοὺς ἐπιβάτας ἀπὸ τῆς καταδυσάσης νεὸς βάλλοντες ἀπήραξαν καὶ ἐπέβησάν τε καὶ ἔσχον αὐτήν. [3] ταῦτα γενόμενα τοὺς Ἴωνας ἐρρύσατο· ὡς γὰρ εἶδε σφέας Ξέρξης ἔργον μέγα ἐργασαμένους, ἐτράπετο πρὸς τοὺς Φοίνικας οἷα ὑπερλυπεόμενός τε καὶ πάντας αἰτιώμενος, καὶ σφεων ἐκέλευσε τὰς κεφαλὰς ἀποταμεῖν, ἵνα μὴ αὐτοὶ κακοὶ γενόμενοι τοὺς ἀμείνονας διαβάλλωσι.

[4] ὅκως γάρ τινα ἴδοι Ξέρξης τῶν ἑωυτοῦ ἔργον τι ἀποδεικνύμενον ἐν τῇ ναυμαχίῃ, κατήμενος ὑπὸ τῷ ὄρεϊ τῷ ἀντίον Σαλαμῖνος τὸ καλέεται Αἰγάλεως, ἀνεπυνθάνετο τὸν ποιήσαντα, καὶ οἱ γραμμάτισται ἀνέγραφον πατρόθεν τὸν τριήραρχον καὶ τὴν πόλιν.

[handwritten annotations: how, look, point out, sit, man, face, inquire, scribe, write down, from, captain, city]

8.90.1

ἐγένετο δὲ καὶ τόδε ἐν τῷ θορύβῳ τούτῳ A summary sentence that refers to 8.89, where Herodotus had described the chaotic situation at Salamis following the Battle of Salamis.

τῶν αἱ νέες Here, τῶν is a relative pronoun.

διεφθάρατο Pluperfect, indicative, passive, 3rd, plural of διαφθείρω.

ὡς δι᾽ ἐκείνους ἀπολοίατο αἱ νέες, ὡς προδόντων This clause contains the slander of the Phoenicians.

ἀπολοίατο Aorist, optative, middle, 3rd, plural of ἀπόλλυμι. The use of the optative indicates that this was the charge (or calumny) of the Phoenicians and not necessarily the view of Herodotus.

ὡς προδόντων The syntax is loose here, but ὡς with the genitive participle clearly means "with the intent of betraying [the Persian side]."

συνήνεικε Aorist, indicative, active, 3rd, singular of συμφέρω. Used impersonally, it means "It [so] happened."

ὦν = οὖν.

τοιόνδε μισθόν More than a touch of irony here.

8.90.2

τούτων ταῦτα λεγόντων Genitive absolute construction.

Σαμοθρηικίη For the specific location of this Aegean island, see map in Landmark *ad* 8.86. Technically speaking, it was not part of Ionia.

κατεδύετο Note the force of the imperfect tense.

ἐπιφερομένη "Attacking."

Αἰγιναίη For the location of Aegina, see map in Landmark *ad* 8.86.

ἐόντες Used as a circumstantial participle. "Since they were…"

ἀπήραξαν Aorist, indicative, active, 3rd, plural of ἀπαράσσω.

8.90.3

ἐρρύσατο Aorist, indicative, middle, 3rd, singular of ἐρύω.

οἷα ὑπερλυπεόμενός τε καὶ πάντας αἰτιώμενος "Given that he was in a rage and blaming all of them."

8.90.4

ὅκως = ὅπως.

κατήμενος Present, middle, masculine, nominative, singular participle of κάτημαι (= κάθημαι).

πατρόθεν τὸν τριήραρχον In other words, Xerxes' scribes noted the trierarch's personal name and his patronymic (i.e., his father's name).

CB

8.98.1-2 Persian Express

This passage contains Herodotus' description of the legendary courier system of the Persian empire, where distances were enormous—about 2,000 miles, for example, between the Lydian capital of Sardis and the royal city of Susa. (In an earlier part of the *Histories* [3.126], we saw that this system had been operational already during the reign of Darius.) Although Herodotus qualifies the accuracy of his description of the Persian system with a well-placed λέγουσι, his account is largely corroborated in Xenophon's *Cyropaedia* (8.6.18). The sentence which describes the determination of the Persian messengers to complete their rounds is the unofficial motto of the U.S. Postal Service, and it gave rise to the well-known paraphrase Mark Twain created to describe the Pony Express, a courier system which required riders to travel from Missouri to California: "No matter whether it was winter or summer, raining, snowing, hailing, or sleeting, or whether his 'beat' was a level straight road or a crazy trail over mountain crags and precipices,...he must be always ready to leap into the saddle and be off like the wind!"

ταῦτά τε ἅμα Ξέρξης ἐποίεε καὶ ἔπεμπε ἐς Πέρσας ἀγγελέοντα τὴν παρεοῦσάν σφι συμφορήν. τούτων δὲ τῶν ἀγγέλων ἐστὶ οὐδὲν ὅ τι θᾶσσον παραγίνεται θνητὸν ἐόν· οὕτω τοῖσι Πέρσῃσι ἐξεύρηται τοῦτο. λέγουσι γὰρ ὡς ὁσέων ἂν ἡμερέων ᾖ ἡ πᾶσα ὁδός, τοσοῦτοι ἵπποι τε καὶ ἄνδρες διεστᾶσι κατὰ ἡμερησίην ὁδὸν ἑκάστην ἵππος τε καὶ ἀνὴρ τεταγμένος· τοὺς οὔτε νιφετός, οὐκ ὄμβρος, οὐ καῦμα, οὐ νὺξ ἔργει μὴ οὐ κατανύσαι τὸν προκείμενον αὐτῷ δρόμον τὴν ταχίστην. [2] ὁ μὲν δὴ πρῶτος δραμὼν παραδιδοῖ τὰ ἐντεταλμένα τῷ δευτέρῳ, ὁ δὲ δεύτερος τῷ τρίτῳ· τὸ δὲ ἐνθεῦτεν ἤδη κατ᾽ ἄλλον καὶ ἄλλον διεξέρχεται παραδιδόμενα, κατά περ ἐν Ἕλλησι ἡ λαμπαδηφορίη τὴν τῷ Ἡφαίστῳ ἐπιτελέουσι. τοῦτο τὸ δράμημα τῶν ἵππων καλέουσι Πέρσαι ἀγγαρήιον.

8.98.1

παρεοῦσάν σφι συμφορήν The reference is to the Battle of Salamis.

ὁσέων...ἡμερέων Genitive of measure.

διεστᾶσι Perfect, indicative, active, 3rd, plural of διίστημι. "Are stationed at regular intervals."

τεταγμένος Perfect, passive, masculine, nominative, singular participle of τάσσω. "Posted."

8.98.2

τὰ ἐντεταλμένα "Instructions" or "messages."

παραδιδόμενα Translate with τὰ ἐντεταλμένα.

κατά περ "Just as...."

ἡ λαμπαδηφορίη "The torch relay race."

ἀγγαρήιον Herodotus displays (again) a linguist's acumen.

☜

8.109.1-5 Themistokles Opposes Chasing After the Persians

The slippery Themistokles is at it again. After failing to convince the allied Greek commanders to give chase to the Persians and destroy the pontoon bridges at the Hellespont (cf. 8.108), he changes his tactics and argues for the opposite course of action (this time, however, to an exclusively Athenian audience). Even if Themistokles actually gave such a speech, and even if Herodotus' informants were able to report to him the gist of the speech, we can be fairly certain that what we have here is essentially Herodotus' own creation. And what a speech it is! Indeed, it is one of the most elaborately constructed of the speeches in the *Histories*. In some ways, it can be even described as Thucydidean, in that ellipses abound, participles proliferate, and, in general, the rules of syntax appear at times to be ignored. (One eminent 19th century commentator, R.W. Macan, despaired of the more difficult constructions and described them as "intolerably harsh.") Fortunately, some parts of the speech bring us back to the Herodotus we know: when Themistokles talks about Xerxes receiving his just deserts for his arrogant and reckless ways, we are back in the familiar world of jealous gods punishing hubristic mortals…and the Greek becomes concomitantly easier. The passage ends on a note of Herodotean Realpolitik (not that different from the type professed by Thucydides), where our author opines that Themistokles' prime motive in saying what he did was so he could assure for himself safe haven with the Persians, in case he ever ran politically afoul of the Athenians. (Cf. 8.110, where Herodotus reports on the secret message that Themistokles is alleged to have sent to Xerxes.)

ὡς δὲ ἔμαθε ὅτι οὐ πείσει τούς γε πολλοὺς πλέειν ἐς τὸν Ἑλλήσποντον ὁ Θεμιστοκλέης, μεταβαλὼν πρὸς τοὺς Ἀθηναίους (οὗτοι γὰρ μάλιστα ἐκπεφευγότων περιήμεκτεον, ὁρμέατό τε ἐς τὸν Ἑλλήσποντον πλέειν καὶ ἐπὶ σφέων αὐτῶν βαλόμενοι, εἰ οἱ ἄλλοι μὴ βουλοίατο) ἔλεγέ σφι τάδε· [2] "καὶ αὐτὸς ἤδη πολλοῖσι παρεγενόμην καὶ πολλῷ πλέω ἀκήκοα τοιάδε γενέσθαι, ἄνδρας ἐς ἀναγκαίην ἀπειληθέντας νενικημένους ἀναμάχεσθαί τε καὶ ἀναλαμβάνειν τὴν προτέρην κακότητα. ἡμεῖς δέ, εὕρημα γὰρ εὑρήκαμεν ἡμέας τε αὐτοὺς καὶ τὴν Ἑλλάδα, νέφος τοσοῦτο ἀνθρώπων ἀνωσάμενοι, μὴ διώκωμεν ἄνδρας φεύγοντας. [3] τάδε γὰρ οὐκ ἡμεῖς κατεργασάμεθα, ἀλλὰ θεοί τε καὶ ἥρωες, οἳ ἐφθόνησαν ἄνδρα ἕνα τῆς τε Ἀσίης καὶ τῆς Εὐρώπης βασιλεῦσαι ἐόντα ἀνόσιόν τε καὶ ἀτάσθαλον· ὃς τά τε ἱρὰ καὶ τὰ ἴδια ἐν ὁμοίῳ ἐποιέετο, ἐμπιπράς τε καὶ καταβάλλων τῶν θεῶν τὰ ἀγάλματα· ὃς καὶ τὴν θάλασσαν ἀπεμαστίγωσε πέδας τε κατῆκε. [4] ἀλλ'

(εὖ γὰρ ἔχει ἐς τὸ παρεὸν ἡμῖν, νῦν μὲν ἐν τῇ Ἑλλάδι καταμείναντας ἡμέων τε αὐτῶν ἐπιμεληθῆναι καὶ τῶν οἰκετέων, καὶ τις οἰκίην τε ἀναπλασάσθω καὶ σπόρου ἀνακῶς ἐχέτω, παντελέως ἀπελάσας τὸν βάρβαρον· ἅμα δὲ τῷ ἔαρι καταπλέωμεν ἐπὶ Ἑλλησπόντου καὶ Ἰωνίης." [5] ταῦτα ἔλεγε ἀποθήκην μέλλων ποιήσασθαι ἐς τὸν Πέρσην, ἵνα ἢν ἄρα τί μιν καταλαμβάνῃ πρὸς Ἀθηναίων πάθος ἔχῃ ἀποστροφήν· τά περ ὦν καὶ ἐγένετο.

8.109.1

ἔμαθε The subject is Themistokles, who realizes that he could not persuade the majority of his fellow Greek commanders (τούς γε πολλοὺς) to go to the Hellespont and destroy the bridges there.

ἐκπεφευγότων περιημέκτεον "Were aggrieved over the Persians having gotten away."

ὁρμέατό Pluperfect, indicative, middle, 3rd, plural of ὁρμάω. "Had been eager to…."

8.109.2

πολλοῖσι παρεγενόμην "I have been present at many [situations]."

πολλῷ πλέω ἀκήκοα τοιάδε γενέσθαι "I have heard of many more such things taking place."

ἀκήκοα Perfect, indicative, active, 1st, singular of ἀκούω.

ἄνδρας ἐς ἀναγκαίην ἀπειληθέντας… The accusative/infinitive construction (really, an indirect statement) expands on what sorts of things (τοιάδε) Themistokles had heard.

ἀπειληθέντας Aorist, passive, masculine, accusative, plural participle of ἀπειλέω. "Having been driven."

νενικημένους This second participle is probably circumstantial.

εὕρημα γὰρ εὑρήκαμεν An idiom where εὕρημα is the cognate object of εὑρήκαμεν. "We have been lucky."

ἡμέας τε αὐτοὺς καὶ τὴν Ἑλλάδα Perhaps these accusatives can be construed as accusatives of respect. So, Themistokles would be saying, "We have been lucky in respect to ourselves and Greece."

νέφος τοσοῦτο ἀνθρώπων An interesting metaphor!

8.109.3

ἀτάσθαλον "Reckless."

τά τε ἱρὰ καὶ τὰ ἴδια ἐν ὁμοίῳ ἐποιέετο "Treated alike sacred things and our own private property."

ἐμπιπράς Aorist, active, masculine, nominative, singular participle of ἐμπίμπρημι.

8.109.4

ἀλλ᾽ εὖ γὰρ ἔχει ἐς τὸ παρεὸν ἡμῖν "But at the present time things are going well for us."

ἐπιμεληθῆναι The infinitive seems to be used in a hortatory sense: "Let's attend to."

ἀναπλασάσθω…ἐχέτω Both are imperatives.

ἀπελάσας Aorist, active, masculine, nominative, singular participle of ἀπελαύνω. It modifies τις, the subject of ἀναπλασάσθω and ἐχέτω.

8.109.5

ἀποθήκην μέλλων ποιήσασθαι ἐς τὸν Πέρσην The phrase seems to utilize a metaphor from
the world of commerce: "Intending to store up for himself a [goodwill] credit with the
Persian."

ὦν = οὖν.

ⳤ

8.114.1-2 Xerxes Never Learns

Herodotus' account of the events immediately following the Battle of Salamis has the
feel of loosely connected entries from a personal journal. The one overriding theme in
these closing chapters of Book VIII is the retreat of Xerxes' army and the arrangements
the King made with Mardonios, who stayed behind in Greece to fight another day with
his 300,000 or so handpicked soldiers. The passage below presents a scene from the camp
of Xerxes, who was still in Thessaly—it is strange to see how leisurely his retreat actually
was—and who is approached by heralds from Sparta. Xerxes reacts to the demands of these
heralds with a scornful laugh (cf. 7.103 and 7.105 for other instances of Xerxes laughing)
and dismisses the Greeks with a contemptuous and deliciously ironic remark.

ἐν δὲ τούτῳ τῷ χρόνῳ, ἐν τῷ Μαρδόνιός τε τὴν στρατιὴν διέκρινε καὶ Ξέρξης
ἦν περὶ Θεσσαλίην, χρηστήριον ἐληλύθεε ἐκ Δελφῶν Λακεδαιμονίοισι,
Ξέρξην αἰτέειν δίκας τοῦ Λεωνίδεω φόνου καὶ τὸ διδόμενον ἐξ ἐκείνου
δέκεσθαι. πέμπουσι δὴ κήρυκα τὴν ταχίστην Σπαρτιῆται, ὃς ἐπειδὴ κατέλαβε
ἐοῦσαν ἔτι πᾶσαν τὴν στρατιὴν ἐν Θεσσαλίῃ, ἐλθὼν ἐς ὄψιν τὴν Ξέρξεω
ἔλεγε τάδε· [2] "ὦ βασιλεῦ Μήδων, Λακεδαιμόνιοί τέ σε καὶ Ἡρακλεῖδαι
οἱ ἀπὸ Σπάρτης αἰτέουσι φόνου δίκας, ὅτι σφέων τὸν βασιλέα ἀπέκτεινας
ῥυόμενον τὴν Ἑλλάδα." ὁ δὲ γελάσας τε καὶ κατασχὼν πολλὸν χρόνον, ὥς
οἱ ἐτύγχανε παρεστεὼς Μαρδόνιος, δεικνὺς ἐς τοῦτον εἶπε· "τοιγὰρ σφι
Μαρδόνιος ὅδε δίκας δώσει τοιαύτας οἵας ἐκείνοισι πρέπει."

8.114.1

διέκρινε Mardonios was selecting the troops who were to stay behind with him in Greece.

ἐληλύθεε Pluperfect, indicative, active, 3rd, singular of ἔρχομαι.

δέκεσθαι = δέχεσθαι. The Spartans were instructed by Delphi to accept whatever response
they received from Xerxes.

τὴν ταχίστην Supply ὁδόν. "By the quickest way possible."

8.114.2

πολλὸν χρόνον Accusative of extent of time.

παρεστεὼς Perfect, active, masculine, nominative, singular participle of παρίστημι. Translate with ἐτύγχανε.

δεικνὺς "Having pointed."

πρέπει Supply διδόναι.

ᴄ�

8.118.1-4 Men Overboard!

Herodotus lets his readers know that he was aware of at least two different accounts of how Xerxes sailed back to Asia following the Battle of Salamis. The story that he presents in this chapter, by far the longer and more interesting of the two *nostoi* ("homecoming stories"), is expertly told. (As for the other version, it is hurriedly told in 8.120.) Herodotus even concedes (8.119) that this longer story about a storm-driven Xerxes, who demands the ultimate sacrifice from his subjects, is most likely false. For Herodotus, the quality story clearly trumped the true story. The better of the two stories also allowed Herodotus to expand his character portrait of Xerxes as the cruel, despotic monarch, whose subjects still had to grovel at his feet even before they threw themselves overboard to save his life. The playwright Aeschylus also relished the topic of a fleeing Xerxes and tells the story of the King ingloriously falling into a suddenly thawed Strymon River, chariot and all (*Persae* 480-514).

ἔστι δὲ καὶ ἄλλος ὅδε λόγος λεγόμενος, ὡς ἐπειδὴ Ξέρξης ἀπελαύνων ἐξ Ἀθηνέων ἀπίκετο ἐπ' Ἠιόνα τὴν ἐπὶ Στρυμόνι, ἐνθεῦτεν οὐκέτι ὁδοιπορίῃσι διεχρᾶτο, ἀλλὰ τὴν μὲν στρατιὴν Ὑδάρνεϊ ἐπιτράπει ἀπάγειν ἐς τὸν Ἑλλήσποντον, αὐτὸς δ' ἐπὶ νεὸς Φοινίσσης ἐπιβὰς ἐκομίζετο ἐς τὴν Ἀσίην. [2] πλέοντα δέ μιν ἄνεμον Στρυμονίην ὑπολαβεῖν μέγαν καὶ κυματίην. καὶ δὴ μᾶλλον γάρ τι χειμαίνεσθαι (γεμούσης τῆς νεός,) ὥστε ἐπὶ τοῦ καταστρώματος ἐπεόντων συχνῶν Περσέων τῶν σὺν Ξέρξῃ κομιζομένων, ἐνθαῦτα ἐς δεῖμα πεσόντα τὸν βασιλέα εἰρέσθαι βώσαντα τὸν κυβερνήτην εἴ τις ἔστι σφι σωτηρίη, [3] καὶ τὸν εἶπαι· "δέσποτα, οὐκ ἔστι οὐδεμία, εἰ μὴ τούτων ἀπαλλαγή τις γένηται τῶν πολλῶν ἐπιβατέων." καὶ Ξέρξην λέγεται ἀκούσαντα ταῦτα εἰπεῖν "ἄνδρες Πέρσαι, νῦν τις διαδεξάτω ὑμέων βασιλέος κηδόμενος· ἐν ὑμῖν γὰρ οἶκε εἶναι ἐμοὶ ἡ σωτηρίη." [4] τὸν μὲν ταῦτα λέγειν, τοὺς δὲ προσκυνέοντας ἐκπηδᾶν ἐς τὴν θάλασσαν, καὶ τὴν νέα ἐπικουφισθεῖσαν οὕτω δὴ ἀποσωθῆναι ἐς τὴν Ἀσίην. ὡς δὲ ἐκβῆναι τάχιστα ἐς γῆν τὸν Ξέρξην, ποιῆσαι τοιόνδε· ὅτι μὲν ἔσωσε βασιλέος τὴν ψυχήν, δωρήσασθαι χρυσέῃ στεφάνῃ τὸν κυβερνήτην, ὅτι δὲ Περσέων πολλοὺς ἀπώλεσε, ἀποταμεῖν τὴν κεφαλὴν αὐτοῦ.

8.118.1

ἀπίκετο = ἀφίκετο.

ἐπ᾽ Ἠιόνα τὴν ἐπὶ Στρυμόνι For the location of Eion and of the Strymon River, see map in Landmark *ad* 8.121.

8.118.2

ἄνεμον Στρυμονίην ὑπολαβεῖν Herodotus switches to an indirect statement (accusative/ infinitive) construction.

ἄνεμον Στρυμονίην The same wind is said to have kept Agamemnon at Aulis (cf. Aeschylus, *Agamemnon* 192f.).

μᾶλλον γάρ τι χειμαίνεσθαι Supply Ξέρξην as accusative subject. "Was more and more distressed by the storm."

γεμούσης τῆς νεός Genitive absolute construction.

ὥστε "Inasmuch as."

ἐπεόντων συχνῶν Περσέων Genitive absolute construction.

εἰρέσθαι = ἐρέσθαι.

8.118.3

εἶπαι Rare first aorist infinitive of εἶπον. Indirect statement continues.

ἀπαλλαγή "Removal."

νῦν τις διαδεξάτω ὑμέων βασιλέος κηδόμενος "Now let each one of you show how much he cares for his King."

διαδεξάτω Aorist, imperative, active, 3rd, singular of διαδείκνυμι.

οἶκε "It seems."

8.118.4

ἐπικουφισθεῖσαν Aorist, passive, feminine, accusative, singular participle of ἐπικουφίζω.

ἐς τὴν Ἀσίην "Until [the ship reached] Asia."

☙

8.123.1-2 When Second Prize Becomes First Prize

In this amusing passage, Herodotus reports that all the Greek commanders who had fought at Salamis voted for themselves to receive the award for having been the most "distinguished." Presumably, Themistokles, who received the second-place vote of all his fellow generals, had also voted the top prize for himself. The question comes to mind of how it was possible for these commanders to have gathered at the Isthmus of Corinth for the sole purpose of distributing prizes, when a Persian force of 300,000 hand-picked soldiers were poised to resume the war. What were they thinking? In any case, the story underscores the highly agonistic ancient Greek outlook, as well as the fractured state of political affairs among the Greeks, this in spite of the fact that they had just recently (and barely) escaped destruction at the hands of the Persians.

μετὰ δὲ τὴν διαίρεσιν τῆς ληίης ἔπλεον οἵ Ἕλληνες ἐς τὸν Ἰσθμὸν ἀριστήια δώσοντες τῷ ἀξιωτάτῳ γενομένῳ Ἑλλήνων ἀνὰ τὸν πόλεμον τοῦτον. [2] ὡς δὲ ἀπικόμενοι οἱ στρατηγοὶ διένεμον τὰς ψήφους ἐπὶ τοῦ Ποσειδέωνος τῷ βωμῷ, τὸν πρῶτον καὶ τὸν δεύτερον κρίνοντες ἐκ πάντων, ἐνθαῦτα πᾶς τις αὐτῶν ἑωυτῷ ἐτίθετο τὴν ψῆφον, αὐτὸς ἕκαστος δοκέων ἄριστος γενέσθαι, δεύτερα δὲ οἱ πολλοὶ συνεξέπιπτον Θεμιστοκλέα κρίνοντες. οἱ μὲν δὴ ἐμουνοῦντο, Θεμιστοκλέης δὲ δευτερείοισι ὑπερεβάλλετο πολλόν.

8.123.1

δώσοντες The future infinitive indicates purpose.

ἀριστήια The prize may have been more than just honorific.

8.123.2

ἀπικόμενοι = ἀφικόμενοι.

διένεμον τὰς ψήφους The generals (or admirals) cast their votes for first place and for second place. They probably had separate jars in which they could deposit the sherds or pebbles that represented first or second place votes.

Θεμιστοκλέα κρίνοντες Supply τὸν δεύτερον εἶναι.

ἐμουνοῦντο The meaning seems clear: "They all had only one vote each."

δὲ δευτερείοισι ὑπερεβάλλετο πολλόν Supply τοὺς ἄλλους στρατηγούς as the object of ὑπερεβάλλετο. "He surpassed by far the other generals for [the prize of] second place."

9.5.1-3 The Story of an Athenian Quisling

Herodotus writes (8.140 ff.) that after Mardonios had failed in his initial attempt to convince the Athenians to medize, he decided to try again and sent Mourychides the Hellespontine to Salamis (where the Athenians had set up a government in exile). This Mourychides spoke to the Athenian Boule—probably the Council of 500—and presented another offer from Mardonios. Only one of the Athenian councilors was won over, a man by the name of Lykides, who subsequently made a motion to the Boule that Mardonios' offer be presented to the Athenian people for a vote. (Herodotus seems to know about the workings of the Athenian Boule and the Ekklesia and uses the correct terminology in his description of Lykides' ill-advised motion.) Herodotus then reports, without comment, on the strongly negative reaction to Lykides' motion and the harsh punishment that was meted out to this hapless councilor and his family. A similar story is told by the fourth century B.C. Athenian orator Demosthenes, but with different names and a different setting (de Corona 204).

τούτων μὲν εἵνεκα ἀπέπεμψε Μουρυχίδην ἐς Σαλαμῖνα, ὁ δὲ ἀπικόμενος ἐπὶ τὴν βουλὴν ἔλεγε τὰ παρὰ Μαρδονίου. τῶν δὲ βουλευτέων Λυκίδης εἶπε γνώμην ὡς ἐδόκεε ἄμεινον εἶναι δεξαμένους τὸν λόγον, τόν σφι Μουρυχίδης προφέρει, ἐξενεῖκαι ἐς τὸν δῆμον. [2] ὁ μὲν δὴ ταύτην τὴν γνώμην ἀπεφαίνετο, εἴτε δὴ δεδεγμένος χρήματα παρὰ Μαρδονίου, εἴτε καὶ ταῦτά οἱ ἑάνδανε· Ἀθηναῖοι δὲ αὐτίκα δεινὸν ποιησάμενοι, οἵ τε ἐκ τῆς βουλῆς καὶ οἱ ἔξωθεν ὡς ἐπύθοντο, περιστάντες Λυκίδην κατέλευσαν βάλλοντες, τὸν δὲ Ἑλλησπόντιον Μουρυχίδην ἀπέπεμψαν ἀσινέα. [3] γενομένου δὲ θορύβου ἐν τῇ Σαλαμῖνι περὶ τὸν Λυκίδην, πυνθάνονται τὸ γινόμενον αἱ γυναῖκες τῶν Ἀθηναίων, διακελευσαμένη δὲ γυνὴ γυναικὶ καὶ παραλαβοῦσα ἐπὶ τὴν Λυκίδεω οἰκίην ἤισαν αὐτοκελέες, καὶ κατὰ μὲν ἔλευσαν αὐτοῦ τὴν γυναῖκα κατὰ δὲ τὰ τέκνα.

9.5.1

τούτων μὲν εἵνεκα ἀπέπεμψε "Mardonios" is the implied subject. His previous attempt to persuade the Athenians to medize had failed (τούτων μὲν εἵνεκα), and so he sent (ἀπέπεμψε) Mourychides the Hellespontine to see if he could win them over.

εἵνεκα = ἕνεκα.

ἀπικόμενος = ἀφικόμενος.

τά "What things he had heard from Mardonios."

δεξαμένους τὸν λόγον Supply "councilors" to go with the participle. "That the councilors, having accepted the proposal…."

ἐξενεῖκαι (= ἐξενέγκαι). Aorist, active infinitive of ἐκφέρω

9.5.2

δεδεγμένος Perfect, middle, masculine, nominative, singular participle of δέχομαι.

εἴτε καὶ ταῦτά οἱ ἑάνδανε For the alternative explanation as to why Lykides did what he did, Herodotus uses a finite verb (imperfect, indicative, active, 3rd, singular of ἀνδάνω) instead of a participle to match δεδεγμένος.

δεινὸν ποιησάμενοι "Having become indignant."

9.5.3

γενομένου δὲ θορύβου Genitive absolute construction.

τὸ γινόμενον "That which had happened." γινόμενον = γιγνόμενον.

παραλαβοῦσα Supply γυνὴ γυναῖκα.

κατὰ μὲν ἔλευσαν An instance of tmesis, where the prepositional prefix is separated from the verb (καταλεύω).

ଔଃ

9.13.1-3 Athens Is Destroyed…Again

With this section of Book IX, Herodotus is setting the stage for the climactic Battle of Plataea. Mardonios, frustrated by the Athenian refusal to medize and worried about the approach of the Spartans, decides to leave Attica. Before he sets out, he unleashes yet another holocaust on an already severely damaged city. This time, Mardonios' soldiers targeted the lower city, as opposed to the Acropolis, which had already been sacked on the occasion of the first Persian invasion (cf. 8.51-55). (The extent of the destruction in Athens may have been overstated by Herodotus: Thucydides writes [1.89] that some buildings and portions of walls survived the devastation.) Herodotus deserves some praise here for his thorough understanding of the strategic considerations behind Mardonios' decision to withdraw to Boeotia.

ὁ μὲν δὴ εἴπας ταῦτα ἀπαλλάσσετο ὀπίσω, Μαρδόνιος δὲ οὐδαμῶς ἔτι πρόθυμος ἦν μένειν ἐν τῇ Ἀττικῇ, ὡς ἤκουσε ταῦτα. πρὶν μέν νυν ἢ πυθέσθαι ἀνεκώχευε, θέλων εἰδέναι τὸ παρ' Ἀθηναίων, ὁκοῖόν τι ποιήσουσι, καὶ οὔτε ἐπήμαινε οὔτε ἐσίνετο γῆν τὴν Ἀττικήν, ἐλπίζων διὰ παντὸς τοῦ χρόνου ὁμολογήσειν σφέας· [2] ἐπεὶ δὲ οὐκ ἔπειθε, πυθόμενος πάντα λόγον, πρὶν ἢ τοὺς μετὰ Παυσανίεω ἐς τὸν Ἰσθμὸν ἐσβαλεῖν, ὑπεξεχώρεε ἐμπρήσας τε τὰς Ἀθήνας, καὶ εἴ κού τι ὀρθὸν ἦν τῶν τειχέων ἢ τῶν οἰκημάτων ἢ τῶν ἱρῶν, πάντα καταβαλὼν καὶ συγχώσας. [3] ἐξήλαυνε δὲ τῶνδε εἵνεκεν, ὅτι οὔτε ἱππασίμη ἡ χώρη ἦν ἡ Ἀττική, εἴ τε νικῷτο συμβαλών, ἀπάλλαξις οὐκ ἦν ὅτι μὴ κατὰ στεινόν, ὥστε ὀλίγους σφέας ἀνθρώπους ἴσχειν. ἐβουλεύετο ὦν ἐπαναχωρήσας ἐς τὰς Θήβας συμβαλεῖν πρὸς πόλι τε φιλίῃ καὶ χώρῃ ἱππασίμῳ.

9.13.1

ὁ μὲν δὴ εἴπας Referring to the Argive messenger, who had warned Mardonios (9.12) that the Spartans were moving northward.

πρίν…ἢ Translate with the (aorist, middle) infinitive πυθέσθαι. πρὶν ἢ + the infinitive is common in Herodotus (cf. infra 9.13.2).

ἀνεκώχευε A nautical metaphor: "He stayed anchored."

τὸ παρ' Ἀθηναίων "The situation at Athens."

οὔτε ἐπήμαινε οὔτε ἐσίνετο There is no substantial difference in meaning between the two verbs.

9.13.2

πάντα λόγον "The whole story."

ὑπεξεχώρεε Imperfect, indicative, active, 3rd, singular of ὑπεκχωρέω.

ἐμπρήσας Aorist, active, masculine, nominative, singular participle of ἐμπίπρημι.

κού = πού.

9.13.3

ἐξήλαυνε Without an object, it means "marched out."

εἴ τε νικῷτο συμβαλών "Having concluded that, if he were defeated,…"

ὅτι μή "Except."

κατὰ στεινόν Probably the pass across Mt. Cithaeron. See map in Landmark *ad* 9.17.

ὀλίγους…ἀνθρώπους The accusative subject of ἴσχειν.

ଔ

9.16.1-5 Thebans and Persians Share Couches

There is much to recommend this passage. For one, Herodotus explicitly identifies his source, something we see him do on only three other occasions (2.55, 3.55, 4.76). For another, Herodotus usually ignores language issues when he presents Greeks and Persians carrying on a conversation, but here he specifies that a certain (unnamed) Persian actually spoke in Greek while he was sharing a banquet couch with Thersandros the Theban. And then there is the matter of what this anonymous Persian said and how he said it. In a moment of great insight, brought on perhaps by his having shared a dining couch with a Greek, the Persian speaks pessimistically about life in general, and the battle to come in particular…and then he bursts into tears. The scene is quite moving, and the philosophical musings of the Persian seem heartfelt.

ἐχόντων δὲ τὸν πόνον τοῦτον τῶν βαρβάρων, Ἀτταγῖνος ὁ Φρύνωνος ἀνὴρ Θηβαῖος παρασκευασάμενος μεγάλως ἐκάλεε ἐπὶ ξείνια αὐτόν τε Μαρδόνιον καὶ πεντήκοντα Περσέων τοὺς λογιμωτάτους, κληθέντες δὲ οὗτοι εἵποντο· ἦν δὲ τὸ δεῖπνον ποιεύμενον ἐν Θήβησι. τάδε δὲ ἤδη τὰ ἐπίλοιπα ἤκουον Θερσάνδρου ἀνδρὸς μὲν Ὀρχομενίου, λογίμου δὲ ἐς τὰ πρῶτα ἐν Ὀρχομενῷ. ἔφη δὲ ὁ Θέρσανδρος κληθῆναι καὶ αὐτὸς ὑπὸ Ἀτταγίνου ἐπὶ τὸ δεῖπνον τοῦτο, κληθῆναι δὲ καὶ Θηβαίων ἄνδρας πεντήκοντα, καί σφεων οὐ χωρὶς ἑκατέρους κλῖναι, ἀλλὰ Πέρσην τε καὶ Θηβαῖον ἐν κλίνῃ ἑκάστῃ. [2] ὡς δὲ ἀπὸ δείπνου ἦσαν, διαπινόντων τὸν Πέρσην τὸν ὁμόκλινον Ἑλλάδα γλῶσσαν ἱέντα εἰρέσθαι αὐτὸν ὁποδαπός ἐστι, αὐτὸς δὲ ὑποκρίνασθαι ὡς εἴη Ὀρχομένιος. τὸν δὲ εἰπεῖν· "ἐπεὶ νῦν ὁμοτράπεζός τέ μοι καὶ ὁμόσπονδος ἐγένεο, μνημόσυνά τοι γνώμης τῆς ἐμῆς καταλιπέσθαι θέλω, ἵνα καὶ προειδὼς αὐτὸς περὶ σεωυτοῦ βουλεύεσθαι ἔχῃς τὰ συμφέροντα. [3] ὁρᾷς τούτους τοὺς δαινυμένους Πέρσας καὶ τὸν στρατὸν τὸν ἐλίπομεν ἐπὶ τῷ ποταμῷ στρατοπεδευόμενον· τούτων πάντων ὄψεαι ὀλίγου τινὸς χρόνου διελθόντος ὀλίγους τινὰς τοὺς περιγενομένους." ταῦτα ἅμα τε τὸν Πέρσην λέγειν καὶ μετιέναι πολλὰ τῶν δακρύων. [4] αὐτὸς δὲ θωμάσας τὸν λόγον εἰπεῖν πρὸς αὐτόν· "οὐκῶν Μαρδονίῳ τε ταῦτα χρεόν ἐστι λέγειν καὶ τοῖσι μετ᾽ ἐκεῖνον ἐν αἴνῃ ἐοῦσι Περσέων;" τὸν δὲ μετὰ ταῦτα εἰπεῖν· "ξεῖνε, ὅ τι δεῖ γενέσθαι ἐκ τοῦ θεοῦ ἀμήχανον ἀποτρέψαι ἀνθρώπῳ· οὐδὲ γὰρ πιστὰ λέγουσι ἐθέλει πείθεσθαι οὐδείς. [5] ταῦτα δὲ Περσέων συχνοὶ ἐπιστάμενοι ἑπόμεθα ἀναγκαίῃ ἐνδεδεμένοι, ἐχθίστη δὲ ὀδύνη ἐστὶ τῶν ἐν ἀνθρώποισι αὕτη, πολλὰ φρονέοντα μηδενὸς κρατέειν." ταῦτα μὲν Ὀρχομενίου Θερσάνδρου ἤκουον, καὶ τάδε πρὸς τούτοισι, ὡς αὐτὸς αὐτίκα λέγοι ταῦτα πρὸς ἀνθρώπους πρότερον ἢ γενέσθαι ἐν Πλαταιῇσι τὴν μάχην.

9.16.1

ἐχόντων δὲ τὸν πόνον τοῦτον τῶν βαρβάρων A genitive absolute construction, it refers to the Persian efforts to construct a base camp in Boeotia (the topic in 9.15).

παρασκευασάμενος μεγάλως "Having made extensive preparations."

εἵποντο "They accepted [the invitation]."

Ὀρχομενίου For the specific location of Orchomenos, a city in Boeotia, see map in Landmark *ad* 9.17.

λογίμου δὲ ἐς τὰ πρῶτα ἐν Ὀρχομενῷ "A man who was held in the highest regard in Orchomenos."

ἔφη δὲ ὁ Θέρσανδρος Much of the following narrative will be in indirect statement.

κληθῆναι Aorist, passive infinitive of καλέω.

σφεων οὐ χωρὶς ἑκατέρους κλῖναι "Both groups [the Thebans and the Persians] were reclining not far apart from one another." That is, one Greek and one Persian were paired on each of the dining couches (as is made clear in ἀλλὰ Πέρσην τε καὶ Θηβαῖον ἐν κλίνῃ ἑκάστῃ).

9.16.2

διαπινόντων Genitive absolute construction. "As they were toasting one another."

Ἑλλάδα γλῶσσαν ἱέντα "Speaking in Greek."

τὸν δὲ εἰπεῖν The τόν refers to the "Persian"

ὁμοτράπεζός τέ μοι καὶ ὁμόσπονδος Wonderfully descriptive words.

μνημόσυνά τοι γνώμης τῆς ἐμῆς "Memorials of my life philosophy."

ἔχῃς As is often the case, the verb ἔχειν means "To be able."

9.16.3

τόν A relative pronoun here.

ὀλίγου τινὸς χρόνου διελθόντος Genitive absolute construction.

9.16.4

τοῖσι μετ᾽ ἐκεῖνον ἐν αἴνῃ ἐοῦσι Περσέων "To those of the Persians who are men of influence under him [Mardonios]."

λέγουσι Dative, active participle, with πιστά as its object.

9.16.5

Περσέων συχνοὶ "Many of us Persians."

ἐνδεδεμένοι Perfect, passive, masculine, nominative, plural participle of ἐνδέω.

πρότερον ἤ Translate with the infinitive γενέσθαι. Cf. the use of πρὶν ἤ + the infinitive in 9.13.2.

CB

9.46.1-3 Maneuvers and Counter-Maneuvers

Herodotus has a very long lead-up to the actual Battle of Plataea. He describes several skirmishes (cf. 9.22 where a well-armed and well-armored Persian defies the multiple spear thrusts of the Greeks); he presents some long made-up speeches about which city's forces should constitute which wing of the Greek army (9.26-28); and he estimates (9.28-30) the numbers of combatants on both sides (for once, the estimates seem to be somewhat realistic). The present passage, which is still part of the lead-up to Plataea, has been roundly criticized by both ancients and moderns. Plutarch (*de Malignitate Herodoti* 42) thought it impossible that Pausanias, the Spartan regent, could ever have requested that the Spartans be allowed to change battle positions with the Athenians. Modern critics dismiss Herodotus' story on the grounds that the kind of pre-battle maneuvers which are described in this passage could not have been executed within the time span of a single day (cf. HW *ad* 9.46).

οἱ δὲ στρατηγοὶ τῶν Ἀθηναίων ἐλθόντες ἐπὶ τὸ δεξιὸν κέρας ἔλεγον Παυσανίῃ τά περ ἤκουσαν Ἀλεξάνδρου. ὁ δὲ τούτῳ τῷ λόγῳ καταρρωδήσας τοὺς Πέρσας ἔλεγε τάδε· [2] "ἐπεὶ τοίνυν ἐς ἠῶ ἡ συμβολὴ γίνεται, ὑμέας μὲν χρεόν ἐστι τοὺς Ἀθηναίους στῆναι κατὰ τοὺς Πέρσας, ἡμέας δὲ κατὰ τοὺς Βοιωτούς τε καὶ τοὺς κατ' ὑμέας τεταγμένους Ἑλλήνων, τῶνδε εἵνεκα· ὑμεῖς ἐπίστασθε τοὺς Μήδους καὶ τὴν μάχην αὐτῶν ἐν Μαραθῶνι μαχεσάμενοι, ἡμεῖς δὲ ἄπειροί τέ εἰμεν καὶ ἀδαέες τούτων τῶν ἀνδρῶν· Σπαρτιητέων γὰρ οὐδεὶς πεπείρηται Μήδων· ἡμεῖς δὲ Βοιωτῶν καὶ Θεσσαλῶν ἔμπειροι εἰμέν. [3] ἀλλ' ἀναλαβόντας τὰ ὅπλα χρεόν ἐστι ἰέναι ὑμέας ἐς τόδε τὸ κέρας, ἡμέας δὲ ἐς τὸ εὐώνυμον." πρὸς δὲ ταῦτα εἶπαν οἱ Ἀθηναῖοι τάδε· "καὶ αὐτοῖσι ἡμῖν πάλαι ἀπ' ἀρχῆς, ἐπείτε εἴδομεν κατ' ὑμέας τασσομένους τοὺς Πέρσας, ἐν νόῳ ἐγένετο εἰπεῖν ταῦτα τά περ ὑμεῖς φθάντες προφέρετε· ἀλλὰ ἀρρωδέομεν μὴ ὑμῖν οὐκ ἡδέες γένωνται οἱ λόγοι. ἐπεὶ δ' ὦν αὐτοὶ ἐμνήσθητε, καὶ ἡδομένοισι ἡμῖν οἱ λόγοι γεγόνασι καὶ ἕτοιμοί εἰμεν ποιέειν ταῦτα."

9.46.1

ἐπὶ τὸ δεξιὸν κέρας The Spartans were stationed there.

τά περ ἤκουσαν Ἀλεξάνδρου Alexandros the Macedonian had reported (9.45) that Mardonios would attack at dawn on the next day.

καταρρωδήσας A somewhat surprising reaction from a Spartan.

9.46.2

γίνεται = γίγνεται.

στῆναι Aorist, active infinitive of ἵστημι.

εἵνεκα = ἕνεκα.

πεπείρηται Perfect, indicative, middle, 3rd, singular of πειράω.

9.46.3

ἐς τὸ εὐώνυμον Note the euphemism.

πάλαι ἀπ᾽ ἀρχῆς An exaggeration?

ἐν νόῳ ἐγένετο "It occurred [to us]."

τά Here, a relative pronoun.

φθάντες προφέρετε "You proposed first."

ଓ

9.48.1-4 Mardonios' Taunt

Mardonios' messenger belittles the Spartans for their unwillingness to line up opposite the Persians. In what is a devastating put-down for the Spartans (but even more so for the Thebans), he reminds the Spartans that the Thebans, their preferred opponents in the battle to come, were slaves of the Persians. How much of this episode really happened? Scholars (cf. HW *ad* 9.48) think Herodotus tapped into a revisionist and unreliable tradition which belittled the Spartans and exalted the Athenians. The speech of the Persian messenger seems less than genuine, as it refers to his fellow Persians as "barbarians" (πρὸ δὲ τῶν βαρβάρων).

ἐπεὶ δὲ κατέστησαν ἐς τὰς ἀρχαίας τάξις, πέμψας ὁ Μαρδόνιος κήρυκα ἐς τοὺς Σπαρτιήτας ἔλεγε τάδε· "ὦ Λακεδαιμόνιοι, ὑμεῖς δὴ λέγεσθε εἶναι ἄνδρες ἄριστοι ὑπὸ τῶν τῇδε ἀνθρώπων, ἐκπαγλεομένων ὡς οὔτε φεύγετε ἐκ πολέμου οὔτε τάξιν ἐκλείπετε, μένοντές τε ἢ ἀπόλλυτε τοὺς ἐναντίους ἢ αὐτοὶ ἀπόλλυσθε. [2] τῶν δ᾽ ἄρ᾽ ἦν οὐδὲν ἀληθές· πρὶν γὰρ ἢ συμμῖξαι ἡμέας ἐς χειρῶν τε νόμον ἀπικέσθαι, καὶ δὴ φεύγοντας καὶ στάσιν ἐκλείποντας ὑμέας εἴδομεν, ἐν Ἀθηναίοισί τε τὴν πρόπειραν ποιευμένους αὐτούς τε ἀντία δούλων τῶν ἡμετέρων τασσομένους. [3] ταῦτα οὐδαμῶς ἀνδρῶν ἀγαθῶν ἔργα, ἀλλὰ πλεῖστον δὴ ἐν ὑμῖν ἐψεύσθημεν. προσδεκόμενοι γὰρ κατὰ κλέος ὡς δὴ πέμψετε ἐς ἡμέας κήρυκα προκαλεύμενοι καὶ βουλόμενοι μούνοισι

Πέρσῃσι μάχεσθαι, ἄρτιοι ἐόντες ποιέειν ταῦτα οὐδὲν τοιοῦτο λέγοντας ὑμέας εὕρομεν ἀλλὰ πτώσσοντας μᾶλλον. νῦν ὦν ἐπειδὴ οὐκ ὑμεῖς ἤρξατε τούτου τοῦ λόγου, ἀλλ᾽ ἡμεῖς ἄρχομεν. [4] τί δὴ οὐ πρὸ μὲν τῶν Ἑλλήνων ὑμεῖς, ἐπείτε δεδόξωσθε εἶναι ἄριστοι, πρὸ δὲ τῶν βαρβάρων ἡμεῖς ἴσοι πρὸς ἴσους ἀριθμὸν ἐμαχεσάμεθα; καὶ ἢν μὲν δοκέῃ καὶ τοὺς ἄλλους μάχεσθαι, οἱ δ᾽ ὦν μετέπειτα μαχέσθων ὕστεροι· εἰ δὲ καὶ μὴ δοκέοι ἀλλ᾽ ἡμέας μούνους ἀποχρᾶν, ἡμεῖς δὲ διαμαχεσώμεθα· ὁκότεροι δ᾽ ἂν ἡμέων νικήσωσι, τούτους τῷ ἅπαντι στρατοπέδῳ νικᾶν."

9.48.1

τὰς ἀρχαίας τάξις "The original formations."

τῇδε "In these parts." That is, in Hellas.

ἐκπαγλεομένων Modifies τῶν…ἀνθρώπων. "Struck with amazement."

9.48.2

ἄρ᾽ "In reality."

πρὶν…ἤ "Earlier than." That is, "Before." πρὶν…ἤ + infinitive/accusative (συμμῖξαι ἡμέας) is a common construction in the *Histories*.

ἐν Ἀθηναίοισί τε τὴν πρόπειραν ποιευμένους "Making the first trial among the Athenians." That is, having the Athenians first take on the Persians.

αὐτούς τε ἀντία δούλων τῶν ἡμετέρων τασσομένους "And arraying yourselves opposite our slaves."

9.48.3

ἐν ὑμῖν "In regard to you."

κατὰ κλέος "Based on your reputation."

προκαλεύμενοι καὶ βουλόμενοι Both participles modify the subject ("you") of the verb πέμψετε.

ὦν = οὖν.

ἐπειδὴ οὐκ ὑμεῖς ἤρξατε τούτου τοῦ λόγου "Since you have not initiated this proposal."

9.48.4

δεδόξωσθε Perfect, indicative, passive, 2nd, plural of δοξόομαι.

ἀριθμόν Accusative of respect.

μαχέσθων Present, imperative, middle, 3rd, plural of μαχέομαι.

ἡμέας μούνους ἀποχρᾶν "We alone [that is, we Persians and you Spartans] are enough."

ὁκότεροι = ὁπότεροι.

☙

9.59.1-2 The Battle of Plataea, Part I

Finally, the Battle of Plataea is underway (late summer, 479 B.C.). In contrast to most of the battle narratives in the *Histories*, the one for Plataea is fairly extensive and takes up most of seven chapters. (Cf. the much briefer account of the Battle of Salamis in Book VIII.) In telling the story of Plataea, Herodotus shows some familiarity with the confusion which usually attends battles at all stages, but especially at the start: for example, he explains that Mardonios' preemptive attack was prompted by a misunderstanding of the movements of the Greeks. In the last sentence of this chapter, Herodotus gives us a clue as to the final outcome of the battle: already at this early phase of the fighting, the Persians were attacking the Greeks without any discernible order.

ταῦτα εἴπας ἦγε τοὺς Πέρσας δρόμῳ διαβάντας τὸν Ἀσωπὸν κατὰ στίβον τῶν Ἑλλήνων ὡς δὴ ἀποδιδρησκόντων, ἐπεῖχέ τε ἐπὶ Λακεδαιμονίους τε καὶ Τεγεήτας μούνους· Ἀθηναίους γὰρ τραπομένους ἐς τὸ πεδίον ὑπὸ τῶν ὄχθων οὐ κατώρα. [2] Πέρσας δὲ ὁρῶντες ὁρμημένους διώκειν τοὺς Ἕλληνας οἱ λοιποὶ τῶν βαρβαρικῶν τελέων ἄρχοντες αὐτίκα πάντες ἤειραν τὰ σημήια, καὶ ἐδίωκον ὡς ποδῶν ἕκαστος εἶχον, οὔτε κόσμῳ οὐδενὶ κοσμηθέντες οὔτε τάξι.

9.59.1

ταῦτα εἴπας Referring to Mardonios' pre-battle speech to his troops. Mardonios is also the subject of the next three verbs.

τὸν Ἀσωπόν For the location of this river (which was probably nothing more than a stream in late summer), see map in Landmark *ad* 9.66.

τῶν Ἑλλήνων ὡς δὴ ἀποδιδρησκόντων The particle δὴ indicates that this was the (mistaken) surmise of the Persians (and not of Herodotus).

ἐπεῖχέ "He was directing his attack against…."

Τεγεήτας For the location of Tegea, a city in Arcadia, see map in Landmark *ad* 9.46.

ὑπό "As a result of."

9.59.2

Πέρσας δὲ ὁρῶντες ὁρμημένους διώκειν τοὺς Ἕλληνας οἱ λοιποὶ τῶν βαρβαρικῶν τελέων ἄρχοντες The nominative participle ὁρῶντες goes with οἱ λοιποί…ἄρχοντες.

ὡς ποδῶν ἕκαστος εἶχον Idiomatically, "As quickly as each could "

☙

9.60.1-3 The Battle of Plataea, Part II

Herodotus utilizes the speech of a Spartan messenger to explain the situation on the battlefield: a large portion of the Greek army had put itself beyond harm's reach; the Athenian and Spartan forces were occupying separate parts of the plain of Plataea and were operating semi-independently of one another; the Spartans were in dire need of Athenian help, as they had come under attack by the Persian cavalry. Critics have questioned whether this visit from the Spartan knight ever took place—we cannot be sure that the Spartans even had cavalry at Plataea—and have suggested that what we have here is yet another example of Herodotus drawing on biased Athenian sources, which placed the Athenians (and, in this case, the Tegeans also) into the best possible light and disparaged the Spartan contribution to the battle.

καὶ οὗτοι μὲν βοῇ τε καὶ ὁμίλῳ ἐπήισαν ὡς ἀναρπασόμενοι τοὺς Ἕλληνας· Παυσανίης δέ, ὡς προσέκειτο ἡ ἵππος, πέμψας πρὸς τοὺς Ἀθηναίους ἱππέα λέγει τάδε· "ἄνδρες Ἀθηναῖοι, ἀγῶνος μεγίστου προκειμένου ἐλευθέρην εἶναι ἢ δεδουλωμένην τὴν Ἑλλάδα, προδεδόμεθα ὑπὸ τῶν συμμάχων ἡμεῖς τε οἱ Λακεδαιμόνιοι καὶ ὑμεῖς οἱ Ἀθηναῖοι ὑπὸ τὴν παροιχομένην νύκτα διαδράντων. [2] νῦν ὦν δέδοκται τὸ ἐνθεῦτεν τὸ ποιητέον ἡμῖν· ἀμυνομένους γὰρ τῇ δυνάμεθα ἄριστα περιστέλλειν ἀλλήλους. εἰ μέν νυν ἐς ὑμέας ὥρμησε ἀρχὴν ἡ ἵππος, χρῆν δὴ ἡμέας τε καὶ τοὺς μετ' ἡμέων τὴν Ἑλλάδα οὐ προδιδόντας Τεγεήτας βοηθέειν ὑμῖν· νῦν δέ, ἐς ἡμέας γὰρ ἅπασα κεχώρηκε, δίκαιοι ἐστὲ ὑμεῖς πρὸς τὴν πιεζομένην μάλιστα τῶν μοιρέων ἀμυνέοντες ἰέναι. [3] εἰ δ' ἄρα αὐτοὺς ὑμέας καταλελάβηκε ἀδύνατόν τι βοηθέειν, ὑμεῖς δ' ἡμῖν τοὺς τοξότας ἀποπέμψαντες χάριν θέσθε. συνοίδαμεν δὲ ὑμῖν ὑπὸ τὸν παρεόντα τόνδε πόλεμον ἐοῦσι πολλὸν προθυμοτάτοισι, ὥστε καὶ ταῦτα ἐσακούειν."

9.60.1

ὡς ἀναρπασόμενοι ὡς and the future participle indicate purpose.

προσέκειτο ἡ ἵππος "The [enemy] cavalry was coming down hard [on them]."

ἀγῶνος μεγίστου προκειμένου Genitive absolute construction.

ἐλευθέρην εἶναι ἢ δεδουλωμένην τὴν Ἑλλάδα This accusative/infinitive construction is triggered by ἀγῶνος: "Struggle [to determine] whether...."

τὴν παροιχομένην νύκτα "Last night."

9.60.2

ὦν = οὖν.

δέδοκται Perfect, indicative, passive, 3rd, singular of δοκέω. "It has become apparent," or "it is clear."

τὸ ἐνθεῦτεν "From now on."

ποιητέον Verbal adjective (from ποιέω), indicating necessity. ἡμῖν is dative of agent.

ἀμυνομένους γάρ…περιστέλλειν Accusative/infinitive construction, because of δέδοκται.

εἰ μέν νυν ἐς ὑμέας ὅρμησε ἀρχὴν ἡ ἵππος The protasis ("if" clause) of a past, contrary to fact condition.

νῦν δέ "But as things are,…"

ἅπασα Supply ἡ ἵππος.

κεχώρηκε Perfect, indicative, active, 3rd, singular of χωρέω.

9.60.3

καταλελάβηκε Perfect, indicative, active, 3rd, singular of καταλάμβανω. Used impersonally, it means "it has come about" and takes an accusative/infinitive construction.

ἀποπέμψαντες χάριν θέσθε "Do us the favor of sending."

☙

9.61.1-3 The Battle of Plataea, Part III

The Athenians, who are again portrayed in a positive way, were prevented from assisting the Spartans in spite of their call for help (9.60). Accordingly, the Spartans (along with their helots, who outnumbered the Spartans by a ratio of seven to one) had to fend for themselves, while they were being showered with Persian arrows. (The plight of the Spartans at Plataea brings to mind the remark made by the anonymous Spartan prior to the Battle of Thermopylae [7.226] about "fighting in the shade.") With his usual keen eye for detail, Herodotus notes that the pre-battle ritual sacrifices of the Spartans turned out unfavorably, which meant that many of the Spartans died or were wounded before they could enter the fray. The passage ends with a particularly moving scene, where Pausanias casts a glance at a nearby shrine to Hera and utters what seems, for all intents and purposes, a "prayer" to the goddess.

ταῦτα οἱ Ἀθηναῖοι ὡς ἐπύθοντο, ὁρμέατο βοηθέειν καὶ τὰ μάλιστα ἐπαμύνειν· καὶ σφι ἤδη στείχουσι ἐπιτίθενται οἱ ἀντιταχθέντες Ἑλλήνων τῶν μετὰ βασιλέος γενομένων, ὥστε μηκέτι δύνασθαι βοηθῆσαι· τὸ γὰρ προσκείμενον σφέας ἐλύπεε. [2] οὕτω δὴ μουνωθέντες Λακεδαιμόνιοι καὶ Τεγεῆται, ἐόντες σὺν ψιλοῖσι ἀριθμὸν οἱ μὲν πεντακισμύριοι Τεγεῆται δὲ τρισχίλιοι (οὗτοι γὰρ οὐδαμὰ ἀπεσχίζοντο ἀπὸ Λακεδαιμονίων), ἐσφαγιάζοντο ὡς συμβαλέοντες Μαρδονίῳ καὶ τῇ στρατιῇ τῇ παρεούσῃ. [3] καὶ οὐ γάρ σφι ἐγίνετο τὰ σφάγια χρηστά, ἔπιπτον δὲ αὐτῶν ἐν τούτῳ τῷ χρόνῳ πολλοὶ καὶ πολλῷ πλέονες ἐτρωματίζοντο· φράξαντες γὰρ τὰ γέρρα οἱ Πέρσαι ἀπίεσαν τῶν τοξευμάτων πολλὰ ἀφειδέως, οὕτω ὥστε πιεζομένων τῶν Σπαρτιητέων καὶ τῶν σφαγίων οὐ γινομένων ἀποβλέψαντα τὸν Παυσανίην πρὸς τὸ

Ἥραιον τὸ Πλαταιέων ἐπικαλέσασθαι τὴν θεόν, χρηίζοντα μηδαμῶς σφέας ψευσθῆναι τῆς ἐλπίδος.

9.61.1

ἐπιτίθενται "Attacked."

οἱ ἀντιταχθέντες "Those posted opposite [the Athenians]." These medizing Greeks were the Boeotians.

τὸ γὰρ προσκείμενον "The pressure of the enemy."

9.61.2

Τεγεῆται For the location of Tegea, see map in Landmark *ad* 9.46.

ἀριθμὸν Accusative of respect.

ὡς συμβαλέοντες "Seeing as how they were about to engage in battle." Note that the participle is future.

9.61.3

οὐ...χρηστά "Unfavorable."

πολλοὶ Referring to the Spartans.

φράξαντες γὰρ τὰ γέρρα "Having stuck their wicker shields [into the ground] to make a defensive wall."

ἀπίεσαν Imperfect, indicative, active, 3rd, plural of ἀπίημι (= ἀφίημι).

πιεζομένων τῶν Σπαρτιητέων καὶ τῶν σφαγίων οὐ γινομένων Genitive absolute constructions.

ἀποβλέψαντα τὸν Παυσανίην...ἐπικαλέσασθαι Accusative/infinitive construction in a result clause, as introduced by ὥστε.

ࣳ

9.62.1-3 The Battle of Plataea, Part IV

According to Herodotus, Pausanias' prayer brought results, and the pre-battle omens finally turned out to be favorable. This meant that the Spartans could at last engage the enemy, but since they were still preoccupied with their omens, the Tegeans (see map in Landmark *ad* 9.46) preempted them and launched an attack against the Persians. Herodotus' description of the fight at the wicker-shield wall shows some understanding of battle strategy, and if we take into account the praise he gives the Persians for their valor and strength, it even appears to be fair and balanced. His explanation as to what turned the tide in the battle also seems to have been carefully considered.

ταῦτα δ᾽ ἔτι τούτου ἐπικαλεομένου προεξαναστάντες πρότεροι οἱ Τεγεῆται ἐχώρεον ἐς τοὺς βαρβάρους, καὶ τοῖσι Λακεδαιμονίοισι αὐτίκα μετὰ τὴν εὐχὴν τὴν Παυσανίεω ἐγίνετο θυομένοισι τὰ σφάγια χρηστά· ὡς δὲ χρόνῳ κοτὲ ἐγένετο, ἐχώρεον καὶ οὗτοι ἐπὶ τοὺς Πέρσας, καὶ οἱ Πέρσαι ἀντίοι τὰ τόξα μετέντες. [2] ἐγίνετο δὲ πρῶτον περὶ τὰ γέρρα μάχη. ὡς δὲ ταῦτα ἐπεπτώκεε, ἤδη ἐγίνετο ἡ μάχη ἰσχυρὴ παρ' αὐτὸ τὸ Δημήτριον καὶ χρόνον ἐπὶ πολλόν, ἐς ὃ ἀπίκοντο ἐς ὠθισμόν· τὰ γὰρ δόρατα ἐπιλαμβανόμενοι κατέκλων οἱ βάρβαροι. [3] λήματι μέν νυν καὶ ῥώμῃ οὐκ ἥσσονες ἦσαν οἱ Πέρσαι, ἄνοπλοι δὲ ἐόντες καὶ πρὸς ἀνεπιστήμονες ἦσαν καὶ οὐκ ὅμοιοι τοῖσι ἐναντίοισι σοφίην, προεξαΐσσοντες δὲ κατ' ἕνα καὶ δέκα, καὶ πλέονες τε καὶ ἐλάσσονες συστρεφόμενοι, ἐσέπιπτον ἐς τοὺς Σπαρτιήτας καὶ διεφθείροντο.

9.62.1

ταῦτα δ' ἔτι τούτου ἐπικαλεομένου Genitive absolute construction; it refers to the prayer of Pausanias (9.61).

προεξαναστάντες Had the Tegeans been sitting before they sprang to their feet?

θυομένοισι Translate with τοῖσι Λακεδαιμονίοισι.

ἐγίνετο = ἐγίγνετο.

ὡς δὲ χρόνῳ κοτὲ ἐγένετο An idiom: "Finally, after some time had lapsed."

κοτέ = ποτέ.

9.62.2

τὰ γέρρα A defensive wall, made of wicker shields, from which the Persians had shot their fusillade of arrows.

ἐπεπτώκεε Pluperfect, indicative, active, 3rd, singular of πίπτω.

ἐς ὅ "Until."

ἀπίκοντο Aorist, indicative, middle, 3rd, plural of ἀπικνέομαι (= ἀφικνέομαι).

9.62.3

λήματι μέν νυν καὶ ῥώμῃ "Now in courage and in physical strength."

σοφίην Accusative of respect.

☙

9.63.1-2 Battle of Plataea, Part V

Mardonios has been a key player in the second half of the Histories. We were introduced to him in Book VI as Xerxes' first cousin and as the commander of the fleet which was mostly destroyed off the coast of Mt. Athos (6.43-45). We even had a chance to look "inside his head" during the debate he supposedly had with Artabanos over the advisability of Xerxes' expedition (7.5-6). Since the Battle of Salamis, he has been in near constant view as the commander-in-chief of the Persian forces which stayed behind after the Battle of Salamis. And now we see him abruptly exit from center stage. All we are told is that Mardonios perished (ἀπέθανε) while riding a white horse (cf. 8.113) in the company of a 1,000 hand-picked troops. Instead of focusing on how Mardonios died, Herodotus quickly returns to the theme of the complete inadequacy of the Persian infantry when faced with its heavily-armored Greek counterpart.

τῇ δὲ ἐτύγχανε αὐτὸς ἐὼν Μαρδόνιος, ἀπ' ἵππου τε μαχόμενος λευκοῦ ἔχων τε περὶ ἑωυτὸν λογάδας Περσέων τοὺς ἀρίστους χιλίους, ταύτῃ δὲ καὶ μάλιστα τοὺς ἐναντίους ἐπίεσαν. ὅσον μέν νυν χρόνον Μαρδόνιος περιῆν, οἱ δὲ ἀντεῖχον καὶ ἀμυνόμενοι κατέβαλλον πολλοὺς τῶν Λακεδαιμονίων· [2] ὡς δὲ Μαρδόνιος ἀπέθανε καὶ τὸ περὶ ἐκεῖνον τεταγμένον ἐὸν ἰσχυρότατον ἔπεσε, οὕτω δὴ καὶ οἱ ἄλλοι ἐτράποντο καὶ εἶξαν τοῖσι Λακεδαιμονίοισι. πλεῖστον γὰρ σφεας ἐδηλέετο ἡ ἐσθὴς ἔρημος ἐοῦσα ὅπλων· πρὸς γὰρ ὁπλίτας ἐόντες γυμνῆτες ἀγῶνα ἐποιεῦντο.

9.63.1

τῇ Translate in combination with ταύτῃ. "Where…there."
ἐπίεσαν Subject is "Spartans." Aorist, indicative, active, 3rd, plural of πιέζω.
ὅσον μέν νυν χρόνον Accusative of extent of time. "For as long a time as."

9.63.2

καὶ τὸ περὶ ἐκεῖνον τεταγμένον "Those posted around him."
τεταγμένον Perfect, passive, neuter, nominative, singular participle of τάσσω.
εἶξαν Aorist, indicative, active, 3rd, plural of εἴκω.
ἡ ἐσθὴς ἔρημος ἐοῦσα ὅπλων A roundabout way of saying that the Persians did not wear heavy armor.

ୣ

9.64.1-2 Battle of Plataea, Part VI

Herodotus turns off his anti-Spartan tone and heaps enormous praise on Pausanias, calling Plataea the greatest of all victories. As a mark of the honor he accords to the Spartan, he mentions not only his personal patronymic but also his father's. In a genealogical note which modern readers may find a bit unsettling, Herodotus reminds us of an earlier claim (7.204), that if one went back far enough in time, he would discover that both Pausanias and Leonidas had Herakles as a common ancestor.

ἐνθαῦτα ἥ τε δίκη τοῦ Λεωνίδεω κατὰ τὸ χρηστήριον τοῖσι Σπαρτιήτῃσι ἐκ Μαρδονίου ἐπετελέετο, καὶ νίκην ἀναιρέεται καλλίστην ἁπασέων τῶν ἡμεῖς ἴδμεν Παυσανίης ὁ Κλεομβρότου τοῦ Ἀναξανδρίδεω. [2] τῶν δὲ κατύπερθέ οἱ προγόνων τὰ οὐνόματα εἴρηται ἐς Λεωνίδην· ωὐτοὶ γάρ σφι τυγχάνουσι ἐόντες. ἀποθνήσκει δὲ Μαρδόνιος ὑπὸ Ἀειμνήστου ἀνδρὸς ἐν Σπάρτῃ

λογίμου, ὃς χρόνῳ ὕστερον μετὰ τὰ Μηδικὰ ἔχων ἄνδρας τριηκοσίους
συνέβαλε ἐν Στενυκλήρῳ πολέμου ἐόντος Μεσσηνίοισι πᾶσι, καὶ αὐτός τε
ἀπέθανε καὶ οἱ τριηκόσιοι.

9.64.1

κατὰ τὸ χρηστήριον It is mentioned in 8.114.

ἐκ Μαρδονίου "Through [the death] of Mardonios."

ἴδμεν = ἴσμεν. Perfect, indicative, active, 1st, plural of *εἴδω.

9.64.2

ὡυτοὶ = οἱ αὐτοί.

μετὰ τὰ Μηδικὰ "After the wars with the Medes [= Persian Wars]."

συνέβαλε ἐν Στενυκλήρῳ See map in Landmark ad 9.66.

πολέμου ἐόντος Genitive absolute construction.

Μεσσηνίοισι πᾶσι The Third Messenian War (465-464) was fought between Sparta and the Messenian helots, who had revolted against their Spartan overlords. For the location of Messenia, see map in Landmark ad 9.66.

✵

9.65.1-2 The Battle of Plataea, Part VII

Herodotus recounts here still another miraculous event from the Persian Wars. The Greeks massacred countless Persians during and after the Battle of Plataea (cf. 9.70), and yet, according to Herodotus, the body of not a single Persian could be found on the sacred grounds of the temple of Demeter, in spite of the fact that it was the epicenter for the battle. Our author proffers an explanation for this oddity: the goddess kept away from her temple those who had set fire to her celebrated shrine at Eleusis (see map in Landmark ad 9.66). This is the only time Herodotus mentions the burning of the "Telesterion" (initiation hall) at Eleusis, which must have been part of the widespread destruction in Attica wrought by the Persians a year earlier (cf. 8.50).

ἐν δὲ Πλαταιῇσι οἱ Πέρσαι ὡς ἐτράποντο ὑπὸ τῶν Λακεδαιμονίων, ἔφευγον
οὐδένα κόσμον ἐς τὸ στρατόπεδον τὸ ἑωυτῶν καὶ ἐς τὸ τεῖχος τὸ ξύλινον τὸ
ἐποιήσαντο ἐν μοίρῃ τῇ Θηβαΐδι. [2] θῶμα δέ μοι ὅκως παρὰ τῆς Δήμητρος
τὸ ἄλσος μαχομένων οὐδὲ εἷς ἐφάνη τῶν Περσέων οὔτε ἐσελθὼν ἐς τὸ
τέμενος οὔτε ἐναποθανών, περί τε τὸ ἱρὸν οἱ πλεῖστοι ἐν τῷ βεβήλῳ ἔπεσον.
δοκέω δέ, εἴ τι περὶ τῶν θείων πρηγμάτων δοκέειν δεῖ, ἡ θεὸς αὐτή σφεας
οὐκ ἐδέκετο ἐμπρήσαντας τὸ ἱρὸν τὸ ἐν Ἐλευσῖνι ἀνάκτορον.

9.65.1

οὐδένα κόσμον "In no order." The dative is the more common case for this expression (cf. 9.59.2).

τό Relative pronoun.

9.65.2

ὅκως = ὅπως.

ἐφάνη Aorist, indicative, passive, 3rd, singular of φαίνω. "Was seen."

ἐν τῷ βεβήλῳ Refers to the area in the vicinity of a temple which was not considered sacred.

ἐμπρήσαντας Aorist, active, masculine, accusative, plural participle of ἐμπίπρημι.

☞

9.70.1-5 The Massacre and Battle Statistics

The Battle of Plataea is essentially over except for some mopping-up activities at the wooden fort. The Tegeans are shown here performing decisively, while the Spartans are described as hapless, because they were inexperienced in siege tactics. Herodotus not only provides a wealth of specific details about the post-battle events but also strongly implies that he had done an autopsy of the battlefield and had actually seen some of the trophies, like the all-bronze horse trough which the Tegeans plundered from the King's tent. (This tent was eventually brought to Athens and may have been the model for the Odeion or "practice hall" which Pericles had ordered built at the foot of the Acropolis.) The massacre which followed the capture of the wooden fort is described, as usual, with no comment from our author. The passage concludes with some casualty figures which seem to be grossly exaggerated for the Persians and very much underestimated for the Greeks.

οὗτοι μὲν δὴ ἐν οὐδενὶ λόγῳ ἀπώλοντο· οἱ δὲ Πέρσαι καὶ ὁ ἄλλος ὅμιλος, ὡς κατέφυγον ἐς τὸ ξύλινον τεῖχος, ἔφθησαν ἐπὶ τοὺς πύργους ἀναβάντες πρὶν ἢ τοὺς Λακεδαιμονίους ἀπικέσθαι, ἀναβάντες δὲ ἐφράξαντο ὡς ἠδυνέατο ἄριστα τὸ τεῖχος· προσελθόντων δὲ τῶν Ἀθηναίων κατεστήκεέ σφι τειχομαχίη ἐρρωμενεστέρη. [2] ἕως μὲν γὰρ ἀπῆσαν οἱ Ἀθηναῖοι, οἱ δ' ἠμύνοντο καὶ πολλῷ πλέον εἶχον τῶν Λακεδαιμονίων ὥστε οὐκ ἐπισταμένων τειχομαχέειν· ὡς δέ σφι Ἀθηναῖοι προσῆλθον, οὕτω δὴ ἰσχυρὴ ἐγίνετο τειχομαχίη καὶ χρόνον ἐπὶ πολλόν. τέλος δὲ ἀρετῇ τε καὶ λιπαρίῃ ἐπέβησαν Ἀθηναῖοι τοῦ τείχεος καὶ ἤριπον· τῇ δὴ ἐσεχέοντο οἵ Ἕλληνες. [3] πρῶτοι δὲ ἐσῆλθον Τεγεῆται ἐς τὸ τεῖχος, καὶ τὴν σκηνὴν τὴν Μαρδονίου οὗτοι ἦσαν οἱ διαρπάσαντες, τά τε ἄλλα ἐξ αὐτῆς καὶ τὴν φάτνην τῶν ἵππων ἐοῦσαν χαλκέην πᾶσαν καὶ θέης ἀξίην. τὴν μέν νυν φάτνην ταύτην τὴν Μαρδονίου ἀνέθεσαν ἐς τὸν νηὸν τῆς Ἀλέης Ἀθηναίης Τεγεῆται, τὰ δὲ ἄλλα ἐς τὠυτό, ὅσα περ ἔλαβον, ἐσήνεικαν τοῖσι Ἕλλησι. [4] οἱ δὲ βάρβαροι οὐδὲν ἔτι στῖφος ἐποιήσαντο πεσόντος τοῦ τείχεος, οὐδέ τις αὐτῶν ἀλκῆς ἐμέμνητο, ἀλύκταζόν τε οἷα ἐν ὀλίγῳ χώρῳ πεφοβημένοι τε καὶ πολλαὶ μυριάδες κατειλημέναι ἀνθρώπων· [5] παρῆν τε τοῖσι Ἕλλησι φονεύειν οὕτω ὥστε τριήκοντα μυριάδων στρατοῦ, καταδεουσέων τεσσέρων τὰς ἔχων Ἀρτάβαζος ἔφευγε, τῶν λοιπέων μηδὲ τρεῖς χιλιάδας περιγενέσθαι. Λακεδαιμονίων δὲ τῶν ἐκ Σπάρτης ἀπέθανον οἱ πάντες ἐν τῇ συμβολῇ εἷς καὶ ἐνενήκοντα, Τεγεητέων δὲ ἐκκαίδεκα, Ἀθηναίων δὲ δύο καὶ πεντήκοντα.

9.70.1

οὗτοι Refers to the Greek allies who, once they learned of the Persian rout, decided to show up at Plataea, only to be attacked and decimated by the Boeotian cavalry (9.69).

ἔφθησαν ἐπὶ τοὺς πύργους ἀναβάντες πρὶν ἤ "Mounted the towers ahead of…."

ἔφθησαν Aorist, indicative, active, 3rd, plural of φθάνω.

ἀπικέσθαι Aorist, middle, infinitive of ἀπικνέομαι (= ἀφικνέομαι).

ὡς ἠδυνέατο ἄριστα "As best they could."

προσελθόντων δὲ τῶν Ἀθηναίων Genitive absolute construction.

9.70.2

ὥστε οὐκ ἐπισταμένων τειχομαχέειν "Since they [the Spartans] were inexperienced in siege warfare."

ἐγίνετο = ἐγίγνετο.

ἤριπον Aorist, indicative, active, 3rd, plural of ἐρείπω.

ἐσεχέοντο "Poured in."

9.70.3

Τεγεῆται For the location of Tegea, see map in Landmark *ad* 9.66.

τὠυτό = τὸ αὐτό. "The same stockpile."

ἐσήνεικαν Aorist, indicative, active, 3rd, plural of ἐσφέρω (= εἰσφέρω).

9.70.4

στῖφος ἐποιήσαντο "Stayed in formation."

πεσόντος τοῦ τείχεος Genitive absolute construction.

ἐμέμνητο Pluperfect, indicative, middle, 3rd, singular of μιμνήσκω. Takes the genitive.

οἷα "Seeing as how."

9.70.5

παρῆν "It was possible."

καταδεουσέων "Except for."

τεσσέρων Supply μυριάδων.

τάς Here, a relative pronoun.

μηδὲ τρεῖς χιλιάδας περιγενέσθαι. In other words, less than 3,000 survived.

CB

9.76.1-3 The Concubine from Cos

The main purpose of this story of the concubine from Cos (see màp in Landmark *ad* 9.80) may have been to delineate further the differences between Greeks and Persians. But what a strange setting Herodotus chose to display Greek clemency: we are told that, when the Coan woman approached Pausanias to beg for mercy, the slaughter of the Persians inside the wooden fort was still going on. It may be worth noting that, following his victory at Plataea, Pausanias had a number of misadventures which culminated in his forming a relationship with the Persian king's daughter. He was eventually returned to Sparta, convicted of sedition, and entombed alive in a temple called the Brazen House (cf. Thucydides 1.130-131). Was the encounter with the concubine from Cos the beginning of Pausanias' downfall?

ὡς δὲ τοῖσι Ἕλλησι ἐν Πλαταιῆσι κατέστρωντο οἱ βάρβαροι, ἐνθαῦτά σφι ἐπῆλθε γυνὴ αὐτόμολος· ἣ ἐπειδὴ ἔμαθε ἀπολωλότας τοὺς Πέρσας καὶ νικῶντας τοὺς Ἕλληνας, ἐοῦσα παλλακὴ Φαρανδάτεος τοῦ Τεάσπιος ἀνδρὸς Πέρσεω, κοσμησαμένη χρυσῷ πολλῷ καὶ αὐτὴ καὶ ἀμφίπολοι καὶ ἐσθῆτι τῇ καλλίστῃ τῶν παρεουσέων, καταβᾶσα ἐκ τῆς ἁρμαμάξης ἐχώρεε ἐς τοὺς Λακεδαιμονίους ἔτι ἐν τῇσι φονῇσι ἐόντας, ὁρῶσα δὲ πάντα ἐκεῖνα διέποντα Παυσανίην, πρότερόν τε τὸ οὔνομα ἐξεπισταμένη καὶ τὴν πάτρην ὥστε πολλάκις ἀκούσασα, ἔγνω τε τὸν Παυσανίην καὶ λαβομένη τῶν γουνάτων ἔλεγε τάδε· [2] "ὦ βασιλεῦ Σπάρτης, ῥῦσαί με τὴν ἱκέτιν αἰχμαλώτου δουλοσύνης. σὺ γὰρ καὶ ἐς τόδε ὤνησας, τούσδε ἀπολέσας τοὺς οὔτε δαιμόνων οὔτε θεῶν ὄπιν ἔχοντας. εἰμὶ δὲ γένος μὲν Κῴη, θυγάτηρ δὲ Ἡγητορίδεω τοῦ Ἀνταγόρεω· βίῃ δέ με λαβὼν ἐν Κῷ εἶχε ὁ Πέρσης." ὁ δὲ ἀμείβεται τοισίδε· [3] "γύναι, θάρσεε καὶ ὡς ἱκέτις καὶ εἰ δὴ πρὸς τούτῳ τυγχάνεις ἀληθέα λέγουσα καὶ εἶς θυγάτηρ Ἡγητορίδεω τοῦ Κῴου, ὃς ἐμοὶ ξεῖνος μάλιστα τυγχάνει ἐὼν τῶν περὶ ἐκείνους τοὺς χώρους οἰκημένων." ταῦτα δὲ εἴπας τότε μὲν ἐπέτρεψε τῶν ἐφόρων τοῖσι παρεοῦσι, ὕστερον δὲ ἀπέπεμψε ἐς Αἴγιναν, ἐς τὴν αὐτὴ ἤθελε ἀπικέσθαι.

9.76.1

τοῖσι Ἕλλησι Dative of agent.

κατέστρωντο Pluperfect, indicative, passive, 3rd, plural of καταστορέννυμι.

ἀπολωλότας Perfect, active, masculine, accusative, plural participle of ἀπόλλυμι.

παλλακή "Concubine."

τῶν παρεουσέων The concubine had maid-servants and a travel wardrobe.

ἀκούσασα Had she heard about Pausanias in her original homeland (Cos), or while she was in the company of important Persians, like Pharandates?

9.76.2

βασιλεῦ Pausanias was a regent, and not a king, but it was probably more prudent for the concubine to address him this way.

ῥῦσαί με τὴν ἱκέτιν αἰχμαλώτου δουλοσύνης "Free me, a suppliant, from the slavery of someone captured in war."

καὶ ἐς τόδε "Even before this."

ὤνησας Aorist, indicative, active, 2nd, singular of ὀνήνυμι. Supply ἐμέ.

ὄπιν ἔχοντας "Having respect for." Takes the genitive.

9.76.3

ἀληθέα λέγουσα Translate as supplementary to τυγχάνεις.

τῶν ἐφόρων The ephors were the five "overseers" of the Spartan kings.

☙

9.79.1-2 Pausanias Plays by the Rules

In the preceding chapter (9.78), Herodotus mentioned a certain Lampon of Aegina, who implored Pausanias to avenge the Persians' abuse of Leonidas' body by impaling the corpse of Mardonios. Herodotus describes this proposal as "most unholy" (ἀνοσιώτατον), and Pausanias himself is said to have rejected Lampon's suggestion. (Aeginetans such as Lampon fare badly in the *Histories*, perhaps because of the drawn-out conflict between Athens and Aegina through much of the 5th century and our author's friendly pre-disposition towards the Athenians.) Modern readers might find it confusing that the Pausanias who is shown behaving virtuously in this passage is the general who oversaw the slaughter of countless Persians inside the wooden fort at Plataea (cf. 9.70 and 9.76).

ὁ μὲν δοκέων χαρίζεσθαι ἔλεγε τάδε, ὁ δ᾽ ἀνταμείβετο τοισίδε· "ὦ ξεῖνε Αἰγινῆτα, τὸ μὲν εὐνοέειν τε καὶ προορᾶν ἄγαμαί σευ, γνώμης μέντοι ἡμάρτηκας χρηστῆς· ἐξαείρας γάρ με ὑψοῦ καὶ τὴν πάτρην καὶ τὸ ἔργον, ἐς τὸ μηδὲν κατέβαλες παραινέων νεκρῷ λυμαίνεσθαι, καὶ ἢν ταῦτα ποιέω, φὰς ἄμεινόν με ἀκούσεσθαι· τὰ πρέπει μᾶλλον βαρβάροισι ποιεῖν ἢ περ Ἕλλησι· [2] καὶ ἐκείνοισι δὲ ἐπιφθονέομεν. ἐγὼ δ᾽ ὦν τούτου εἵνεκα μήτε Αἰγινήτησι ἅδοιμι μήτε τοῖσι ταῦτα ἀρέσκεται, ἀποχρᾷ δέ μοι Σπαρτιήτησι ἀρεσκόμενον ὅσια μὲν ποιεῖν, ὅσια δὲ καὶ λέγειν. Λεωνίδῃ δέ, τῷ με κελεύεις τιμωρῆσαι, φημὶ μεγάλως τετιμωρῆσθαι, ψυχῆσί τε τῆσι τῶνδε ἀναριθμήτοισι τετίμηται αὐτός τε καὶ οἱ ἄλλοι οἱ ἐν Θερμοπύλησι τελευτήσαντες. σὺ μέντοι ἔτι ἔχων λόγον τοιόνδε μήτε προσέλθῃς ἔμοιγε μήτε συμβουλεύσῃς, χάριν τε ἴσθι ἐὼν ἀπαθής."

9.79.1

ὁ μὲν δοκέων χαρίζεσθαι ἔλεγε τάδε Lampon of Aegina is being referred to here (see 9.78).

τὸ μὲν εὐνοέειν τε καὶ προορᾶν These two articular infinitive constructions are the objects of ἄγαμαί ("I am grateful for").

ἡμάρτηκας Perfect, indicative, active, 2nd, singular of ἁμαρτάνω.

ἐξαείρας Aorist, active, masculine, nominative, singular participle of ἐξαίρω.

ἐς τὸ μηδὲν κατέβαλες Idiomatically, "You have ruined [dashed] everything."

ἄμεινόν με ἀκούσεσθαι "I would have a better reputation."

9.79.2

ἐκείνοισι Referring to the barbarians who committed such atrocities.

ὦν = οὖν.

τούτου εἵνεκα "For this very reason."

εἵνεκα = ἕνεκα.

ἅδοιμι Aorist, optative, active, 1st, singular of ἀνδάνω.

τοῖσι Both the relative pronoun and its antecedent are in this one word.

ἀποχρᾷ δέ μοι The verb is used impersonally: "It is enough for me that...."

τῷ Here, a relative pronoun.

τετιμωρῆσθαι Perfect, passive infinitive of τιμωρέω. "Vengeance has been taken for him."

προσέλθῃς Aorist, subjunctive, active, 2nd, singular of ἔρχομαι. The aorist subjunctive + μή indicates prohibition.

χάριν τε ἴσθι Literally, "know gratitude." Idiomatically, "be grateful."

ἴσθι Perfect, imperative, active, 2nd, singular of εἴδω.

☙

9.82.1 For This He Invaded Greece?

This chapter interrupts a section of Book IX where Herodotus describes in some detail the treasures which the Persians left behind in Greece and which were divided among the victors. Clearly, he could not resist a good story, even if it had little to do with the subject at hand. The anecdote appears to have been passed down (λέγεται) by story-tellers as a kind of morality tale which emphasized the differences between the simple Spartan lifestyle and Persian opulence. As told by Herodotus, the story concludes with Pausanias making a joke—perhaps uncharacteristically—about the folly of the Persian King, who came to Greece to steal wretched food, like the infamous Spartan "black broth." There is at least a tinge of irony in this tale, since Herodotus' audience was doubtless aware of what happened to Pausanias a year or two after Plataea, when he was indeed seduced by Persian opulence. (For the story of Pausanias' fall from grace, see Thucydides 1.130-131.)

δὲ καὶ τάδε γενέσθαι, ὡς Ξέρξης φεύγων ἐκ τῆς Ἑλλάδος Μαρδονίῳ τὴν κατασκευὴν καταλίποι τὴν ἑωυτοῦ· Παυσανίην ὦν ὁρῶντα τὴν Μαρδονίου κατασκευὴν χρυσῷ τε καὶ ἀργύρῳ καὶ παραπετάσμασι ποικίλοισι κατεσκευασμένην, κελεῦσαι τούς τε ἀρτοκόπους καὶ τοὺς ὀψοποιοὺς κατὰ ταὐτὰ καθὼς Μαρδονίῳ δεῖπνον παρασκευάζειν. [2] ὡς δὲ κελευόμενοι οὗτοι ἐποίευν ταῦτα, ἐνθαῦτα τὸν Παυσανίην ἰδόντα κλίνας τε χρυσέας καὶ ἀργυρέας εὖ ἐστρωμένας καὶ τραπέζας τε χρυσέας καὶ ἀργυρέας καὶ παρασκευὴν μεγαλοπρεπέα τοῦ δείπνου, ἐκπλαγέντα τὰ προκείμενα ἀγαθὰ κελεῦσαι ἐπὶ γέλωτι τοὺς ἑωυτοῦ διηκόνους παρασκευάσαι Λακωνικὸν δεῖπνον. [3] ὡς δὲ τῆς θοίνης ποιηθείσης ἦν πολλὸν τὸ μέσον, τὸν Παυσανίην γελάσαντα μεταπέμψασθαι τῶν Ἑλλήνων τοὺς στρατηγούς, συνελθόντων δὲ τούτων εἰπεῖν τὸν Παυσανίην, δεικνύντα ἐς ἑκατέρην τοῦ δείπνου παρασκευήν· "ἄνδρες Ἕλληνες, τῶνδε εἵνεκα ἐγὼ ὑμέας συνήγαγον, βουλόμενος ὑμῖν τοῦδε τοῦ Μήδων ἡγεμόνος τὴν ἀφροσύνην δέξαι, ὃς τοιήνδε δίαιταν ἔχων ἦλθε ἐς ἡμέας οὕτω ὀϊζυρὴν ἔχοντας ἀπαιρησόμενος." ταῦτα μὲν Παυσανίην λέγεται εἰπεῖν πρὸς τοὺς στρατηγοὺς τῶν Ἑλλήνων.

9.82.1

τὴν κατασκευήν "His tent."

Παυσανίην Accusative in indirect statement (after λέγεται).

ὦν = οὖν

9.82.2

ταὐτά Crasis (two words combined into one) for τὰ αὐτά.

ἐστρωμένας Perfect, passive, feminine, accusative, plural participle of στορέννυμι. The couches (κλίνας) were beautifully "covered."

ἐκπλαγέντα Aorist, passive, masculine, accusative, singular participle of ἐκπλήσσω. The participle, though passive, takes the accusative in τὰ προκείμενα. "Astounded at what goods lay before him."

ἐπὶ γέλωτι "As a joke."

9.82.3

τῆς θοίνης ποιηθείσης Genitive absolute construction.

ὡς...ἦν πολλὸν τὸ μέσον "As there was a huge difference [between the Spartan and Persian meals]."

συνελθόντων δὲ τούτων Genitive absolute construction.

εἵνεκα = ἕνεκα.

δέξαι Aorist, active infinitive of δείκνυμι.